Amphibians and Reptiles

A GUIDE TO

Amphibians and Reptiles of Costa Rica

TWAN LEENDERS
PREFACE BY ADRIAN FORSYTH

A ZONA TROPICAL PUBLICATION

ISBN 0-9705678-0-4

Editor: David Featherstone
Book design: Ingalls + Associates
Designers: Thomas Ingalls, Motoko Tamura

Published by Distribuidores Zona Tropical, S.A.
S.J.O. 1948
P.O. Box 025216
Miami, FL 33102-5216

Acknowledgements:
Special thanks are due Michael Fogden and Peter Mudde for their attentive review of this book in manuscript form. The author would also like to thank Jay Savage and the people of Rara Avis for their generous cooperation. Finally, we must acknowledge all the photographers who contributed to this project.

Except when otherwise indicated, photographs and drawings are by Twan Leenders.

CONTENTS

PREFACE

Just a handful of countries such as England, the United States, Canada, and parts of Europe, for example, have a significant body of modern field guides. Few things could be more useful for the long-term fate of our species. How is a nation ever to manage its natural resources if its people do not know the names and fundamental ecology of the animals and plants that comprise natural communities and make ecosystems?

The tropics, where most of the world's terrestrial biodiversity is concentrated, are sadly short of information on their flora and fauna. Happily, Costa Rica is an exception. This small but biologically complex country is rapidly developing a rich set of tools for the naturalist and ecologist. This book ranks among the best of these tools. It enables one to identify most of some 400 of Costa Rica's amphibians and reptiles. But to call this work a field guide hardly does it justice, for it encompasses a great breadth of knowledge concerning breeding behavior, feeding ecology, morphological adaptation, and the like. Although ostensibly about Costa Rican species, the text in fact provides a large amount of general herpetological and natural history information. Moreover, many of the species, genera, and families described in this book occur widely in the neotropics. It is hard to imagine any neotropical naturalist who would not rejoice in this book.

My two sons, Darwin and Adam, like all boys, delight in capturing tadpoles, snakes, salamanders, lizards, and frogs. Being young and inquisitive, their absorption of herpetological information now proceeds more rapidly than that of their father. Thus, although I have never met Twan Leenders, I am already deeply in his debt. On our next tropical vacation, this book will help me keep pace with them as they discover some of the living treasures that slither and leap and croak and climb in Costa Rica.

Adrian Forsyth

INTRODUCTION

This book, which is intended for nonspecialists and specialists alike, describes a majority of the nearly 400 currently identified species of amphibians and reptiles in Costa Rica. Because its principal purpose is to aid in identifying species in the field, certain species have not been described because they would be impossible to identify in anything other than laboratory conditions. A secondary purpose of this book, one at times somewhat at odds with the primary purpose, is to provide a lively introduction to the diversity of amphibian and reptilian fauna in Costa Rica. The author thus describes some species because interesting natural history information exists for them, even though they may be difficult to identify. Any selection process involves some arbitrary elements, and it must be admitted that, in several cases, species were included because they were in some manner interesting, or simply beautiful.

Although this book does not describe all Costa Rican species, material provided in family descriptions and other sections should allow the reader to assign any Costa Rican amphibian or reptile to the proper taxonomic family, if not to identify the exact species. Specialists will certainly want to consult Appendix 3, which contains a list of all currently identified species.

It is customary to discuss amphibians and reptiles in a single book, as the author has done here, even though each is a distinct class of animal. The popular imagination tends to lump amphibians and reptiles together, surely because both groups are generally viewed as slimy, unattractive, and threatening. Biologists link the two groups in a branch of zoology dealing with amphibians and reptiles called herpetology. This linkage is not arbitrary, since both groups are related on the evolutionary tree; but, in fact, reptiles and birds are more closely related than are reptiles and amphibians. This book heeds convention and discusses both classes of animals, and the body of the text provides interesting examples of the significant differences between them.

Research, Diversity, and Prospects for Survival

Since the middle of the nineteenth century, the number of species of amphibians and reptiles in Costa Rica that have been described has increased significantly. Although new species are occasionally added to the list of Costa Rican herpetofauna, the rate of discovery has slowed considerably. One might, therefore, expect that contemporary research efforts would be directed toward studying the biology and natural history of the already-identified species, particularly since current understanding is far from complete and, in many cases, has been derived solely from the examination of preserved museum specimens. Unfortunately, this is not the case. Field research of herpetofauna is exceedingly difficult, and discovering new species tends to be a faster route to scientific notoriety. Attention thus still seems to be focused on taxonomic issues, either the description of new species or the reclassification of already-identified ones.

At the time of this writing, nearly 400 species of amphibians and reptiles are known to inhabit Costa Rica, a very high number for such a small country. There are several explanations for this. First, Costa Rica is quite literally a land bridge between North and South America. Several groups of amphibians and reptiles whose primary range is in North America reach their southern limit in Costa Rica; likewise, several groups in South America reach their northern limit in Costa Rica. Second, the country offers a variety of habitats, including a dry, savanna-like forest, several types of rainforest, and even scrub vegetation near the summit of some of its highest mountains. There is, so to speak, something for everyone. Indeed, one finds many endemic, or native, amphibian and reptile species in habitat islands in different parts of the country. In most cases, these endemic species are found in highland areas, where they have survived since ancient eras, when the landscape, climate, and fauna of the area now called Costa Rica was very different. Two other endemic species, the Pacific dwarf gecko (*Sphaerodactylus pacificus*) and Townsend's anole (*Norops townsendi*) are only found on Cocos Island. Third, in recent years, several species have arrived as stowaways on ships from Caribbean and more remote destinations. Populations of introduced species, such as the Puerto Rican crested anole (*Ctenonotus cristatellus*), occur in and near port cities such as Limón.

While one is tempted to celebrate the diversity of the Costa Rican herpetofauna, one must also acknowledge that prospects for the future are not cheerful. Many known species are disappearing at an alarming rate, and undiscovered species may disappear before scientists have the chance to record them. Massive changes to original habitat, destruction of habitats, and excessive hunting and collection of natural populations are some of the threats Costa Rican amphibians and reptiles face. Wide-ranging, possibly global, environmental changes, also appear to have a major effect on Costa Rican fauna. (See page 49 on the disappearance of amphibian species in Costa Rica.)

Geography, Climate, and Seasons

Costa Rica is a small country (51,100 km^2/19,730 sq mi). The Caribbean and Pacific coasts are separated by four mountain chains (called *cordilleras* in Spanish) that run roughly in a northwest to southeast direction: the Guanacaste, Tilarán, Central, and Talamanca ranges. These mountains include the highest peak in Central America, Mount Chirripó (3,820 m/12,530 ft), and several active volcanos. The Central Valley, or Meseta Central, where the majority of Costa Ricans live, is a large highland valley enclosed on all sides by the mountains of the Central range and the northern part of the Talamanca range. The Caribbean side of the country consists mainly of a large, flat coastal plain that is widest near the Nicaraguan border and narrows toward the southern border with Panama. The Pacific side of the country can be divided into two climate regions: the dry northern region, which encompasses the lowland plains of Guanacaste and the Nicoya Peninsula, and the wet Osa Peninsula and the adjacent lowlands in the south.

Costa Rica lies within the tropics and is about halfway between the Tropic of Cancer and the Equator. At any given place in the country, the average temperature in the hottest month of the year does not exceed the average temperature in the coolest month by more than 5°C/9°F. This small variance is strikingly different from the large changes in temperature

Map of Costa Rica indicating key landmarks.

that can occur locally on a daily basis. In some areas it is invariably hot during the day, but may be cool at night. With temperatures relatively constant, seasons in the tropics are not defined by temperature differences, but by variation in rainfall.

Costa Rica experiences a dry season and a rainy season. The dry season generally begins toward the end of November and lasts until April or May, when the rainy season begins. This general pattern varies significantly in different parts of the country; even during the dry season, it is not uncommon for the Caribbean slope to continue to receive rainfall. In fact, there is a marked difference in the amount of rainfall received by the Pacific and Caribbean slopes. The Pacific slope has a maximum annual precipitation of around 2,500 mm (98 inches), while the Caribbean foothills may receive more than twice as much. Nevertheless, most places in the country receive a lot of rain in comparison with temperate zones to the north. At one specific site (Hacienda Cedral), reports indicate rain fell on 359 days in 1968, which is thought to be a world record.

The northwestern part of Costa Rica, north of the Tarcoles River and including the Nicoya Peninsula, is very hot, and substantially drier than the rest of the country. Annual precipitation there ranges from 1,300 to 2,300 mm (51 to 91 inches). The forest in this part of the country has a low canopy, with trees usually less than 15 m (49 ft) tall. The trees generally lose their leaves during the dry season, which is particularly harsh and may last up to eight months, starting around October. Many of the amphibian and reptile species of this dry forest zone are not found anywhere else in the country.

The majority of amphibians and reptiles inhabit the wetter lowland areas, and the number of both species and individuals is higher in these regions than in any other part of the country. The wettest lowland areas are found in the northern Caribbean region and north and east of Golfo Dulce on the southern Pacific coast. In most of these evergreen forests, it rains almost year-round, and some areas may receive more than 6,000 mm (236 inches) of rain annually. In most of the remaining lowland areas, the rainfall is much less extreme, with a yearly range of 2,500 to 4,000 mm (98 to 157 inches).

At elevations above roughly 1,500 m (4,900 ft), a cool, highland climate prevails, with temperatures between 10 and 16°C (50 and 61°F). Near the summit of some of the higher peaks, at elevations above 3,500 m (11,500 ft), there is occasional frost. Because most highland regions are frequently covered in clouds, the resulting ground-level mist creates the very humid conditions that are prerequisite for most species of amphibians. Whereas the lowland regions are home to the greatest number of species and individuals, the highlands, above roughly 1,500 m (4,900 ft), are home to the more elusive, and often endemic, species. Many of Costa Rica's endemic species are restricted to one or a few mountains, isolated from neighboring mountains by intolerably hot and/or dry lowlands.

Seasonal changes in rainfall can significantly affect both the size of amphibian and reptile populations and species diversity. During year-round sampling of the leaf-litter herpetofauna at La Selva Biological Station, a Caribbean lowland location near Puerto Viejo de Sarapiquí, the highest number of individual animals was recorded in February and the lowest in August. The months with the highest and lowest species diversity (March and October, respectively) correspond roughly with the population findings. These data indicate that the greatest diversity and abundance of herpetofauna occurs between the end of the dry season and the onset of the rainy season. As the dry season progresses, falling leaves contribute to the abundance of leaf litter on the forest floor, thus increasing the size of the preferred habitat of these species.

Taxonomy and Scientific Names

At present, about 9,850 species of amphibians and reptiles are known to walk, hop, crawl, or slither on our planet. Taxonomy, the branch of biology concerned with the classification of living things into groups, offers a convenient method of categorizing and discussing these nearly ten thousand kinds of animals. Currently, classification is based on what we know or hypothesize about the evolution of an organism. In practice, our knowledge of such an organism's evolutionary history is mainly based on differences and similarities in morphological traits, such as patterns of scales, the presence or absence of a tail, or dentition, to name but a few traits. This process involves a good deal of interpretation, and it is possible for two experts who agree on classification criteria to disagree on how to categorize a specific organism.

Since Carolus Linnaeus' invention of binomial nomenclature almost 250 years ago, biologists have been naming each plant and animal species with a unique combination of a genus name and a species name. These names are generally derived from Greek or Latin and are usually italicized in literature. For example, the scientific name of the jumping pit viper is *Atropoides nummifer*. *Atropoides* is the name of the genus, a taxonomic group that includes a few species of closely related snakes; *nummifer* identifies a single species within that genus.

The combination of *Atropoides* and *nummifer* thus uniquely identifies a single species and is used worldwide to ensure that scientists are able to communicate clearly. *Atropoides* is derived from Greek and means "having the nature of Atropos," a Greek goddess whose task was to sever the "life thread" at death, a clear reference to the fact that snakes in this genus are venomous; *nummifer*, from Latin, means "bearing coins," which perhaps refers to the pattern of saddlelike blotches on this snake's back.

As our understanding increases, it sometimes becomes clear that a species has been assigned to the wrong genus. Since its original description in 1845, *Atropoides nummifer* has been variously named *Atropos nummifer*, *Bothrops nummifer*, *Bothriechis nummifer*, and *Porthidium nummifer*. In other words, over time it has been placed in five genera. By convention, a change in scientific name does not become official until the change is justified and published in a peer-reviewed herpetological journal. In cases where the taxonomy of a species included in this book is under debate, the most commonly applied scientific name has been favored.

Scientific names, though indispensable for communication in scientific circles, are often awkward for the nonspecialist. Therefore, each species in this book is also identified by its English common name, and, in a few cases, by its local Spanish common name. For more information on the taxonomy of amphibians and reptiles see page 23.

Observing and Identifying Amphibians and Reptiles

Most members of the Costa Rican herpetofauna are shy, and many are well camouflaged and active only at night. If sighting herpetofauna can be a challenge, at times it is even more difficult to identify what one has seen. Some species require close inspection, since the distinguishing characteristics may be very subtle. Success in this endeavor requires a good deal of patience, a bit of luck, and practice. Following are pointers that will improve chances for success.

Amphibians and reptiles are often called cold-blooded, although their body temperatures can sometimes reach a level equal to that of humans. In technical terms, amphibians and reptiles are ectotherms, which means they depend on external sources of heat for regulating body temperature, unlike humans, who generate heat through metabolism. The body heat of amphibians and reptiles is derived from solar energy, either directly (e.g., by basking in sunny spots), or indirectly (e.g., by conduction from the ground or rocks on which they rest). Some species are thermally passive and simply adopt the prevailing ambient temperature, while others actively maintain a specific high body temperature by moving in and out of sun-exposed areas.

Many reptile species can be seen sunning themselves during the day. Amphibians, on the other hand, generally shy away from direct exposure to sunlight. Their thin, moist skin permits rapid escape of fluids (unlike the dry and scaly skin of reptiles); in a warm and dry climate, water will evaporate from their bodies, resulting in dehydration and ultimately death. Amphibians can replenish their internal water supply by absorbing water through their skin, from either the ground, the air, or bodies of water. Curiously, they do not replenish their internal water supply by drinking, as reptiles do. For this reason, amphibians are mostly found in areas with high humidity or where they can enter water. In addition, most Costa Rican amphibians are active mainly at night, when cool and humid climate conditions are much more favorable. Those amphibian species active during the day are mostly found in water, or in moist and heavily shaded habitats.

Amphibians and reptiles can be difficult to spot. Note how well this rain frog blends in with its surroundings.

Areas with "disturbed" plant life, such as forests where trees have been cut down, or pastures and plantations, often still harbor amphibians and reptiles. In some cases, herpetofauna may be present in higher densities in disturbed areas than in primary rainforests. However, the number of species living in an undisturbed forest, with its very large trees and understory of palms, lianas, epiphytes, and other plant life, is invariably higher than in any secondary forest or cultivated area. Population patterns of Costa Rican herpetofauna are typical of the New World tropics in that there are a few extremely abundant species and a very large number of rare ones. It is the abundant species that are found in large numbers in disturbed areas; many of the rarer rainforest species do not survive in disturbed habitats.

There are certain habitats in Costa Rica where, with a little careful observation, you are much more likely to find amphibians and reptiles. During the day, while hiking in a lowland rainforest, for example, you are very likely to see several species of anoles (genus *Norops*), rain frogs (genus *Eleutherodactylus*), and poison-dart frogs, as well as an occasional snake.

Boat trips on lowland rivers offer excellent opportunities to observe several species of conspicuous large reptiles. Freshwater turtles are fond of basking on logs or riverbanks, often accompanied by spectacled caimans (*Caiman crocodilus*) and occasionally even an American crocodile (*Crocodylus acutus*). Along the riverbanks, you may see basilisks, also known as Jesus Christ lizards, running away or darting across the water, while the tops of the trees that line the river are home to large green iguanas (*Iguana iguana*).

Species of basilisk lizards and whip-tailed lizards inhabit the vegetation lining most Costa Rican beaches, often in large numbers. Along the Pacific Coast, these lizards share their habitat with the large black spiny-tailed iguana (*Ctenosaura similis*). On some nights, beaches on either coast are the scene of one of natures most poetic spectacles, the nesting of sea turtles. Under no circumstances should you disturb these highly endangered animals; using flashlights or electronic flashes for cameras is not permitted on beaches where sea turtles nest.

On night walks, even the smallest creature can be spotted with the aid of a powerful flashlight. When you hold the flashlight next to your eyes and point it toward the forest, it is often possible to see the red reflections of amphibian and reptile eyes, even of individuals at a considerable distance. While walking slowly along a rainforest trail, point the flashlight toward the forest floor and tree trunks and vegetation; in addition to night-active frogs and snakes, you may also spot diurnal lizards and snakes that are sleeping.

Ponds prove best for observing frogs and frog-eating snakes, and on many nights the sound of male frogs announcing their presence to female frogs can be heard from far away.

Although a flashlight is the essential tool for observing amphibians and reptiles, a pair of close-focussing binoculars, a magnifying glass, and a plastic freezer bag can be useful accessories for more enthusiastic "herp-watchers." Small amphibians and reptiles are easily hurt, and they may overheat if you hold them in your hand. To examine an individual more closely, place it carefully in a clear plastic bag, and hold it away from direct sunlight. After a brief inspection, gently release the individual where you found it. Generally, it is best to avoid direct contact with these animals. However, when handling one, make sure your hands are free of sunscreen and insect repellent; they contain chemicals that can harm or kill reptiles and amphibians

How to Use This Book

With the aid of this book, you will be able to identify the majority of the nearly 400 currently identified species of amphibians and reptiles in Costa Rica. Some species of amphibians and reptiles are very difficult to identify and pose problems to even the most experienced herpetologist. The identification of these animals is normally based on minute characteristics that are only visible on preserved museum specimens. Such distinguishing features are of little use in the field, and in this book the emphasis is placed on externally visible characteristics. In many cases, you should be able to identify an amphibian or reptile without having to handle it.

The "Getting Started" section that follows provides a chart with a simple set of rules for placing any amphibian or reptile in its general group. The chapters on amphibians begin on page 27; the chapters on reptiles begin on page 121. Throughout those chapters, you will find narrative descriptions of the identifying characteristics of various groups, along with charts that list a summary of those characteristics. This feature is very useful for quick reference in the field. Distinguishing characteristics are also depicted in drawings and photographs. You will also find schematic drawings of generalized, representative members of each family; these should further aid in placing a field specimen in its proper family.

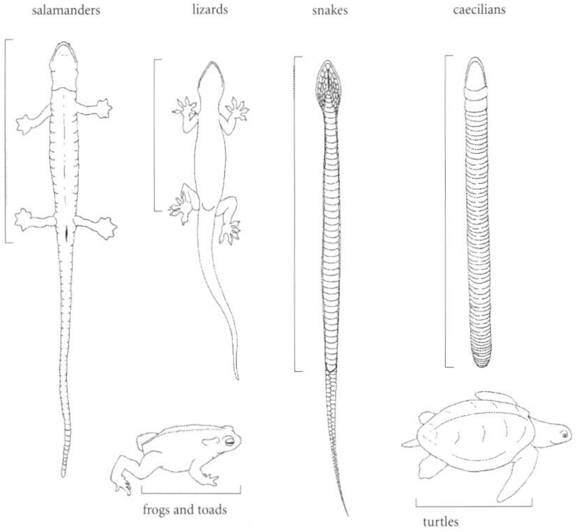

The size of a reptile or amphibian is generally expressed as the snout-vent length (SVL). This is the straight line distance between the tip of the snout and the edge of the vent that is furthest away from the snout. The illustration shows how the SVL is measured in salamanders, lizards, snakes, caecilians, and frogs and toads. An exception is made for turtles, whose size is expressed by the straight line distance between the front and the back of the shell.

Each species' description in this guide generally begins with a brief listing of a specific characteristic or combination of characteristics that are unique to that species. Next, a more extensive description of body shape, size, color, and pattern is given to further aid in correctly identifying the species. The general distribution range is also indicated, along with more specific information about where the animal occurs in Costa Rica. When available, the species description also includes information about its natural history.

The tails of salamanders and lizards, and of some snakes, break off easily. To avoid confusion, therefore, the length of an amphibian or reptile is normally measured from the tip of the snout to the vent and is called snout-vent length (or sometimes standard length). Unless stated otherwise, the sizes of animals discussed in this book are snout-vent lengths. The size of turtles is determined by measuring the distance in a straight line between the front and rear of the shell (carapace).

Although technical jargon has generally been avoided in the text, economy of expression requires the use of technical terminology at times. A glossary of technical terms begins on page 301.

Getting Started

All Costa Rican vertebrates (animals with backbones) that do not have hair, feathers, or fins, are either amphibians or reptiles. If the individual has moist, nonscaly skin, it is an amphibian; otherwise, it is a reptile.

Table 1: Physical Distinctions between Amphibians and Reptiles

	Amphibian	*Reptile*
	moist skin/no scales	scales
no limbs	caecilian	snake
four limbs, with tail	salamander	lizard or crocodilian
four limbs, no tail	frog or toad	n/a
shell	n/a	turtle

A quick glance at table 1 reveals two possible areas of confusion. First, both caecilians and snakes are limbless, and while caecilians do not actually have tails, they appear to have one. However, since there are only four species of caecilians in Costa Rica and they spend most of their time burrowing underground, you are generally much more likely to see a snake than a caecilian. Caecilians are elongated in shape and have no externally visible eyes. They have thin, moist skin that appears segmented, giving them a wormlike appearance. Snakes, on the other hand, have scales and generally have clearly visible eyes. Also they have long, whip-like tails.

Second, both salamanders and lizards have four limbs and a tail. In practice, salamanders and lizards are fairly easy to distinguish. Salamanders have noticeably moist, smooth skin; lizards have dry, scaly skin.

As for other groups, there should be little chance for confusion. Even the nonspecialist can quickly identify an animal as a crocodile or a caiman, though distinguishing between the two may not be so easy; and the distinct body shape of frogs and toads, as well as turtles, should make identifying them easy.

You should note one additional source of confusion: Some snakes, most lizard species, and many salamanders have the ability to shed their tails as a defense mechanism, although when the tail has been shed, usually a short stump remains. Among amphibians and reptiles, the only truly tailless species are the frogs and toads. If you encounter another animal without a tail, keep in mind that it may have been shed.

Literature

Coen 1983.

Systematics of Amphibians and Reptiles

The desire to identify, categorize, and label is apparently inherent in humans; but until the mid-eighteenth century, most plants and animals had only local names, and these names were not applied in a systematic, logical manner. The invention of binomial nomenclature by the Swedish botanist Carolus Linnaeus drastically altered this situation. He proposed a unique genus-species label for each species of plant and animal. Linnaeus also argued that organisms should be placed in a series of hierarchical groups; thus, similar species could be placed in the same genus, similar genera placed in the same family, and so on.

Linnaeus conducted his studies during an era in which religious dogma influenced—even controlled—much scientific thinking. His interest in the reproductive organs of plants, the very notion of which affronted the Catholic Church, perhaps exacerbated the skepticism with which his ideas were originally met. However, over time the usefulness of the unique genus-species label became apparent to scientists, and today Linnaeus's work still forms the backbone of systematics.

Systematics consists of two disciplines, taxonomy and phylogeny. Taxonomy, the strict classification of living organisms, views the natural world as a snapshot in time; phylogeny, which is fundamentally a historical discipline, deals with more or less philosophical questions of how certain organisms or groups are related to a greater or lesser degree.

Taxonomy principally concerns itself with the classification of species, which are generally classified on the basis of unique morphological traits. Species that have specific traits in common are thought to be more closely related than those that do not.

A fundamental problem in taxonomy is that no two animals are exactly the same. When an individual animal is assigned to a certain species, it is done based on the fact that a particular individual has typical characteristic features that fall within the variation known for the species. If it falls outside of that specific variation, either we are dealing with a new species or the original species should be considered more variable than previously thought.

Perhaps recollections of high school biology may lead one to offer a simple way of resolving whether an individual is a member of a given species. If the definition of a species is the set of all animals capable of mating and producing fertile offspring, then an individual animal could be put to this test. Though in theory this is correct, the realities of field research make this solution a practical impossibility. Furthermore, there are exceptions to this rule. In the family Ranidae, for example, three European species are able to interbreed and produce *fertile* hybrids. Also, the females of several lizards, including a few Costa Rican species, are able to reproduce without mating. In the absence of any males, all female populations of these species are able to produce fertile offspring through the process of parthenogenesis. In this case, all offspring produced are females.

In some cases, biologists believe that a species contains members that should be assigned to a new species, or, similarly, that a genus contains species that should probably belong to another genus. They maintain such "incorrect" classifications until new information can resolve the issue. An example of this is found in the amphibian genera *Hyla* and *Eleutherodactylus*; both are large genera containing a great diversity of individuals. Undoubtedly these genera contain individuals that will someday be assigned to other genera, or even other families.

While taxonomy's job is to describe the animal world as we find it today and to bring order to the immense variety within that world, it often does so at the price of obscuring the relationships between groups. For example, taxonomy classifies tetrapods in this manner:

Class Amphibia (amphibians)
Class Reptilia (reptiles)
  Order Chelonia (turtles)
  Order Crocodylia (crocodilians)
  Order Squamata (lizards, snakes, amphisbaenians)
  Order Rhynchocephalia (tuataras)
Class Aves (birds)
Class Mammalia (mammals)

This classification, which places amphibians, reptiles, birds, and mammals at the same level, obscures the fact that, while they all share a common ancestor, these classes did not all originate at the same time. To better understand the ancestral, evolutionary relationships between groups, one must turn to the related field of phylogeny. The principal tool of phylogenetic research is the analysis of genetic material. This analysis provides an indication of the age of a species and the relationships between species. While a key tool, the analysis of genetic material is only one tool among many for resolving phylogenetic issues. The results of genetic analysis are subject to interpretation, and this may lead to conflicting interpretations.

Phylogenetic research classifies tetrapods according to their ancestral relationships:

Tetrapoda (vertebrates with four limbs, although some species may have lost those again over time)
- -Amphibians (the most primitive tetrapods, with jelly-coated eggs, a larval stage, and a metamorphosis)
- -Amniota (tetrapods with three embryonic membranes)
  - -Mammalia (mammals)
  - -Reptilia (the animals we call reptiles, and birds)
    - -Testudinata (turtles)
    - -Sauria (archosaurs and lepidosaurs)
      - -Archosauria (crocodilians and birds)
      - -Lepidosauria (tuataras, amphisbaenians, lizards, and snakes)

While the traditional taxonomic classification of amphibians, reptiles, birds, and mammals views each as simply taxa on the same hierarchical level, phylogeny is concerned with charting relationships on the evolutionary tree. It describes the order in which the taxa appeared as well as their ancestral relationships.

The traditional taxonomic scheme hides the connections between, for example, reptiles and birds, but phylogeny shows that birds descended from reptiles. When carefully examined, birds and reptiles have much in common. For example, the scales that typically cover the entire body in reptiles are still present on birds' feet and legs. Although several species of contemporary reptiles are live-bearing, primitive species are thought to all have laid shelled eggs, just as birds do.

Literature
Greene 1997.

AMPHIBIANS

Table 2: Taxonomy of Costa Rican Amphibians

Order	*Family*	*Number of Species*
Gymnophiona	Caeciliaidae (Caecilians)	4
Caudata	Plethodontidae (Lungless salamanders)	37
Anura	Rhinophrynidae (Mexican burrowing toads)	1
	Bufonidae (Toads)	14
	Centrolenidae (Glass frogs)	13
	Dendrobatidae (Poison-dart frogs)	8
	Hylidae (Tree frogs)	43
	Leptodactylidae (Leptodactylid frogs)	46
	Microhylidae (Narrow-mouthed frogs)	3
	Ranidae (True frogs)	5

Introduction to Amphibians

Amphibians are found in all parts of the world, except in Antarctica and on some oceanic islands; they are also absent from oceans and other saltwater habitats. Present day amphibians are divided into three major groups, or orders: the caecilians (order Gymnophiona, burrowing wormlike animals), the salamanders (order Caudata), and the frogs and toads (order Anura). At present, there are slightly more than 150 different species of caecilians known throughout the world, along with about 400 species of salamanders and almost 4,000 species of frogs and toads. Representatives of all three orders occur in Costa Rica; to date 174 species of amphibians have been identified there.

Each of the three amphibian orders is divided into smaller groups, called families, whose member species share distinctive characteristics. Only one family of caecilians and one family of salamanders occur in Costa Rica, while there are eight families of frogs and toads (see table 2). Each family and at least one of its representative species are described in this book.

Amphibians (Class Amphibia) form an intermediate group of vertebrates between the completely aquatic fish and the land-dwelling reptiles, birds, and mammals (some mammals, such as whales and dolphins, have returned to life in the water). Amphibians were the first vertebrates to develop paired front and hind legs, although they were not the first to evolve mechanisms for breathing out of water; several fish had developed lungs earlier. Paleontologists believe that, roughly 350 million years ago, the first ancestors of the amphibians we know today left the water and populated land.

As with other large taxonomic animal groups, the diversity among species of amphibians is so great that it is very difficult to say with any degree of specificity what it is that makes an amphibian an amphibian. Although numerous morphological characteristics exist, these are often impossible to perceive without dissecting the animal. Therefore, many definitions center on the role that water plays in the natural history of amphibians, particularly with respect to the development of their young and to habitat selection.

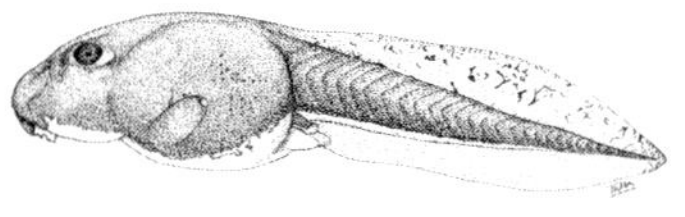

A typical anuran tadpole. **Yellow toad** (*Bufo luetkenii*).

Although there are many exceptions, most species of amphibians begin their lives as aquatic larvae (commonly known as tadpoles) and transform into land-dwelling adults; this process is called metamorphosis. During their aquatic phase, amphibians use gills, the surface of their skin, and the thin skin inside their mouths to absorb oxygen from the surrounding water. During metamorphosis, their gills disappear and are replaced by lungs, which allow the animals to breathe air and begin living on land.

This transformation from gills to lungs could serve as the perfect identifying characteristic for amphibians, except for the fact that a few species of salamanders never loose their gills and live their entire lives in water. Also, species of a large family of salamanders, the lungless salamanders (Plethodontidae), never develop lungs, although, as adults, they are able to breathe air and live on land. Even though the vast majority of adult amphibians have lungs, they continue to absorb perhaps 50% of their oxygen requirement through the skin and the lining of the mouth. Such oxygen absorption only works when the skin is thin, moist, and permeable, traits found in all adult amphibians.

The permeability of amphibian skin has one major drawback: it makes amphibians extremely vulnerable to the dehydrating effects of life on dry land. Since dehydration can be fatal, amphibians have developed a variety of strategies to maintain body moisture. Some species continue to live a primarily aquatic existence, even as adults. These species are the only amphibians that can afford to live in areas exposed to direct sunlight without risk of dehydration. Among the Costa Rican amphibians, only some of the true frogs (family Ranidae) are partially aquatic. They are sometimes seen in ponds, rivers, or streams during the day.
All other day-active amphibians have found different ways to avoid excessive dehydration. Some species, including those in the poison-dart frog family (family Dendrobatidae), live in permanently moist leaf litter, below the closed-canopy forest. This habitat receives only a small percentage of the available sunlight, since dense foliage overhead blocks out the majority of it. Other amphibians, like the harlequin toads (genus *Atelopus*), inhabit the spray-zones of either waterfalls or rapids in fast-flowing mountain streams and absorb moisture from the air and the rocks they perch on.

The majority of Costa Rican amphibians, however, avoid dehydration by shifting their period of main activity to the night. Amphibian activity patterns are also influenced by seasonal climate changes. In northwestern Costa Rica, for example, a pronounced dry season forces amphibians to seek refuge in humid shelters for extended periods of time.

Because amphibians are preyed upon by many different animals, including insects, spiders, birds, reptiles, mammals, and even other amphibians, they rely on a number of fascinating defense strategies. While mucus glands help maintain skin moisture in adults, amphibians also have another type of skin gland, the so-called granular gland, that produces toxic secretions. In all species, these toxins protect the skin against infections caused by bacteria and fungi, while in some species the toxins are sufficiently strong to serve as a defense against predators. Among the most toxic species in Costa Rica are the poison-dart frogs of the genera *Dendrobates* and *Phyllobates*, the toads of the genera *Bufo* and *Atelopus*, and the salamanders of the genus *Bolitoglossa*. The toxins that amphibians carry may cause convulsions, obstruct breathing, influence the heart rate, or even cause death.

Often, toxic species are brightly colored to ward off potential predators. Most amphibians, however, do not have strong skin toxins and rely on camouflage (cryptic coloration) to escape detection by predators. Other amphibian defense mechanisms include the erratic path traced by hopping frogs, which leaves a discontinuous scent trail and thus throws off pursuing snakes; lungs that inflate to make the animal look larger and thus more intimidating and more difficult to eat; and the ability many salamanders have to "release" the tail when it is grabbed by a predator.

In early life, most amphibians—as tadpoles—move through the water using a muscular tail. With metamorphosis, the means of locomotion changes radically, and most adult frogs, toads, and salamanders develop two pairs of limbs. In salamanders, the front and hind limbs are similarly structured, each consisting of a thigh, heel, and foot. In contrast, frogs and toads have arms (front limbs) that consist of three segments (upper arm, lower arm, and hand) and legs (hind limbs) that have four (thigh, heel, tarsus, and foot). All Costa Rican amphibians have four fingers and five toes, except for the strange Mexican burrowing toad (*Rhinophrynus dorsalis*), which has four fingers and *four* toes.

Different species have evolved hands and feet adapted to specific functions. Some have adhesive disks useful for climbing, or skinlike webbing between the digits for swimming; others have spadelike tubercles for burrowing. The locomotion of caecilians (order Gymnophiona) is entirely distinct from that of frogs, toads, and salamanders. Caecilians, the most primitive amphibians, are limbless creatures with adaptations highly specialized for a burrowing lifestyle. Their body is elongate, and their bullet-shaped head is designed for pushing through the earth.

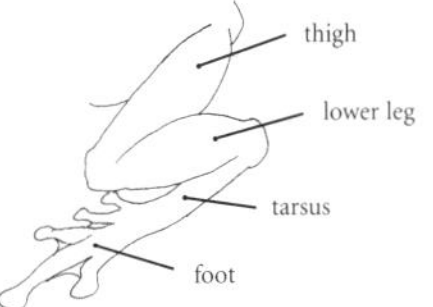

Four sections of anuran hind limb.

Most tadpoles feed mainly on algae and decaying plant matter. In some species, tadpoles are carnivorous and feed on amphibian eggs or other tadpoles. All adult amphibians are strictly carnivorous, predominantly feeding on invertebrates (mostly insects and spiders); the larger frogs and toads occasionally eat vertebrates such as other frogs, reptiles, and small mammals.

The mouth of a tadpole usually consists of a horny serrated beak (also referred to as a larval beak), several rows of hard, filelike teeth, and a sucker around the mouth to cling to rocks or logs while grazing for algae. This entire organ disappears during metamorphosis and is restructured into a mouth that can be opened widely and closed completely; it is often lined with small teeth. In addition, most adult Costa Rican amphibians have a long tongue that is attached to the front of the mouth and fires out, projectile like, to capture prey. In most frogs, toads, and salamanders, the tongue has a sticky tip.

Caecilians differ from other amphibians in that they have no free-swimming tadpole stage. All Costa Rican species are live-bearers. Embryos develop within the mother's body and utilize fetal teeth specialized for gathering a nutritious secretion from the walls of the oviducts where they develop. Shortly after birth, these fetal teeth are replaced by regular dentition suitable for eating insect prey.

The males of many species of frogs and toads produce calls to establish territorial rights and to attract the attention of potential mates. Each species produces a distinctive call. In frogs and toads, the most important sound receptors are the external ears, although vibrations from low-frequency sounds are also detected through the front limbs. Frogs and toads also have well-developed senses of smell and sight, and there is evidence that visual cues, in addition to calls, play a role in communication between individuals of the same species. How communication takes place in salamanders and caecilians is poorly understood; they most likely rely on chemical signals, as indicated by the presence of paired chemosensory organs on the head of lungless salamanders (family Plethodontidae) and of caecilians.

In frogs and toads, mating is generally initiated by a sexually active female, who selects a calling male. After a brief courtship, the male climbs onto the female's back and "embraces" her with his arms, clasping her tightly near the armpits. This sexual embrace, called amplexus, may last from a few hours to several weeks, depending on the species. In all Costa Rican frogs and toads, fertilization of the eggs takes place outside the female's body; in general, female frogs and toads lay their eggs, and the male, who is usually still located on the female's back, releases his sperm over the eggs as they leave the female's body. Most frogs and toads lay their eggs in bodies of water (see page 32 for more information on different reproductive strategies employed by Costa Rican amphibians).

In Costa Rican salamanders and caecilians, there is no amplexus. Salamanders have a dancelike courtship display that differs from species to species; the courtship and mating patterns of caecilians are poorly understood. In both salamanders and caecilians, the eggs are fertilized while still inside the mother's body. Male caecilians have a penislike organ that is inserted into the female's cloaca to deposit sperm. Male salamanders, on the other hand, deposit a spermatophore, a cone-shaped structure capped with a jellylike package of sperm, on the ground. During the courtship ritual, the female picks up the sperm with the lips of her cloaca. The sperm is stored inside the cloaca until the female lays her eggs. Just before the eggs leave the female's body, they are fertilized by the stored sperm.

Costa Rican salamanders do not lay their eggs directly in water, but in a moist spot on land, usually on the forest floor. The larvae complete their development and undergo metamorphosis inside the egg before hatching as tiny salamanders. In one frog genus, *Eleutherodactylus*, metamorphosis also takes place within the egg. Caecilians take this reproductive strategy even further; their larvae hatch inside the body of the female, making these animals one of the very few live-bearing amphibians.

In general, amphibians lay small eggs surrounded by a jellylike capsule that swells when it comes into contact with water. The eggs have no protective shell or embryonic membrane, unlike reptilian eggs, which have a hard or leathery shell and three embryonic membranes.

S U M M A R Y

How to identify members of the different amphibian orders:

- Order Gymnophiona (caecilians): limbless animals with an elongate, wormlike body; the eyes are degenerate, but the mouth is clearly visible; the body is covered with moist, glandular skin that is arranged in annular folds.
- Order Caudata (salamanders): animals with four limbs and a tail; the skin is moist and glandular.
- Order Anura (frogs and toads): animals with four limbs and no tail; the skin is moist and glandular.

Literature

Duellman & Trueb 1986; Savage & Villa 1986; Zug 1993.

Variations on a Theme: Amphibian Reproduction

Most temperate-zone amphibians lay eggs in a body of water, where the eggs hatch into free-swimming tadpoles. Tadpoles metamorphose into small frogs, toads, or salamanders that come to shore, leaving the aquatic habitat behind until they are ready to reproduce. In tropical regions, however, amphibians have developed several fascinating variations on this theme. This section describes the various reproductive strategies used by Costa Rican amphibians.

Live-bearing amphibians

Caecilians are the only live-bearing amphibians in Costa Rica. Females of all four species retain the eggs in the oviduct, where they hatch and develop into juvenile caecilians before leaving the mother's body. During development, the larvae feed on secretions from the inner lining of the female's oviduct.

Direct development: eggs hatch as miniature versions of the adult, with no free-swimming tadpole stage

No Costa Rican salamander has a free-swimming tadpole stage; the same is true for all rain frogs of the genus *Eleutherodactylus*. These amphibians lay large-yolked eggs in a humid depression in the forest floor, hidden from view by leaf litter, a log, or a rock. Some species with an arboreal lifestyle lay the clutch of eggs in a moist place often far above the ground, on a mossy branch or inside a bromeliad. The larvae of lungless salamanders and rain frogs undergo a highly specialized development that is completed inside the egg; they hatch as a salamander or tiny froglet. Amphibians that reproduce through direct development of the larvae produce large eggs with a very high yolk content. Since it requires more energy to produce such eggs, females of direct-developing species generally produce smaller clutches than those whose eggs result in free-swimming aquatic tadpoles.

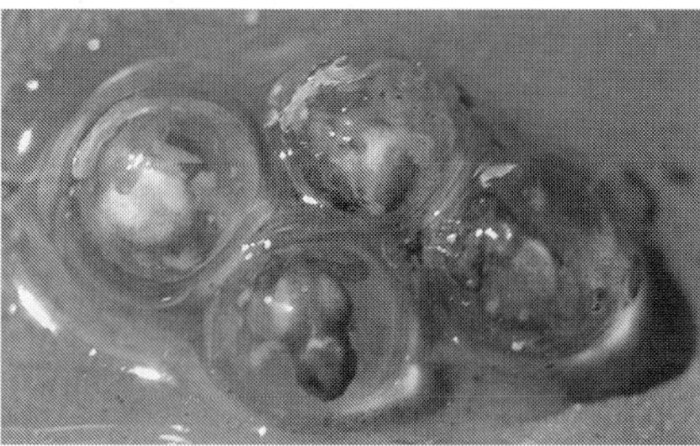

Eleutherodactylus diastema eggs. Unlike most frogs and toads, which begin life as free-swimming tadpoles, the larvae of the genus *Eleutherodactylus* develop into tiny froglets within the egg.

Larvae of the horned marsupial tree frog, *Gastrotheca cornuta*, also complete their entire development inside the egg. In this species, however, the eggs are carried around by the female in a pouch on her back. After hatching, little tree frogs emerge from the pouch.

All other Costa Rican amphibians are thought to have an aquatic tadpole stage, although the tadpoles of these 14 species still remain undiscovered: *Atelopus chiriquiensis*, *Atelopus senex*, *Bufo melanochloris*, *Crepidophryne epiotica*, *Centrolenella ilex*, *Cochranella albomaculata*, *Cochranella euknemos*, *Hyalinobatrachium chirripoi*, *Hyalinobatrachium pulveratum*, *Hyalinobatrachium talamancae*, *Hyalinobatrachium vireovittatum*, *Duellmanohyla lythrodes*, *Hyla miliaria*, and *Hyla xanthosticta*.

A female **horned marsupial tree frog** (*Gastrotheca cornuta*) carrying her eggs in a pouch on the back.

Eggs hatch on land, tadpoles carried to water

This reproductive strategy is employed by all 8 Costa Rican poison-dart frogs (Dendrobatidae). All lay eggs in a moist spot in the leaf-litter layer or on the forest floor. After the tadpoles hatch, a parent carries its offspring to water on its back, and the tadpoles develop there. One species, *Colostethus nubicola*, deposits its tadpoles in small streams, while the other species generally place their tadpoles in water-filled treeholes, fallen palm fronds, bromeliads, leaf axils, or other small basins. The larvae either feed on available organic matter or, in the case of *Dendrobates pumilio* and *Dendrobates granuliferus*, are fed nutritive eggs by the female parent.

Eggs hatch on vegetation, tadpoles drop into water

As far as is known, all Costa Rican glass frogs lay their eggs on the upper or lower surface of a leaf overhanging a fast-flowing stream. The eggs hatch during a nighttime rain, and the tadpoles wash off the leaf into the stream, where they hide between the debris on the bottom.

Some members of the tree frog family (all *Agalychnis* species, *Phyllomedusa lemur*, *Hyla ebraccata*, *Hyla calypsa*, and *Hyla lancasteri*) place their eggs on vegetation, but the body of water where the tadpoles develop differs from species to species. For example, the tadpoles of Lancaster's tree frog (*Hyla lancasteri*) drop into a stream, whereas the eggs of the spurred yellow-eyed leaf frog (*Agalychnis calcarifer*) were observed overhanging a small water-filled depression in a fallen log. Most of these tree frogs, however, place their eggs over temporary ponds.

Eggs of **red-eyed leaf frog** (*Agalychnis callidryas*). Sometimes parents fold over the leaf where the eggs are deposited, thus protecting the developing tadpoles from direct sunlight.

When the arboreal eggs hatch, the tadpoles are usually larger and have reached a further stage of development than do aquatic tadpoles at the time of hatching. Eggs deposited on vegetation are usually larger than those in water, and they contain more yolk; the number of eggs laid in water, on the other hand, is often twice as large as those placed on a leaf surface.

Both eggs and tadpoles develop in tree holes or in other arboreal basins

Four species of tree frogs are known to lay their eggs in water-filled tree holes or in water-filled bromeliads. Two small tree frogs, Zetek's bromeliad frog (*Hyla zeteki*) and Picado's bromeliad frog (*Hyla picadoi*) spend most of their lives in bromeliads and also reproduce there. Their tadpoles are specially adapted to life in a small basin of water; they can, for example, survive in water with a very low oxygen content. The crowned tree frog (*Anotheca spinosa*) places its eggs in water-filled tree cavities and feeds its offspring with nutritive eggs. The highland fringed-limbed tree frog (*Hyla fimbrimembra*), and possibly the closely related lowland fringed-limbed tree frog (*Hyla miliaria*) also breed in tree holes.

Eggs and tadpoles develop in a body of water

This is by far the most common reproductive strategy in Costa Rican amphibians, although a few variant forms exist, the most distinctive of which is the unique breeding pattern of the gladiator tree frog, *Hyla rosenbergi*, which constructs a special basin for its eggs and tadpoles.

The Costa Rican species of the genus *Leptodactylus* and the tungara frog (*Physalaemus pustulosus*) are distinctive in making a floating foam nest that contains their eggs. The emerging tadpoles leave the foam nest and drop into a temporary pool, where they complete their development.

Most Costa Rican anurans reproduce in temporary pools. In large permanent bodies of water, which are rare in Costa Rica, the danger of predation by fish is great. Giant toads (*Bufo marinus*) and green-eyed frogs (*Rana vibicaria*) are known to breed occasionally in permanent bodies of water. Mexican burrowing toads (*Rhinophrynus dorsalis*), all toads of the genus *Bufo*, many tree frogs, all true frogs (genus *Rana*) and all narrow-mouthed frogs (family Microhylidae) predominantly breed in temporary ponds; the tadpoles complete their metamorphosis in the same pool. The tadpoles of the genus *Rana*, and some of the genus *Bufo*, are sometimes found in slow-moving parts of streams.

Thousands of tadpoles of the **giant toad** (*Bufo marinus*) congregate to form a large group in the middle of a temporary pond.

The remainder of the tree frogs, such as the stream-breeding tree frogs (genus *Duellmanohyla*), and variable harlequin frogs (*Atelopus varius*) lay their eggs in streams, where they are often anchored to rocks or other large objects. Their tadpoles live in quiet parts of the stream, or have a large suction disk that they use to hold on to objects in order to resist the water current.

Literature

Donnelly 1994; Jaramillo et al. 1997; Jungfer 1996; Lips & Savage 1996b; Scott & Limerick 1983.

ORDER: **Gymnophiona** (Caecilians)
CLASS: Amphibians

It is hard to imagine that these dull-looking creatures belong to the same class of animals as some of the most delicate, gemlike frogs. Caecilians are limbless, elongate creatures that are found only in the tropics. They have no ear openings, and their eyes are reduced. In all species of caecilians found in Costa Rica, the eyes are covered by skin and are barely discernible. In one species, *Gymnopis multiplicata*, the eye sockets are even covered over with bone, which lies below a layer of skin.

Caecilians look like giant earthworms—both animals have segmented bodies and generally lack externally visible features. They distinguish themselves from the latter by a variety of features, the most visible of which is a large mouth.

Limbless, earless, and essentially eyeless, these animals appear to be a kind of null entity. Nevertheless, even the limited information available about their natural history and biology reveals a highly specialized creature, greatly adapted to a burrowing life, with features not found in other animals.

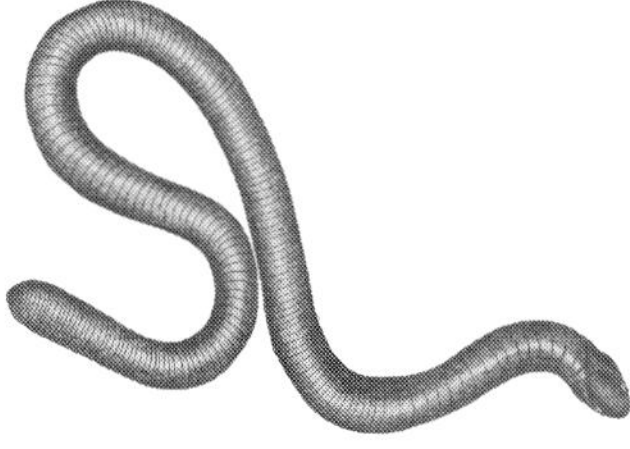

Purple caecilian (*Gymnopis multiplicata*).

Caecilians spend most of their time hunting for prey underground or hiding beneath logs, rocks, or leaf litter. Occasionally, during or after extremely heavy rains, caecilians are found on the surface of the forest floor, perhaps in order to forage or simply because their burrows have been flooded.

An excellent burrower, a caecilian creates tunnels by bracing its body against the earth and pushing its bullet-shaped head forward into soft soil. The head is covered with smooth skin that contains numerous tiny glands. These glands produce a slimy substance that helps reduce friction as the animal burrows. Also, tiny nostrils, along with eyes covered by skin and/or bone, reduce irritation to the nose and eyes when the caecilian pushes through the soil.

The only features of the head that protrude slightly are a pair of short, retractable tentacles, one on each side of the head. These tentacles, which sense chemical cues, are primarily used for locating prey.

Caecilians possess several biological traits that are otherwise unknown or highly unusual among amphibians. For example, fertilization takes place inside the female's body; the male inseminates the female by inserting a penislike structure, called a phallodeum, into the female's cloaca. Copulation is very uncommon among amphibians; in most species, fertilization takes place outside the female's body. Also highly unusual is the fact that most caecilians bear live young (as opposed to laying eggs). Although some caecilian species reproduce by laying eggs, as far as we know, all Costa Rican species are live-bearing. The larvae develop within the mother's body and feed on a highly nutritious substance that is secreted from the lining of the female's oviducts (the tubes that transport eggs from the ovary). The unborn young have special fetal teeth they use to scrape food from the oviduct walls; this scraping, in turn, stimulates the continued production of nutritious secretions. Shortly after birth, the babies' fetal teeth are replaced by regular adult teeth suitable for eating invertebrate prey. Caecilian larvae undergo metamorphosis, much like tadpoles do. However, they complete the part of the life cycle that tadpoles complete in an aquatic environment within the confines of the mother's body. At the time of birth, the larvae have developed into fully formed, miniature caecilians.

SUMMARY

How to identify Costa Rican caecilians:

- Caecilians are amphibians that look like large worms, except for a clearly visible mouth. The moist, sticky skin is creased into ringlike folds that encircle the body.
- All Costa Rican caecilians are in the family Caeciliaidae.

FAMILY: **Caeciliaidae** (Caecilians)
ORDER: Gymnophiona

All four caecilian species found in Costa Rica belong to the family Caeciliaidae. Two species, *Dermophis gracilior* (formerly known as *Dermophis mexicanus*) and *Dermophis parviceps*, are closely related and belong to the same genus; the extremely rare *Oscaecilia osae* (known only from a single individual) and the fourth Costa Rican caecilian, *Gymnopis multiplicata*, are each in a different genus.

All caecilians have skin folds (annuli) that encircle the body. The so-called primary folds appear at more or less regular intervals. Their number is related to the skeletal structure of the animal: there is one primary fold for each vertebra. Secondary folds are those skin folds that are located between two primary skin folds. Each species has a distinctive combination of primary and secondary skin folds. *Dermophis parviceps*, for example, has an extremely low number of secondary skin folds, which appear only near the vent. Other species have a greater number of secondary folds, giving them a more segmented appearance.

Gray caecilian (*Dermophis gracilior*). The tentacle is located halfway between the eye spot and the nostril.

A second distinguishing feature, which is easier to observe, is the location of the two tentacles; they are between the eye and nostril in *Dermophis*, close to the nostril in *Oscaecilia*, and near the eye in *Gymnopis*.

SPECIES DESCRIPTIONS

Dermophis parviceps
Slender caecilian (plate 1)

Dermophis parviceps is the most slender Costa Rican caecilian. Its eyes are clearly visible through the skin; a short tentacle is located between the eye and the nostril on each side of the head.

The body is a lavender purple with tiny light specks. The head, which is relatively elongate, is grayish brown. The throat and lower jaw, as well as the area around the vent, are whitish. *Dermophis parviceps* reaches a total length of at least 425 mm (17 inches).

Dermophis parviceps is known to occur in Costa Rica and Panama, from near sea level to at least 700 m (2,300 ft). In Costa Rica, it has been reported from the wet rainforests in the northeast and southwest.

Like all caecilians, *Dermophis parviceps* is a secretive animal. It is sometimes found under rocks or logs. Although caecilians rarely venture out into the open, one individual of this species was found crawling through an open, grassy clearing after an early-afternoon rain shower.

Gymnopis multiplicata
Purple caecilian
Dos cabezas (plate 1)

Gymnopis multiplicata is the only caecilian in Costa Rica that has a short, retractable tentacle on each side of the head, just below the eye. In the other commonly seen species, *Dermophis gracilior*, the tentacle is located between the eye and the nostril. *Gymnopis multiplicata* is the only Costa Rican caecilian whose eyes are not only covered by skin, but also by bone. The location of the eyes is indicated by a light spot on each side of the head. This spot also encircles the base of the tentacle.

Gymnopis multiplicata owes its common name, purple caecilian, to its coloration, which ranges from a grayish purple to lavender. This is a large species, reaching a maximum length of 510 mm (20 inches).

The purple caecilian, the most widespread caecilian in Costa Rica, ranges countrywide, from sea level to elevations of at least 1,400 m (4,600 ft). It mostly resides in forested areas, where it is found under rocks or logs, burrowed into soil, under leaf litter, between buttress roots of large trees, and in other wet places. Individuals sometimes surface to the forest floor at night or during heavy rains—presumably to forage, but possibly only to escape flooded burrows.

The caecilian diet consists of a variety of ground-dwelling or burrowing invertebrates, such as worms and insect larvae. Prey is not restricted to small invertebrates; records exist of caecilians eating small- to medium-sized lizards. Caecilians mainly use airborne chemical cues for locating prey, detecting scent particles with their sensitive tentacles.

In the confines of their dark subterranean burrows, eyes are more of a burden than an advantage since burrowing activity would irritate or damage true eyes. This is probably why caecilians have lost the use of their eyes over time. They are basically blind; at best they can distinguish between light and dark.

The main predators of caecilians appear to be birds and snakes. Coral snakes, in particular, are known to eat the occasional caecilian.

Gymnopis multiplicata gives birth to live young. Litters of two to ten babies, measuring 125 to 131 mm (4⅞ to 5⅛ inches), are produced, probably every other year. Biologists do not know the length of the gestation period, but the closely related *Dermophis gracilior* has a gestation period of about one year.

Literature

Hayes et al. 1989; Lahanas & Savage 1992; Savage & Villa 1986; Savage & Wake 1972; Taylor 1952a; Wake 1983; Zug 1993.

ORDER: **Caudata** (Salamanders)
CLASS: Amphibians

Salamanders and salamander-like animals (such as newts and axolotls) are also referred to as the tailed amphibians. This order includes eight families, and its members are very diverse in body shape and size.

Although most salamanders are small, the giant salamanders of Japan and China (genus *Andrias*) sometimes grow to over 150 cm (5 ft) in length. Salamanders are primarily found throughout temperate America and Eurasia. One family, however, the lungless salamander (family Plethodontidae), is widespread in Central and South America. All 37 salamander species known to occur in Costa Rica are in this family.

The general form and structure of a salamander's body is very similar to that of the first prehistoric amphibians. Salamanders have long tails and distinct heads, unlike frogs, toads, or caecilians, whose heads appear to be mere extensions of the body. Usually, front and hind limbs are present, although these may be very slender and short in relation to the size of the body.

Nonspecialists often confuse salamanders and lizards because their body shapes are similar. Salamanders, however, lack the scaly skin, claws, and external ear openings that lizards have.

In temperate climates, one can find salamander species that are land-dwelling (terrestrial), that live in water (aquatic), or that inhabit both environments. Even those species that spend their time on land, however, normally begin life in a body of water, first as an egg, then as a larva. In contrast, the salamanders that inhabit the tropics are either terrestrial or, in some cases, arboreal. Like all amphibians, salamanders depend on environmental moisture for survival. Tropical humidity and rainfall provide salamanders with sufficient moisture to prevent dehydration, and make them less dependent on standing bodies of water than species living in temperate climates.

All Costa Rican salamanders have developed a completely terrestrial life and, interestingly, have even lost the free-swimming larval stage. The female deposits her eggs in a moist place (e.g., leaf litter, wet moss, or under a log or rock), but never in water. The larvae develop within the watery confines of the egg, undergo metamorphosis there, and hatch as miniature replicas of their parents.

Salamanders do not copulate. Males have special glands in their cloaca that produce a gelatinous, cone-shaped structure called a spermatophore, which is capped with a small packet of sperm. During mating, a pair of sexually active salamanders initiates a courtship ritual in which the male places a spermatophore on the ground and then coerces the female to move over it. The female then picks up the packet of sperm with the lips of her cloaca and stores it there. When the environmental conditions are suitable, the female finds a place to lay her eggs; as the eggs pass through the female's cloaca, the stored sperm is released onto them and fertilization takes place. In some species of tropical salamanders, sperm can remain within the female's body for more than a year prior to egg laying.

Courtship patterns, as well as the size and shape of the male's spermatophore, differ from species to species, thus preventing cross-breeding between species.

SUMMARY

How to identify Costa Rican salamanders:

- Salamanders are amphibians with four limbs, an elongate body, and a long tail (though salamanders are capable of breaking off parts of the tail to escape predators, and in some animals part of the tail may be missing). The skin is smooth and moist, and never bears bony scales.
- All Costa Rican salamanders are in the family Plethodontidae.

Literature

Duellman & Trueb 1986; Lips 1993a,b,c,d; Savage & Villa 1986; Stebbins 1980; Zug 1993.

FAMILY: **Plethodontidae** (Lungless Salamanders)
ORDER: Caudata (Salamanders)

Plethodontidae, the largest family of salamanders, is the only family found in tropical regions. Plethodontids occur in North, Central, and South America, in northern Italy, and on the island of Sardinia. Costa Rica has three genera of lungless salamanders: *Bolitoglossa* (16 species), *Nototriton* (7 species), and *Oedipina* (14 species).

In the tropics and subtropics, lungless salamanders seem to display a preference for cool, humid habitats, like those found in forested mountain ranges. Costa Rican lungless salamanders, for example, are most abundant at moderate or high elevations in the Central and Talamanca mountain ranges. Nevertheless, with the exception of the relatively dry lowlands in northwestern Costa Rica, salamanders can be found in any suitable habitat throughout the country, from elevations near sea level to the summit of some of the highest peaks in the country—wherever there is high annual rainfall and no pronounced dry season.

Ridge-headed salamander (*Bolitoglossa colonnea*).

As their common name indicates, plethodontid salamanders are lungless. Because they breathe through their thin skin, and because gas exchange is facilitated by skin moisture, their survival depends on keeping their skin moist. Humid tropical air not only prevents adult salamanders from dehydrating, but also protects the terrestrial egg clutches from drying out, which would eventually kill the embryos.

All Costa Rican salamanders show direct development, which means that their embryos develop inside the egg into tiny salamanders. Metamorphosis, the transition from tadpole to salamander, thus takes place before hatching. Compared to frogs and toads, which sometimes lay egg clutches of tens of thousands of eggs, female salamanders produce relatively small egg clutches, usually between 10 and 30 eggs. Their eggs have a large yolk supply, which feeds the developing embryo. The time between egg-laying and hatching can be very long by amphibian standards; an egg clutch of the species *Bolitoglossa compacta* was reported to hatch about 250 days after being laid, a period of over eight months.

In many species, the female (sometimes the male) coils around the egg clutch during embryo development. The parent protects the eggs against predators, and contact between parent and eggs helps to regulate incubation temperature and humidity. At times, the parent will agitate the eggs to ensure they receive sufficient oxygen. Skin secretions from the parent seem to reduce fungal and bacterial growth that may infect the eggs. Observations of abandoned egg clutches of the mountain salamander (*Bolitoglossa subpalmata*) indicate that clutches not attended by a parent invariably die. A report on the successful reproduction in captivity of another *Bolitoglossa* species, on the other hand, showed that parental attendance of an egg clutch is not critical in all *Bolitoglossa* species, since those eggs developed into perfectly healthy young without any adult attention.

The life expectancy of salamanders, especially those living in cool climates, commonly exceeds ten years; most frogs and toads do not live longer than four to five years. A Japanese species, the Japanese giant salamander (*Andrias japonicus*), lived 55 years in captivity. One species of lungless salamander found in Costa Rica, the mountain salamander (*Bolitoglossa subpalmata*), reaches an estimated maximum age of 18 years. In a population study of this species, males were found to reach sexual maturity after 6 years, whereas females reached sexual maturity after 12 years. Most species of lungless salamanders first reproduce 0.5 to 3.5 years after hatching.

Salamanders lack an outer and middle ear, but do possess inner ear structures. Although they are thought to have a poorly developed sense of hearing, their capacity to hear remains largely unstudied. With very few exceptions, salamanders are voiceless. Most have acute vision, and see especially well at night or in dark burrows.

Chemoreception, the perception of chemical cues, is probably their most important sense. It helps salamanders locate food, identify potential mates, and perhaps avoid predators. All plethodontids have nasolabial grooves, visible on each side of the snout as a furrow connecting the nostril and the upper lip. These organs appear to play an important role in the reception of chemical traces. Crawling salamanders can often be seen tapping their nose on the substrate. Experiments have shown that the waterborne chemicals present in the film of moisture that covers everything in the salamander's humid environment are carried through the nasolabial grooves to a highly sensitive sensory organ.

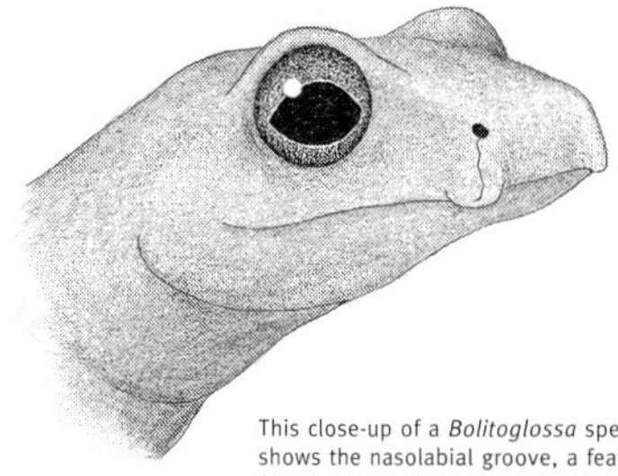

This close-up of a *Bolitoglossa* species shows the nasolabial groove, a feature found exclusively in plethodontid salamanders.

Several salamanders have noxious skin secretions that are bitter and burn the eyes or the lining of the mouth of would-be predators. In some species of *Bolitoglossa*, including those found in Costa Rica, these secretions can cause predators to regurgitate their prey. In severe cases of poisoning, they can impair coordination, or even kill the predator.

A specialized means of escaping predation that is widespread in the family Plethodontidae is pseudoautotomy, or tail breakage after the tail has been grasped. After an animal loses its tail, a replacement grows back completely, including vertebrae and all other tissues (unlike lizards, which develop a new, secondary tail that does not have vertebrae). Many species of *Bolitoglossa* have a slight constriction at the tail base—immediately behind the cloaca—where tail breakage occurs most often. Neither *Nototriton* nor *Oedipina*, the other two genera of Costa Rican salamanders, have a constriction at the tail base. At least some species of the genus *Oedipina* are capable of pseudoautotomy, however. There are no studies on pseudoautotomy in *Nototriton*.

Alvarado's salamander (*Bolitoglossa alvaradoi*) using prehensile tail.

Salamanders are not easy to observe. They are scarce compared to frogs and toads, and they have secretive habits. Generally, salamanders in the genera *Bolitoglossa* and *Nototriton* climb well. Their extensively webbed hands and feet adhere to the climbing surface, and their prehensile tails help anchor them to branches. Species of the genus *Bolitoglossa* often inhabit even the highest regions of the forest canopy, far from human sight, while moss salamanders (genus *Nototriton*) are mostly found in moss mats that hang in trees or bushes, or in the moss that covers tree trunks and large boulders. The genus *Oedipina* appears to be more terrestrial, but these salamanders are still difficult to see since they usually live concealed in leaf litter or in clumps of moss.

If salamanders are difficult to observe, they are practically impossible to identify in the field because distinguishing features, such as the number of teeth and the amount of webbing between fingers and toes, can only be observed properly using a microscope. You should never attempt to examine such microscopic features on a living salamander; it would cause excessive stress to the animal.

Seven species of Costa Rican lungless salamanders are described in the following sections. The mountain salamander (*Bolitoglossa subpalmata*) is the most commonly observed Costa Rican salamander species and probably the most studied. The ring-tailed salamander (*Bolitoglossa robusta*) is included simply because it is one of the few species

Bolitoglossa hand and foot

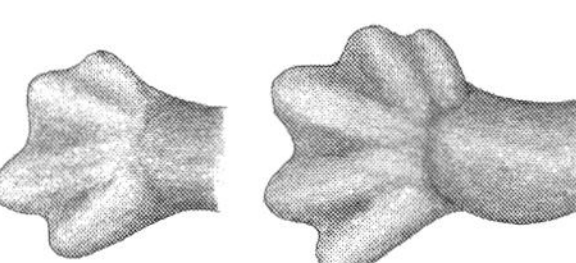

Oedipina hand and foot

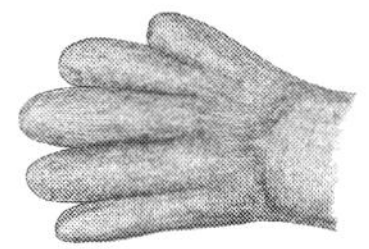

Bolitoglossa species have wide hands and feet that may be twice as wide as the limbs to which they are attached. *Oedipina* species (worm salamanders) have narrow hands and feet that are not much wider than their limbs.

that is easy to identify in the field. The worm salamanders (*genus Oedipina*) are described since, as a genus, they are easily recognized. Brief descriptions are also included for *Bolitoglossa alvaradoi, Bolitoglossa colonnea, Bolitoglossa lignicolor,* and *Bolitoglossa striatula,* to indicate the diversity within this family.

SPECIES DESCRIPTIONS

Bolitoglossa alvaradoi

Alvarado's salamander (plate 2)

Alvarado's salamander is a rather large, arboreal species with a maximum known length of 159 mm (6¼ inches), including the tail. It is a robust salamander with almost completely webbed hands and feet. The color pattern is highly variable and even changes within a single individual; the daytime and nighttime coloration of this species is strikingly different. During the daylight hours, this species can be almost completely black, save for a few large, islandlike patches of a lighter color (cream to tan). At night, the dark ground color of the body and tail lightens to gray, tan, or reddish brown, with a pattern of irregularly scattered black or dark brown spots. Sometimes the body coloration lightens so much that the light patches visible in the daytime coloration are barely discernible.

Bolitoglossa alvaradoi is only known from Costa Rica, where it has been found in a few locations on the Caribbean slope at elevations between approximately 700 and 1,150 m (2,300 and 3,750 ft). Occasionally, adults are seen perched on vegetation at night, but apart from the general knowledge derived from other *Bolitoglossa* species as a group, little is known about the biology of this species.

Bolitoglossa colonnea

Ridge-headed salamander (plate 2)

In Costa Rica, *Bolitoglossa colonnea* is one of the more commonly seen salamanders. A distinguishing feature is the pronounced fleshy ridge that runs between the eyes.

This medium-sized species may reach 130 mm (5⅛ inches) including the tail. Its fingers and toes are almost completely enveloped in skinlike webbing; the hands and feet resemble fleshy pads. A protuberance bearing a naso-labial groove is clearly visible on each side of the snout.

During the day, *Bolitoglossa colonnea* has a dark-brown mottled coloration. At night, this becomes significantly lighter, and changes to a uniform salmon to tan coloration that is sometimes marked by small dark specks.

This species has been found in Costa Rica and Panama. In Costa Rica, it inhabits the Caribbean slope and the southwestern region of the country, from near sea level to at least 1,000 m (3,300 ft).

At rest, *Bolitoglossa colonnea* curls up, with the tail wrapped around the body. On warm, humid nights, they are sometimes found perched on leaves in low vegetation. One individual was found during the day under the loose bark of a dead tree.

Bolitoglossa lignicolor

Bark-colored salamander (plate 3)

Bolitoglossa lignicolor is a poorly known species found in southwestern Costa Rica. This salamander owes its common name to the lichenous, barklike coloration that makes it hard to see when it is perched on a tree trunk. Generally, the barklike coloration is restricted to the back and tail of this species; the lower half of the sides and the underside are usually of a uniform dark color (gray, brown, or black).

Like other Costa Rican species of *Bolitoglossa*, this species is active at night, when it can be seen climbing through foliage. During the day, these salamanders retreat into hiding, often in a crevice or under the bark of a tree.

Bolitoglossa robusta

Ring-tailed Salamander (plate 3)

Bolitoglossa robusta is the most readily identifiable species of the Costa Rican salamanders. The combination of a uniform, dark (brown to black) dorsal coloration and a light-colored ring (white, cream, yellow, orange, or reddish) around the base of the tail is unique among Costa Rican salamanders. The dark coloration on the upper parts of the body is sometimes interrupted by white or reddish flecking, especially on the upper surfaces of the tail and limbs. The belly and the underside of the tail are black or slate.

Another distinguishing feature is its size; *Bolitoglossa robusta* is the largest salamander in Costa Rica. The head and body measure 115 mm (4½ inches); including the tail, this species may reach 210 mm (8¼ inches). The body is robust and heavy-set, with large, strong limbs and wide hands and feet. The hands and feet are not completely webbed, and the tips of at least two fingers and toes protrude from the skinlike webbing.

Bolitoglossa robusta has been found at low, intermediate, and high elevations of the Tilarán, Central, and Talamanca mountain ranges; it appears to occur most often at elevations of 1,500 m (4,900 ft) and higher. This species mainly inhabits the leaf litter, where it forages for ants and beetles during the night. Individuals have been found during the day hidden under logs and rocks, inside decaying stumps, or even in arboreal bromeliads.

Bolitoglossa striatula

Striated salamander (plate 4)

This beautiful salamander is the only Costa Rican species with a striped pattern. Irregular dark brown stripes, which run the length of the body, stand out clearly from the tan or reddish-brown background color. This is a medium-sized salamander, reaching a total length of about 140 mm (5½ inches), of which a little less than half is tail.

Rarely seen in Costa Rica, *Bolitoglossa striatula* is known only from a few locations in the northeastern lowlands. It is also known from scattered locations in adjacent Nicaragua. Interestingly, there is an isolated population on the slopes of Mombacho Volcano, near Granada, Nicaragua, hundreds of miles from its main distribution range.

These salamanders are most frequently encountered during rainy nights, perched on leaves that overhang water or a road. Individuals have been found in both cultivated zones and severely disturbed habitats, as well as in dense, primary forest. During the day, they retreat under logs or leaf litter.

Bolitoglossa subpalmata

Mountain salamander (plate 4)

Bolitoglossa subpalmata is perhaps the most frequently encountered salamander in Costa Rica. In some areas it reaches population densities unknown for any other Costa Rican salamander, although its numbers dropped markedly after the late 1980s. Populations near the summit of Cerro de la Muerte used to exceed 9,000 individuals per hectare (2.5 acres). Below 2,400 m (7,850 ft), *Bolitoglossa subpalmata* is significantly less abundant.

Bolitoglossa subpalmata has a slender body, short legs, and slightly webbed hands and feet; all but the innermost fingers and toes are free from webbing for a considerable distance. This is a medium-sized species, reaching a snout-vent length of 67 mm (2⅝ inches), and a total length (including the tail) of 131 mm (5⅛ inches).

Bolitoglossa subpalmata has an extremely variable coloration, and even individuals living within the same geographical area may vary greatly. Until recently, several color forms were described as separate species; even today, the taxonomic status of this species is uncertain. The background color of the upper surfaces varies from blackish brown or gray brown through gray to olive, and can be either uniform or with spots of varying size and color. In most individuals, the belly is dark (brown, gray, or black); sometimes the belly coloration extends onto the sides. The legs are red, pink, cream, or yellowish, and the chin and throat are reddish, pink, or cream, usually of a lighter color than the belly. Considering the variability of this species, it is hard to present an accurate description. Many individuals, however, can be distinguished from other species by the presence of a pink or reddish coloration on the chin, throat, arms, and legs, a dark belly, and a lighter brownish or grayish back.

As indicated by their common name, mountain salamanders live at high altitudes. They can be found in the Tilarán, Central, and Talamanca mountain ranges, at elevations from 1,500 to 3,300+ m (4,900 to 10,800+ ft). Within this altitude range, *Bolitoglossa subpalmata* occurs in a variety of habitats and has been found in leaf litter, in or under logs, in clumps of moss, and even in bromeliads in the high canopy, more than 30 meters (100 ft) above the ground. Active salamanders have been observed on nights when temperatures were between 6.4 and 12.8°C (43.5 and 55°F); at lower temperatures, they remain in hiding. During the drier months of the year, this species restricts its surface activity since dry, windy nights significantly increase the risk of dehydration. On nights when the temperature and humidity conditions are suitable, individuals can be observed actively exploring crevices for insect prey. Prey is captured using a projectile tongue.

When confronted by a snake, individual *Bolitoglossa subpalmata* have been observed to position their body in such a way to direct the snake's attack toward a section of the salamander's skin containing a high number of glands that excrete toxic substances. In experimental conditions, snakes that bit *Bolitoglossa subpalmata* became completely motionless as quickly as 45 seconds after the attack. Some snakes suffered from what appeared to be a paralysis of the mouth—the lower jaw relaxed and then fell open, in extreme cases allowing the salamander to scurry from the attacker's mouth. Skin secretions of a Guatemalan salamander species, *Bolitoglossa rostrata*, killed 40% of the snakes that tried to eat it. Noxious, or even toxic, skin secretions constitute an effective antipredator mechanism; and although data is lacking for most species, such secretions appear to be widespread in the genus *Bolitoglossa*.

A population of *Bolitoglossa subpalmata* in Monteverde is thought to belong to a separate species, and will certainly be described as such in future literature.

Oedipina species

Worm salamanders (plate 5)

Distinguishing between species of the genus *Oedipina* is nearly impossible under field conditions. Many of the distinctive features, such as the number of teeth, or the length of the limbs, cannot be observed on a living salamander without causing it extreme distress. However, as a group, worm salamanders are easily recognized.

Members of this genus are distinguished from all other Costa Rican amphibians by an extremely slender, elongate body and tail and tiny limbs. Individuals generally do not exceed 75 mm (3 inches), or, including the tail, 210 mm (8¼ inches). Salamanders of the genus *Oedipina* have 17 to 22 transverse skin folds on the sides of the body (costal folds), while *Bolitoglossa* and *Nototriton* species all have less than 15 costal folds. These costal folds, although often barely discernible, are found on the side of the body, between the front and hind limbs.

Members of this genus are of a very similar build. Except for the presence of tiny front and hind limbs, they are almost wormlike in appearance. All species have a long and fragile tail that may be well over twice the length of the body when unbroken. The head is slightly wider than the neck, the snout is short, and the eyes, which have a black iris, are relatively large and bulging. The coloration of many

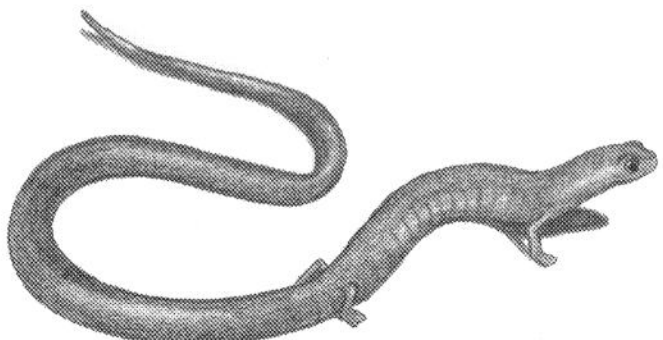

An *Oedipina* species with the tiny limbs and elongate body and tail that characterize this genus.

species is a uniform dark tone, usually tan, dark brown, gray, slate, or black. Slight differences in the intensity of the background color may appear on the head, belly, tail, or limbs. A pale lateral line on each side of the body, bordering the coloration of the belly, is reported for Poelz's worm salamander (*Oedipina poelzi*).

A few species (e.g., *Oedipina altura*) are restricted to high elevations in Costa Rica's mountain ranges, and other species, such as *Oedipina uniformis* (see plate 5), occur from near sea level to high altitudes; but the majority of the Costa Rican species of *Oedipina* are found in the Atlantic lowlands, below 1,500 m (4,900 ft). Worm salamanders can be found in habitats that range from dense primary rainforest to heavily disturbed areas; individual salamanders have also been taken from underneath rocks at the edge of streams.

In general, worm salamanders are strictly terrestrial and are rarely seen in Costa Rica. They live a secretive and nocturnal life, hidden from view in leaf litter, under wet moss mats, in or under decaying logs, in soft mud or loose soil, or in old insect burrows. These fast-moving, agile animals are often detected as a flash of motion seen out of the corner of the eye.

Literature

Brame 1968; Brodie & Ducey 1991; Brown 1968; Donnelly 1994; Hayes et al. 1989; Jiménez 1994; Mudde & van Dijk 1984e; Pounds 2000; Savage & Villa 1986; Schmidt & Köhler 1996; Scott 1983b; Stebbins 1980; Taylor 1952a; Vial 1968; Wake & Dresner 1967.

Disappearing Amphibians

Studies on extinct species are no longer the strict domain of fossil-examining paleontologists; since the late 1980s, an alarming number of amphibian species have disappeared worldwide, and this trend continues. The International Union for Conservation of Nature (IUCN) has formed a special Declining Amphibian Populations Taskforce to investigate the global demise of these animals and to take action wherever possible. Although the words *declining amphibian populations* appear on dozens of scientific papers each year, biologists have yet to arrive at a conclusive, widely agreed-upon explanation or set of explanations for the decline of amphibian populations.

The environmental changes wrought by civilization may be categorized as either global or local. Global effects include global warming and the greenhouse effect, depletion of the ozone layer, pollution of the air with exhaust fumes, and expanding deserts. Effects on a local scale include problems such as deforestation, the introduction of predatory fish in natural streams, and the pollution of water by fertilizers, pesticides, or detergents. Even though local, these problems occur in many places and often have a profound effect on the environment. Since the amphibian decline is clearly a global phenomenon, most research is being done on threats to the environment that have a worldwide effect. One of the reasons most frequently suggested for the demise of amphibians is the depletion of the ozone layer.

In areas in the world where the ozone layer has been diminished, more ultraviolet radiation reaches Earth than where the ozone layer is relatively unchanged. This type of radiation has been shown to damage DNA in amphibian eggs and thus contribute to the rapid decline of a population. A recent study, however, has demonstrated that a reduction in the ozone layer does not necessarily affect all amphibian species in a specific area to the same extent. Many amphibian eggs possess an enzyme, called photolyase, that is capable of repairing DNA damaged by excess radiation. Amphibians that produce eggs with high photolyase content are relatively safe, while other species in the same area may produce eggs that have a low photolyase content and thus may be more severely affected by radiation. In laboratory tests on eggs with low photolyase content, those eggs produced healthier offspring when incubated in an environment protected from ultraviolet radiation.

Golden toads *(Bufo periglenes). Photograph by M. & P. Fogden, courtesy of AUDIOVISE.*

Although this theory seems to explain the disappearance of many species, it does not adequately explain the disappearance of Costa Rican amphibian species such as the golden toad (*Bufo periglenes*). The abrupt decline of the golden toad between 1987 and 1988 seems better explained by a high rate of adult mortality, rather than by unsuccessful breeding. These animals spend almost 95% of their time in retreats protected from the harmful effects of ultraviolet radiation. Another frequently mentioned agent in the decline of amphibians, acid rain, is known to kill amphibian embryos but not adults, so it also does not seem to explain the decline of the golden toad.

When the golden toad first began to decline, many observers thought they were perceiving a natural population fluctuation rather than the beginning phase of a mass extinction. But when the pattern of amphibian disappearance in the Monteverde Cloud Forest Preserve in the Tilarán mountain range of Costa Rica was compared to models of expected population dynamics, biologists concluded that the population declines could not be explained by population fluctuations: 20 species of frogs and toads, or 40% of the anuran fauna in Monteverde, have disappeared since 1987. Amphibian species that survived the 1987 crash are still present in highly reduced numbers, and they do not appear to have yet recovered.

In the case of the Monteverde Cloud Forest Preserve, three hypotheses have been proposed as possible explanations for the extinction of the golden toad, the variable harlequin frog (*Atelopus varius*), and possibly other species. Two of these hypotheses are linked to extreme droughts brought on by the 1986–1987 *El Niño* weather patterns. The first hypothesis suggests that the extremely dry weather of 1987 may have desiccated breeding pools, everyday habitats, and even subterranean retreats so severely that the frogs died from dehydration. This idea is supported by the observation that, just before the variable harlequin frogs disappeared, they were gathered in extraordinary high densities around the last remaining wet areas in drying streams. If the lack of water does not in itself explain the extinction, a related explanation is that the animals, weakened by dehydration, may have fallen prey to parasitic, bacterial, fungal or viral infections.

A second hypothesis for the 1987 crash in amphibian numbers suggests a sudden deposition of high concentrations of pesticides on the reserve, carried there by the ever-present mist and clouds. Because of the relative lack of rainfall, insecticides, herbicides, and fungicides, which are used massively in surrounding areas, may have evaporated from exposed soils, only to be deposited, practically undiluted by the rainwater, onto the reserve.

The third hypothesis results from analysis of the daily weather patterns in the Monteverde Cloud Forest Preserve during the 1977–1998 period. Three crashes in the size of amphibian populations—in 1987, 1994, and 1998—coincided with unusually high numbers of dry days. Evidence suggests that sea surface temperatures, which have risen as a result of global warming, have caused an increase in the number of dry, cloudy days in the Monteverde area. In addition to affecting frog populations, these periods of dryness seem to have also reduced some lizard and bird populations. While anuran populations naturally fluctuate with changes in climate, and populations sometimes disappear from an area and then later recolonize that same area, there are indications that the ability of some species to adapt to changing weather conditions has been overtaxed in recent years.

It may be too soon to say that specific species are gone forever, but golden toads and variable harlequin frogs have not been seen in Monteverde since 1989. Other Costa Rican amphibian species, such as *Atelopus senex*, *Bufo holdridgei*, *Rana vibicaria*, and many more, have dramatically dropped in number, and some may have disappeared as well.

Very recently, biologists have uncovered evidence that fungal infections may explain the death of large numbers of frogs in certain populations worldwide, in cultivated areas as well as in untouched rainforest environments.

It is now generally accepted that habitat destruction alone does not explain the disappearance of amphibian populations worldwide, although it may be one of the most devastating factors on a local scale. In the search for possible alternative explanations, many different theories have been proposed, debated, and often rejected.

Amphibians are ubiquitous inhabitants of most freshwater, terrestrial, and arboreal habitats. Because of their thin, permeable skin and bi-phasic life cycle (both on land and in the water) amphibians are also twice as susceptible to pollution as animals that strictly live on land or in water. These sensitive animals are exceptional indicators of environmental health, and their mass extinction should serve as a warning to human kind.

Literature

Blaustein et al. 1994; Brodkin et al. 1992; Pounds & Crump 1994; Pounds et al. 1997, 1999.

ORDER: **Anura** (Frogs and Toads)
CLASS: Amphibians

The anurans currently number about 3,800 species, and many new species are identified every year. By far the largest and most successful group of living amphibians, the tailless amphibians, or frogs and toads as they are more commonly called, are a familiar sight throughout most of the world. They are absent only from some oceanic islands and both polar regions.

In spite of a wide variety in size, habitat, and biology, present-day frogs and toads share a surprisingly similar body shape. All have a reduced and shortened backbone, lack a distinct neck (the head appears to be attached directly to the body), and, as adults, are tailless (unlike salamanders, which have a tail). Most species spend the first part of their lives as tadpoles, during which stage they do possess a tail.

Another common characteristic among frogs and toads is long, muscular arms and legs that are used, particularly in the case of land-dwelling species, to jump and to absorb the shock of landing. Some of the most athletic frogs are capable of jumping a distance equal to 35 times their body length. To match this feat, a human being of average height would need to jump well over 60 meters, or 200 feet. Although most anurans seem to jump their way through life, many species use their well-developed limbs for other purposes: toads often walk rather than jump; narrow-mouthed frogs burrow; tree frogs, naturally, climb trees; and more aquatic frogs use their powerful legs for swimming. Typically, anuran hind limbs consist of four clearly discernible segments (thigh, lower leg, tarsus, and foot), whereas all other amphibians and reptiles have hind limbs with only three segments (thigh, lower leg, and foot).

Frogs and toads, like all amphibians, have thin, moist skin that is permeable to water and oxygen. All frogs and toads that venture outside their hiding places during the heat of the day face the threat of dehydration, especially in hot tropical environments, so most are active at night. To a varying degree, all anurans depend on water for their survival and reproduction, and most species are found in or near water, or at least in moist environments.

During the reproductive season, the male generally produces an advertisement call, usually from or near a body of water, to attract a female. A pair is formed when a male climbs on top of a female and clasps her with his front limbs (this behavior is called amplexus). While thus linked, the pair searches for a suitable place to lay the eggs. With very few exceptions—none of which is found in Costa Rica—the fertilization of frog and toad eggs takes place outside the body; the female lays the eggs, and the male fertilizes them immediately after they leave her body. The eggs hatch into free-swimming tadpoles that later transform into tiny froglets through a process called metamorphosis. Many reproductive variations are found in different species of anurans, especially in tropical regions. For example, some species lack a free-swimming tadpole stage and complete their development into tiny froglets inside terrestrial eggs; other species develop inside a brood pouch on the back of one of the parents; and still other species lay their eggs on the ground and carry the newly hatched tadpoles to a water-filled hole in a tree. The fascinating breeding biology of various Costa Rican frogs and toads is discussed in more detail on page 32.

Most male frogs and toads use different calls for distinct purposes, including attracting females, defending territories, or signaling distress. These acoustic signals are usually produced by forcing air through a pair of vocal slits in the mouth. Male anurans often have a single or double balloon-like resonating chamber, called a vocal sac, that they inflate to increase the volume, and thus the range, of their calls. This vocal sac may be either internal or external. An external vocal sac expands from the throat, or, in some cases, from the corners of the mouth.

Male and female frogs and toads have excellent hearing capacity, and in most species a conspicuous eardrum is visible on each side of the head.

Although the tadpoles of many species eat algae and other plant matter, adult anurans are exclusively carnivorous and eat a wide variety of insects, spiders, and other invertebrates. Larger species may also occasionally devour a small vertebrate. Frogs and toads locate their prey primarily by eyesight; their vision is particularly acute when recording rapid motion. A long, projectile tongue attached to the front of the mouth is used to capture prey.

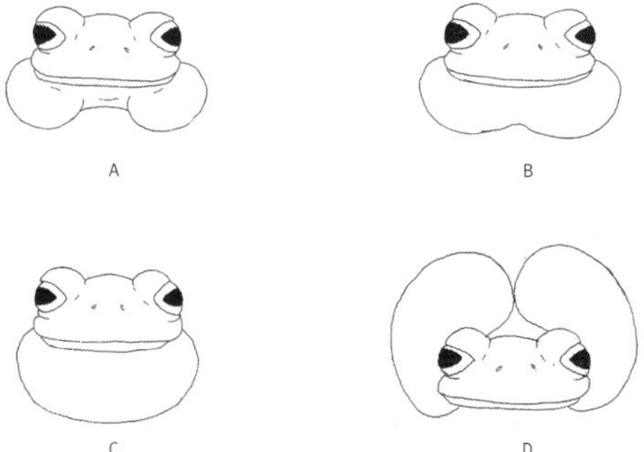

Calling male frogs display four types of external vocal sacs (some frogs have an internal vocal sac): (A) paired vocal sacs extending from the throat region (*Hyla pseudopuma*); (B) pseudo-paired vocal sacs extending from the throat region (e.g. *Smilisca* species); (C) a single vocal sac extending from the throat region (most frogs and toads); and (D) paired vocal sacs extending from the corner of the mouth (e.g. *Phrynohyas* and *Rana* species).

Costa Rica has 133 species of frogs and toads in 8 families. All of the anuran families found in Costa Rica are presented in this section, along with descriptions of representative species of each family.

A note on terminology: All "true" toads are members of the family Bufonidae, although, confusingly, some members of this family are commonly called frogs. To make matters more confusing, some "true" frogs are commonly referred to as toads. Common names notwithstanding, if a species is a member of the family Bufonidae, it is a toad; otherwise it is a frog.

SUMMARY

How to identify Costa Rican anurans:

- Anurans (frogs and toads) are amphibians that have no tail as adults. The larvae, better known as tadpoles, do have tails.
- The skin may be smooth or warty, but is invariably moist to the touch; there are never any visible bony scales present.
- The hind limbs of all frogs and toads consist of four clearly discernible segments (thigh, lower leg, tarsus, and foot), as opposed to all other amphibians and reptiles, whose hind limbs have only three segments (thigh, lower leg, and foot).

Literature

Duellman & Trueb 1986; Lips & Savage 1996b; Savage & Villa 1986; Zug 1993.

FAMILY: **Rhinophrynidae** (Mexican Burrowing Toads)
ORDER: Anura (Frogs and Toads)

Rhinophrynus dorsalis, commonly known as the Mexican burrowing toad, is the only living member of the family Rhinophrynidae. The description of the family is therefore incorporated into the following species description.

SUMMARY

How to identify Mexican burrowing toads:
- The Mexican burrowing toad is the only Costa Rican anuran with just four toes on the hind limb, as opposed to five in all others.

SPECIES DESCRIPTION

Rhinophrynus dorsalis
Mexican burrowing toad
Sapo borracho (plate 5)

The Mexican burrowing toad is a primitive and bizarre species. It has no breastbone, no ribs, no teeth, and only four toes on the hind feet, rather than the five toes found on all other Costa Rican amphibians (all amphibians found in Costa Rica, including the Mexican burrowing toad, have four fingers on each front limb). Its tongue is attached to the back of its mouth, unlike all other frogs and toads, whose tongues are attached to the front of their mouth (except for the Pipidae, a tongueless family of aquatic frogs not found in Costa Rica).

This unusual-looking amphibian differs unmistakably from any other Costa Rican frog or toad. It has a somewhat egg-shaped body and looks as if its skin is at least one size too big. Its head is small and pointed, with a calloused snout that is used for digging. Tiny, beady eyes with moveable eyelids and vertical pupils are located on the top of the head, which is further adorned with upwardly directed nostrils. The eardrums are not visible.

The arms and legs are short and stocky, and the hind limbs are partly enclosed by the smooth, loose skin. The feet are large and have only four toes. Unlike the unwebbed hands, the feet have extensive webbing; each foot is also equipped with a pair of enlarged, spade-like tubercles.

The color pattern of the Mexican burrowing toad is also very distinctive. Its body is chocolate-brown, purplish-brown, or dark gray, with a broad yellow to reddish-orange stripe down the middle of the back. Usually, the back and sides have an irregular pattern of spots, which are the same color as the stripe down the back. The belly is generally a uniform grayish color.

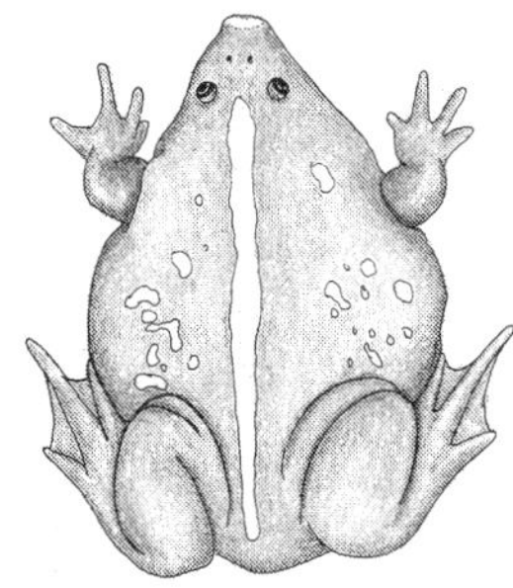

Mexican burrowing toad (*Rhinophrynus dorsalis*).

Because of their cone-shaped head and egg-like body, Mexican burrowing toads somewhat resemble the narrow-mouthed frogs (family Microhylidae). However, the latter always have a distinct transverse skin fold across the back of the head. Also, adult Mexican burrowing toads are larger than any

Costa Rican microhylid, with an average length of 60 to 65 mm (2⅜ to 2½ inches) and a maximum recorded size of 89 mm (3½ inches).

The Mexican burrowing toad ranges from southern Texas into Mexico and Central America; it reaches the southern limit of its distribution in the dry coastal lowlands of northwestern Costa Rica. It is found at elevations from sea level to 600 m (1,950 ft). The preferred habitat of this species is the dry seasonal forests of Guanacaste, but it is also found in cultivated areas in that province, provided the soil is suitable for burrowing.

The name *Rhinophrynus* is derived from the Greek *rhino* (nose) and *phrynos* (toad), probably referring to its heavily calloused snout. The function of the protective snout patch is uncertain, although it may be to protect the delicate amphibian skin during digging, or possibly to ward off the ferocious attacks of termite soldiers when the toad breaks through a termite-tunnel wall to forage.

The diet of Mexican burrowing toads consists of ants and termites. They forage by stationing themselves near an ant trail, or by sticking their calloused snout inside a termite tunnel. They then wait for insects to pass by and ensnare them with the tip of their rod-like tongue, which is extended through a groove in the front of the mouth.

Mexican burrowing toads are excellent burrowers, as their name implies, and they make use of paired spades on each hind foot to shuffle backward into the soil. At the onset of the dry season, each individual constructs a subterranean chamber in which it is able to survive long periods of drought without suffering dehydration. A captive Mexican burrowing toad managed to survive nearly two years in a burrow in its terrarium without any water or food. Because this species spends most of its time underground and is active on the surface generally only at night, it is not often seen.

The reproductive season of Mexican burrowing toads, which lasts only a few days, coincides with the first heavy rains of the rainy season. When pastures start to flood and ditches and dried-out ponds begin filling up, the toads leave their burrows and congregate at these temporary bodies of water. At night, large unorganized choruses of male burrowing toads call from the water's surface. Their advertisement call is a very loud, moaning "*uwoooo*" that, according to some herpetologists, is not unlike the sound of human regurgitation. When producing this call, the males' paired internal vocal sacs are inflated to such an enormous size that the animal resembles a floating balloon. The animal also uses this balloon-like posture when it is frightened; it inflates its body to almost twice normal size in order to intimidate predators.

Pairs are formed when a female approaches a calling male and bumps into him, nudging him with her snout. The male then clasps the female around her waist from behind (inguinal amplexus). The female typically lays several thousands of eggs in small clumps; they are immediately fertilized by the male as they exit the female's body. Tadpoles hatch within a few days. The tadpoles of this species often form large schools, over a meter in diameter, that consist of several thousand tadpoles. An aggregation of many tiny tadpoles may give the impression of being a single large animal, and the behavior is perhaps a strategy to ward off predators. Such structured social organization is not very common among tadpoles, but this defensive strategy is comparable to that displayed by schools of fish and herds of zebras.

Literature

Duellman 1967b; Foster & McDiarmid 1983; Fouquette 1969; Fouquette & Rossman 1963; Lee 1996; Sasa & Solórzano 1995; Savage & Villa 1986; Zug 1993.

FROGS & TOADS

FAMILY: **Bufonidae** (Toads)
ORDER: Anura (Frogs and Toads)

The Costa Rican members of the family Bufonidae can be divided into two distinct subgroups: toads and harlequin frogs.

The first subgroup includes the rare *Crepidophryne epiotica*, a small, obscure toadlet that occurs in the Talamanca mountain range, and ten species of the genus *Bufo*, although three of these species, *Bufo fastidiosus*, *Bufo holdridgei*, and *Bufo periglenes*, are almost certainly extinct (see page 49 on disappearing amphibians).

The second subgroup includes three species of harlequin frogs, all in the genus *Atelopus*. Note that while harlequin frogs are in the toad family, the common name *toad* is usually applied only to the genus *Bufo*. All three Costa Rican species of *Atelopus*, *Atelopus chiriquiensis*, *Atelopus senex*, and *Atelopus varius*, have disappeared from the areas where they were once common, and may be extinct.

Giant toad (*Bufo marinus*). Note the conspicuous paratoid gland; all members of this genus have a paratoid gland on each side of the neck.

Originally, "true" toads of the genus *Bufo* lived nearly everywhere except for Australia and New Guinea. After the introduction of *Bufo marinus* to those countries in the 1930s, this genus achieved cosmopolitan status and today lives on every continent except Antarctica. Although members of this genus may vary widely in color and size, nearly all have robust, plump bodies and thick, warty skin. Most Costa Rican members of the genus *Bufo* can easily be identified by the presence of both a poison gland (paratoid gland) on each side of the neck and a series of bony crests on the head. One exception is the smooth-skinned toad (*Bufo haematiticus*), which has neither bony crests on its head nor warty skin; nevertheless, as the only Costa Rican amphibian with both paratoid glands and smooth skin, it is fairly easy to identify. A small, toadlike species of frog, the tungara frog (*Physalaemus pustulosus*) in the family Leptodactylidae, also has a pair of paratoid glands, but it can be distinguished from the genus *Bufo* by the extremely warty skin on the top of its head, instead of the bony crests found in most members of the genus *Bufo*.

The paratoid glands secrete a viscous, white liquid when the toad is under severe stress. The secretion contains both bufogenin and bufotoxin, two powerful toxins that, when ingested by potential predators, are exceedingly distasteful and, in extreme cases, can cause death.

Toads are generally nocturnal, but their activity is strongly influenced by the weather. On rainy days, they may sometimes leave their hiding places before the sun sets; but on warm, rainless nights during the dry season, they may not emerge at all. Metamorphosing tadpoles and small juveniles are frequently sighted during the day.

The rough and warty skin of members of the genus *Bufo* is dry to the touch and less permeable than the thin, smooth skin of most amphibians. The specialized skin structure and texture block the evaporation of body fluids and enables toads to survive better under more arid conditions than most other amphibians. Nevertheless, all toads depend on the presence of a body of water, usually a temporary pool or a slowly moving stream, for depositing their eggs. Toad eggs are laid in long strands, unlike frog eggs, which are generally laid in clumps or in a layer that floats on the water surface.

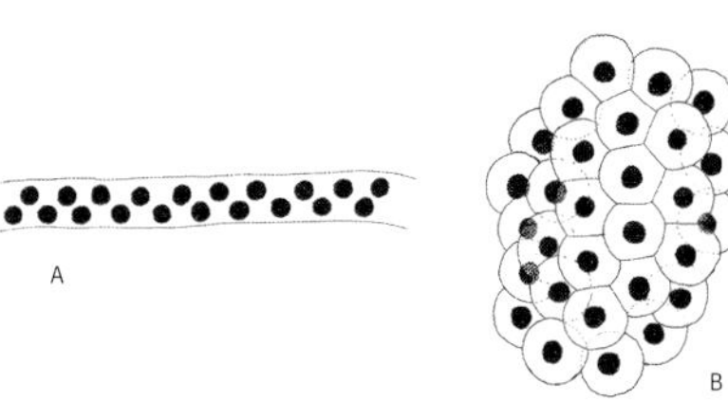

Toads produce long strands of eggs (A) that lie submerged in water. Frogs lay clumps (B) or sheets of eggs that float on or near the surface of water.

The harlequin frogs of the genus *Atelopus* are closely related to the genus *Bufo*. These toads are endemic to the New World tropics, ranging from South America to northwestern Costa Rica. Active exclusively during the day, members of the genus *Atelopus* are brightly colored and therefore very noticeable. They generally live near small, rapidly-moving streams and were formerly found throughout the country, in mountainous areas (at middle and high elevations) and in a few lowland areas. Mist from the spray zone of fast-flowing, cascading streams minimizes the dehydrating effects of direct sunlight. Harlequin frogs were once a common sight in Costa Rica, but this situation has changed dramatically over the last ten to fifteen years (see page 49 on disappearing amphibians).

Members of the genus *Atelopus* have inconspicuous paratoid glands and scattered skin glands that contain a strong toxin, tetrodotoxin, which protects them from most predators. Unlike other terrestrial anurans that move about by hopping or leaping, harlequin frogs move from place to place with a very distinctive gait. Their hands and feet are fleshy pads.

These anurans reproduce during the rainy season when water levels in streams are high. Eggs are laid in strings (like those of toads of the genus *Bufo*). All known *Atelopus* tadpoles are highly adapted to life in fast-moving streams, and they characteristically develop a strong suction disc on their belly that enables them to anchor themselves on rocks and other objects to avoid being swept away by currents.

SUMMARY

How to identify Costa Rican toads:
This family consists of two subgroups with different characteristics.

- Anurans with conspicuously enlarged poison glands in the neck region, bony crests on the head, and a dry and warty skin belong to the toad genus *Bufo*. An exception to this rule is *Bufo haematiticus*, which has smooth skin.
- Anurans with inconspicuous poison glands scattered over the head and back, and whose hands and feet are transformed into fleshy pads, belong to the harlequin frog genus *Atelopus*. These anurans usually have a bright, contrasting color pattern and an angular, cadaverous appearance.

SPECIES DESCRIPTIONS

Atelopus chiriquiensis
Chiriquí harlequin frog (plate 6)

This highland toad lives in the cloudforests of the Talamanca mountain range in Costa Rica and adjacent Panama, at altitudes from 1,400 to 2,500 m (4,600 to 8,200 ft). The Chiriquí harlequin frog prefers a relatively cool and humid climate. Males are most often seen near streams, while females display a preference for shaded forests. These enigmatic amphibians are highly variable in color. Males are generally a uniform yellow, green, or brownish red; female coloration is even more variable. Many female Chiriquí harlequin frogs have an orange stripe that begins at the snout, then splits and runs along each side of the back. The eyes of this species are normally either orangish or greenish. One report notes a male with one greenish eye and one orange eye.

Biologists have not described the tadpoles of either *Atelopus chiriquiensis* or another species of *Atelopus* found in Costa Rica, *Atelopus senex*—this little-studied frog was found solely on Barva Volcano and in the northernmost part of the Talamanca mountain range that forms the southern border of the Central Valley, at elevations above 2,000 m (6,550 ft). However, it has not been reported in recent years, and may be extinct.

Atelopus varius
Variable harlequin frog (plate 6)

Those in an anthropomorphic mood might describe this bony creature as "sickly," or perhaps "cadaverous." This aspect of its appearance, along with its conspicuous coloration and gaitlike walk, makes this small toad rather unmistakable. The variable harlequin frog is a smooth-skinned toad species with a very angular body and long, sticklike limbs. The head has a pointed snout that protrudes beyond the mouth. The eyes are large, with greenish irises and horizontally elliptical pupils that often appear to be round. Externally, the animal appears to have no ears. The underside of the hands and feet are padlike, wrinkled, and fleshy. The thumb is much shorter than the second finger and sometimes appears to be missing. There is a trace of webbing only between the inner two fingers, whereas the toes are connected by an extensive skinlike webbing.

In most populations, males reach a maximum size of 35 mm (1⅜ inches); females, which are typically larger, up to one and a half times the size of adult males, usually measure between 40 and 45 mm (1⅝ and 1¾ inches). Females also differ from males in having a more slender body and a longer, more pointed snout. As a general rule, if the distance from the eyes to the tip of the snout is longer than the diameter of the eye, the individual is a female.

The extremely variable color pattern of this species formerly led some herpetologists to believe they were dealing with individuals from different subspecies, or even different species. Studies in the early 1970s nevertheless showed that, although individuals from different populations often appear strikingly dissimilar, they in fact are of the same species. Without exception, all variable harlequin frogs are very boldly colored, and most individuals have a yellow, yellow-orange, or lime-green background color overlaid with a pattern of black lines, spots, or blotches. In some populations, juveniles are yellow and black, but adults develop an increasing amount of red or orange pigment on the back, head, and limbs. Old individuals may be red, yellow, and black—or even completely red and black above, with no trace of the original yellow background color remaining. The belly, which is usually light yellow or yellowish-green, may range from immaculate to heavily patterned with black blotches or spots. The bellies of some individuals may be patterned with green or bluish spots. A population of golden-yellow individuals from the Valle de Anton area in Panama has also been described.

The variable harlequin frog lives exclusively in Costa Rica and Panama. Most populations live at elevations between 1,200 and 2,000 m (3,950 and 6,550 ft), although some populations inhabit the Pacific lowlands, where individuals have been found at 16 m (52 ft) above sea level. Until 1987, this species was a common sight along fast-flowing mountain streams in forested regions on the slopes of the Tilarán, Central, and the Talamanca mountain ranges, but its numbers have dropped dramatically and they are now considered an endangered species.

During the day, harlequin frogs perch on boulders in or near streams, fully exposed to direct sunlight. Mist from cascading streams and moisture absorbed from the surfaces on which they sit protect them from the dehydrating effect of the sun. Interestingly, these frogs are not aquatic and are very poor swimmers. At night they sleep on the leaves of low vegetation or in rock crevices. Both males and females are territorial and defend their home range against intruders. They also appear to be extremely attached to their territory—some individuals have been observed to occupy the same boulder for up to two years. Individuals that are washed away by rising waters return to their territory, though it is not understood how they orient themselves on the return journey.

The reproductive season of harlequin frogs coincides roughly with the rainy season. Pairs in sexual embrace (amplexus) have been seen from July through early December. The male firmly clasps the female behind the arms (axillary amplexus) and remains in this position until the eggs are laid, at which time he fertilizes them. Frogs of the genus *Atelopus* remain in amplexus for prolonged periods of time—several weeks is not uncommon. The record is held by a Venezuelan species (*Atelopus oxyrhynchus*); in one observation, a male remained on the female's back for 125 days, during which time he did not eat anything.

The eggs are deposited in long strings, similar to those of the "true" toads (genus *Bufo*), but in flowing water. The strands of small, white eggs are attached to rocks, logs, or tree roots and hatch after 4 to 7 days. The tadpoles initially hide in loose gravel or debris on the bottom of rivers. During this first period, their mouth parts quickly develop into a strong suction device that they use to cling to rocks and logs, as well as to feed on algae. The tadpoles of this species are black, with yellowish-white dots; they have a very short, poorly developed tail.

The variable harlequin frog is of interest because it has no eardrums and no middle-ear cavity, and it also lacks some of the bones normally required for the transduction of sound waves; yet its ears are fully functional. In a laboratory study, the hearing capabilities of the Chiriquí harlequin frog (*Atelopus chiriquiensis*) were found to be the same as those of a similarly sized tree frog that did not lack these ear structures. Some amphibian species are known to "hear" sounds by perceiving vibrations through their arms, but it is not known whether this is the case with *Atelopus*.

Adult males have a single internal vocal sac. Three types of calls have been recorded: a "buzz," a "whistle," and a "chirp" or "twitter" call. All of these calls seem to play a role in interactions between males and apparently are used during confrontations over territory. In this species, visual communication may be more important in the process of mate selection than acoustic signaling, which may partly explain the bright coloration. This reduction in the use of sound for signaling to mates, and the consequent loss of external ears and middle ear structures, is perhaps a result of life amidst the permanent noise of rushing waters, where sound does not travel far.

The variable harlequin frog lacks the distinct poison glands (paratoid glands) that characterize the "true" toads of the genus *Bufo*, but it does have indistinct poison glands scattered throughout the skin on the back, head, and limbs. These glands produce tetrodotoxin, which is a very strong nerve toxin. There are no studies on the effects of this poison on humans, but it serves as an effective means of protection against most potential predators. Warned by the frog's bright colors, most predators avoid harlequin toads as they make their sluggish walkabouts. However, at least one species of snake, the fire-bellied snake (*Liophis epinephelus*) appears to be immune to harlequin frog skin toxins and occasionally eats them. Another predator, reported from the Monteverde area, is a carnivorous fly, *Notochaeta bufonivora*, whose name refers to its toad-eating habits. Females of this fly deposit their eggs on the harlequin frog; when the maggots hatch, they eat their way into the victim's body, where they eat the frog's intestines and cause it to die within a few days.

Bufo coccifer

Dry forest toad (plate 7)

Toads are relatively well-adapted to a life in dry areas. Their thick skin does not allow water to pass through as easily as does the delicate, moist skin of other amphibians. Among the toads, the dry forest toad, *Bufo coccifer*, seems to thrive under hot and dry conditions; within Costa Rica, its distribution is restricted to the Central Valley and the Guanacaste lowlands, areas where such conditions prevail.

Bufo coccifer is a medium-sized toad that reaches a size of about 80 mm (3 inches). Its color is yellowish to brown, with a pattern of scattered dark blotches. Usually, a thin light stripe runs down the middle of the back. Another distinguishing characteristic is an overall spiky appearance, created by the cone-shaped warts that cover this toad's body. The poison glands (paratoid glands) of this species are oval and are slightly larger in size than the upper eyelid.

Bufo coniferus

Green climbing toad (plate 7)

This is a medium-sized toad; males grow to 72 mm (2⅞ inches), females may reach 94 mm (3¾ inches). A distinguishing trait is a series of distinctly enlarged, spine-tipped warts that form two rows, one on each side of the body. Each row extends from one of the two poison glands (paratoid glands) in the neck to the hind limbs. These warts give the skin a sandpaper-like texture. Another distinguishing trait is the triangular shape of the poison glands. These small glands are roughly the same size as the area of the upper eyelid. In some individuals, the glands can be difficult to discern. Distinct bony crests adorn the top of the head. The second finger is longer than the thumb, and there are large skinlike webs between the outer three toes.

Bufo coniferus' coloration is extremely variable, ranging from shades of green, brown, olive, and yellow to brick red. Juveniles are generally more colorful than adults, often with a bright green background color and reddish-brown warts. The eyes have a green or brown iris, and a horizontally elliptical pupil.

Bufo coniferus is widely distributed in both the Caribbean and southwest Pacific areas of Costa Rica, from near sea level to an elevation of about 1,300 m (4,250 ft). Its distribution range extends from northern Costa Rica to Ecuador.

This species is a skilled climber; individuals fold their fingers in a claw-like fashion and use their long legs to ascend tree trunks or dense tangles of vegetation—an unusual trait among Costa Rican toads. During the day, individuals have been observed several meters high in epiphytic vegetation, on top of a tree fern, or in a hole in the trunk of a dead tree.

Although green climbing toads are mainly nocturnal, juveniles are sometimes active during rainy, overcast days. Occasionally, males start calling in late afternoon, sitting in or at the edge of shallow pools of rainwater.

These toads reproduce throughout the year, whenever there is enough rain to fill up their temporary breeding ponds. The male's mating call is a relatively high-pitched melodious trill. When a female and a male form a couple, the male clasps the female's armpits (axillary amplexus). The female deposits her eggs in a small pool of rainwater, and the male fertilizes the eggs as they exit from her body.

Tadpole development in this species is very fast, and newly metamorphosed toadlets have been observed to leave the water only 35 days after eggs are deposited. This rapid development from tadpole to toad minimizes the time the tadpoles must spend in temporary pools of water that can dry out after only a few days without rain. It thus also minimizes the possibility of an untimely death. This raises the question of why green climbing toads deposit their eggs in these shallow, sun-exposed rain puddles. One major advantage of doing so is that temporary pools of water do not contain fish and other large, aquatic predators.

A very unusual breeding site of these toads was discovered on top of a 20 m (60 ft) waterfall in the rainforests of Sarapiquí. There, tadpoles inhabit "kettle holes" that are surrounded by a rapidly flowing river. These cylindrical holes are formed in fluvial boulders by the drilling action of small rocks that initially settle into shallow depressions in the boulders and are then spun, top-like, by the powerful force of the river. Although a myriad of seemingly ideal breeding puddles is present in the area, breeding toads bypass these, traverse the river to reach their preferred kettle-hole breeding site, and thus risk being washed down the waterfall.

Nevertheless, tadpoles of this species are not entirely safe from predation; they have been observed being eaten by the carnivorous tadpoles of the Central American bullfrog, *Leptodactylus pentadactylus*, which sometimes share the same puddles. Also, a juvenile fire-bellied snake (*Liophis epinephelus*) was observed eating tadpoles of this species.

The green climbing toad, like other toads, feeds on invertebrate prey, although large adults sometimes eat small vertebrates as well.

Bufo haematiticus

Smooth-skinned toad (plate 8)

Although *Bufo haematiticus* lacks the warty skin that distinguishes most toads, the presence of a large poison gland (paratoid gland) behind each eye indicates it belongs to the genus *Bufo*. In Costa Rica, smooth-skinned toads inhabit the leaf-litter layer of forests in the Caribbean and southern Pacific lowlands. At the end of the dry season, individuals congregate and reproduce in pools that are left behind by receding streams and rivers.

Except during the reproductive season, these toads are not often seen. The call emitted by males during the breeding season has been described as a series of uniform chirps that resembles the sound of a baby chick crying for food.

Bufo marinus

Giant toad
Sapo grande (plate 8)

The most striking feature of *Bufo marinus* is its enormous size. Females, which are generally larger than males, can weigh over 1.5 kg (3⅓ lbs) and grow longer than 230 mm (9 inches). Another distinguishing feature is the large size of the triangular poison glands (paratoid glands) on both sides of the neck. These glands often appear swollen. The top of the head is adorned with conspicuous bony ridges. The skin of both sexes is covered with irregularly scattered warts. In sexually active males, each wart bears one or more small keratinized spine. Small juveniles

This Nicaraguan highland frog (*Rana maculata*) rapidly released a juvenile *Bufo marinus* after attempting to eat it. Strong skin toxins protect *Bufo marinus* against predators.

have no visible eardrum; neither the bony crests on the head nor the paratoid glands are sufficiently developed to be noticeable.

Bufo marinus is generally a uniform brown or olive color. Often, indistinct blotches and variously sized, rounded warts are scattered randomly over the surface of the body. The belly is dirty white to cream, with irregularly spaced brown blotches. The back and sides of females and immature males are a more uniform yellow-brown color, the yellow being more pronounced on the sides.

Natural populations of *Bufo marinus* occur throughout Central America and northern South America, but its range has expanded dramatically since the late nineteenth century, when it was introduced into Australia and several Pacific and Caribbean islands in an attempt to control beetles that feed on sugar cane. In Australia, where *Bufo marinus* has no natural predators, populations have exploded, and this toad is now considered a pest.

Because it is highly adaptable, *Bufo marinus* is commonly found in a wide variety of habitats, from sea level to approximately 1,600 m (5,250 ft). At night, it can be seen by the waterline on most Costa Rican beaches. Carolus Linnaeus, the eighteenth-century Swedish biologist, named this species *Bufo marinus* because he erroneously believed that this toad lived both on land and in the sea.

These toads appear better-suited to survive habitat destruction and other ecological catastrophes wrought by man than virtually all other amphibians. Originally, *Bufo marinus* probably inhabited natural clearings in forested regions as well as the edges of the forests surrounding those clearings. Deforestation continues to create clearings in forested regions, and thus expands greatly the preferred habitat (and range) of *Bufo marinus*. Today, the giant toad is very common around human settlements throughout the tropics; the only place where it is still absent is closed-canopy rainforest.

Bufo marinus feeds on a large variety of prey; it mainly eats invertebrates (insects and spiders) and small vertebrates (frogs), but also plant material and fruit in dire times. In urban areas, it can survive on cat and dog food intended for pets, and it has been reported to eat mice and rats occasionally, and even small pets such as kittens.

The mating call produced by the male has been accurately described as a low-pitched machine-gun trill. Breeding takes place year-round. Female giant toads are extremely prolific and deposit between 5,000 and 25,000 eggs in the shallow margins of permanent or temporary pools, which are typically located in open areas.

Toxins play a key role in protecting *Bufo marinus* from predation during every stage of its existence. The jelly surrounding the eggs is toxic, glands in tadpoles' skin produce toxins that make them unpalatable, and adult poison glands produce highly toxic secretions. In fact, the amount of toxin present in the poison glands of an adult toad is powerful enough to kill large mammals, including humans. Some snake species that specialize in eating toads (e.g., the false terciopelo, *Xenodon rabdocephalus*) seem to have developed an immunity to the toad's toxins and are capable of eating them without any signs of discomfort.

A component of one of the toxins produced by the poison glands is bufotenin, which is reputed by some to possess hallucinogenic properties. In some early experiments, this chemical substance produced hallucinogenic effects comparable to those of LSD or mescaline, and some studies described bufotenin as "violently hallucinogenic." More recent studies, however, failed to produce hallucinogenic experiences, even at doses higher than ever before tested. Although controlled laboratory experiments have failed thus far to produce conclusive evidence, cultures throughout the world continue to believe in the psychoactive powers of the toad's skin and continue to seek hallucinogenic experiences through its use. Methods range widely, and include smoking dried toad skin, licking the skin of a living *Bufo marinus*, and boiling the toads and drinking the resulting concoction. Additionally, there are indications that the ancient indigenous peoples of northern Central America, including the Mayans, used frogs and toads to bring about mystical states of consciousness in their religious ceremonies.

The psychoactive properties of the skin secretions of *Bufo marinus* remain a matter of debate, but what is indisputable is their potentially lethal effect on healthy human beings. Those in search of altered states of consciousness should consider other avenues.

Bufo periglenes

Golden toad
Sapo dorado (plate 9)

While almost certainly extinct, *Bufo periglenes* is referred to here in the present tense, this in deference to the theoretical possibility that it is *not* extinct.

Bufo periglenes is one of four mysterious species of highland toads that inhabit locations within the central mountain ranges of Costa Rica and Panama. Each of the four has an extremely limited distribution range: *Crepidophryne epiotica* is known from a few individuals from the Atlantic slope of the Talamanca mountain range; *Bufo fastidiosus* inhabits the high peaks of the Talamanca range; *Bufo holdridgei* is found only in the Central mountain range; *Bufo periglenes*, the most famous species of the four, has a tiny geographic range, probably less than 10 km^2 (2,500 acres), that lies between elevations of 1,480 and 1,600 m (4,850 and 5,250 ft) within the Monteverde Cloud Forest Preserve, located in the Tilarán mountain range.

The brilliant coloration of *Bufo periglenes* is unmistakable. Males are uniformly yellow to orange, while females have a pattern of yellow-outlined red spots on a black background. Juveniles display a faded version of the female color pattern. Male toads have an average size of 43 mm (1¾ inches); female toads have an average size of 50 mm (2 inches). Like all other Costa Rican species of *Bufo*, *Bufo periglenes* has a poison gland (paratoid gland) on each side of the neck; in this species it is small and elongate.

Golden toads are "explosive" breeders. When it is not mating season, they are rarely seen; but, with the first early rains in March or April, they emerge en masse from their burrows and congregate around small puddles to mate.

Since males greatly outnumber females, there may be 8 to 20 times more males than females around the breeding pools. These few females are in high demand, and there is fierce competition among the male toads. In the process of trying to find a potential mate, males grasp virtually anything that moves; they have been observed frantically hugging other desperate males, different species of frogs that happen to pass by, and even an observer's foot. If a male encounters a single female, he climbs onto her back and embraces her with his arms, tightly holding her armpits (axillary amplexus). Amplexus may last over 24 hours, and during that time the male may be attacked from all sides by other males that try to dislodge him from the female's back. Observers have noted "toad balls" of up to ten toads grappling with each other for the right to a female. The male fertilizes the eggs as they are released from the female's body.

In the mating season, which lasts from March to June, *Bufo periglenes* is mainly active during the day, although egg laying appears to occur predominantly at night. The average clutch size of 200 to 250 eggs is small compared to the several thousands of eggs that most toads produce, but *Bufo periglenes*' eggs are definitely larger than those of most other toads, with an average diameter of 3 mm (⅛ inch). Eggs are deposited in the small to very small rain pools found, for example, in shallow depressions between tree roots, or even human footprints. When the tadpoles metamorphose into miniature toads, in about 6 weeks, they measure about 30 mm (1⅛ inches). Juveniles require at least two years to reach maturity.

The four Costa Rican species of mountain toads all lack external ear openings, vocal slits, and a vocal sac. However, these animals are not necessarily deaf or voiceless. Two types of calls have been recorded for *Bufo periglenes*. One is a release call, a low trill emitted by a male toad when he is accidentally clasped by another male; the other is a soft "*tep-tep-tep*" sound, likened to the noise produced when two wooden spoons are clicked together. The latter call may serve to attract females, although the bright coloration of these toads and the extreme differences in coloration and pattern between the sexes suggest that visual signals play a more important role in sexual selection than calls.

Although these extraordinary toads were discovered in 1964, knowledge of their existence remained limited until their description in 1966. The creation of the Monteverde Cloud Forest Preserve in 1972 protected their minute distribution range. Until 1987, the status of *Bufo periglenes* seemed secure; but when the breeding season of 1988 started, only a single toad appeared at the most important known breeding pond, instead of the more than 1,500 seen there the previous year. In 1989, only a few toads were observed, and none has been seen since. The International Union for the Conservation of Nature (IUCN) lists the golden toad as endangered in its *Red Data Book*, but in recent years there has been no sign of *Bufo periglenes*, in spite of intensive surveys. The decline of the golden toad is not an isolated incident, and amphibian species are declining worldwide. More information on this topic can be found on page 49.

Bufo valliceps

Gulf Coast toad (plate 9)

The Gulf Coast toad is a medium-sized species; males may reach 76 mm (3 inches) while females may measure 84 mm (3⅜ inches). The head has distinct crests and a deep concave depression between the eyes. A single row of pointed warts extends from each paratoid gland (which is roughly the same size as the eye) to the groin.

The ground color of the back and head is reddish-brown to brown, and a light vertebral stripe is usually present. Bold, dark triangles sometimes run along each side of the vertebral stripe. The back may also display dark mottling. The hind limbs, which are usually darker than the back, may be banded. In most individuals a light blotch is present on the upper lip directly below each eye. This light blotch is often bordered by a larger dark spot that covers the eardrum. The series of prominent warts on each side of the body is white or cream, bordered below by a dark band.

This species ranges from the southern United States into northeastern Costa Rica. Throughout its distribution range it is found at low and moderate elevations. In Mexico and most of Central America, it lives in open, dry areas. In Costa Rica, however, *Bufo valliceps* inhabits wet forests, where it seems to prefer the small clearings created by tree falls. Generally common throughout most of its range, it occurs in smaller numbers in Costa Rica.

Although *Bufo valliceps* is terrestrial, reports note cases of individuals that climb trees in search of daytime retreats in hollows 3 to 5 m (10 to 15 ft) above the ground.

Bufo valliceps is very similar in appearance to the elusive foothill stream toad (*Bufo melanochloris*), which co-occurs in northeastern Costa Rica (and also inhabits the southern Caribbean foothills and the Golfo Dulce area of Costa Rica). In *Bufo melanochloris* the crests on the head and the row of pointed warts are less pronounced.

Literature

Behler & King 1979; Carneiro 1970; Cocroft et al. 1990; Crump 1986; Crump & Pounds 1989; Durant & Dole 1974; Easteal 1986; Fabing & Hawkins 1956; Franzen 1987; Furst 1972, 1974; Hayes et al. 1989; Jacobson & Vandenberg 1991; Jaslow & Lombard 1996; Jungfer 1988; Kim et al. 1975; Knip 1992; LaBarre 1970; Lee 1996; Leenders 1995a; Licht 1968; Licht & Low 1968; Lips & Savage 1996b; Livezey 1986; Mudde 1992a, 1993; Novak & Robinson 1975; Porter 1970; Pounds 2000; Pounds & Crump 1987, 1994; Savage 1966, 1972a,b; Savage & Kluge 1961; Savage & Villa 1986; Schultes & Hoffman 1973; Scott 1983c; Tyler 1976; Wassersug 1971; Weimer et al. 1993b; Zug 1983, 1993.

FAMILY: **Centrolenidae** (Glass Frogs)
ORDER: Anura (Frogs and Toads)

More than 100 species of glass frogs inhabit the tropical and subtropical regions of South and Central America, and in some regions new species are discovered every year. In Costa Rica, however, the last two decades have seen no additions to the country's 13 species of glass frogs. Researchers nonetheless have had their hands full investigating the natural history of those known species; for example, the tadpoles of almost half of the Costa Rican species of glass frogs are still unknown.

Fleischmann's glass frog
(*Hyalinobatrachium fleischmanni*).

The common name of these delicate little frogs derives from their lightly pigmented, or even completely pigmentless, bellies—observers can see the frog's intestines and bones through the translucent skin of the belly. The backs are usually a translucent shade of green, with yellow, white, blue, red, or black markings. This translucent coloration allows ambient colors to pass through the body of the frog; thus, glass frogs seem to blend in perfectly with their background. Individuals perched on a leaf are virtually invisible.

Glass frogs are sometimes confused with some small species of tree frogs. But these can be distinguished by comparing the orientation of the eyes. In glass frogs, the eyes face forward; in tree frogs, the eyes are directed sideways.

The orientation of the eyes may distinguish a glass frog from a small tree frog. In glass frogs, the eyes tend to face forward; in tree frogs, the eyes are directed to the side.

Centrolenids are strictly arboreal; the tips of their fingers and toes are slightly expanded and bear adhesive disks, an adaptation to life in the trees.

Parental care is common among glass frogs, and a single male may guard one to several egg clutches, in some species up to 24 hours a day. All glass frogs lay their eggs on vegetation over rapidly flowing streams, sometimes several meters above the surface of the water. Some species deposit their eggs on the upper surface of leaves, and others place them on the underside. Typically, species that lay eggs on the top of leaves produce dark clutches—usually dark brown or black—while species that deposit eggs on the underside of leaves produce eggs that are white, cream, or light green. This form of camouflage makes the eggs less visible to predators.

The number of eggs produced per clutch is relatively small, usually between 20 and 40. The tadpoles undergo their initial development within the egg and typically hatch when it is raining; they wriggle themselves free from the egg and drop into the stream below. Timing the moment of hatching so as to coincide with a period of rain increases the chance that tadpoles that get washed off the leaf and land on the banks of the stream below will ultimately reach the water. Also, the turbidity of the stream during a downpour makes hatchlings less visible to predators. After the tadpoles enter the stream, their body coloration becomes bright red, and they bury themselves in the leaf litter and debris that collect in quiet eddies. Sometimes tadpoles are found in the small puddles that are left behind after a stream's water level goes down. The tadpoles complete their development into small frogs several months after hatching.

The thirteen species of Costa Rican glass frogs are divided into three genera: *Centrolenella, Cochranella,* and *Hyalinobatrachium*. Until 1991, all species from these three genera were thought to belong to a single genus, *Centrolenella*. Studies comparing morphological characteristics and aspects of their biology have lead biologists to the current system of classification, which is thought to more accurately represent the relationships within the glass frog family. In most of the older literature, however, all Costa Rican glass frogs are referred to as *Centrolenella*.

Four of the more frequently observed Costa Rican glass frogs are presented here.

SUMMARY

How to identify Costa Rican glass frogs:

- Glass frogs are tiny arboreal frogs with a somewhat flattened appearance, large forward-directed eyes, and adhesive disks on the fingers and toes.
- The upper surfaces of glass frogs are often green. They usually have a transparent belly, through which the intestines are visible.

SPECIES DESCRIPTIONS

Centrolenella ilex

Ghost glass frog (plate 10)

Centrolenella ilex is the largest glass frog in Central America. With a maximum known length of 37 mm (1½ inches), it is sometimes twice as large as its relatives. The most extraordinary features of this frog are its prominent, forward-directed eyes, which have a silver iris with a black reticulum. The horizontally elliptical pupil may be reduced to a very small slit when exposed to bright light, making the eyes appear even more striking.

The ghost glass frog is a slender, long-limbed frog with a large head that is semicircular when seen from above. The back, head, and limbs are a uniform leaf-green color; the throat and belly are light green or whitish. These frogs have yellowish hands and feet. Individuals with scattered white dots on the back have been reported. The bones of this species are green. Unlike some glass frog species, *Centrolenella ilex* has a white skinlike membrane covering its intestines, which are thus hard to see through the skin of the belly.

The closely related emerald glass frog (*Centrolenella prosoblepon*) attains a comparable size and also has a uniform leaf-green color and green bones. However, males and some females of this species have a distinctive pointed spur on the forearms, a feature absent in *Centrolenella ilex*. Another distinguishing feature is *Centrolenella ilex*' protuberant nostrils, which are located on a slightly elevated ridge. In *Centrolenella prosoblepon* the nostrils are not elevated.

The ghost glass frog is an uncommon species. In Costa Rica, it inhabits the foothills of the Central and Talamanca mountain ranges, and has also been found in a few scattered locations on the northern Pacific slope. It also occurs in Nicaragua and Panama.

Centrolenella ilex appears to prefer wet to very wet forests, where it is usually found on the low-lying leaves of large-leafed plants in the spray zone of streams or waterfalls. During the day it sleeps on exposed leaves, often subject to direct sunlight. The humid environment prevents dehydration.

The frog's deep green coloration, which modifies in intensity to match the substrate, enables it to blend in perfectly with the background.

Centrolenella prosoblepon

Emerald glass frog (plate 10)

Centrolenella prosoblepon reaches a maximum size of 33 mm (1¼ inches). The smooth skin of the back is a uniform dark emerald green, often with small dark spots. The distinctly visible bones are green, but the intestines are covered by a white membrane and are not clearly discernible. The large bulging eyes have a horizontally elliptical pupil, and a grayish or silvery iris.

A pointed spur on each upper arm identifies the males of this species. Although some females also have a spur on the upper arm, it is much smaller than that of males. In territorial fights between males, these spurs are used to get a good hold on the opponent. The struggle, which takes place on top of a leaf or as the two males hang from the underside of a leaf, normally ends with the winner pushing the subdued male off the leaf.

Centrolenella prosoblepon is mostly active on rainy or misty nights. It seems to prefer undisturbed, primary forests, where it inhabits banks of streams covered with dense vegetation that reaches close to the surface of the water. This species usually occupies much lower sites on vegetation than does *Hyalinobatrachium fleischmanni*, another common glass frog that is often found in the same habitat. Its behavior also differs from the latter species in that *Centrolenella prosoblepon* usually moves about actively, calling occasionally, while *Hyalinobatrachium fleischmanni* usually calls from fixed calling sites. Finally, unlike *Centrolenella prosoblepon*, which calls when perched on the top of a leaf, *Hyalinobatrachium fleischmanni* calls as it hangs from the underside of a leaf. The mating call of *Centrolenella prosoblepon* is a sharp series of usually three notes: "*dik-dik-dik*." The darkly colored eggs are deposited on the upper surface of a large leaf.

Centrolenella prosoblepon ranges from the highlands of northern Nicaragua southward through Costa Rica and Panama. It is found in a wide variety of habitats within Costa Rica, and can be found at low, intermediate, and high elevations throughout the country, except for the dry northwest.

Hyalinobatrachium fleischmanni

Fleischmann's glass frog (plate 11)

Hyalinobatrachium fleischmanni is probably the most abundant glass frog in Costa Rica. A tiny, translucent frog, it has a leaf-green back that is marked with small yellow dots, and yellow, translucent hands. One can observe tiny white bones through its transparent belly, although the heart, which is covered by a white, skinlike membrane, is not directly visible. The body is somewhat flattened; the head is broad, with a rounded snout and large, forward-directed eyes. The pupil is horizontally elliptical, and the iris is gold-colored. The eardrum is small and barely discernible. These diminutive, fragile-looking froglets measure between 22 and 25 mm (⅞ inch and 1 inch).

Hyalinobatrachium fleischmanni is both the most widespread and the northern-most member of the glass frog family, ranging from Mexico to Ecuador, Colombia, Venezuela, and the Guianas. Also a widespread species within Costa Rica, it may be present near swift-flowing streams from sea level to 1,600 m (5,200 ft); it is not found in Guanacaste, however, which is inhospitably dry for these frogs.

Hyalinobatrachium fleischmanni is strictly arboreal. It is usually seen perched above a stream, on the underside of a leaf sometimes up to several meters above the water. It should be noted, however, that egg clutches have been found less than 20 cm (8 inches) above the surface of the water.

Their leaf-green coloration and small size, along with the fact that these frogs cease movement on discovery, can make finding them a frustrating activity, particularly when one is surrounded by their calls. Males call from underneath leaves; the call consists of a single, high-pitched, and bell-like "peep." There seem to be different intensities of calls, and some individuals call louder than others. The frog with the loudest call appears to initiate a series of response calls from other frogs that react to the dominant frog's initial call. The loudness of the call seems to be an indication of dominance; it is unknown whether these calls serve territorial or courtship purposes, though most species of frogs produce a different call for each purpose. Territorial conflicts between males of *Hyalinobatrachium fleischmanni* have been reported, and such aggressive encounters sometimes end in a miniature arboreal wrestling match.

A female glass frog actively searches for her favorite calling male, and amplexus usually follows as soon as the female approaches within an inch of the male. She deposits a clutch of 25 to 50 small, sticky, greenish eggs, each measuring about 1.5 mm (1/16 inch) in diameter, on the underside of a leaf, where they are fertilized by the male. The egg clutch normally covers an oval surface roughly the size of an adult glass frog. After oviposition, the pair separates, and the male occasionally returns to attend the eggs. Males have been observed perched on top of the clutch, as if brooding the eggs. The most probable purpose of this "brooding" behavior is to protect the eggs from desiccation.

Hyalinobatrachium fleischmanni has a prolonged breeding season, and calling males have been heard from early March to late November, whenever there is sufficient rainfall. During the breeding season, these frogs appear to be active on nights when there is a slight drizzle or mist. Although high humidity helps protect adults and their eggs from drying out, and although some rain is required for the hatching eggs, these frogs generally stay in hiding during strong rains. They are frequently knocked off leaves by falling rain, and individual glass frogs have even been observed to die from the direct impact of a single raindrop.

Hyalinobatrachium valerioi
Reticulated glass frog (plate 11)

The back of this small glass frog has large pale-yellow round spots on a green background that is sprinkled with tiny black dots. Interestingly, this coloration gives the frog an appearance that very closely mimics the appearance of its own egg clutches. Among the frogs of the genus *Hyalinobatrachium*, the reticulated glass frog has perfected the art of parental care. The female deposits the eggs on the underside of a leaf, where the eggs' sticky jelly coating keeps them in place. After the male has fertilized the eggs, he releases his amplexial hold on the female and positions himself near the egg clutch, guarding it 24 hours a day. Because the male resembles the egg clutch, he attracts certain insects, generally drosophilid flies, that attack glass frog eggs. These flies normally lay their eggs in the frog's clutch, and the fly maggots feed on the developing tadpoles. When the insects approach the male, mistaking him for an egg clutch, he eats them, thus simultaneously feeding himself and protecting the egg clutch.

Several egg clutches may be deposited on the same leaf on consecutive nights, and males have been seen protecting up to three clutches in different stages of development. Other males that approach the eggs are aggressively attacked by the attending male.

Literature

Donnelly 1994; Duellman 1967b; Duellman & Trueb 1986; Hayes 1991; Hayes et al. 1989; Jaramillo et al. 1997; Lips & Savage 1996b; McDiarmid 1983; McDiarmid & Adler 1974; Pounds 2000; Ruiz-Carranza & Lynch 1991; Savage & Starrett 1967; Savage & Villa 1986; Starrett & Savage 1973; Villa 1977, 1984; Weimer et al. 1993b; Zug 1993.

FAMILY: **Dendrobatidae** (Poison-dart Frogs)
ORDER: Anura (Frogs and Toads)

Costa Rican members of this family include eight species in three genera: three species of *Colostethus* (*Colostethus flotator, Colostethus nubicola*, and *Colostethus talamancae*), three species of *Dendrobates* (*Dendrobates auratus, Dendrobates granuliferus*, and *Dendrobates pumilio*), and two species of *Phyllobates* (*Phyllobates lugubris* and *Phyllobates vittatus*).

Frogs of this family differ from all other frogs by having two shieldlike flaps on the top of the fingers and toes, although it is sometime hard to see these without a magnifying glass. Most dendrobatids are easily recognized by their bright coloration, which appears to advertise the presence of skin toxins, although some species, primarily in the genus *Colostethus*, are cryptically colored and not poisonous

Dendrobatids are small to very small frogs that inhabit rainforests of southern Central America and tropical regions of South America. This family's common name derives from the skin toxins mainly found in the genera *Dendrobates* and *Phyllobates*. Frogs of the genus *Phyllobates* have skin toxins that can be particularly strong; the skin of a South American species, *Phyllobates terribilis*, contains toxin sufficient to kill twenty thousand mice or ten adult humans. This is the strongest animal toxin known to biologists.

Indigenous people from the Chocó region in Colombia are keenly aware of the extreme toxicity of these frogs. When they rub the tips of their arrows and blowgun darts on the frog's back, they hold a leaf folded around the animal to prevent poison from coming into contact with the palms of their hands. Sometimes, they hold the frog over a fire or pierce it with a sharp stick to cause it to secrete more of its defensive toxins. The secretion covering the darts and arrows carries a strong neurotoxin that may cause total paralysis, or even cardiac arrest, within minutes. Tribal hunters use these darts for hunting monkeys or sloths, animals that are usually high in the forest canopy; if a monkey is as much as grazed by a poison-laden dart and some of the frog's toxins enters its bloodstream, it will succumb quickly and fall paralyzed to the forest floor.

Recent studies have revealed that the source of the alkaloids, or chemical compounds, responsible for the toxicity of the skin secretions may be the food the frogs eat. Although many insect species that this frog consumes contain alkaloids, more species of ants contain alkaloids than do any other insect group. Interestingly, ants made up 50% to 73% of the diet of boldly-colored, toxic species of *Dendrobates*, while the percentage of ants consumed by the nontoxic *Colostethus* was only 12% to 16%. This theory is further substantiated by the observation that captive-bred poison-dart frogs invariably lose their toxicity when kept on a diet that does not include ants.

All Costa Rican dendrobatids lay their eggs in leaf litter on the forest floor. One of the parents guards the clutch until the eggs hatch; and, at least in *Dendrobates* and *Phyllobates*, the male parent frequently empties his bladder on the eggs to keep them moist. On hatching, the tadpoles slither onto the back of one of the parents, who subsequently carries them to a small pool or water-filled bromeliad, where they complete their development. The tadpoles of *Dendrobates* and *Phyllobates* are invariably found in a variety of small bodies of standing water, never in streams; *Colostethus* tadpoles, on the other hand, are usually found in streams, although sometimes they occur in small pools as well.

Striped rocket frog (*Colostethus nubicola*) carrying tadpoles.

Since these beautiful frogs are diurnal, they are among the more easily observed Costa Rican amphibians. During the day, males call from fixed, elevated sites, such as trunks, logs, or rocks, to attract females and to keep other males at a distance. The males are extremely territorial and literally wrestle intruders out of their territory.

In the following pages are descriptions of at least one species from each of the three Costa Rican genera of dendrobatids.

SUMMARY

How to identify Costa Rican poison-dart frogs:

- Poison-dart frogs are small, diurnal frogs that typically have two shield-like flaps on the tip of each finger and toe.
- Most poison-dart frogs are easily recognized by their color pattern of bright red, orange, yellow, green, blue, or purple. They may also have brightly colored stripes or spots on a contrasting black background.
- Some poison-dart frogs are brown, but those invariably have a pattern of white stripes on each side of the body.

SPECIES DESCRIPTIONS

Colostethus talamancae

Talamanca rocket frog (plate 12)

Although the three species of *Colostethus* found in Costa Rica (*Colostethus flotator, Colostethus nubicola*, and *Colostethus talamancae*) are members of the poison-dart frog family, they lack the toxins and bright coloration characteristic of that family. Each is a small frog, and not spectacular in appearance. The body is brown; light, longitudinal stripes run along the back and sides. These frogs are commonly referred to as rocket frogs because of the way they launch themselves headfirst into streams when startled. After doing so, they tend to drift with the current for a while, climbing back onto shore when danger appears to have passed.

Colostethus talamancae has a chocolate-brown back and light-colored belly. A broad dark band runs along each side of the body and head; two white stripes run along the top and bottom of this dark band.

The fingers and toes lack webbing, and the digits lack expanded disks. A pair of shieldlike flaps adorns the top of each finger and toe; all members of the poison-dart frog family share this feature.

Male *Colostethus talamancae* reach a maximum size of 22 mm (⅞ inch); females reach a maximum of 24 mm (1 inch). The skin on the throat is black in males, but white, cream, or yellow in females. In addition, the third finger appears swollen in males.

Colostethus talamancae ranges from southern Costa Rica to Panama, Colombia, and Ecuador. It usually lives near rapid-flowing, clear mountain streams at elevations between sea level and 750 m (2,450 ft), although it has also been found at some distance from any stream.

Colostethus talamancae are strictly active during the day, but prefer periods of low light; males call in the early morning and late afternoon, or during cloudy spells. The advertisement call resembles a rapid, high-pitched trill, with a pause before the fourth beat: "*peet-peet-peet. . . peet.*" This call is repeated steadily in bursts of 10 to 20 seconds.

In most species of frogs and toads, the male aggressively defends his territory against other males and uses advertisement calls to attract females. However, in *Colostethus talamancae*, the female energetically defends her territory, and it is the males who seek out the female, although the male still relies on advertisement calls to woo the female.

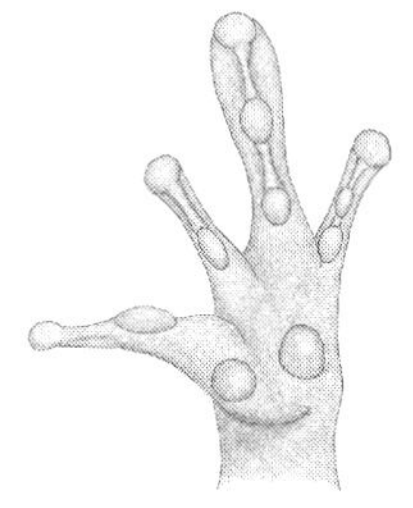

Note swollen third finger of male *Colostethus*.

Colostethus talamancae displays parental-care behavior very similar to that of *Phyllobates*. The female deposits her eggs in moist leaf litter. One of the parents carries from one to ten newly hatched tadpoles to small bodies of water, such as water-filled depressions in logs and rocks, or shallow puddles near streams. The tadpoles have a characteristic umbrella-shaped mouth that is directed forward; this design appears to help them gather food particles floating on the surface of the water.

Dendrobates auratus

Green and black poison-dart frog (plate 12)

Dendrobates auratus is the largest poison-dart frog in Costa Rica. Adults measure from 30 to 39 mm (1⅛ to 1½ inches). It is also the only frog in the country with a highly variable pattern of yellow-green, bluish-green, or blue spots on a black background. The Latin name, *auratus*, literally means *golden* and derives from Panamanian populations whose individuals have metallic gold spots on a brown background.

Dendrobates auratus is found from southern Nicaragua to northwestern Colombia, from sea level to 800 m (2,600 ft). In Costa Rica, it inhabits rainforests on the Caribbean coast, though a geographically isolated population also occurs on the southern Pacific coast.

Dendrobates auratus is a shy species and is generally found deeper in the forest interior than the other two Costa Rican *Dendrobates* species. Most activity takes place early mornings, especially after it has rained. Males are in constant motion, calling occasionally between hops. This frog's call, which is a fairly high-pitched, insectlike buzz, "*cheez-cheez-cheez*," serves to attract females and to keep competing males at a distance. If a male wanders into another male's territory, the resident male jumps onto the intruder's back and wrestles him to the ground. The dominant male's body often twitches and trembles as the defeated male slowly retreats, head kept low.

The reproductive behavior of *Dendrobates auratus* is similar to that of *Dendrobates granuliferus* and *Dendrobates pumilio*, but certain differences justify a brief description. In all three species, the female selects the mate. Female *Dendrobates granuliferus* and *Dendrobates pumilio* usually nudge the selected male to indicate interest; the female *Dendrobates auratus*, however, is not as subtle and jumps on top of the selected male, prodding him with her hands.

When poison-dart frogs mate, the male does not clasp the female (amplexus) as do males of most species of frogs and toads. Instead the partners face opposite directions, with their vents in contact. Eggs are fertilized outside the female's body, as soon as they emerge. The female *Dendrobates auratus* lays four to six eggs in a moist location on the forest floor. If the eggs do not hatch at roughly the same time, considerable size differences may develop between tadpoles of the same clutch; and occasionally, the largest tadpole turns cannibalistic and eats his smaller brethren. This never happens among tadpoles of *Dendrobates granuliferus* or *Dendrobates pumilio* because they are fed nutritive eggs by the mother. The tadpoles of *Dendrobates auratus* eat algae, detritus, protozoans, insect larvae, and, at times, each other.

The male parent takes a single tadpole on his back and carries it to a suitable small body of water, such as a water-filled tree hole or a water-filled bromeliad. These often are some distance from the ground, and reports mention males that have climbed higher than 13 m (43 ft) to reach their destination. When a tadpole-carrying male reaches a potentially suitable basin, he investigates the site and goes in for a dip. Once the basin is approved, the male floats vertically in the water with its legs spread while the tadpole wriggles free. Nine to fifteen weeks after being deposited in their water basins, the tadpoles complete metamorphosis and emerge as dull-colored replicas of their parents. Captive individuals have reached the impressive age of eight years, although life-expectancy in the wild is probably lower.

Dendrobates granuliferus

Granular poison-dart frog (plate 13)

Dendrobates granuliferus closely resembles *Dendrobates pumilio*. Both species have a red head and back, and bluish hind limbs. Both are small; *Dendrobates granuliferus*, slightly more slender than *Dendrobates pumilio*, measures from 19 to 23 mm (¾ to ⅞ inch). There are also significant correspondences between the natural history of the two species; both, for example, are diurnal, and both display comparable reproductive and parental-care behavior.

Nonetheless, there are at least three distinguishing features. First, *Dendrobates granuliferus* has an extremely granular dorsal surface, while *Dendrobates pumilio* has a smooth dorsal surface. Second, they inhabit distinct geographic regions. *Dendrobates granuliferus*, which is endemic to Costa Rica, lives along the Pacific coast, inhabiting lowland areas from Quepos southward to the Osa Peninsula and Golfo Dulce. It ranges from sea level to an elevation of approximately 100 m (330 ft). *Dendrobates pumilio*, on the other hand, is found throughout the Caribbean lowlands, on the opposite side of the country. Third, while coloration is very similar (both have bright red to orange heads and backs), there are significant, if subtle, differences. In *Dendrobates granuliferus*, the belly is greenish to turquoise-blue; in *Dendrobates pumilio*, the belly, like the head and back, is bright red to orange. In *Dendrobates granuliferus*, the hind legs and hands are greenish to turquoise-blue; in *Dendrobates pumilio*, the hind legs and hands are bright blue to purplish. There is an isolated population of *Dendrobates granuliferus* in the Pacific lowlands north of Quepos that displays unique color characteristics. Although these frogs are similar to the normal red variety in morphology and natural history, their back is olive-yellow, as is a portion of the belly and the front limbs (with the exception of the fingers).

Dendrobates granuliferus prefers the steeply sloping banks of fast-flowing streams that run through the humid forests of the southwestern lowlands. As deforestation proceeds, this species is increasingly forced into disturbed or cultivated areas.

The male's advertisement call is an insectlike "*buzz-buzz-buzz*," lasting several seconds; it is very similar to the calls of *Dendrobates pumilio* and *Dendrobates auratus*, although the latter species calls at a slightly higher pitch. Calling starts at sunrise and lasts until mid-morning; it resumes in late afternoon and ends at dusk, although the calling during this second round is less intense. Males call from fixed calling sites, which are invariably elevated, usually between 20 cm and 150 cm (8 and 60 inches) above the forest floor. Each male has one to three of these fixed calling sites and uses them throughout the rainy season. The male leaves his territory with the onset of the dry season, but returns to his previous calling sites when the rainy season arrives. The calls of male *Dendrobates granuliferus* may serve both to attract females and to ward off males that invade their territories. When an intruding male ignores the acoustic signals and trespasses into another male's territory, the resident male invariably tries to remove the intruder from his domain.

Dendrobates pumilio

Strawberry poison-dart frog,
Blue-jeans frog
Ranita roja (plate 13)

Dendrobates pumilio is undeniably among the most conspicuous of Costa Rican frogs. Its bright red head and back and bluish-purple legs are very distinctive; this frog shares a resemblance with only one other species, the closely related granular poison-dart frog (*Dendrobates granuliferus*). *Dendrobates pumilio* has smooth skin on its back, while *Dendrobates granuliferus* invariably has coarse, granular skin.

In Costa Rica, the head, back, and belly of *Dendrobates pumilio* are orange to scarlet, usually marked with some diminutive streaks or spots, colored either blue or black. The hind limbs and the lower half of the front limbs are patterned with bright blue or purple spots on a black background (the blue legs in this species give rise to its nickname, "blue-jeans frog"). Male frogs have a brown patch on the throat, indicating the presence of a vocal sac; this feature is absent in females. Several populations of *Dendrobates pumilio* in the Bocas del Toro region of northeastern Panama lack the red coloration characteristic of Costa Rican populations; they are extremely variable in color and pattern, often with blue, green, or olive on the back, and patterned with white, yellow, or brown spots. In 2000, an entirely blue *Dendrobates pumilio* was found in La Selva Biological Station. This unusual color form was previously only known from Panama, where it is common in some locations.

Individuals of this species are small and measure from 19 to 24 mm (¾ to 1 inch). Generally active during the day, *Dendrobates pumilio* is abundant in humid areas in the Caribbean lowlands of Costa Rica, from sea level to 900 m (2,950 ft).

In areas without a prolonged dry season, *Dendrobates pumilio* seems to reproduce year-round. Males can be heard calling incessantly throughout the day, and sometimes at night when a full moon floods the forest with light. Even heavy rains do not seem to discourage males from producing their insectlike "*buzz-buzz-buzz*," a call to attract potential mates.

The reproductive behavior of this species is a fascinating story of parental care unrivaled among other amphibians. Courtship begins when a female approaches a calling male. The male then leads the way to a suitable egg-laying

FROGS & TOADS

site, such as a concave leaf or a shallow depression in the ground. These sites are invariably located in moist leaf litter. Poison-dart frogs do not perform amplexus when breeding; instead they position themselves vent to vent. The female lays 3 or 4 eggs on the forest floor. The eggs are immediately fertilized by the male. After mating, the female departs. The male remains with the clutch, occasionally emptying its bladder on the eggs to keep them from drying out. Sometimes, a single male attends to more than one egg clutch at a time, and up to three clutches have been found on a single leaf. The male parent eats eggs infected with fungi or those that fail to develop; and when a male encounters an unattended egg-clutch fertilized by another male, he may also eat those eggs.

After about one week, the terrestrial eggs hatch into tadpoles. The female parent now returns to the clutch and sits among her offspring, waiting for one of the tadpoles to wriggle onto her back. One by one, the female carries the tadpoles to a water-filled crevice formed by the juncture between a leaf stem and the supporting stem of a plant. Preferred plants include bromeliads and species of *Dieffenbachia*. The offspring of a single clutch are not necessarily placed in the same plant, but are often distributed among several plants. Tadpole-carrying females prefer to deposit their offspring at locations close to the ground. If no suitable sites are available, however, they go elsewhere; they have been observed scaling enormous rainforest trees in search of such locations.

During their entire development, *Dendrobates pumilio* tadpoles feed on unfertilized eggs provided by their mother. On her feeding trips, the female climbs a plant containing one of her tadpoles and starts by searching for the appropriate crevice. The resident tadpole indicates its presence by vibrating its tail, which is a sign for the female to back down into the leaf crevice and deposit from 1 to 5 nutritional eggs. The number of eggs depends on the size and appetite of the tadpole. Smaller tadpoles suck out the egg yolk through a little hole they bite in the egg's jellylike coating, whereas larger tadpoles often eat the entire egg. Until their metamorphosis into miniature frogs, some 43 to 52 days after hatching, the female parent feeds the tadpoles every 4 days, on average; thus, during its development, the tadpole will feed between 9 and 13 times. The female only provides food to her own offspring and, while caring for her brood, abstains from mating.

Male *Dendrobates pumilio* are very territorial and remain in the same area for several weeks at a time. Individuals typically have a territory measuring between 5 and 30 m^2 (45 and 270 sq ft). An ideal territory includes several elevated calling sites (e.g., a log or rock), potential nest sites, plants with water-filled leaf crevices for depositing tadpoles, and usually a buffer zone, which is vigorously defended against intruding males. In experiments, two-thirds of males that were taken from their territory and moved several meters away returned to their territory. This experiment also indicates that these frogs are capable of remembering and recognizing their environment, a trait called spatial memory.

Dendrobates pumilio eats large numbers of small invertebrates, particularly tiny ants, which comprise up to 86% of recorded prey. Ants contain high concentrations of alkaloids, which are important components of the skin toxin in dendrobatids, and the diet of *Dendrobates pumilio* is at least partly responsible for its toxicity.

Adult frogs of this species seem to have very few predators. Reports indicate that the Central American bullfrog (*Leptodactylus pentadactylus*) is its only known predator. The bright red warning coloration seems to scare off potential attackers. In its natural environment, *Dendrobates pumilio* may reach the respectable age of 5 or 6 years. Dendrobatid eggs are more vulnerable. Unprotected by toxins, they fall prey to fungi, worms, snakes, and members of their own species.

Although dendrobatids in general are collectively known as poison-dart frogs, only three species of South American poison-dart frogs (*Phyllobates aurotaenia, Phyllobates bicolor*, and *Phyllobates terribilis*) have ever been used by Colombian tribes to poison their blowgun darts. A potent skin toxin is definitely present in all species of the genus *Dendrobates*, but these frogs are not dangerous to man. However, it is always advisable to wash your hands after handling any amphibian, since the effects of some of their skin secretions are largely unknown. The author, after having handled several frogs, wiped the sweat off his face with his hand and accidentally ingested some of the toxin residue—for the following half hour, he experienced a very uncomfortable feeling in his throat, as though something were physically obstructing his swallowing and breathing.

Phyllobates lugubris

Striped poison-dart frog (plate 14)

Phyllobates lugubris is somewhat smaller than *Phyllobates vittatus*; males reach 21 mm (⅞ inch), females reach 24 mm (1 inch). The two species have a similar color pattern, although the paired stripes on the back of *Phyllobates lugubris* are narrower (and yellowish rather than reddish) than those on the back of *Phyllobates vittatus*. Both species have a black background color, though the mottling on the limbs is yellowish-green in *Phyllobates lugubris*, bluish-green in *Phyllobates vittatus*.

Phyllobates lugubris inhabits the Caribbean lowlands of Costa Rica and Panama, from sea level to 650 m (2,150 ft). Distinguishing between the two *Phyllobates* species is not a problem, since they are geographically separated. However, *Phyllobates lugubris* shares its range with another species of frog, *Eleutherodactylus gaigeae* (the false poison-dart frog), a small black frog whose paired, red stripes on the back might be a source of confusion. As its common name implies, this froglet is not a poison-dart frog, but a nontoxic imposter. When a harmless species (*Eleutherodactylus gaigeae*) gains protection by resembling a dangerous species (*Phyllobates lugubris*), biologists label the phenomenon *mimicry*, a survival strategy not uncommon among amphibians and reptiles (see page 252 for more information on mimicry).

The call of *Phyllobates lugubris* is a constant high trilling that lasts several seconds. Like *Phyllobates vittatus, Phyllobates lugubris* males call from a hidden spot.

Poison-dart frogs of the genus *Phyllobates* are among the most toxic frogs known. Although both Costa Rican species are not as dangerously poisonous as some of their South American relatives, you should always wash your hands after handling these frogs.

Phyllobates vittatus

Golfo Dulce poison-dart frog (plate 14)

Phyllobates vittatus, which is endemic to Costa Rica, is one of two species of *Phyllobates* that reside in the country. The other species, the striped poison-dart frog (*Phyllobates lugubris*), is very similar in appearance and biology. There is no problem distinguishing between the two, however, since each inhabits a distinct geographic region. *Phyllobates vittatus* is restricted to the wet forests of the Golfo Dulce area in the southwestern part of the country, at elevations between 30 and 70 m (100 and 230 ft). *Phyllobates lugubris* lives in the Caribbean lowlands.

Male *Phyllobates vittatus* reach a maximum size of 26 mm (1 inch); females grow somewhat larger, reaching a maximum size of 31 mm (1¼ inches). The back and sides are black, with a pair of wide, reddish-orange or orange stripes that run along the back from the level of the hind limbs to the tip of the snout. The belly and the limbs are also black, but mottled with blue-green.

Phyllobates vittatus lives in the leaf litter of forested stream valleys. When approached, these shy creatures hide in holes found between roots or in rock crevices. Frogs of the genus *Phyllobates* are highly territorial, and warnings to approaching intruders often escalate into vigorous grappling and wrestling.

Male *Phyllobates vittatus* usually call in the early morning and late afternoon, generally on cloudy days, hidden from view in leaf litter or underneath vegetation. Their call is a constant high trilling produced in short bouts lasting 4 to 6 seconds; on many occasions, males have been heard responding to each other's call. As soon as one male starts calling, a second joins in shortly after.

Mating occurs without the male clasping the female, as is common in most species of frogs and toads; instead, the male and female sit with their rear ends touching. The female lays 10 to 25 eggs, preferring to deposit them in a little depression or hole in the ground. The male fertilizes the eggs immediately after they are deposited. The female abandons the eggs, and the male remains, guarding the clutch and emptying his bladder on the eggs at irregular intervals to keep them moist.

When the eggs hatch, approximately 18 days after deposition, the male carries the tadpoles on his back to small puddles on the forest floor. Unlike species of *Dendrobates* that usually carry only one tadpole at a time, male *Phyllobates* have been seen with as many as six tadpoles on their back. Free-swimming tadpoles have been observed in areas where water has collected, including small pools formed in depressions in logs, water-filled palm fronds that have fallen to the forest floor, calm water near rapid streams, and even in discarded cans and bottles.

During development, tadpoles feed on plant matter. As they approach metamorphosis, some two months after having hatched, they usually develop the bright orange stripes that will characterize them as adults.

Literature

Brust 1993; Bunnel 1973; Caldwell 1996; Duellman & Trueb 1986; Dunn 1941; Eaton 1941; Heselhaus 1984; Ibanez & Smith 1995; Jörgens 1994; McVey et al. 1981; Mudde & van Dijk 1983; Savage 1968; Savage & Villa 1986; Wassersug 1971; Weimer et al. 1993b; Wijngaarden, van & van Gool 1994; Young 1979; Zug 1993.

FAMILY: **Hylidae** (Tree Frogs)
ORDER: Anura (Frogs and Toads)

Worldwide, this very large and extremely diverse family includes over 700 species. While the family Hylidae reaches its greatest diversity in the New World tropics, species are also found throughout the Americas, Eurasia, Australia, and northern Africa. This is one of the largest amphibian families in Costa Rica, and is represented there by 43 species, distributed among ten genera.

This family's common name, tree frog, misleadingly suggests that all member species are tree-dwelling. In fact, some members of this family live on the forest floor or, even more surprisingly, burrow below its surface. This notwithstanding, all Costa Rican tree-frog species *do* spend their lives in trees. Invariably, they have rounded, adhesive disks on the tips of the toes and fingers that help them stick to vertical surfaces. For maximum adhesion, a specialized joint structure in the fingers and toes allows the frogs to keep the adhesive disks flat against the climbing surface, regardless of the angle formed between that and the frog's limbs. While earth-dwelling frog species move from place to place by hopping, Hylidae predominantly rely on climbing or walking, although all are capable of jumping great distances. Some species are even known to jump from the tree canopy to descend to breeding ponds.

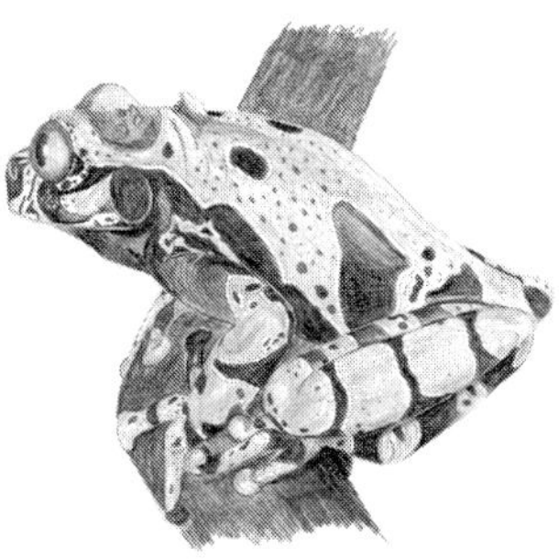

Crowned tree frog *(Anotheca spinosa).*

The tree frogs of Costa Rica are extremely variable in shape and size. They range in size from the tiny *Hyla zeteki*, whose adult males reach approximately 23 mm (7⁄8 inch), to "giants" like *Phrynohyas venulosa,* whose size can exceed 110 mm (4 3⁄8 inches).

Hylids live in a wide variety of habitats and climates, including, at one extreme, the hot, dry lowlands of Guanacaste, and, at the other, the sometimes freezing cold, frequently wet summits of Costa Rica's mountains. In many parts of Costa Rica, hylids are often the most conspicuous amphibians, particularly on warm, rainy nights, when large numbers of breeding males fill the air with their sometimes deafening advertisement calls.

All Costa Rican hylid tadpoles, except for those of one species, pass through a free-swimming stage. Depending on the species, the watery habitats parents may select for the development of their tadpoles include rapid mountain streams, temporary ponds, and treetop bromeliads. The single and fascinating exception is the horned marsupial tree frog (*Gastrotheca cornuta*); the female of this species carries the fertilized eggs in a pouch on her back. After completing their entire development inside the egg, the larvae hatch and emerge from their mother's pouch as tiny froglets.

Many hylid species are extremely hard to identify in the field. Some are so small that accurate identification requires a microscope. Other species are so similar in appearance to related species, or so variable in appearance, that identification must be based on comparisons with museum specimens. Other species are extremely rare, and the chances of encountering them are marginal at best. *Hyla xanthosticta*, for example, is only known from a single individual.

Small tree frogs sometimes resemble glass frogs. However, the eyes of tree frogs are directed sideways, while the eyes of glass frogs are directed forward. In addition, glass frogs have transparent skin on the belly; tree frogs do not.

It is beyond the scope of this book to include complete descriptions of all Costa Rican Hylidae. The following pages describe species that are commonly encountered and/or easily identified.

SUMMARY

How to identify Costa Rican hylids:

- Tree frogs have rounded, enlarged adhesive disks on the tips of the fingers and toes and also have skinlike webbing between both fingers and toes.
- Tree frogs have a somewhat flattened body and large bulging eyes that are directed sideways. The pupil can be vertically or horizontally elliptical, but is never round. Tree frogs never have a transparent belly.

SPECIES DESCRIPTIONS

Agalychnis callidryas

Red-eyed leaf frog, Red-eyed tree frog (plate 15)

Agalychnis callidryas is probably the most photographed frog in the world. In Costa Rica, its image appears on T-shirts, postcards, and posters. It is also possible to see *Agalychnis callidryas* in its natural setting, provided one knows where and when to look.

Agalychnis callidryas is most definitely a tree frog, but is so different from the "true" tree frogs of the genus *Hyla*, for example, that it is placed in a separate subfamily, the Phyllomedusinae, whose members are commonly called leaf frogs. All Phyllomedusinae are medium- to large-sized frogs, with a very skinny body, a green or brownish back, and a light belly (white, yellow, or orange). However, the two distinguishing features are eye color (red, yellow, or silver) and vertical pupils. Five members of the family Hylidae (*Duellmanohyla lythrodes, Duellmanohyla rufioculis, Duellmanohyla uranochroa, Hyla debilis* and *Hyla legleri*) also have red eyes and green or brownish bodies, but they invariably have horizontal pupils.

Costa Rica has six species of phyllomedusids, or leaf frogs; five in the genus *Agalychnis* (*Agalychnis annae, Agalychnis calcarifer, Agalychnis callidryas, Agalychnis saltator,* and *Agalychnis spurrelli*) and the closely related ghost frog (*Phyllomedusa lemur*). Some of these species are very rarely encountered.

Unquestionably, *Agalychnis callidryas* is the most common phyllomedusid in Costa Rica. It has red eyes and vertical pupils, as do two other Costa Rican members of the same genus, *Agalychnis saltator* and *Agalychnis spurrelli*. However, what distinguishes

Agalychnis callidryas from the other two species—indeed from all other Costa Rican frogs—is a pattern of pale cream, yellow, or white vertical bars on both sides of the body. These light bars are normally on a blue or purple background, although in some Pacific populations the background is brown. The back is a bright leaf-green, often with one or several small white or pale-yellow spots. The belly and throat are white; brilliant hues of blue trace the upper arms and legs, and bright orange colors the hands and feet. When the frog closes its eyes, one can observe a transparent lower eyelid marked with a beautiful golden reticulum.

Agalychnis callidryas are fairly large frogs; males reach 56 mm (2¼ inches), while females reach 71 mm (2¾ inches).

Although sometimes found at intermediate elevations, up to 1,200 m (3,950 ft), *Agalychnis callidryas* is a lowland species. It ranges from Mexico to eastern Panama; in Costa Rica it mainly lives along the Caribbean coast. An isolated population inhabits the Pacific lowlands of Costa Rica.

Agalychnis callidryas lives in forests. During the day—and generally during the dry season—individuals remain hidden in treetops. In the rainy season, the frogs move back and forth between tree canopy and breeding pond, generally displaying slow hand-over-hand movements, but sometimes parachuting rapidly from elevated positions (for comparison, see description of the parachuting red-eyed leaf frog, *Agalychnis saltator*, p. 82).

Breeding activity, which centers around both permanent and temporary ponds, usually begins in late May or early June, triggered by the first rains of the rainy season. At dusk, while descending to a perch near the surface of the water, males start emitting their advertisement call, a short single or double "*chuck*." Calling males do not remain in one position for very long. They move about between adjacent perches, often turning to call in different directions, in an attempt to increase the chances of attracting a female.

When a female is attracted to the calls of a particular male, she moves toward him in a straight line, sometimes passing by other calling males. Once the two frogs are only an inch apart, the female turns around and the male climbs onto her back, holding on tight with his hands near her armpits. The female then starts to walk, searching for a suitable place to lay her eggs, meanwhile carrying her mate, who resembles an oversized backpack.

Occasionally, two males fight over the female; and when a solitary male comes upon a couple, he may try to dislodge the attached male from the female's back. Every so often, a bold interloping male manages to attach himself to the female next to the original male. If he manages to maintain this position until egg-laying, more than one male may fertilize the egg clutch.

Prior to egg-laying, the pair descends into a pond and remains there for several minutes, during which time the female fills her bladder with water, probably through absorption. After the female emerges from the pond and selects a suitable site, she deposits a clutch of 20 to 50 sticky eggs, which are instantly fertilized by the male. The female then empties her recently-filled bladder on the eggs, which absorb the water and swell up. After laying her eggs, the female, with the male still on her back, may return to a pond in order to refill her bladder and begin the process anew; females may lay up to five clutches in the course of a single night. Before dawn, the frogs disengage and climb back to the forest canopy with a hand-over-hand motion. Each settles down on the underside of a broad leaf, folds its limbs beneath the body, and sleeps during the day.

Eggs are most frequently deposited either on the upper or lower surface of a broad leaf overhanging a body of water. When the eggs are placed on top of a leaf, where they would be exposed to sunlight and predators, the parents may fold the leaf over their egg clutch. The folded-over leaf is held in place by the gluelike jelly coating of the eggs.

If *Agalychnis callidryas* eggs are knocked from their leaf and fall into the pond below, and if this happens at an early stage of larval development, the eggs will die—an irony, since most frog eggs die from *lack* of moisture. If the same thing happens at a late stage of larval development, the embryo will survive; but it will leave its egg sooner than it would have had it been allowed to develop under normal conditions on its leafy, air-exposed perch.

Hatching tadpoles free themselves by wriggling rigorously until the egg capsule breaks. The tadpole then drops into the water below. Sometimes newly hatched tadpoles land at the edge of the pond rather than in it, or they are not able to roll off the leaf because they have become stuck to the jelly of other eggs. In both cases, the tadpoles generally survive, since they can live out of water for several hours and are experts at using their tail to flip about until they reach water.

As noted earlier, these frogs place their eggs above both permanent and temporary ponds. For the tadpole, the advantage of temporary pools is that they contain few or no fish or other large predators. *Agalychnis callidryas* tadpoles do occasionally eat tadpoles of other frog species, however.

Adult *Agalychnis callidryas* are eaten by a variety of predators, including birds, bats, and snakes, despite the presence of skin toxins. These toxins are apparently not very powerful, although a possible case of poisoning has been reported. A frog collector who had been handling several *Agalychnis callidryas* individuals later smoked a cigarette and presumably inhaled some of the toxins in the process. He reported fits of coughing and a general feeling of discomfort that lasted an entire day.

Agalychnis saltator

Parachuting red-eyed leaf frog
(plate 15)

This is a small species of *Agalychnis*. Adult males measure between 34 and 54 mm (1⅜ and 2⅛ inches); females grow a little larger, from 57 to 66 mm (2¼ to 2⅝ inches).

Agalychnis saltator is very similar to *Agalychnis callidryas* (the red-eyed leaf frog), but differs from the latter in having uniform dark blue or purple flanks instead of the vertical white, yellow, or cream-colored bars on that species' flanks. There is another striking difference between the two species: during the day, *Agalychnis saltator* is a uniform leaf-green color, sometimes with darker green transverse lines; at night, the green surfaces become tan or brown. *Agalychnis callidryas* does not change its green color; although it does modify the intensity of its color.

Nevertheless, the two species are more alike than dissimilar. Both have large red eyes with a vertical pupil; the hands and feet are orange. The limbs have a structure typical of tree frogs, with skinlike webbing between the fingers and toes and large adhesive disks on the tip of each digit.

Agalychnis saltator is found in the humid Caribbean lowlands of Nicaragua and Costa Rica, from near sea level to 780 m (2,550 ft). It often shares its habitat with the red-eyed leaf frog (*Agalychnis callidryas*).

Spectacular aggregations of breeding *Agalychnis saltator* are sometimes seen on vines that overhang temporary ponds in forested areas. After periods of exceptionally heavy rain, large, wriggling clumps of frogs—aggregations of 25 to 400 individuals have been reported—may gather on only a few yards of vertical vines, mating and laying eggs in the early morning hours. Clasping pairs plaster their egg clutches amidst the mosses that cover the vines, until the entire vine is covered with a layer of eggs. Because of the great number of frogs present, it is impossible to assess whether the male tree frogs actually fertilize the eggs of the female they embrace. It is thought that some eggs may be fertilized by more than one male.

Such large concentrations of frogs and eggs are a potential feast for predators, and adults and eggs fall prey to a variety of animals. Long columns of ants have been seen on the egg-covered vines, carrying small amounts of egg yolk to their nests. The northern cat-eyed snake (*Leptodeira septentrionalis*), a well-known night-active predator that feeds on both eggs and adults, has been observed in these breeding aggregations. Yellow blunt-headed vine snakes (*Imantodes inornatus*) are also frequent nocturnal predators of these frogs, while the parrot snake (*Leptophis ahaetulla*) tends to prey on adults during the day. Other predators reported to feed on adult frogs found in breeding aggregations include hawks and white-faced capuchin monkeys.

These aggregations of breeding *Agalychnis saltator* are most likely triggered by weather conditions such as extreme rainfall. In order to move rapidly from the forest toward the site where these large aggregations form, individual frogs leap from considerable heights onto large-leafed plants. During the descent, the frog extends its limbs and spreads out the skin between its fingers and toes to increase the surface area. This "parachuting" behavior slows down the fall and allows the tree frog to steer toward a suitable landing area. Large swaying leaves absorb some of the frog's impact on landing.

When ascending trees, *Agalychnis saltator* climbs vines and lianas with a rapid hand-over-hand motion that, along with parachuting, is an adaptation to life in trees. Parachuting has also been observed in some other Costa Rican tree frogs, including two other species of *Agalychnis* (*Agalychnis callidryas* and *Agalychnis spurrelli*), *Hyla miliaria, Phrynohyas venulosa*, and *Scinax boulengeri*.

Anotheca spinosa

Crowned tree frog (plate 16)

This rare species is known only from a few scattered locations in Mexico, Costa Rica, and Panama. In Costa Rica, it has been found on the Caribbean slope at elevations between 300 and 1,200 m (1,000 and 3,950 ft); a few additional individuals have been found in the southwest of the country near San Vito, at elevations between 1,150 and 1,250 m (3,750 and 4,100 ft).

Anotheca spinosa is the only frog in Costa Rica with dark spots encircled by white and with a series of sharp, bony spines on the back of the head and between the eyes.

Anotheca spinosa has a breeding biology that is very unusual for tree frogs. The eggs are laid just above the water surface in water-filled tree cavities, glued to the inside wall of the cavity. Only about 5% of the eggs hatch into small tadpoles. These tadpoles are capable of breathing atmospheric oxygen immediately after hatching, unlike most tadpoles, which initially absorb oxygen from the water through external gills. The tadpoles of this species are fed with unfertilized food eggs by their mother, very much in the way female strawberry poison-dart frogs (*Dendrobates pumilio*) feed their offspring. The nutritive eggs and the ability of the newly-hatched larvae to take air at the water surface are both thought to be adaptations to life in a small body of water with a very low oxygen content and with hardly any organic matter on which to feed.

Duellmanohyla uranochroa

Red-eyed stream frog (plate 16)

Costa Rica is home to three species of *Duellmanohyla: Duellmanohyla lythrodes, Duellmanohyla rufioculis,* and *Duellmanohyla uranochroa*. These were formerly placed in the genus *Hyla*.

Duellmanohyla uranochroa is a small species that measures up to 40 mm (1⅝ inches) in maximum size. This beautifully colored frog has a green back and head, and bright red eyes with horizontal pupils. A distinct white line along the upper lip passes below the eardrum to the groin on each side of the body. Its belly, hands, feet, and the back of each thigh are bright yellow. The throat is usually a somewhat paler yellow. Thin white lines run along the back of the arms and legs and above the vent.

The three *Duellmanohyla* species occur exclusively in the foothills and mountains of Costa Rica and western Panama. *Duellmanohyla uranochroa* inhabits humid and wet evergreen forests from 500 m (1,650 ft) to over 1,700 m (5,600 ft). It is found at lower elevations on the Atlantic slope than the Pacific, where it is rarely found below 1,400 m (4,600 ft). This is probably due to the fact that the Pacific slope, which is drier than the Atlantic slope, offers sufficient humidity only at higher elevations.

Red-eyed stream frogs inhabit dense forest areas and, sometimes, secondary growth, but invariably live near small, rocky streams. Males call at night from low vegetation, often at some distance from the water—other tree frogs generally call from vegetation in or near the water. The call of *Duellmanohyla uranochroa* is a single, melodic bell-like note that is repeated in rapid succession. For some undiscovered reason, calls seem to become more frequent as the air temperature increases. Breeding activity reaches its peak during the onset of the rainy season, and is especially intense on rainy nights. The female lays her sticky eggs in streams and attaches them to rocks and aquatic vegetation. Tadpoles of this species are bottom-dwellers that can be found in the debris on the bottom of quiet stream pools.

During the day, inactive red-eyed stream frogs are found clinging to small trees and perched on leaves or in bromeliads.

Duellmanohyla uranochroa was formerly a common species, and could be found congregated during the breeding season in considerable numbers. However, in the last two decades, its numbers have decreased drastically throughout its range. Within the Monteverde Cloud Forest Preserve, this species seemed to have disappeared from several locations, but has now returned to these locations in small numbers. Unfortunately, it has disappeared entirely from other areas.

Hyla ebraccata

Hourglass tree frog (plate 17)

A yellow to tan background color and large brown spots on the head, back, and limbs distinguish this tiny, delicate tree frog from all other Costa Rican frogs. The background color changes to a brilliant yellowish orange at night or in other dark conditions. The bold pattern of large chocolate-brown spots contrasts intensely with the lighter background. Usually, one large and roughly hourglass-shaped spot is present on the back, which explains its common name. The arms and legs of *Hyla ebraccata* are mostly banded brown and orange, but the thighs are invariably a uniform yellow. According to one interpretation, the Latin name *ebraccata* means "without trousers," a reference to the unpatterned thighs of these frogs.

Hyla ebraccata is a small species; males average roughly 25 mm (1 inch) in length, females are slightly larger. The head is short and wide, with a bluntly rounded snout and large bulging eyes, which have a horizontally elliptical pupil and a coppery iris. The long limbs end in extensively webbed hands and feet; the tips of all fingers and toes have expanded adhesive disks. A distinct thin sheet of skin in the armpits, called an axillary membrane, is invariably present.

This species is distributed from Mexico to Panama, mainly in areas with heavy rainfall throughout most of the year and no pronounced dry season. During the rainy season (roughly May to December), when most breeding activity takes place, *Hyla ebraccata* can be observed near many temporary ponds in the Caribbean lowlands of Costa Rica. Two individuals were once taken from a bromeliad about 30 m (100 ft) above the forest floor on the Caribbean slope. This was before the onset of the rainy season, suggesting that *Hyla ebraccata* leaves the vicinity of its pond during periods of less rainfall. A geographically isolated population lives in the Golfo Dulce region in the Pacific lowlands. Though mainly found at low altitudes, these frogs can be found at elevations of up to 1,200 m (3,950 ft).

Hyla ebraccata sometimes shares its habitat with two other tree-frog species, both of which resemble it in several respects. In the Golfo Dulce

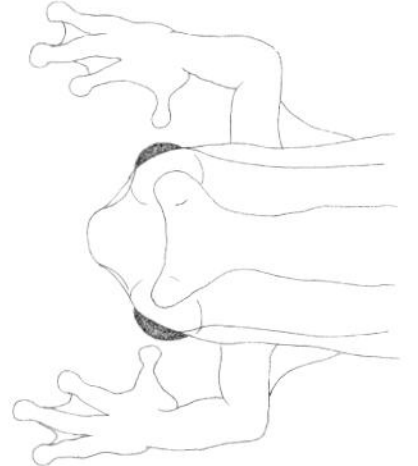

Note axillary membranes in *Hyla ebraccata.*

region, *Hyla ebraccata* sometimes occurs with the small-headed tree frog (*Hyla microcephala*). On the Caribbean slope, it may occur with the veined tree frog (*Hyla phlebodes*). These two other species are of a size and shape similar to *Hyla ebraccata*. Also like *Hyla ebraccata*, they are brownish in coloration, have uniform yellow thighs, and have axillary membranes. However, each frog has a feature that distinguishes it from *Hyla ebraccata. Hyla microcephala* has a thin, dark-bordered, white stripe from the tip of the snout along each side of the body; the pattern on the back of *Hyla phlebodes* consists of irregular brown blotches on a slightly lighter background, but it never has the large, contrasting dark spots characteristic of *Hyla ebraccata.*

When the first heavy rains of the rainy season begin flooding pastures and filling up impressions in the forest floor, *Hyla ebraccata* commences its breeding season. In the wet Pacific lowlands of Golfo Dulce, this may be as early as March; populations on the Caribbean slope usually need to wait another month or two before their ponds fill up. *Hyla ebraccata* breeds in almost any type of standing water that is filled with vegetation and/or surrounded by extensive vegetation.

During the breeding season, *Hyla ebraccata* stays close to its breeding grounds and passes the daylight hours hiding in the vegetation growing in or around the pond. Males generally call from a position close to the water surface, either on emergent herbs or grasses, or from the leaves of bushes that closely overhang the water. They commence calling at dusk and usually continue until early morning (4:00 A.M.), seemingly unaffected by rainfall or the bright light from a full moon. Their call, a surprisingly loud, insectlike "*creek*" sometimes followed by a few short clicks, serves two purposes. It is both an advertisement call that attracts females and an aggressive call intended to keep competing males at a distance. The calling behavior of this tree frog has been studied extensively, and several interesting findings have been uncovered.

In most breeding choruses of *Hyla ebraccata*, males are two to fourteen times more numerous than females; each female thus selects her ideal mate from a large number of potential partners. In several observations, females moved past several calling males until reaching their chosen male. This observation suggests that females select mates exclusively on the basis of their advertisement calls.

Once a female selects a calling male, she approaches to within 10 cm (4 inches) of the male, turns one side of her body toward him, and waits; the male then responds by jumping on her back and embracing her with his front limbs, clinging tightly to her armpits (axillary amplexus)

Sometimes, noncalling males will try to intercept and clasp a female that is heading toward a calling male. If this sexual parasite is not to the female's liking, she will try to escape his grasp. In one instance, a female was observed squeezing herself through a tiny opening between a fallen branch and the ground, knocking off the attached male in the process. Males do not always wait passively for a female, however, and have been observed fighting over a single female.

Once a pair of *Hyla ebraccata* is in amplexus, the couple locates a suitable place to deposit the eggs. The female typically places her eggs on the upper surface of a leaf overhanging water, where they are immediately fertilized by the male. An egg clutch from this species generally consists of a single coherent mass of 20 to 80 eggs surrounded by a sticky gelatinous layer. After hatching, the tadpoles fall into the water, where they stay until they complete their development into tiny tree froglets. They are very shy and usually hide between dense clumps of water plants in shallow parts of the pond.

The exact function of the so-called aggressive call in this species is still poorly understood. Observations of small choruses indicate that individual males answer to one another's call. There also appears to be a relationship between the distance between males and the number of aggressive calls produced; if males are situated more closely together, the call frequency seems to increase. Usually, both advertisement and aggressive call types are produced simultaneously, allowing a male to keep intruders away while at the same time attracting females.

Hyla loquax

Loquacious tree frog (plate 17)

This medium-sized tree frog, about 40 mm (1⅝ inches) long, is characterized by gray, brown, or tan coloration, along with bright red or orange coloration on the back of the thighs and on the webbing between the fingers and toes. The only other Costa Rican tree frog with red webbing on hands and feet is *Hyla rufitela*, which is a green frog.

Hyla loquax ranges from Mexico to Costa Rica. In Costa Rica it is found exclusively in the northeast, at elevations below 1,000 m (3,300 ft).

Hyla loquax is mainly a rainforest species that breeds in relatively deep bodies of standing water. In the breeding season, which takes places during the initial stages of the rainy season, males produce a loud "*kaaack*" while perched on floating aquatic plants or hidden in the vegetation on the pool's margin. Females lay eggs in small clumps that float on the surface of the water.

Hyla microcephala

Small-headed tree frog (plate 18)

Hyla microcephala lives on Costa Rica's Pacific slope, where it is one of the more frequently encountered tree frogs. This species resembles both the hourglass tree frog (*Hyla ebraccata*) and the veined tree frog (*Hyla phlebodes*). All three species are small—with a maximum size of about 25 mm (1 inch)—and are yellowish or tan with unpatterned yellow thighs. However, *Hyla microcephala* is the only species of the three with a longitudinal dark brown line that extends from the nostril to the vent on each side of the body. This dark marking is often bordered above by a thin white line.

Hyla microcephala is predominantly found in pastures, cut forests, and other disturbed areas; it appears to be absent from virgin rainforests. In contrast with *Hyla ebraccata*, the eggs of this species are not deposited on leaves above the water surface, but directly in the water. Other aspects of this species' breeding biology are very similar to those of *Hyla ebraccata*. In the reproductive season, male *Hyla microcephala* advertise their presence by a loud, high-pitched "*creek-eek*" call.

Hyla miliaria

Lowland fringe-limbed tree frog (plate 18)

Costa Rica is home to two species of giant fringe-limbed tree frog, the lowland fringe-limbed tree frog (*Hyla miliaria*) and the highland fringe-limbed tree frog (*Hyla fimbrimembra*). Both species are rarely seen because they inhabit the rainforest canopy, far from the view of observers on the ground. Their presence in an area is indicated by loud, growling calls.

Hyla miliaria is most easily distinguished from *Hyla fimbrimembra* by its granular back and limbs; the back and limbs of the latter species are generally smooth. Also, *Hyla miliaria* has small, spine-tipped tubercles on its belly; the tubercles on the belly of *Hyla fimbrimembra* do not have spines.

The lowland fringe-limbed tree frog is one of the largest tree frogs in Costa Rica, and may attain a body length of over 100 mm (4 inches). One of its most striking features is its enormous hands and feet, which are extensively webbed. The finger and toe disks are also large.

Hyla miliaria is extremely well camouflaged. The tubercles and skin fringes obscure the outline of its body; the color pattern of mottled light brown with irregular green spots blends in perfectly with the background. The hind limbs are adorned with dark brown or dark olive green bands. The belly is a dark color, usually brown, with a pattern of small whitish markings. The iris of *Hyla miliaria* is a dark, chocolate brown color.

This species ranges from Nicaragua to Colombia. It inhabits wet forests at elevations between 600 and at least 1,200 m (1,950 and 3,900 ft). Its close relative, *Hyla fimbrimembra*, is only known from an elevation of approximately 1,500 m (4,900 ft) on the Caribbean slope of Poás Volcano in Costa Rica.

Bony plates embedded in the skin on top of the head of *Hyla miliaria* form a protective helmet. Some South American tree frogs with similar head armor live in tree holes, positioning themselves in order to plug the entrance with the top of the head. This behavior helps prevent excessive dehydration in the arid canopy environment; it may also protect them from predators. The Costa Rican fringe-limbed tree frogs possibly display similar behavior.

Large adhesive disks and extensive webbing on the hands and feet of this species are an adaptation to life in the forest canopy. A lowland fringe-limbed tree frog once jumped from its perch and glided, using the large surface area created by its spread digits and skin fringes to slow its descent. It covered a distance of approximately 3 meters (10 ft), while descending less than 1 meter (3 ft).

Hyla phlebodes

Veined tree frog (plate 19)

Hyla phlebodes is a small brown to tan frog. The backs of its thighs are yellow. The maximum size of this species is approximately 25 mm (1 inch).
In Costa Rica, *Hyla phlebodes* is the Caribbean counterpart of its close relative *Hyla microcephala*, which it resembles in size, coloration, call, and natural history. It differs from the latter species in lacking the dark longitudinal lines that extend to the vent, although in some individuals a short dark line running from the nostril to the shoulder region may be present on each side of the body. *Hyla phlebodes* is mostly found in humid lowland forests below 700 m (2,300 ft), where it breeds in shallow rain pools.

Calling males produce a loud "*creek-eek-eek-eek-eek*" while perched on grasses emerging from temporary pools. Small clumps of eggs are glued to the grasses on, or even below, the surface of the water. Because of its wet environment, this species may breed almost year-round.

Hyla rosenbergi

Gladiator tree frog (plate 19)

This species' combativeness and the sharp, curved spikes on its hands give rise to its common name, gladiator tree frog.

By the standard of tree frogs, this species is very large. Individuals found in Costa Rica generally measure 70 to 75 mm (2¾ to 3 inches), but may measure more than 90 mm (3½ inches). Several features distinguish *Hyla rosenbergi* from all other Costa Rican tree frogs: it is one of the largest species; it has diffuse, dark vertical bars over the groin area; and it has a distinct dark stripe that begins at the snout and continues along the middle of the back. It is further distinguished by a protrusion at the base of each thumb called a prepollex. This feature is seen most clearly in males, since their prepollex is tipped by a sharp, curved spine. Unlike the large highland and lowland fringe-limbed tree frogs (*Hyla fimbrimembra* and *Hyla miliaria*), both of which also have distinct spines on the prepollex, *Hyla rosenbergi* does not have a fringe of loose skin along its lower arms.

Additional characteristics include enlarged disks on the toes and fingers, a substantial amount of skinlike webbing between all toes and between the outer fingers, large silvery or whitish eyes with a horizontally slit pupil, and a large, round eardrum.

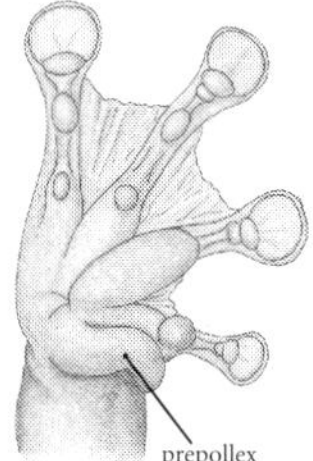

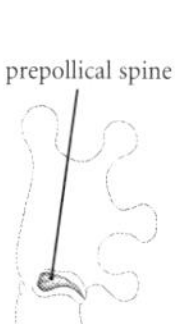

The prepollex is a fleshy protuberance just below the thumb that conceals most of the prepollical-spine; only the tip of the spine is visible.

Hyla rosenbergi has relatively smooth dorsal skin. The cream or white undersurfaces are smooth in the area of the chin, throat, and chest, but tend to become granular toward the hind limbs. The upper surfaces of this species may be a mottled cream, tan, brown, or reddish-brown, with or without obscure markings on the back, sides, and limbs. Males usually have a darker background color than do females, and usually have more distinct markings. Females are generally more uniformly colored.

Hyla rosenbergi ranges from northwestern Ecuador and Columbia to the Pacific lowlands of Panama and Costa Rica. It lives at low elevations in southwestern Costa Rica, in the Golfo Dulce area, the Osa Peninsula, and the coastal lowlands slightly north of the peninsula. *Hyla rosenbergi* inhabits forested areas with a high to very high average rainfall.

This species has a very prolonged breeding season that, in Costa Rica, may begin in early March and last until September. The two main periods of reproduction coincide with the end of the dry season, generally in May, and with the end of the *veranillo*, Costa Rica's version of Indian Summer, which generally begins in July or August and lasts a couple of weeks.

Hyla rosenbergi searches for bodies of water that have nearly dried up. At the edge of these pools, the male scoops out a bowl-like depression, generally with a diameter between 15 and 50 cm (6 and 20 inches). These depressions fill up with water that seeps through from the adjacent stream or pond. On the night after the nest construction is finished, the male enters his artificial pond and starts calling to attract females. The mating call of this species, which can be heard from a great distance, has been described as a series of low, short notes resembling the hammering of a stick on a hollow log.

When a female can be induced to mate, the male climbs on the female's back and clasps her using his prepollical spines for a better grip. The eggs are deposited on the nest's water surface in a floating layer and are fertilized by the male when they leave the female's body.

Male *Hyla rosenbergi* attend the egg clutch during its development. They are very territorial and aggressively defend the nest area against intruders. They are especially on their guard for competing male *Hyla rosenbergi* that try to invade their nest and break the surface tension of the water within the basin. When the surface tension is broken, the eggs sink to the bottom and die from lack of oxygen. For this reason, males actively patrol the perimeter of their nest and fight off every trespasser, often using the sharp spines on their thumbs to get a better grip on their slippery opponents. Males are often seriously injured during these fights, and are sometimes killed.

Phrynohyas venulosa
Milk frog
Rana lechosa (plate 20)

Phrynohyas venulosa is the only Central American representative of the genus *Phrynohyas*; four additional species are found in South America. Because its coloration is highly variable, Central American *Phrynohyas venulosa* was long thought—incorrectly—to comprise three distinct species.

This very large tree frog is unique among Costa Rican frogs in having thick, glandular skin on its back. Additionally, calling males of this species can instantly be recognized by the presence of two large, inflatable vocal sacs, one on each side of the head, behind the angle of the jaw.

Milk frogs are probably the largest tree frogs in Costa Rica; males attain a maximum size of 100 mm (4 inches), and females reach 114 mm (4½ inches). In addition to their thick, glandular dorsal skin, they have very grainy skin on the belly. The hands and feet are webbed, and the tips of all digits are expanded into large adhesive disks. The large, protuberant eyes have a horizontally elliptical pupil and a very beautiful iris, which has a golden background and an intricate pattern of black lines, sometimes arranged in a crosshair pattern.

Phrynohyas venulosa displays such a wide range of colors and patterns that a precise description is very difficult. In general terms, however, the upper surfaces of most individuals have a pattern of large, dark spots on a lighter background (gray, yellow, reddish or brown). These spots are often outlined in black, although in some individuals the spots may be so indistinct that the top of the frog appears to have a uniform color. Distinct transverse bands adorn the limbs. *Phrynohyas venulosa* does not have vertical bars on its lips, a feature of the otherwise similar-looking *Smilisca baudinii* (Mexican tree frog).

In Costa Rica, *Phrynohyas venulosa* is found mainly in the Pacific lowlands, below 1,000 m (3,300 ft). A widespread species that ranges from Mexico to Brazil, mostly in areas with a prolonged dry season, *Phrynohyas venulosa* seems to favor relatively dry areas, where it is active during the rainy season and survives the dry months hidden in humid, cool places such as tree holes or bromeliads, or under the bark of standing trees. These frogs are not extremely picky in selecting their habitat, and it is not uncommon to find them in agricultural areas or even clinging to the sides of houses in Pacific lowland villages.

Phrynohyas venulosa is an explosive breeder; its reproductive activity is triggered by the first rain storms of the rainy season, and mating and egg-laying is restricted to a few rainy nights every year. At dusk they come down from their hiding places toward breeding ponds. One study suggests that *Phrynohyas venulosa* is able to parachute, by jumping from an elevated place with its hands and feet spread to slow down and direct the descent. However, that study may not be representative of behavior in a natural situation, since the tested frogs were thrown off a 43-m (140-ft) tower.

Males aggregate in large numbers at shallow temporary or permanent ponds, where they call from partly submerged water plants or while floating on the surface of the water to attract nearby females. The males' large vocal sacs give them such buoyancy that they float high in the water; in some individuals with particularly large vocal sacs, the inflated sacs may rise from each side of the frog's head and end up touching above the head. The call of *Phrynohyas venulosa* is a very loud and far-carrying growl with a raucous, nasal quality that some biologists have likened to the roar of a bull.

If a male succeeds in attracting a female, he climbs on her back and hugs her tightly while holding on firmly to her armpits (axillary amplexus). The female, who is sitting in very shallow water, lifts her abdomen a few millimeters above the water surface; as soon as the eggs leave the female's body they are fertilized by the male. The eggs are deposited in a single floating layer that may comprise a surface area of 1.5 m^2 (16 sq ft). After the entire clutch is laid, the parents remain motionless for a few minutes until the eggs have stabilized. The pair then leaves the pond. This strategy of laying the eggs in a thin sheetlike surface layer is an adaptation to the low oxygen content present in small bodies of warm, standing water; other Costa Rican frogs that share this behavior include *Smilisca baudinii*, *Smilisca phaeota*, and *Hyla rosenbergi*.

Phrynohyas venulosa tadpoles typically hatch very quickly, often within one day. Newly hatched tadpoles sometimes hang vertically, their large external gills spread out at the surface of the water. This morphological and behavioral trait seems another adaptation to life in waters with relatively low oxygen content. Tadpoles complete their development into froglets between 37 and 47 days. Froglets measure between 13 and 16 mm (½ and ⅝ inch).

The thick skin that covers the upper surfaces of *Phrynohyas venulosa* contains mucous and poison glands. When threatened, the frogs secrete a sticky, white substance from these glands; it is this secretion that has led to the common name of milk frog. The secretions can cause a burning sensation to those who touch them. In some people, mere proximity to the skin toxins induces sneezing, even when the subject has not touched the frog.

Although the skin secretion of *Phrynohyas venulosa* repels potential predators, it may also serve to protect the frogs from drying out. The sticky substance is not water soluble and possibly forms a protective layer around the frog; anyone who has ever tried to wash the sticky secretion from his hands has experienced how difficult it is to remove. An old report on the behavior of this species notes that *Phrynohyas venulosa* lines the inside of its tree hole retreat with this skin secretion.

It has been suggested that the similarity in appearance of *Phrynohyas venulosa* and the Mexican tree frog (*Smilisca baudinii*) is a case of mimicry, a defensive strategy in which a harmless species, *Smilisca baudinii*, imitates a noxious species, *Phrynohyas venulosa*. Nevertheless, *Phrynohyas venulosa* can be distinguished from *Smilisca baudinii* because the former species lacks dark vertical bars on its lips, has glandular dorsal skin, and has cream and black mottling on its flanks.

Scinax elaeochroa

Olive tree frog (plate 20)

Scinax elaeochroa, one of the most common tree frogs in the Caribbean lowlands of Costa Rica, is a flat-bodied tree frog with a long, protruding snout and very little webbing between the fingers and the two inner toes. One of the most striking features of this species is its dark green bones, which are visible most easily through the skin on the underside of the hind limbs.

The long, flat head bears a snout that is rounded when seen from above and large, bulging eyes. The pupil is horizontally elliptical, and the iris is a dull bronze; the lower half of the eye is usually suffused with gray. The color of this species varies, and individuals may be a uniform ochre, a patterned dark brown, or even striped with alternating bright beige and dark brown bands.

Adult females reach a maximum size of about 40 mm (1⅝ inches), while adult males are substantially smaller, generally attaining a length of not more than 35 mm (1⅜ inches).

Scinax elaeochroa is found at elevations below 1,000 m (3,300 ft) in the Caribbean lowlands between central Nicaragua and western Panama, as well as in the Pacific lowlands of the Golfo Dulce area in southwestern Costa Rica and adjacent Panama. This species is absent from the dry northwestern regions of Costa Rica, where the very similar-looking Stauffer's tree frog (*Scinax staufferi*) takes its place.

Scinax elaeochroa is highly arboreal—individuals have been found in bromeliads in the rainforest canopy more than 25 m (75 ft) above the ground. It is most frequently observed sitting on the top of leaves, which bend under the added weight, thus leaving the frog in a vertical, head-down position. This vertical position can be maintained because of the mobile inner toes and inner fingers that are characteristic of the genus *Scinax*. These digits can be directed straight up, opposite to the outer digits, which point down. This creature is also able to adhere to the vertical leaf by pressing its entire flattened body against the leaf; in this manner, the body functions as a large suction cup.

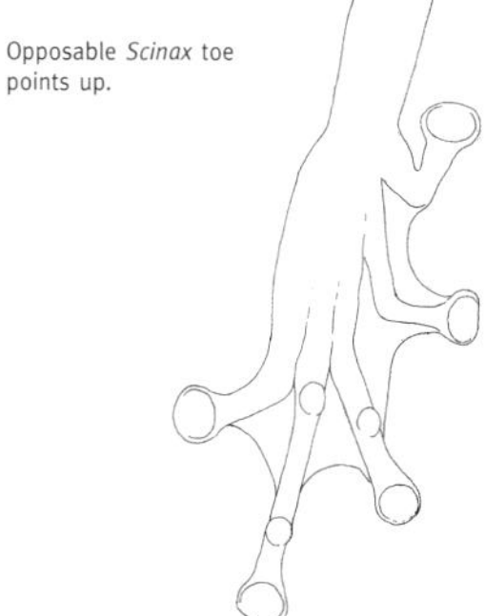
Opposable *Scinax* toe points up.

In its humid, lowland rainforest environment, *Scinax elaeochroa* appears to be active year-round, except perhaps for the driest months. During heavy rains, males call from emergent vegetation or from low bushes near the edge of temporary ponds; in some areas, large choruses of several dozen calling males are formed. One lonely male was spotted calling from the water reservoir of a flush toilet in an isolated jungle lodge. Eggs are laid in a large mass that is often attached to floating water plants; tadpoles live in the shallow margins of the ponds, where they hide between the vegetation.

Two other tree frog species in the genus *Scinax* inhabit Costa Rica: *Scinax boulengeri* and *Scinax staufferi*. These species, like *Scinax elaeochroa*, have a flattened body, a long snout, and an opposable thumb and inner toe. Insights into the taxonomy of these three species have led to several changes in their taxonomic status in the last decades. They were formerly placed in either the genus *Hyla* or *Ololygon;* thus *Scinax elaeochroa* was formerly labeled *Hyla elaeochroa* or *Ololygon elaeochroa*.

Scinax staufferi

Stauffer's tree frog (plate 21)

Scinax staufferi is very similar in appearance to *Scinax elaeochroa*, but is smaller—measuring less than 30 mm (1⅛ inches)—and has a more pointed snout when seen from above. It also lacks the distinct green bones. This species ranges from Mexico to Panama; in Costa Rica it occurs only in the dry northwest region. It is fairly common in disturbed areas and near human settlements.

During the rainy season, males can be heard emitting their advertisement call, a series of short nasal notes, "*ah-ah-ah-ah*," from emergent vegetation in rain pools.

Smilisca baudinii

Mexican tree frog (plate 21)

Five species of *Smilisca* (*Smilisca baudinii, Smilisca phaeota, Smilisca puma, Smilisca sila*, and *Smilisca sordida*) inhabit Costa Rica. Originally included in the genus *Hyla*, this group of tree frogs was later placed in a separate genus on the basis of anatomical features not readily observable in the field (e.g., the relative position of specific muscle groups and the structure of the skull). Costa Rican *Hyla* and *Smilisca* can be distinguished by the shape of the vocal sac of calling males. As a rule of thumb, *Hyla* species have a single balloonlike vocal sac in the throat region, whereas in *Smilisca* this structure has a constriction down the middle, making the expanded vocal sac appear as two small inflatable sacks. The only exception to this rule is *Hyla pseudopuma*, which is the only Costa Rican *Hyla* that has a double vocal sac. However, *Hyla pseudopuma* inhabits mountainous areas between 1,000 and 2,400 m (3,300 and 7,850 ft); at such high elevations one is very unlikely to find any species of *Smilisca*.

Smilisca baudinii and *Smilisca phaeota*, which it closely resembles, are among the most frequently observed tree frogs in Costa Rica. *Smilisca baudinii* is distinguished from *Smilisca phaeota* (and all other Costa Rican tree frogs) by a prominent row of warts along the lower arm and a dark brown bar that extends from below each eye to the upper lip. Adjacent to this bar is a light green, gray, or cream-colored spot.

Smilisca baudinii is highly variable in color and pattern; the upper surface can be a shade of green, tan, or brown, with a pattern of dark irregular blotches. In breeding males, the area on the throat where the vocal sac is located is gray; the remaining undersurfaces are white to creamy yellow. The short-snouted head bears a dark, masklike eye stripe that extends onto the shoulder area. The eardrums are distinctly visible, and the eye has a horizontal pupil with a bronze or silver iris. As in *Smilisca phaeota*, the dorsal surfaces of the hind limbs are marked by dark transverse bars, although in *Smilisca baudinii* there is no distinct white stripe running along the outer edge of the leg and foot.

Among the Costa Rican tree frogs, *Smilisca baudinii* is unquestionably one of the larger species: males attain a length of 76 mm (3 inches); females grow even larger and reach a maximum size of 90 mm (3½ inches).

This species ranges from Mexico to Costa Rica, at low and intermediate elevations on both the Pacific and Caribbean slopes. Within Costa Rica, it is found in the dry tropical forest on the northern Pacific slope, as well as in rainforest environments on the Caribbean coast, generally at elevations below 1,000 m (3,300 ft).

The mating call of these frogs, a series of short "*wonk-wonk-wonk*" notes, is commonly heard on rainy nights near any type of temporary pond within the species' distribution range. *Smilisca baudinii* usually call in duets, with two males often calling in an alternating fashion. Calling males are usually seen on bushes or small trees near the water's edge, and they may be separated by only a few centimeters. The call sequence of one duet may be picked up quickly by other vocalizing individuals, and the resulting chorus may produce a deafening ruckus. Although the intensity of the calls increases gradually as more individuals join a chorus, an entire chorus frequently stops abruptly. After a short interval in which all frogs are silent, one duet will initiate the next massive sing-along.

Smilisca baudinii seems to adapt better to habitat disturbances than most Costa Rican amphibians, and it is often seen in the immediate vicinity of human settlements—on roads, near street lights, or clinging to the walls of buildings. These frogs can be very abundant in some places, although no Costa Rican records currently can compete with the sighting of a breeding congregation of more than 45,000 *Smilisca baudinii* at a pond in Veracruz, Mexico.

Smilisca phaeota

Masked tree frog (plate 22)

Smilisca phaeota is the only large tree frog in Costa Rica that has both a silvery white stripe on the upper lip and a dark, masklike stripe that starts near the nostril and runs along both sides of the head to somewhere near the insertion of the arms, encompassing the eye and eardrum. This latter feature is the obvious origin of its common name, masked tree frog. Many individuals also sport a green spot on each side of the head between the dark mask and the lip.

Adult females of this large species may reach 78 mm (3⅛ inches); males are considerably smaller with a maximum size of 65 mm (2½ inches).

Smilisca phaeota has a somewhat flattened body, skinlike webbing between the toes and fingers, and conspicuously enlarged adhesive disks on all digits. The snout is rounded when seen from above. The eardrums are distinctly visible; the eyes are large, with a horizontally elliptical pupil and an iris that is coppery, with a dark suffusion through its center.

This species is capable of changing color. Its upper surfaces can be either tan or green; they are usually tan during the day and change to green at night. The back is variably patterned with olive-green or brown blotches. On the top of the head, a dark bar connecting the eyes is nearly always present. The undersurfaces are creamy white, though in males the area of the throat where the vocal sac sits is sometimes yellowish, cream, or gray. The hind limbs are adorned with both alternating light and dark transverse bands and a distinct white stripe that runs along the outer edge of the leg and foot.

Smilisca phaeota is primarily an inhabitant of lowland rainforests, though it can be found as high as 1,000 m (3,300 ft). It occurs from northern Nicaragua to northern Colombia. In Costa Rica, *Smilisca phaeota* is found on both the Caribbean and Pacific slopes, although it is absent from the dry Guanacaste area.

Like all other tree frogs, *Smilisca phaeota* is mostly active during the night. Individuals spend the day sleeping on the upper surface of large leaves, but they have also been found on the top of large tree ferns or in rolled-up banana leaves. On two occasions, however, males of this species were found actively climbing on vegetation in the spray zone of a large waterfall in broad daylight.

Males begin producing their calls—a surprisingly loud and harsh "*wrauk*"—at dusk, attempting to persuade a female to join them. They call from the water surface of small rain pools (e.g., drainage ditches or water-filled tire tracks) that are shaded by trees during the day. The eggs of this species, which are laid in small clumps that form a thin layer floating on the water surface, often hatch within a day. Since the puddle they live in may dry out if it fails to rain for a day or two, their environment is highly unstable, requiring tadpoles of *Smilisca phaeota* to develop extremely quickly in comparison with other frogs and toads. Tadpoles may go through metamorphosis and leave their birth pools as tiny tree frogs roughly one month after hatching.

Smilisca sordida

Drab tree frog (plate 22)

Smilisca sordida displays sexual size dimorphism. Males grow to 45 mm (1¾ inches); females may reach an impressive 73 mm (2⅞ inches).

The background color is either a uniform tan, gray-brown, or reddish brown, usually marked by several indistinct darker blotches on the back and head, and faint crossbands on the hind limbs. The back of the thighs is dark brown with cream, tan, or bluish white spots. A distinct skin fold, bordered below by a dark line, passes from behind the eye over the eardrum. The belly is white. The sides have dark spots and flecks.

Smilisca sordida lacks the white stripe on the upper lip, a trait characteristic of *Smilisca phaeota*; it also lacks the light spot below the eye typically seen in *Smilisca baudinii*.

In Costa Rica, *Smilisca sordida* inhabits the Atlantic and Pacific lowlands, and the Central Valley, at elevations up to 1,200 meters (3,950 ft). It also ranges just across the border into extreme western Panama.

Drab tree frogs are most frequently seen when they reproduce, during the dry season. Males, which produce a short rattling call to attract females, perch on branches overhanging water, or on rocks in streams or near the edge of streams. Pairs mate and lay their eggs in shallow sections of rocky, slowly moving streams and rivers. The tadpoles of *Smilisca sordida* are found in pools in clear streams, either on the bottom between collected debris or clinging to rocks.

Smilisca sordida sometimes lives in the same area as the closely related *Smilisca baudinii* and *Smilisca phaeota*, yet each species breeds in a distinct type of water. *Smilisca sordida* breeds in streams; *Smilisca baudinii* breeds in large, temporary pools; and *Smilisca phaeota* breeds in very small puddles.

Literature

Crump & Kaplan 1979; Duellman 1967a,b, 1968a,b, 1970; Fouquette 1960; Hayes et al. 1989; Janzen 1962; Jungfer 1987a, 1996; Kluge 1981; Lee 1996; Morris 1991; Myers & Duellman 1982; Pounds 2000; Pyburn 1970; Roberts 1994; Sasa & Solórzano 1995; Savage & Heyer 1969; Savage & Villa 1986; Scott 1983a; Scott & Starrett 1972; Taylor 1954a; Wassersug 1971; Weimer et al. 1993a,b; Zug 1993; Zweifel 1964b.

Insects and Spiders

Amphibians and reptiles eat a variety of invertebrates, especially insects and spiders. But other interesting relationships exist between amphibians and reptiles and these invertebrates beyond the predator-prey relationship.

In some cases, the predator becomes the prey. Hunting spiders of the genus *Cupiennius* (family Cteniidae) have been observed catching and eating adult hourglass tree frogs (*Hyla ebraccata*) and adult slender anoles (*Norops limifrons*). Juveniles of the latter species have been found caught in spider webs, unable to release themselves; they are likely to die in these spider webs, although not necessarily at the jaws of the resident spider. In addition to spiders, praying mantises, large predatory katydids, and centipedes are also known to eat small amphibians and reptiles on occasion.

A spider of the genus *Cupiennius*.

Though they are sometimes predators of amphibians and reptiles, arthropods are much more commonly parasites. In a tropical environment, clouds of bloodthirsty mosquitoes surround almost every vertebrate animal, ranging from large frogs to humans. In addition to internal parasites, various external ectoparasites are also found on amphibians and reptiles. Snakes and turtles are often infested with ticks; these can be seen feeding through the exposed skin between scales, or even between scutes of a turtle's shell. Tiger rat snakes (*Spilotes pullatus*), which forage in bird and mammal nests, often carry ticks; and giant toads (*Bufo marinus*) that live in or near cattle pastures occasionally do so as well. Tiny red mites can be seen, often in large numbers, between the scales of virtually any lizard or snake. The deep pockets that are located behind the insertion of each forelimb in the ground anole (*Norops humilis*) often contain so many mites that, in German, they are called *Milbentäsche* (mite pockets). Some ectoparasites that are never found on terrestrial snakes have been reported to trouble yellow-bellied sea snakes (*Pelamis platurus*); their body surface may be used as a settling place for barnacles. As with other reptiles, frequent shedding of the skin helps remove these unwanted creatures.

One of the most fascinating sights in nature is insects that mimic reptiles. In Costa Rica, larvae of the several butterflies and moths of the families Papilionidae, Sphingidae, Geometridae, Noctuidae, Oxytenidae, and Notodontidae may have snakelike markings and often display movements that are similar to those of snakes. Occasionally, pupae are found that mimic snakes. One of the most striking examples of such mimicry is the chrysalis of the butterfly *Dynastor darius* (Nymphalidae), which shows a startling resemblance to the head of a pit viper, such as the hog-nosed pit viper (*Porthidium nasutum*), or the fer-de-lance (*Bothrops asper*). When touched, the chrysalis continues its deception and moves in a way that resembles the movements of an attacking snake. This kind of intimidating behavior most likely serves to ward off potential predators.

Chrysalis of the butterfly *Dynastor darius*.

Peanut-head bug (*Fulgora lanternia*).

The bizarre peanut-head bug, or *machaca* (*Fulgora laternaria*, family Fulgoridae), is a cicada with a greatly extended hollow structure on its head that bears a marked resemblance to the head of a lizard (an alligator or caiman according to other authors). What the exact survival value of resembling a lizard might be is a mystery. Many birds that are capable of eating such a large insect would probably not shy away from eating a lizard, either. However, it is a beautiful example of one of the many intricate surprises that can be expected in a tropical rainforest.

Literature

Andrews 1983; Cloudsley-Thompson 1995; Ernst 1992; Janzen 1980; Janzen & Hogue 1983.

FAMILY: **Leptodactylidae** (Leptodactylid Frogs)
ORDER: Anura (Frogs and Toads)

The family Leptodactylidae is extremely large, with over 800 exceptionally diverse species in more than 50 genera. Although most species live in the neotropics, some members of this family occur in Australia. Species vary greatly in appearance; they may be squat and toadlike, streamlined and aquatic, or miniscule and similar in appearance to tree frogs. Among the species living in Costa Rica, the diversity in shape, size, and color is often very confusing, even to the most experienced herpetologists.

One of the few easily recognizable leptodactylids in Costa Rica is the **broad-headed rain frog** (*Eleutherodactylus megacephalus*). See description on page 104.

The number of leptodactylid frog species living in Costa Rica is a matter of debate and continuing investigation. New species are still being added to the list, while the taxonomic status of some of the "known" species has not been satisfactorily resolved. At the time of this writing, 46 species are recognized in three genera: *Physalaemus*, *Leptodactylus*, and *Eleutherodactylus*.

Physalaemus pustulosus, the tungara frog, is the only species in the genus *Physalaemus* that resides in Central America. It is a small terrestrial frog, measuring 35 mm (1⅜ inches), that inhabits dry areas of the Pacific lowlands. It has extremely warty skin and is the only Costa Rican frog with a well-developed wartlike tubercle on the middle of the heel. There is a poison gland (paratoid gland) on each side of the neck; generally, the presence of paratoid glands is more typical of toads (genus *Bufo*) than of frogs. Although both *Physalaemus pustulosus* and toads have paratoid glands, *Physalaemus pustulosus* can be distinguished from all toad species that co-occur within its range in two ways—toads have distinct bony crests on the head and lack the distinct heel tubercle characteristic of *Physalaemus pustulosus*.

Five species of the genus *Leptodactylus* reside in Costa Rica: *Leptodactylus bolivianus*, *Leptodactylus labialis* (formerly known as *Leptodactylus fragilis*), *Leptodactylus melanonotus*, *Leptodactylus pentadactylus*, and *Leptodactylus poecilochilus*. While all are found in the Pacific lowlands, only the black-backed frog (*Leptodactylus melanonotus*) and the Central American bullfrog (*Leptodactylus pentadactylus*) are also found on the Caribbean slope. Species of the genus *Leptodactylus* are somewhat reminiscent of the "true" frogs in the genus *Rana*, having a medium-sized to very large streamlined body, a fairly long snout, and long, muscular hind limbs. The most important difference between *Leptodactylus* and true frogs (*Rana*) is the absence in *Leptodactylus* of skin-like webbing between the toes. Instead, *Leptodactylus* often have narrow fringes of skin on the sides of the toes. They also differ from true frogs by having a conspicuous circular skin fold on the belly; the function of this is unknown, though in some species it may serve as an adhesive organ.

Costa Rican *Leptodactylus* and *Physalaemus* have a free-swimming tadpole stage. Eggs are deposited in a foamy nest composed of mucus, semen, air, and water that the male whips up with his hind legs during mating. Generally the nest floats near the edge of a river or pond, often hidden under vegetation. On hatching, tadpoles leave the nest and complete their development in water. In contrast, all species of the third leptodactylid genus that occurs in Costa Rica, *Eleutherodactylus*, lay a relatively small number of large-yolked eggs (depending on the species, from 10 to 100 eggs per clutch), in a moist retreat on the forest floor or in a tree. The larvae of these species are capable of completing their development into tiny replicas of their parents inside the eggs, away from any body of water. In many species, a parent, either the female or the male, guards the eggs.

Recently hatched *Eleutherodactylus* are extremely small.

The genus *Eleutherodactylus* contains more species than any genus found within the vertebrates. It currently includes over 500 species, with new additions each year. This extremely diverse genus represents a taxonomic nightmare, and it is only a question of time before herpetologists splinter it into multiple genera. At present, the 40 Costa Rican *Eleutherodactylus* are tentatively assigned to 11 so-called species groups (see species list on page 281).

Generally, female *Eleutherodactylus* are larger than males. In some species, the size difference between sexes is extreme, the female being more than double the size of the male. As a result, adult males are often mistaken for juveniles. Another generally observable difference between the genders is the size of the eardrum, although in some species this structure is barely visible or not visible at all. Males usually have larger ears than females; the size of male eardrums measures from two-thirds the diameter of the eye to a length equal the diameter of the eye; the female eardrum usually only measures from half to two-thirds the diameter of the eye. The larger eardrum in males indicates that sound plays an important role in their life. Not much is known about vocalization in these frogs, but most produce a call that is fairly soft in comparison with some of their tree frog relatives in the family Hylidae.

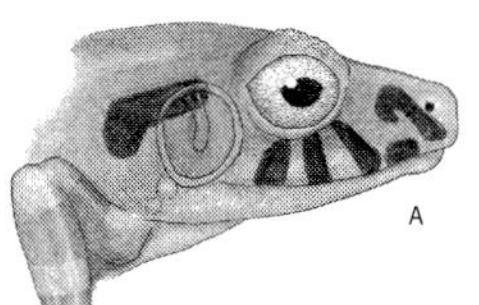

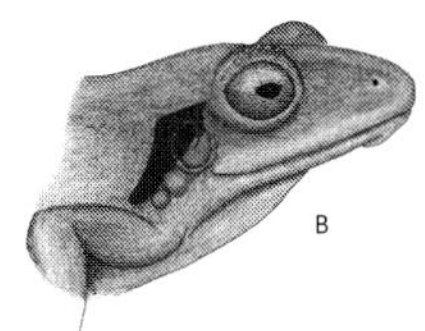

The male *Eleutherodactylus bransfordii* (A) has a distinctly larger eardrum than the female (B).

Most species of *Eleutherodactylus* vary so extremely—not only in size, shape, coloration, and pattern, but also in habitat preference, activity patterns, and other aspects of natural history—that individual frogs are often hard to identify without access to special resources. Positive identification may depend, for example, on examining a series of preserved museum specimens to check whether the individual in question falls within the normal range of variation in a certain species. Further, since many distinguishing characteristics (i.e., those morphological features that vary least from individual to individual) involve very technical issues, or are so minute—such as the shape of the finger disks on a frog that is only slightly larger than a fingernail—positive identification is extremely difficult.

However, members of this genus are generally small- to medium-sized frogs that lack skinlike webs between the fingers, but may have webbed feet. All have a circular skin fold on the belly, although this skin fold is often difficult to discern.

The *Eleutherodactylus* species presented in the following section have been included because they are relatively easy to recognize and/or because they are very common. Nevertheless, positive identification of species in this genus is a true challenge, even for the expert.

SUMMARY

How to identify Costa Rican leptodactylid frogs:
The Costa Rican members of this family are extremely diverse in shape and size. Different characteristics identify the three genera that inhabit the country:

- Members of the genus *Eleutherodactylus* are small- to medium-sized anurans that lack skinlike webs between the fingers, but may have webbed feet. All have a circular skin fold on the belly.
- Members of the genus *Leptodactylus* are large to very large anurans that lack skinlike webbing between the toes, but instead have fringes of skin along the sides of all toes.
- The sole Costa Rican member of the genus *Physalaemus*, the tungara frog (*Physalaemus pustulosus*) is a small, toadlike anuran whose head, back, and sides are covered with an extremely warty skin. It has a toadlike poison gland on each side of the neck, but, unlike toads, it never has bony crests on the head.

SPECIES DESCRIPTIONS

Eleutherodactylus bransfordii
Bransford's litter frog (plate 23)

Eleutherodactylus bransfordii, one of the most abundant amphibians in Costa Rica, is also one of the hardest to identify! No other Costa Rican *Eleutherodactylus* is so variable in skin texture, coloration, and pattern.

Eleutherodactylus bransfordii is a tiny, ground-dwelling species. Males reach sexual maturity at a length of only 14 mm (½ inch), and reach a maximum size of 26 mm (1 inch); adult females usually range between 16 and 30 mm (⅝ and 1⅛ inches). Apart from size, males and females can be told apart by the size of the eardrum, which is about the same size as the eye in males but distinctly smaller in females. These frogs have fairly short legs and arms; they do not have enlarged disks on the tips of the fingers or toes, and webbing between the digits is completely absent. *Eleutherodactylus bransfordii* has wartlike tubercles underneath its hands and feet.

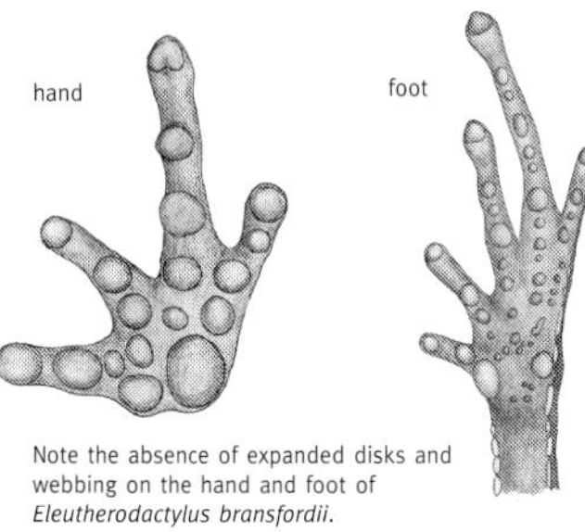

Note the absence of expanded disks and webbing on the hand and foot of *Eleutherodactylus bransfordii.*

The skin texture on the upper surfaces of this species can be either smooth, irregularly granular, or warty; also, various patterns of dorsal ridges may be superimposed on any of these skin types. The background color of the back and head can be uniform tan, gray, cream, or brown with a highly variable pattern of spots. The back is sometimes adorned with a pattern of two broad cream-colored dorsolateral stripes, or, less frequently, a narrow cream or white stripe running along the middle of the back. The belly is dull yellow, and in most individuals the thighs and flanks are suffused with orange or red. Sometimes a dark eye mask is present on each side of the head, and the upper lip may be adorned with alternating dark and light vertical bars.

Eleutherodactylus bransfordii ranges from eastern Nicaragua through Costa Rica (where it lives on both coasts) to western Panama. Although it can be found from sea level up to 1,600 m (5,250 ft), it is most commonly found below 1,400 m (4,600 ft). *Eleutherodactylus bransfordii* is absent from drier areas in Guanacaste Province, such as Santa Rosa National Park.

In many lowland areas in Costa Rica, *Eleutherodactylus bransfordii* is the most abundant leaf-litter amphibian present. Studies of population density in La Selva Biological Station, near Puerto Viejo de Sarapiquí, indicate that as many as 34 of these frogs may live in a 64 m^2 (575 sq ft) plot. This high-density population of *Eleutherodactylus bransfordii* was observed in an abandoned cacao grove. In another plot of equal size, this time in dense rainforest, population size peaked at 13 individuals. *Eleutherodactylus bransfordii* is a very successful colonizer of disturbed areas, and, even in pristine forests, it seems to prefer open trails over the forest interior. The density of this species is normally highest at the end of the dry season (April to May), when the ground is covered with a thick layer of dead leaves that provides many hiding places.

Mainly active during the day, *Eleutherodactylus bransfordii* hops across the layer of fallen leaves on the forest floor. Because its coloration blends in well with the background, it is often difficult to see. If disturbed, it will remain motionless and rely on its camouflage for protection; but when approached too closely, it dives under the leaf litter in two or three short hops. This species is very active and spends most of the day foraging for insect prey. A food generalist, *Eleutherodactylus bransfordii* eats a wide variety of invertebrates, including ants, spiders, mites, beetles, and insect larvae.

This species generally reproduces at night, although on some rainy and overcast days, the mating call of *Eleutherodactylus bransfordii*—a soft "*pew*"—is also heard during the daytime. Males call from under leaf litter or from areas of dense vegetation, particularly areas with tall grass. The terrestrial eggs of *Eleutherodactylus bransfordii* are laid in moist shady places near the calling site, where they complete their development into little froglets.

Initial studies of the countrywide variation in these confusing frogs resulted in the recognition of two closely related and highly variable species: *Eleutherodactylus bransfordii* (Bransford's litter frog) and *Eleutherodactylus podiciferus* (montane litter frog). More recently, research using biochemical and DNA analysis has reclassified *bransfordii*-like frogs into five species: *Eleutherodactylus bransfordii, Eleutherodactylus persimilis, Eleutherodactylus polyptychus, Eleutherodactylus stejnegerianus*, and *Eleutherodactylus underwoodi*. These species resemble one another so closely that identification in the field is nearly impossible.

The very similar-looking and equally variable *Eleutherodactylus podiciferus*, the montane litter frog, lives at higher elevations in the Central, Tilarán, and Talamanca mountain ranges, occurring from 1,100 to 2,100 m (3,600 to 6,900 ft); *Eleutherodactylus bransfordii* is found from sea level to around 1,600 m (5,250 ft). Thus, at elevations between 1,100 and 1,400 m (3,600 and 5,250 ft), both species may live together. Although they are not easy to distinguish, *Eleutherodactylus podiciferus* is somewhat larger than *Eleutherodactylus bransfordii*. Also, the wartlike tubercles underneath the hands and feet of *Eleutherodactylus podiciferus* are fewer in number, and lower and more rounded than those found in *Eleutherodactylus bransfordii*. These differences, however, are hard to assess without direct comparison between individuals of each species.

Eleutherodactylus cerasinus

Clay-colored rain frog (plate 23)

Eleutherodactylus cerasinus is a small to medium-sized, robust rain frog. Males are much smaller than females. They reach 23 mm (7⁄8 inch), while females measure up to 35 mm (1 3⁄8 inches).

A distinctive feature of this species is the W-shaped ridge on the back of the head. Its skin is relatively smooth on the upper surfaces, except for the area around the eardrum, which is very warty. The belly is coarsely granular. *Eleutherodactylus cerasinus* possesses greatly enlarged finger and toe disks on its unwebbed extremities. It typically has a large, conical tubercle on each heel. Interestingly, it lacks the pointed tubercles above each eye which are characteristic of several small species of *Eleutherodactylus*, such as the golden-groined rain frog, *Eleutherodactylus cruentus*.

The clay-colored rain frog owes its common name to its tan to reddish brown coloration. A faint pattern of light and dark bands may be present on the limbs. The back of the thighs is uniform red. This frog does not have the distinctively colored light spots on the groin that characterize some closely related species of *Eleutherodactylus*.

Eleutherodactylus cerasinus inhabits the Atlantic lowlands and foothills of Nicaragua and Costa Rica, and both coasts of Panama. It is found from near sea level to at least 1,300 m (4,250 ft). It appears to be present throughout its range in very low densities—it is not often seen. Although probably arboreal, individuals have been found in leaf litter and perched on low vegetation at night.

Male *Eleutherodactylus cerasinus* have an inflatable vocal sac, although their call is still unknown.

Eleutherodactylus cruentus

Golden-groined rain frog (plate 24)

This delicate, large-eyed frog has been found in humid to wet environments throughout Costa Rica, from near sea level to elevations exceeding 1,600 m (5,250 ft). Sightings are not very common. *Eleutherodactylus cruentus* is a medium-sized frog, with a maximum size of about 38 mm (1½ inches). Large, bright yellow spots on the groin that are normally hidden when the frog is resting distinguish this frog from all other Costa Rican *Eleutherodactylus*. The frog also has two to four spiny projections on the back of the tarsus and one or more hornlike spikes above each eye.

Very little is known about the biology of *Eleutherodactylus cruentus*. On rainy nights, individuals have been observed perched on large leaves among plants close to the ground. It appears to prefer dense and undisturbed cloudforest or rainforest habitats.

Eleutherodactylus diastema

Common tink frog (plate 24)

Eleutherodactylus diastema is found in Nicaragua, Costa Rica, and Panama, from near sea level to 1,800 m (5,900 ft). In Costa Rica, it occurs countrywide, except for in the dry northwestern regions. These miniscule arboreal frogs are difficult to see, but few who visit Costa Rica will miss their call. On virtually any night, you can hear short, bell-like calls in low- and middle-elevation rainforests throughout Costa Rica. Their "*tink!*" call, which resembles the sound of someone tapping a metal fork on the rim of a wineglass, is produced at intervals that range from fifteen seconds to more than one minute.

Eleutherodactylus diastema is a small frog. Adult males reach 20 mm (¾ inch); females, slightly larger, grow to 24 mm (1 inch). This species is strictly a tree-dweller and individual frogs are found from approximately 1.5 m (5 ft) above the forest floor to a height of more than 35 m (115 ft) in the upper tree crowns. These frogs are especially well-equipped for life in the trees; they have greatly enlarged adhesive disks on the fingers and toes. These disks are rounded, except for those on the two outer fingers and toes, which are teardrop-shaped. There is no trace of webbing between the toes or the fingers. The legs and arms are short and stubby; using these, they hop short distances from leaf to leaf or scurry around, somewhat in the manner of a tiny mouse. The skin is smooth, but there may be some scattered tubercles present on the head, the upper eyelids, or the body.

Eleutherodactylus diastema is highly variable in coloration and pattern; to confuse matters more, individuals are capable of considerable color change. During the day the upper surfaces of these frogs are usually gray to brown with a pattern of longitudinal bars, stripes, or spots. At night, individuals may be almost uniformly pink or tan. The belly is invariably a light color (white, cream, yellowish). The eyes are silver with brown speckling and have a horizontally elliptical pupil.

Like all Costa Rican *Eleutherodactylus*, this species does not experience a free-swimming, tadpole stage; the young exit their eggs as miniature copies of their parents. Females may lay up to 10 eggs, each with a large supply of cream-colored yolk. Each egg measures approximately 4 mm (⅛ inch) in diameter. The egg clump is usually deposited within the humid confinement of treetop bromeliads.

A single bromeliad may harbor several individuals that use the leaf axils as daytime retreats. At dusk, the frogs venture out from their hiding places and the males start calling from the upper surfaces of leaves, often within dense leaf tangles, which makes them very hard to see. Males sometimes call in duets, or even in small groups, in which one or more individuals respond to the call of a dominant male, the frog that emits the first call. When the dominant male receives a response to his initial call, he in turn responds, apparently after an interval that equals the length of the interval between his initial call and the first response. It is not known whether this timing of the calls plays a role in reproduction or in territoriality.

A second species of tink frog, the montane tink frog (*Eleutherodactylus hylaeformis*), is so similar to *Eleutherodactylus diastema* in size, appearance, and the sound of its call that distinguishing between the two is difficult. The montane tink frog, as its common name indicates, is a highland species with a distribution restricted to the higher regions of the Central, Talamanca, and Tilarán mountain ranges, above 1,500 m (4,900 ft).

Eleutherodactylus diastema and *Eleutherodactylus hylaeformis* differ in their coloration, however. *Eleutherodactylus diastema* has a white belly and a grayish-brown back patterned with dark spots, whereas *Eleutherodactylus hylaeformis* has a pink belly and, usually, a uniform pink to reddish-brown back.

Eleutherodactylus fitzingeri
Common rain frog (plate 25)

Eleutherodactylus fitzingeri, like the common tink frog (*Eleutherodactylus diastema*), is abundant in Costa Rica, but difficult to see and even more difficult to identify. Nonetheless, you invariably are able to hear its call during a visit to any humid lowland area.

Eleutherodactylus fitzingeri is a medium-sized frog; adult males reach 35 mm (1⅜ inches), and adult females 52 mm (2⅛ inches). The skin on the upper surfaces usually shows considerable ridging and scattered warts. The head is somewhat pointed when viewed from above and has distinctly visible eardrums. This species invariably has long legs with webbing between the toes and unwebbed hands that have small rounded disks on the two inner fingers and blunt widely expanded disks on the outer two fingers.

Since color and pattern may vary greatly from individual to individual, they do not reveal much about its identity. Gray, beige, or brown are the colors that most frequently appear on the back and head. Often a broad yellow or orangish stripe runs down the middle

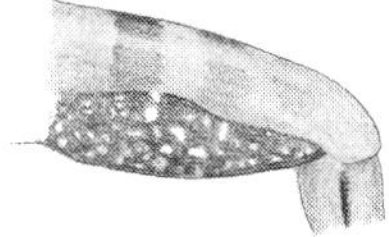

Eleutherodactylus fitzingeri leg.

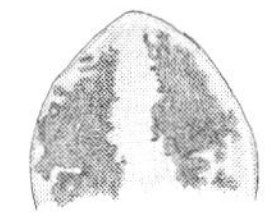

Eleutherodactylus fitzingeri throat.

of the back, or a dark hourglass- or W-shaped spot may be present. When it is possible to examine a frog at close distance, two distinguishing features may be observable. The most important distinguishing feature is the pattern on the back of the thighs; it consists of numerous wormlike, more-or-less fused, pale-yellow spots on a dark brown or black background. This surface is not visible when the legs are folded into a sitting position, however. The second distinguishing feature is the pattern on the underside of the frog: the undersurface is white, changing to cream and yellow near the hind limbs. The throat is white, and mottled to varying degrees with dark pigment. There is invariably also a broad white stripe down the middle of the throat.

Eleutherodactylus fitzingeri is a very common lowland frog, found in humid conditions from eastern Nicaragua through Costa Rica and Panama into northwestern Colombia. In Costa Rica, it is found countrywide at elevations below 1,200 m (3,950 ft).

Although these frogs call mainly at dusk and in the early evening from elevated positions on low vegetation, they are also heard during strong daytime rains. The call, which resembles the sound of someone rapidly clicking two pebbles together, is heard frequently, but it is exceedingly difficult to locate the frogs using the call as an indicator. They are often concealed in leaf litter or in dense clumps of vegetation. *Eleutherodactylus fitzingeri* males call sporadically, perhaps to reduce the possibility of assisting predators in tracking their whereabouts. At least one predator, the fringe-lipped bat (*Trachops cirrhosus*), is known to eat these and other frogs after having located them by their calls.

Unlike most other frogs and toads, *Eleutherodactylus* species do not congregate near a body of water during reproduction. There is no indication that they call in an organized chorus, although in some species, such as *Eleutherodactylus diastema*, calls from an individual male are answered by a nearby individual. *Eleutherodactylus fitzingeri* males seem to call in a random order, but it may be that some underlying order exists beyond the comprehension of the human observer.

Eleutherodactylus fitzingeri appear to be most common around clearings and along streams and rivers, mostly within humid forests. During the day, they inhabit leaf litter in deeply shaded parts of the forest floor. They are mostly seen after dusk. These frogs sometimes sit on the warm pavement of roads at night, but normally they climb onto low vegetation, 30 to 150 cm (12 to 60 inches) above the forest floor, or onto exposed logs or rocks in or near streams or rivers. A very good place to find these frogs is in the reed-like vegetation lining slow-moving rivers in the lowlands, where they sit on top of the foliage. When threatened, they sometimes dive from their perch into the water and hide on the bottom.

Some species of the genus *Eleutherodactylus* exhibit parental care and attend eggs until they hatch into miniature rain frogs. *Eleutherodactylus fitzingeri* lays its eggs in a moist spot on the forest floor. A female frog was observed sitting on 44 eggs deposited under leaves. It is not known whether males also attend the eggs.

Eleutherodactylus megacephalus

Broad-headed rain frog (plate 25)

Among the 46 or so Costa Rican *Leptodactylidae*, four species, *Eleutherodactylus bufoniformis, Eleutherodactylus gulosus, Eleutherodactylus megacephalus*, and *Eleutherodactylus rugosus*, are highly conspicuous because of their extremely broad heads. These species are members of a group known as broad-headed rain frogs; they differ from all other Costa Rican frogs in that the width of some individuals' heads exceeds half their body length. Broad-headed rain frogs have distinguishing bony ridges on their backs. These ridges resemble an hourglass at the center of the back and taper toward the lower back, where they meet to form a V shape. Additional bony crests are present on the snout and between the eyes.

Eleutherodactylus megacephalus is a large species, with a maximum recorded size of 110 mm (4⅜ inches) for adult females. Though toadlike in appearance, *Eleutherodactylus megacephalus* lacks paratoid glands on the neck and thus distinguishes itself from all true toads. The sex of an individual is determined by examining the size of the eardrum. In females, the diameter of the eardrum is about half the diameter of the eye; in males, the diameter of the eardrum is nearly the same as the diameter of the eye.

The background color of the upper surface of *Eleutherodactylus megacephalus* is either a grayish tan, grayish brown, or dark brown. In most individuals, the ridges on the back are outlined by a dark line. There is a dark marking behind each eye that extends above the ear. Another dark marking in the shape of a triangular patch is located at the vent. The dark brown or black belly is patterned with brightly colored (white, yellow, orange, or red) contrasting spots. The groin has a pattern of black and white spots, while the back of the thigh is either a uniform black or a black marked with pale flecks. The underside of the hands and feet is also dark (brown or black). The iris is coppery to gold.

Eleutherodactylus megacephalus occurs at low and moderate elevations, from the Atlantic slope of Honduras south to western Colombia. In Costa Rica, it can be found on the Caribbean slope, from near sea level to approximately 1,000 m (3,300 ft).

The broad-headed rain frog is a relatively uncommon species that is most frequently discovered on the forest floor, concealed in leaf litter. Juveniles appear to be active primarily during the day, while adults can be observed actively hopping about during the day and at night. Individuals are often seen close to holes in the ground, into which they immediately escape when disturbed.

These frogs are sit-and-wait predators; they hunt by ambushing passing prey. Large spiders seem to be a favorite prey, although large millipedes and beetles have also been found in the stomach of *Eleutherodactylus megacephalus*. A broad head and big mouth allow *Eleutherodactylus megacephalus* to tap into food sources that are not accessible to most narrow-headed species.

Eleutherodactylus mimus

Mimicking rain frog (plate 26)

Herpetologists have placed *Eleutherodactylus mimus* and two other species, *Eleutherodactylus gollmeri* and *Eleutherodactylus noblei*, in the Gollmeri Group because these three species are more closely related to each other than to other species within the genus. *Eleutherodactylus mimus* is indeed so similar in appearance and habits to its close relatives that it was only in 1955 that it was recognized as a separate species.

Eleutherodactylus mimus is the only species in the Gollmeri Group that has substantial webbing between its toes—most of the inner four toes are enclosed. It can also be recognized by the presence of a thin light line that runs down the middle of the back and by the dark mask that covers the sides of the head and extends onto the body past the insertion of the front limbs.

This frog inhabits dense lowland forests on the Atlantic slope of Honduras, Nicaragua, Costa Rica, and extreme western Panama. In Costa Rica it has been found from near sea level to an elevation of 640 m (2100 ft).

Eleutherodactylus mimus is most similar in body shape to *Eleutherodactylus gollmeri*, with which it sometimes co-occurs. The finger disks of these two species are nearly uniform in size; in contrast, *Eleutherodactylus noblei* has distinctly widened finger disks on the outer two fingers. *Eleutherodactylus gollmeri* has a distinct wartlike protuberance on its tarsus and can thus be distinguished from *Eleutherodactylus mimus*, which does not.

Eleutherodactylus noblei

Noble's rain frog (plate 26)

Eleutherodactylus noblei and the two other species in the Gollmeri Group are similar-looking small- to medium-sized frogs, with a streamlined, long-snouted body and smooth skin. Unlike other *Eleutherodactylus*, members of this group have a distinctive appearance and are therefore fairly easy to identify. The challenge in this case is distinguishing between members of the group.

Adult males measure between 43 and 53 mm (1¾ and 2⅛ inches); adult females are considerably larger and range between 58 and 66 mm (2⅜ and 2⅝ inches).

Eleutherodactylus noblei has a long, protruding snout that appears pointed when seen from above and is marked on each side with a dark brown mask-like eye stripe that extends beyond the shoulders, well onto the body. The large eyes have a golden iris and a horizontally elliptical pupil.

The three species in the Gollmeri Group are somewhat variable in coloration, but some elements of their color pattern are generally present. They are colored in some shade of tan, bronze, or brown, with a thin, light stripe running down the middle of the back. Usually a distinct dark brown hourglass-shaped spot, which may be outlined by a light border, is present on the back. The flanks are patterned with a series of dark stripes, and the backs of the thighs are invariably uniform brown, sometimes suffused with red. The undersurfaces of these frogs are uniform white or cream.

Eleutherodactylus noblei occurs at low and intermediate elevations from eastern Honduras to the Canal Zone in Panama. In Costa Rica, it is mainly found in the wet forests of the Caribbean slope and in the lower portion of the premontane zone of southwestern Costa Rica, from near sea level to 1,200 m (3,950 ft).

Virtually nothing is known about the life history of this frog. It appears to be active mostly during the day, when it is seen in the leaf-litter layer of humid rainforest environments; on many occasions, however, active adult frogs have been encountered at night sitting on the thin twigs of low bushes, up to 2 m (6½ ft) above the ground. Cryptic coloration enables these frogs to blend in perfectly with the dead leaves on which they sit. When threatened, they rely on their camouflage and remain motionless, pressing their body close against the ground. However, when the source of the threat comes too close, they launch themselves at the last second and, with their powerful legs, bound to safety in the underbrush in a zigzag pattern of long leaps.

It is still unknown how *Eleutherodactylus noblei* find their mates, since no calls have ever been heard. Males lack the vocal sac and vocal slits that are normally present in frogs that produce calls, but the absence of these structures does not necessarily mean that they are incapable of calling. Various frogs that also lack these structures are surprisingly articulate. The presence of prominent eardrums in both males and females indicates they are capable of hearing. On two occasions, a soft, birdlike chirp was heard in areas where a male was later discovered. Whether this particular sound is connected to *Eleutherodactylus noblei* remains to be determined.

Eleutherodactylus ridens

Pygmy rain frog (plate 27)

The pygmy rain frog is one of the lesser known frogs in Costa Rica. It is a tiny species of *Eleutherodactylus* with a maximum size of 25 mm (1 inch) in females, and only 19 mm (¾ inch) in males.

The large adhesive disks on its fingers and toes would suggest that this species is arboreal. This appears to be the case, and individuals have been found hidden in bromeliads at heights of over 30 m (100 ft) in tall rainforest trees. However, sometimes these inconspicuous creatures are found closer to the ground, and several individuals have been observed inside the rolled-up leaves of large *Heliconia* and banana plants. They have even been observed hopping in leaf litter.

In many cases, the pygmy rain frogs found near the forest floor were gravid females. At the end of the dry season, calling males were heard to produce a rapid and soft series of high-pitched clicks, possibly an advertisement call to entice females to mate. It is not known where these frogs lay their eggs, but it is likely that egg clutches are deposited in bromeliads or other arboreal plants. Like other species in the genus *Eleutherodactylus*, the young of *Eleutherodactylus ridens* leave the egg fully developed, as a tiny froglet rather than as a tadpole.

Pygmy rain frogs can be recognized by their red thighs and feet, which are hidden when the frog has its legs folded, and by the presence of one or more pointed warts on top of the upper eyelids. These frogs are otherwise brown, with or without a pattern of dark spots. Another distinctive feature of this species is their nostrils, which are conspicuously raised, giving the impression, when seen from above, that the tip of the snout is almost three-lobed.

Eleutherodactylus ridens primarily inhabits premontane rainforest habitats from near sea level to at least 1,200 m (3,950 ft), from Honduras to Ecuador. In Costa Rica, it has been found on both the Atlantic and the Pacific slopes.

Leptodactylus melanonotus

Black-backed frog (plate 27)

Compared to its impressive cousin, the Central American bullfrog (*Leptodactylus pentadactylus*), *Leptodactylus melanonotus* is small and inconspicuous. It is nevertheless a robust little frog with a maximum size of 45 mm (1¾ inches) and a body shape somewhat reminiscent of true frogs of the genus *Rana*. It differs from the latter, however, in lacking dorsolateral skin folds and well-developed webbing between the toes; instead these frogs have skin fringes on the sides of their fingers and toes. A unique characteristic of this species is the presence of

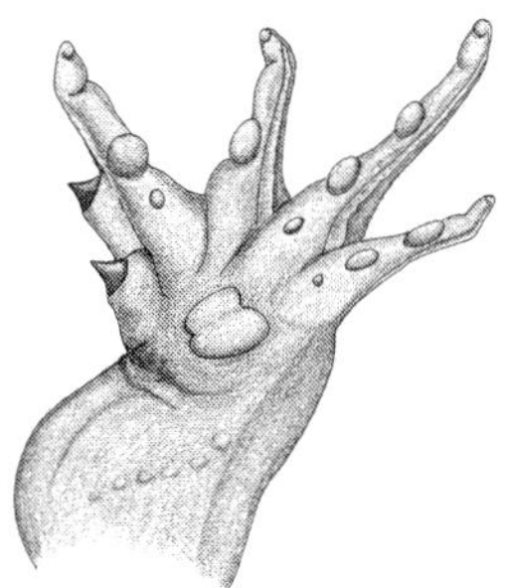

Hand of male *Leptodactylus melanonotus*. Note the two black spikes on the inner fingers.

paired black spikes at the base of the male's inner fingers.

Although its common name suggests otherwise, *Leptodactylus melanonotus* is not black, but generally a dark gray or brown punctuated with various obscure markings. Often, a triangular dark spot is present on the top of the head between the eyes, and the lips are marked with dark bars. The coloration of the belly is extremely variable: Some individuals may have a belly that is a uniform light color; on others, the belly may have dark reticulum on a light background.

Leptodactylus melanonotus is a common to abundant species in Costa Rica, where it is found along the Pacific coast and in the northeastern lowlands, from sea level to roughly 1,440 m (4,700 ft). Though it has great climatic tolerance, it prefers drier habitats, where it inhabits small to very small ponds located on the margins of a larger body of water. It is also found in water-filled hoof prints or flooded pastures. These frogs can be encountered singly, but they are sometimes found in very large congregations; the size of the population seems to be primarily determined by the presence of sufficient hiding places.

Leptodactylus melanonotus signals its presence with a distinctive, often soft "*tuc-tuc-tuc*" call, similar to the sound of a metal object tapping on a dinner plate. Calling males are difficult to locate since they are invariably hidden in vegetation or in a burrow underneath a rock or log. A large chorus of these frogs, which can be heard from a great distance, may sound not unlike an idling engine. Although this is a nocturnal species, it is often heard calling during the day.

Like many other species of *Leptodactylus*, *Leptodactylus melanonotus* breeds in shallow water or on the periphery of larger bodies of water. The eggs are deposited in foam nests and hatch into free-swimming tadpoles. The foam nest protects the eggs and tadpoles from drying out; the exposed exterior of the nest becomes viscous or may even harden somewhat, while the interior remains moist. Sometimes the water around the nest may recede temporarily, and the nest will remain out of water for a few days. The humid climate inside the nest ensures continued development of the eggs, however. Even after the eggs have hatched, the tadpoles may stay inside the nest until the water returns to the surrounding environment. Groups of swimming tadpoles were observed to form tight groups, resembling a single, larger animal. Other tadpoles such as those of the Mexican burrowing toad (*Rhinophrynus dorsalis*) have shown similar behavior.

Leptodactylus pentadactylus

Central American bullfrog
Rana toro, Rana ternero (plate 28)

This species' multiple common names—which include Central American bullfrog, *Rana Toro*, and *Rana Ternero*—suggest the arresting effect its striking appearance has on people. Its sheer size distinguishes it from almost all Costa Rican amphibians, with the possible exception of the giant toad (*Bufo marinus*), which is also large but differs in other respects.

Adult females reach a maximum size of 181 mm (7⅛ inches); males are smaller but reach the still impressive size of 169 mm (6⅝ inches).

Behind each eye run two linear skin folds. One skin fold runs down the back to the groin; the other slants downward over the eardrum and continues onto the side of the body. Breeding males are easily recognized by their greatly swollen arms. Males also have a large black keratinized spine on each

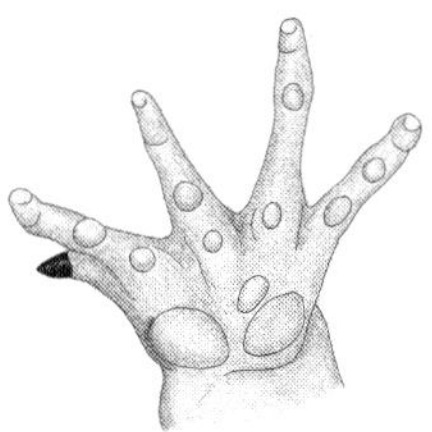

Keratinized spine on thumb of a male *Leptodactylus pentadactylus*.

thumb and a pair of smaller spines on the chest. They use these spines in territorial conflicts with other males; when mating, the spines help the male hold on to the female.

The smooth skin on the back is reddish-brown, brown, or purplish-gray, either uniformly so or with a pattern of spots and bars with faint dark outlines. The upper surfaces of the limbs are distinctly barred, whereas the backs of the thighs have a pattern of white or cream spots on a dark brown background. The lips are boldly marked with chocolate-brown vertical bars or spots. A dark brown stripe extends from the nostril to a point beyond the shoulder.

Leptodactylus pentadactylus ranges from Honduras southward into South America. In Costa Rica, it is widespread on both Atlantic and Pacific slopes, from almost sea level to 1,200 m (3,950 ft).

At the first sign of dusk, a loud and ominous "*wrooop*" reveals the presence of *Leptodactylus pentadactylus*. Males call sporadically from holes in the ground located underneath a log or rock, often where there is dense vegetation. Their calls serve to attract females and, very likely, also to delimit their territory.

Unlike the closely related species of the genus *Eleutherodactylus*, which complete their larval development within terrestrial eggs, frogs of the genus *Leptodactylus* develop as free-swimming tadpoles. No Costa Rican species of *Leptodactylus* lays its eggs directly in water, however; instead they deposit their eggs in foam nests on the periphery of bodies of water. During amplexus, the male hugs the female with his forearms and, as eggs emerge from the female, kicks his legs to create a foamy mass consisting of eggs, sperm, skin secretions, water, and air. This foamy nest, which rests either in a burrow near a body of water or in a shallow depression at the margins of a pond, serves to protect the eggs and larvae from predators and from drying out. A single nest normally contains around 1,000 eggs, measuring roughly 3 mm (⅛ inch) in diameter. As soon as the eggs hatch, the tadpoles leave the nest and disperse into the nearby water.

The free-swimming tadpoles of *Leptodactylus pentadactylus* develop in small rain pools that are usually subject to direct sunlight. When the pool dries out, the tadpoles retreat into burrows in the muddy soil or between roots of adjacent vegetation, only to emerge again when the next rains refill their pond. Tadpoles of this species are resistant to dehydration, and laboratory experiments have shown that they are able to survive up to 156 hours (6.5 days) without water.

Leptodactylus pentadactylus tadpoles are facultative carnivores; they prefer to feed on eggs and tadpoles of either their own or other species, but are also capable of developing solely on a vegetarian diet of algae and plant matter. Adults prey on virtually anything they can gobble up: invertebrates in all shapes and sizes, bird chicks, snakes, and, especially, other frogs, including the toxic poison-dart frogs. Interestingly, *Leptodactylus pentadactylus* is the only New World frog known to eat scorpions.

The frog is itself preyed on by a variety of animals, including coatimundis, snakes, caimans, and sometimes even humans; some Amazonian peoples eat *Leptodactylus pentadactylus*. If these frogs manage to avoid predation successfully, they may survive a long time—captive individuals have lived at least 15 years.

When discovered, these frogs often remain motionless and are easily approached. When seized, *Leptodactylus pentadactylus* sometimes emits a loud, bone-chilling scream that rarely fails to stun an unsuspecting frog collector, or a potential predator. This surprise vocalization may result in a momentary release of the frog, allowing it to escape with long, rapid jumps into the underbrush.

Research on adult frogs taken from their burrows and displaced over short distances has shown that these frogs have an accurate image of their direct vicinity and manage to return to their burrow in a straight line. It is not known what cues they use to recognize their environment.

Physalaemus pustulosus

Tungara frog (plate 28)

This small frog measures up to 35 mm (1⅜ inches). It is the only amphibian in Costa Rica not a member of the toad family (*Bufonidae*) that has a long poison gland on each side of the neck. *Physalaemus pustulosus* further differs from other Costa Rican amphibians in having extremely warty skin; the body, limbs, head, and even the eardrums are covered with warts and pustules (hence *pustulosus*).

Within Costa Rica, *Physalaemus pustulosus* lives in relatively dry parts of the Pacific lowlands. It is usually seen or heard only during the breeding season, at the start of the rainy season. On rainy nights, calling males can sometimes be found in puddles of rainwater producing a characteristic "*mew*" call. The inflatable vocal sac, observable in calling males, is of an enormous size compared with the frog itself. In addition to attracting females, the male's call was also observed to attract an unusual predator, the fringe-lipped bat (*Trachops cirrhosus*). Like species of the genus *Leptodactylus*, these frogs produce a foam nest in which to lay their eggs. The tadpoles develop in rain pools.

In earlier literature, this species is sometimes found under the name *Engystomops pustulosus.*

Literature

Donnelly 1994; Duellman 1967b; Duellman & Trueb 1986; Gregory 1983; Hayes et al. 1989; Heyer 1970; Lee 1996; Leenders 1995a, 1996; Lips & Savage 1996a; Lourenco 1995; Lynch 1975; Lynch & Myers 1983; Miyamoto 1982, 1983; Pröhl 1997; Rand 1983; Rodríguez & Duellman 1994; Savage 1974, 1986, 1997; Savage & Emerson 1970; Savage & Villa 1986; Scott 1983f,g; Taylor 1952b, 1954a, 1955; Tuttle & Ryan 1981; Valerio 1971; Vinton 1951; Weimer et al 1993c, 1994; Zug 1993.

FAMILY: **Microhylidae** (Narrow-mouthed Frogs)
ORDER: Anura (Frogs and Toads)

All Costa Rican microhylids are small, plump-bodied frogs with small heads. A transverse skin fold across the head, just behind the eyes, that appears to separate the head from the body is the key identifying feature for Costa Rican microhylids. In addition, these narrow-mouthed frogs have horny shovel-like tubercles on their feet and short, powerful legs that are used when burrowing backwards into the soil. Costa Rica is home to three microhylid species, each in a separate genus: *Hypopachus variolosus, Nelsonophryne aterrima* and *Gastrophryne pictiventris.*

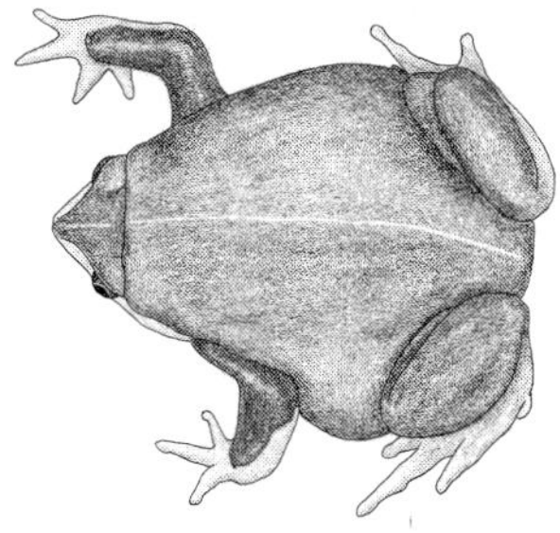

The three Costa Rican microhylids, including the **sheep frog** (*Hypopachus variolosus*) pictured here, have an egg-shaped body and a transverse skin fold across the head.

Microhylids are secretive, nocturnal frogs with a burrowing (fossorial) lifestyle. During the day, they hide in leaf litter, under objects, or in burrows; at night, they surface and actively hunt for small insects. Their diet mainly consists of ants and mites.

The three Costa Rican species seem to prefer rainforest habitats that range from humid to wet, although *Hypopachus variolosus* is also common in the dry Guanacaste area. In Costa Rica, all three species are restricted to the lowlands.

The reproductive season coincides with periods of heavy rains. Females are attracted to males that call from the water surface of temporary ponds. Amplexus is axillary, and the two frogs are held together firmly, partly because of the male's resolute grip, but also due to sticky secretions produced by skin glands on the back of the female. Although some members of this family are known to produce tadpoles that develop directly within terrestrial eggs, all Costa Rican species produce aquatic eggs from which hatch tadpoles that develop in bodies of water.

SUMMARY

How to identify Costa Rican microhylid frogs:

- Costa Rican microhylids all have an egg-shaped body, a tiny head, and a typical transverse skin fold across the head, behind the eyes.
- All are good burrowers and have large spade-like tubercles on the feet.

Hypopachus variolosus

Sheep frog (plate 29)

A skin fold across the back of the head immediately identifies this species as a microhylid, though the fold is more distinct in some individuals than others. *Hypopachus variolosus* differs from the two other Costa Rican representatives of this family in having two prominent spadelike tubercles on each foot, as opposed to a single enlarged tubercle per foot in the other two species.

These little, egg-shaped frogs have a small head with a pointed snout and short, robust limbs. The skin is smooth and moist. Both the hands and the feet are unwebbed, and the digits bear no disks.

Hypopachus variolosus typically has a gray, olive, brown, or reddish-brown dorsal background color, with scattered dark spots and a light yellow or orange line down the middle of the back. Often, the dark dorsal markings are outlined in red, especially on the usually hidden rear surface of the hind limbs. The belly has dark mottling on a white or gray background, with a light stripe down the middle. The sides of the head are marked with a white diagonal stripe that runs from the eye toward the insertion of the front limb. A dark eyemask is usually present. The eyes are yellow to gold, with a round pupil.

The maximum size recorded for this species is 49 mm (1⅞ inches), but most individuals reach a length of between 30 and 40 mm (1⅛ and 1⅝ inches). Larger individuals generally are females. Another trait that distinguishes males and females is that males have a dark throat, while females do not.

Hypopachus variolosus ranges from southeastern Texas to northern Costa Rica, where it occurs on both the Pacific and Caribbean slopes, from about sea level to at least 1,200 m (3,950 ft). The most commonly observed microhylid in the country, it is abundant during rains in preferred habitats (e.g., Santa Rosa National Park). *Hypopachus variolosus* inhabits moist forests and humid places that are surrounded by relatively dry and open areas.

These frogs are strictly nocturnal, and they hide during the day in burrows or underneath rocks or logs. After heavy rains, they surface and are often observed on the still-warm pavement of roads. When discovered, they tend to freeze and rely on their camouflage for protection. In spite of their short, stubby legs, they are capable of escaping with surprisingly long jumps.

Hypopachus variolosus prefers to eat ants and termites, and it actively searches for large concentrations of these insects.

Hypopachus variolosus reproduces during the rainy season in temporary pools, such as those found in flooded pastures or drainage ditches. Breeding activity is initiated by heavy rains. Sexually active males produce a nasal advertisement call with a duration of approximately three seconds. This call is reminiscent of the sound made by a bleating sheep, hence its common name. Females lay their eggs in a floating surface film, and hatching occurs within twenty-four hours. As with most other species that breed in temporary ponds, *Hypopachus variolosus* tadpoles complete their development rapidly, metamorphosing into froglets within a few weeks. The unusual discovery of a single tadpole in a water-filled treehole almost one meter above the ground, suggests that further investigation into the natural history of these little known frogs may yield surprising discoveries.

Nelsonophryne aterrima

Black narrow-mouthed frog (plate 29)

Nelsonophryne aterrima is the only microhylid in Costa Rica with a uniform dark color, which may be dark brown, slate gray, or black. A transverse skin fold is clearly visible behind the eyes.

This is a somewhat featureless species, with a globlike body and a small, bluntly rounded head.

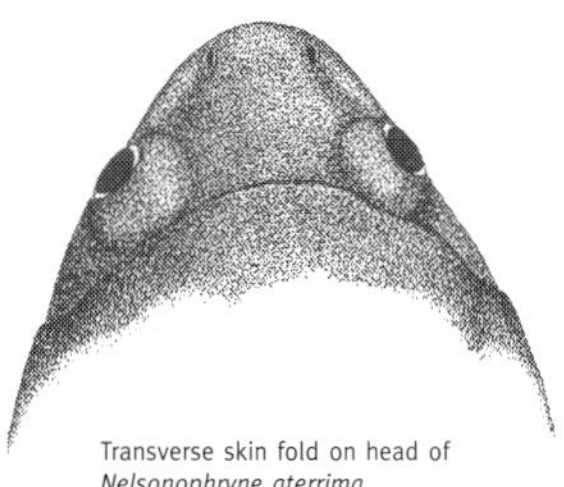

Transverse skin fold on head of *Nelsonophryne aterrima*.

The eardrums are not visible. The bulging eyes have a round pupil that is barely visible because of the darkly colored iris. The tips of the fingers and toes are not expanded, and reduced webbing is visible, mainly between the outer toes. A single enlarged, spadelike tubercle is located on each foot, at the base of the inner toe.

Males range in size from 40 to 60 mm (1⅝ to 2⅜ inches); females range in size from 50 to 70 mm (2 to 2¾ inches). In addition to size, males and females differ in several characteristics. Breeding males have rough patches (nuptial pads) on the inside of their inner three fingers that improve their grip on slippery females. Males also have a gland that covers the entire abdomen and extends onto the undersurface of the upper arms, a feature absent in females. Adult females normally have smooth skin; adult males have rough skin with a glandular appearance.

Nelsonophryne aterrima is known only from scattered locations in Costa Rica, Panama, Colombia, and Ecuador. Within Costa Rica, it has a discontinuous distribution and has been recorded in the lowlands of the southwest and at intermediate elevations of the northern Caribbean slope, to approximately 1,200 m (3,950 ft).

Little is known about the natural history of *Nelsonophryne aterrima*. Limited observations indicate that this species inhabits dense rainforests, where it seeks out clearings, areas where trees have fallen, or disturbed areas. The main period of activity seems to be during nighttime rainfall. One individual was seen emerging from its muddy burrow amidst low herbs during an exceptionally strong downpour in the early afternoon.

In one observation in Panama, a male vibrated its toes during handling and emitted a release call when it was grabbed by the waist. Such release calls are not uncommon among frogs and toads, and are normally used when a male is accidentally clasped by another male that has confused the first male for a female. The Panamanian frog in question may have mistaken the hands of its captor for the grip of a sexually aroused male frog. In some other species, the vibrating toes appear to be a sign of excitement or aggression, usually in male-male interactions (see, for example, *Dendrobates auratus*, page 73).

Nelsonophryne aterrima was previously known as *Glossostoma aterrimum*, and is mentioned as such in most early literature.

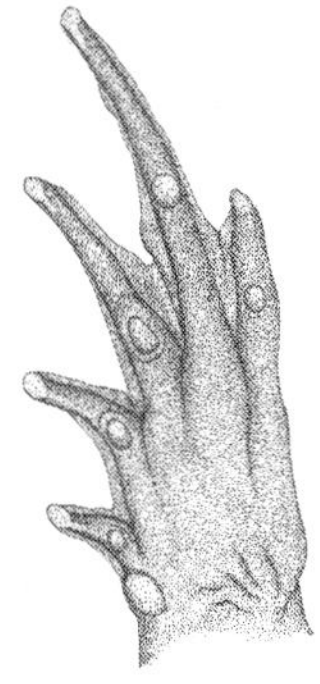

Nelsonophryne aterrima foot.

Literature
Behler & King 1979; Donnelly 1994; Hayes et al. 1989; Jungfer 1988; Lee 1996; McDiarmid & Foster 1975; Nelson 1962; Sasa & Solórzano 1995; Savage & Villa 1986; Zug 1993.

FAMILY: **Ranidae** (True Frogs)
ORDER: Anura (Frogs and Toads)

This very large family occurs almost everywhere in the world, except for Australia, the Sahara Desert, and southern South America. The genus *Rana*, with over 200 species of very similar-looking frogs, is the only genus of the ranids found in the Americas. To most, these streamlined frogs with long legs and smooth-skinned bodies will appear very familiar.

All Costa Rican ranids are characterized by the presence of a pair of glandular dorsolateral skin folds that run from behind the eyes to the groin. The legs are long and muscular, and these frogs are capable of jumping long distances. The feet have extensive webbing and are used for propulsion during swimming. The hands are completely free of webbing.

Vaillant's frog (*Rana vaillanti*). Note dorsolateral skin fold and long muscular legs.

Tadpoles of the genus *Rana* can be found in many ponds, slow-moving rivers, and streams. Among the largest tadpoles in the country, they can reach impressive lengths of well over 10 cm (4 inches).

Five species of *Rana* occur in Costa Rica. Forrer's leopard frog (*Rana forreri*) is found in the dry northwest; the green-eyed frog (*Rana vibicaria*) is a highland species that only occurs at elevations over 1,500 m (4,900 ft) in the Central, Talamanca, and Tilarán mountain ranges. Taylor's frog (*Rana taylori*, formerly known as *Rana pipiens*), the brilliant forest frog (*Rana warszewitschii*), and Vaillant's frog (*Rana vaillanti*, formerly known as *Rana palmipes*), are widespread and common.

SUMMARY

How to identify Costa Rican ranid frogs:

- All ranid frogs have two glandular dorsolateral skin folds; each runs from behind the eye to the groin. These are medium-sized to large frogs with smooth skin, a streamlined body, and long, muscular legs.
- Ranid frogs always have strongly webbed feet, but never have webbing between the fingers.

SPECIES DESCRIPTIONS

Rana vaillanti

Vaillant's frog (plate 30)

Distinct, longitudinal glandular ridges on the hind legs characterize *Rana vaillanti*. Its variable coloration may be dark brown to bright green, uniform or spotted. Juveniles of this species tend to be of a brighter shade of green than adults. The toes are fully webbed. A large frog, this species may reach 110 mm (4⅜ inches).

Rana vaillanti is one of the more aquatic species of *Rana* found in Costa

Rica, and it is a common sight along many lowland ponds, streams, and rivers. It is active both during the day and at night. *Rana vaillanti* lives on the banks of quiet waters; when startled, it escapes into the water, swims a short distance, and hides on the bottom.

Like many other species of *Rana*, Vaillant's frog reproduces in water. The male attracts a female with his advertisement call, which resembles the sound made when one rubs a finger over an inflated balloon. Females deposit a very large clump of eggs in the water that may contain up to several thousand eggs.

Rana vibicaria

Green-eyed frog (plate 30)

Rana vibicaria is an easily recognized frog: it has green eyes and bright red coloration on the back of the thighs. Its other features are typical of members of the family Ranidae. It has a streamlined body and long legs, as well as long, glandular ridges running along each side of the back. Juvenile frogs often have a bright green coloration that later changes into the brassy or brown colors seen in adults.

This species has a very limited distribution; it is only found in the Central, Talamanca, and Tilarán mountain ranges of Costa Rica, at elevations above 1,650 m (5,400 ft). An isolated population of *Rana vibicaria* inhabits the western slopes of Chiriquí Volcano in Panama.

Green-eyed frogs are less aquatic than some of their relatives; this is indicated by the relatively small amount of webbing present between the toes of these frogs and by their nostrils, which are directed more or less sideways. Aquatic frogs usually have their nostrils on top of the snout, pointing up. In the breeding season, which primarily takes place during the rainy parts of the year but may continue almost year-round, green-eyed frogs are seen in ponds and in slow-moving parts of rivers, where they reproduce. Nonreproducing individuals are sometimes encountered in dense forest habitats.

Male *Rana vibicaria*, like all other Costa Rican species in the genus *Rana*, have no vocal sacs or vocal slits, but are still capable of producing a soft call. According to observers, a chorus consisting of approximately 100 calling frogs could no longer be heard at a distance beyond 100 m (300 ft).

Rana warszewitschii

Brilliant forest frog (plate 31)

Rana warszewitschii is a relatively small and elegant *Rana* that differs from all other Costa Rican frogs in having bright red coloration on the underside of the limbs and on the webs between the toes, and in having 2 to 4 large, bright yellow spots on the back of the thighs. This slender frog has a pointed head with a long snout, distinctly visible eardrums, and large golden eyes. A pair of thin dorsolateral skin folds runs from behind the eye to the groin; these folds are somewhat lighter in coloration than the background color of the back and sides. A thin light stripe runs from the tip of the snout to the eye, and a broad white or cream stripe adorns the upper lip. The background color of Costa Rican individuals is bronze, speckled with bright blue or green spots. The sides of the body are often somewhat darker. The belly is normally cream to dusky, but in males it can be blackish.

Rana warszewitschii is a smooth-skinned species. The tips of the fingers and toes are somewhat expanded, but they do not have the disks found in tree frogs or some species of *Eleutherodactylus*. The hands are not webbed, but the feet have extensive webbing between the toes.

Females reach a length of 63 mm (2½ inches); males, slightly smaller, reach a maximum size of 48 mm (1⅞ inches).

Rana warszewitschii is found in Panama, Costa Rica, Nicaragua, and Honduras at elevations from near sea level to about 2,000 m (6,600 ft). It is found in very humid habitats throughout Costa Rica, but is absent from dry areas in the northwest.

Adults are mostly active during daylight hours. Metamorphosing juveniles, however, have been observed crawling on land at night, and small individuals also have been encountered hopping along the forest floor at night.

Rana warszewitschii is one of the least aquatic species among Costa Rican *Rana*. Adults are usually found on the floor of dense rainforests, but normally do not venture too far from the forest ponds or slow-moving streams in which they reproduce year-round. Their eggs, which are attached to the undersides of rocks, hatch into some of the largest tadpoles found in Costa Rica, sometimes reaching the impressive size of 115 mm (4½ inches). A long tail makes up the majority of the tadpole's body; this tail disappears when the tadpole becomes a frog. Initially black, tadpoles change color gradually; older tadpoles usually become gold-brown, with large black spots on the tail and fins.

These frogs, frequently encountered within their range, may be seen fleetingly as they jump and then dive into the leaf litter on the forest floor. When motionless, *Rana warszewitschii* blends in perfectly with its surroundings. It normally relies on its camouflage, but if an animal approaches too closely it escapes with a few long jumps. When the long legs are stretched during a jump, the red undersides and bright yellow spots flash in front of the viewers eyes, but those bright colors disappear when the legs are folded on landing. These so-called flash colors are an effective defensive strategy that serves to confuse potential predators.

Literature

Donnelly 1994; Hillis & de Sa 1988; Robinson 1983a; Savage & Villa 1986; Villa 1990; Zweifel 1964a.

Evolution of Amphibians and Reptiles

More than 350 million years ago, at some point during the Devonian Era, one of the most important steps in the evolution of vertebrates occurred when a fishlike ancestor of present-day amphibians—and also of reptiles, birds, mammals, and humans—crawled onto land. Before that time, all vertebrate life-forms were found strictly in water.

Amphibians are the most primitive group of terrestrial vertebrates and the first four-limbed land dwellers. They evolved from the lobe-finned fishes of the order Crossopterygii, whose sole survivor is the rare coelacanth (*Latimeria chalumnae*), a true living fossil found only in deep water off the east coast of Africa and near Indonesia. For over 100 million years, amphibians were the dominant land animals, reaching peak diversity in the Carboniferous Era (345 to 280 million years ago).

The earliest-known fossil amphibian is *Ichtyostega*, which is thought to have lived about 350 million years ago in what we now call Greenland. Unlike the fins of their fish ancestors, amphibians' limbs have joints and articulated digits and are connected to a well-developed shoulder and pelvic girdle. These limbs are used to support the body and for locomotion.

Early amphibians were large—some of the giants may have reached up to 4.6 m (15 ft) in length. Some species had bony armor plates covering exposed parts of the body. During the peak of amphibian diversity, at least eight orders of amphibians roamed the Earth; now only three remain. Compared to some of their prehistoric ancestors, these surviving orders of amphibians are small and secretive. Even so, the body form and structure of present-day salamanders, for example, still show many similarities to Paleozoic amphibians.

After the amphibians came the reptiles. The first reptiles, like the amphibians, lived partly in water and partly on land. Later species were fully terrestrial. The evolution from lobe-finned fish through amphibians to reptiles did not happen in a straight line, however; these groups lived side-by-side.

It is not known precisely when the evolution of reptiles began, but the oldest-known reptilian fossils are about 340 million years old. When the first reptiles left the shallow coastal waters for land, the many plants and insects already present formed a copious food supply for these colonists. The evolution of the shelled egg was the key for reptile survival on dry land; although the jellylike coating of amphibian eggs protects the egg to a certain degree, it offers little protection against small predators; and the egg would immediately dry out if taken out of the water. The shelled egg thus allowed reptile species to inhabit a greater diversity of habitats than their amphibian ancestors.

Reptiles ruled the land, air, and sea during the entire Mesozoic Era (225 to 65 million years ago). This period, now called the age of the dinosaurs, is the era in which reptilian diversity was greatest. The first dinosaurs arose about 200 million years ago. Originally they were small, some the size of a chicken, and walked on their hind limbs; but soon dinosaur diversity—in shape, size, and habit—increased tremendously. Famous reptiles such as *Brontosaurus*, *Tyrannosaurus*, *Ichtyosaurus*, and *Plesiosaurus* were among the largest and most powerful creatures Earth has ever seen. The largest species must have weighed up to 45 metric tons. Today no true flying reptiles exist, but some species of dinosaur could fly then. In the extinct pterosaurs, one of the fingers on each hand was greatly extended to support a membranelike, featherless wing that allowed them to fly and glide. Some of these flying reptiles reached very large sizes, the absolute winner being *Pteranodon*, with a wingspan of up to 6 m (20 ft).

During the Cretaceous Era (135 to 65 million years ago) the Earth cooled down considerably. Many primitive plant groups disappeared and were replaced by flowering plants. During this period, a shift occurred within the dinosaurs, from mostly carnivorous species to greater numbers of herbivorous species.

The group of reptiles known as dinosaurs died out, perhaps due to climatic changes brought about by the impact of a meteorite 65 million years ago; but four orders of reptiles survive today, turtles, crocodilians, lizards and snakes, and the Rhynchocephalia. Crocodiles and turtles have been around for over 230 million years, having hardly changed since they first evolved. The sole members of the order Rhynchocephalia are two species of tuatara, *Sphenodon guntheri* and *Sphenodon punctatus*; these, like the coelacanth, are true living fossils; they are the only survivors of an otherwise extinct order. These lizardlike reptiles only live on a few small islands off the coast of New Zealand. Because they have a low rate of metabolism, they grow very slowly and may reach a very old age. Some individuals are thought to be almost 120 years old.

REPTILES

Table 3: Taxonomy of Costa Rican Reptiles

Order	*Suborder*	*Family*	*Number of Species*
Crocodylia		Alligatoridae	1
		Crocodylidae	1
Testudines (Turtles)		Cheloniidae	4
		Dermochelyidae	1
		Emydidae	4
		Kinosternidae	3
		Chelydridae	1
Squamata	Lacertilia	Eublepharidae	1
	(Lizards)	Gekkonidae	11
		Corytophanidae	4
		Iguanidae	3
		Polychrotidae	27
		Phrynosomatidae	3
		Scincidae	3
		Gymnophthalmidae	6
		Teiidae	6
		Xantusidae	2
		Anguidae	7
Squamata	Serpentes	Anomalepididae	3
	(Snakes)	Leptotyphlopidae	1
		Typhlopidae	1
		Loxocemidae	1
		Boidae	5
		Colubridae	103
		Elapidae	5
		Viperidae	14

Introduction to Reptiles

More than 6,000 species of reptiles inhabit the earth, and many more extinct species are known from fossilized remains. To date, 221 species of reptiles have been recorded in Costa Rica (see table 3).

The first reptiles, which appeared about 350 million years ago, are thought to have evolved from amphibian ancestors. The oldest still-surviving group of reptiles is the order Testudines, the turtles; they have lived for at least 230 million years, long before the first dinosaur walked the planet. The remaining three orders of reptiles recognized today—Squamata, Crocodylia, and Rhynchocephalia—probably emerged around the same time as did the dinosaurs.

The vast majority of contemporary reptiles, more than 5,700 species, are in the order Squamata, which comprises all lizards, snakes, and amphisbaenians (a group of limbless, lizardlike reptiles not found in Costa Rica). Worldwide, there are over 250 species of turtles in the order Testudines, and 23 crocodilians in the order Crocodylia. In the order Rhynchocephalia, two species of tuatara (*Sphenodon guntheri* and *Sphenodon punctatus*) are the only surviving members of an otherwise extinct group and can be considered true living fossils. These lizardlike reptiles are found only on a few small islands off the coast of New Zealand.

All reptiles have scaly skin, as seen in this **black spiny-tailed iguana** (*Ctenosaura similis*).

An important difference between reptiles and amphibians is that reptiles are substantially less dependent on water for their survival than are amphibians. Reptiles have impermeable, scaly skin, which allows them to retain water within their body more efficiently, even under very dry conditions. In addition, the shelled eggs reptiles lay provide most of the water necessary for the development of the embryo. Instead of laying their eggs in water, reptiles provide their offspring with a "private pool" within an egg. This egg can be deposited virtually anyplace it is safe from predators, and which has the environmental conditions beneficial to the developing embryo.

Reptile eggs do require specific moisture and temperature levels to develop and hatch successfully, so they still remain somewhat dependent on water. Some highly evolved reptiles (several species of lizards and snakes) have become what is called ovoviviparous. This means that they produce eggs without a shell, but with a well-developed membranous covering instead. These eggs are retained inside the female's body during development of the embryo and usually hatch just before they are laid. The visible result is that living young emerge from the mother's body. Although these animals are not truly live-bearing (viviparous), this form of reproduction provides further independence from environmental factors, such as the availability of water. The female's body offers a regulated, humid environment for the eggs; and, as the mother actively regulates her own body temperature by basking in the sun or moving into the shade, she also regulates the incubation temperature of her eggs.

All crocodilians, turtles, lizards, and snakes fertilize internally: males transfer sperm to females through a penislike structure. Interestingly, male lizards and snakes have two copulatory organs, the hemipenes; during mating, however, only one of the two organs is used. The reproductive organs of male lizards and snakes are located at the base of the tail, and the swollen appearance of this part of the body indicates that an individual is male. The sex of snakes is especially hard to distinguish. Apart from the length of the tail (longer in males than in females) and the shape of the tail base (swollen in males, tapering in females) there are no externally visible differences.

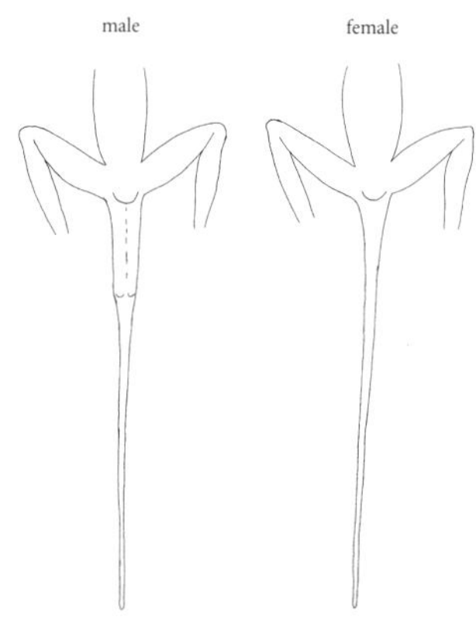

Sexual dimorphism in lizards. The swollen tail base of male lizards indicates the location of the hemipenes.

Like amphibians, all reptiles are ectothermous, which means their body temperature depends on external sources of heat. This is the main reason why herpetofauna is more diverse in warm climates than in cold. Animals that are warm-blooded, such as mammals, need to eat a lot in order to generate enough energy to maintain a stable body temperature. Since reptiles do not have to do this, they can survive with relatively small amounts of food. Some snakes are able to survive for many months without eating. In general, a snake can sustain itself by eating from 55% to 300% of its own body weight in prey in a year. Most reptiles are carnivorous, although there are several species of turtles and lizards that survive solely on a vegetarian diet.

Since reptilian teeth are not suited for cutting, they mainly serve to grab and hold on to animal prey. Therefore, reptiles usually swallow their prey whole. The size of the gape of a particular snake or lizard greatly determines the maximum prey size for that animal. Turtles lack teeth; instead they have a hard sheath with a cutting edge that covers the upper and lower jaws. These sharp jaw sheaths are capable of cutting manageable pieces out of their (often vegetable) food.

Members of several families of snakes and one family of lizards have teeth specially adapted for administering toxins that incapacitate and sometimes kill large, and potentially dangerous, animals. These toxins help break down body tissues and thus also help the animal to digest bulky prey. The only two existing venomous lizards, the beaded lizard (*Heloderma horridum*) and the Gila monster (*Heloderma suspectum*), are found in the southwestern United States, Mexico, and Guatemala. Two families of snakes, the Elapidae (cobras, kraits, mambas, coral snakes, sea snakes, etc.) and the Viperidae (vipers and pit vipers), are considered dangerously venomous. Elapid snakes, represented in Costa Rica by one species of sea snake and four species of coral snakes, have a pair of short, nonmoveable fangs at the front of the mouth fixed to the upper jaw. Each of these fangs is connected to a venom gland that produces a powerful nerve toxin. All viperid snakes, including the Costa Rican pit vipers, have long, moveable fangs on the front of the upper jaw that can be folded against the roof of the mouth when not in use. The venom glands of vipers usually contain large quantities of a cocktail of chemicals that can damage the nervous system, the circulatory system, and body tissues. For more detailed information on snake venoms and venomous snakes, see page 257.

Nonvenomous snakes that are constrictors kill their prey by suffocating it before eating. Those nonvenomous snakes which are not constrictors simply swallow their prey alive.

Lizards and crocodilians grab their prey with a quick lunge and crush small prey to death between powerful jaws. Often, they shake their head from side to side to incapacitate larger animals at the same time that they move their jaws, trying to manipulate the prey to the back of their mouth.

A feature commonly associated with reptiles is the forked tongue. In fact, the forked tongue is only found in snakes and several species of lizard; in all other reptiles, the tip of the tongue is not divided. Reptiles use their tongue—forked or not—to sample scent particles from their environment. Such particles are taken into the mouth when the tongue retracts and smeared against a very sensitive chemical receptor in the roof of the mouth called Jacobson's organ. Using the tongue and Jacobson's organ, reptiles can examine their surroundings for the presence of potential prey, or possibly of mates.

Those reptiles that have a forked tongue enjoy a special advantage. The sensory organ in the roof of the mouth is so sensitive that it can detect differences in concentrations of scent particles between each tip of the tongue. Because of this, a snake or lizard can detect whether it is moving away from a scent trail left by another animal (when there is a big difference between the two tips), or whether it is still right on track (no difference between the two tips). This use of the tongue seems to be confirmed when the different groups of reptiles are considered: the best "trackers," such as snakes and monitor lizards, all have a deeply forked tongue; anoles, which hunt visually, and plant-eating iguanas do not.

Vision is well-developed in most reptiles, and at least some reptiles are capable of distinguishing colors. Anoles, for example, use brightly colored body markings and an extendable throat fan (dewlap) to distinguish gender and for communication.

Although some lizards, turtles, and crocodilians produce sounds, with the exception of some geckos, functional calls are mainly the domain of amphibians. Although vocalization is not a general capacity in reptiles, most do have good hearing abilities. Lizards perceive airborne sounds through an eardrum that, in most species, is located on the surface of the head—in some species, the eardrum is in a shallow depression. The eardrum, whether on the surface of the head or in a shallow depression, is clearly visible behind the eye. Snakes have no external ears, but they can "hear" some low-frequency sounds through vibrations in the ground that are transferred to the bones in their skull. In some parts of the world, snake charmers appear to hypnotize cobras with the tones of a flute or other instrument. In fact, the snake is not responding to the music; rather, it is reared up in defense, keeping an eye on the threatening motion of the charmer's flute, whose owner wisely stays out of striking range of the snake.

The most impressive of the unusual reptilian senses is probably the infrared perception found in pit vipers and some boas. These snakes possess special pits, located either in the lip shields or on each side of the head, between the eye and the nostril, that allow the animal to perceive objects or animals with a temperature that differs from the ambient temperature. The sensitivity of these heat-sensitive organs is sufficient to detect temperature differences of only a few hundredths of a degree. Recent studies indicate that the information these pits gather is merged with visual information, presenting the snake with a visual and thermal image of its surroundings. Pit vipers that hunt at night or in other dark places, such as rodent burrows, rely on the radiation of warm-bodied prey to direct their strike.

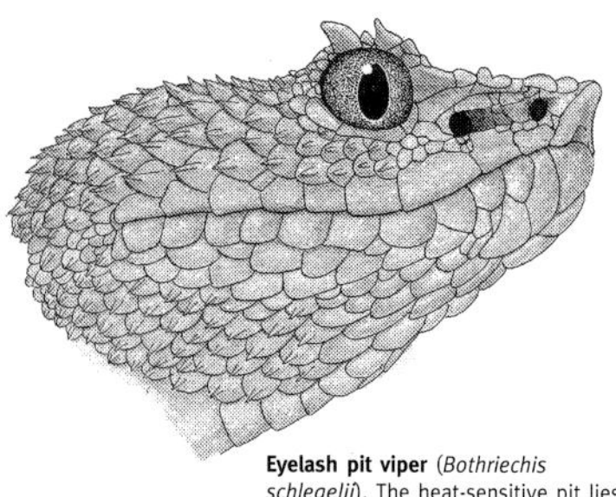

Eyelash pit viper (*Bothriechis schlegelii*). The heat-sensitive pit lies between the eye and the nostril.

Reptiles are preyed upon by a variety of animals, from spiders and katydids to birds, mammals, and even other reptiles. Most species are very well camouflaged and remain still when approached, making detection difficult.

A lizard's tail has fracture points in the vertebrae that allow the tail to break off easily without causing the animal too much discomfort. Many species have the option of breaking off the tail volitionally; in other species, the tail breaks off only when grasped. The severed piece of the tail usually wriggles for a few minutes, keeping a potential predator busy while the lizard escapes. The damaged tail regenerates within a few months, but it looks slightly different than the original. The regenerated part does not contain vertebrae, and thus cannot break again. A few Costa Rican snakes have evolved to using this antipredator strategy; when restrained by the tail, they are able to break off a part. The amputated portion of the tail does not grow back, however.

Many lizards, and all snakes, possess scent glands near the cloaca that are emptied when the animal is under attack. Certain snake species produce some of the most foul-smelling excretions known to man, and it may require several days and many bouts of hand washing to get rid of the smell. Different forms of warnings or threat displays are seen in reptiles, including hissing, vibrating or rattling the tail, flattening the head and/or body—or inflating the neck region—to appear bigger, sham attacks, death-feigning, and mimicking venomous species. What is likely the most effective form of defense is seen in turtles. The hard shell, and the ability to withdraw most vulnerable body parts inside this protective cover, probably explain how these animals have survived for so long.

Like amphibians, many reptiles are now endangered by human kind. Most crocodilians and sea turtles are on the brink of extinction. Habitat destruction, pollution, and the pet trade affect almost every other reptile species on the planet. Costa Rica is no exception to this rule, and several species of its diverse herpetofauna are critically endangered.

In the following chapters, the three reptilian orders found in Costa Rica are presented in more detail, and all extant families and a number of representative species are described.

SUMMARY

How to identify the different Costa Rican reptilian orders and suborders:

- Order Testudines (turtles): reptiles that have no teeth and whose body is encased in a shell.
- Order Crocodilia (crocodilians): large to very large reptiles with four limbs and a markedly compressed tail.
- Order Squamata, suborder Lacertilia (lizards): small to large reptiles with four limbs and a tail that is not compressed.
- Order Squamata, suborder Serpentes (snakes): small to very large limbless reptiles.

Literature

Ernst 1992; Savage & Villa 1986; Schwenk 1994; Zug 1993.

ORDER: **Crocodylia** (Crocodilians)
CLASS: Reptiles

Worldwide there are 23 species of crocodilians, divided among three families: crocodiles, alligators and caimans, and the unique gharial, which is the sole member of its family and which inhabits the Ganges River in India. During the Mesozoic Era, lasting from 225 to 65 million years ago, the diversity of a large number of animal groups arising from the so-called archosaurs increased tremendously. Most of these groups, including the dinosaurs and pterosaurs, disappeared during a mass extinction —probably caused by the impact of a meteorite and the subsequent global climate changes—at the end of the Cretaceous Period, 65 million years ago. Among the archosaur descendants present at that time, only the crocodilians, turtles, and birds have survived until today. Fossil evidence suggests that crocodilians arose around 160 million years ago, and that their general body shape has changed little over time, indicating a design that, from the start, ensured their success in the Darwinian struggle.

Even a nonspecialist can quickly identify an animal as being a member of the order Crocodylia, but several features are nevertheless worth describing. Crocodilians are the only reptiles with four toes on the hind limbs and five digits on the front limbs. The toes have extensive webbing, the front digits have no webbing. Typically, the vent in crocodilians is oriented on the axis that runs along the length of the body; in other reptiles, the vent runs across the base of the tail, *perpendicular* to the body-length axis.

Crocodilians have a muscular, laterally compressed tail that is used to produce the main thrust during swimming. A large, flattened head with elevated eyes and nostrils allows crocodilians to breathe and see even when the body is submerged. Both the ears and the nostrils are equipped with a moveable flap that closes off these body openings when the animal dives. Also, as long as they keep their nostrils above water, a special valve in the roof of the mouth enables crocodilians to breathe even when the mouth is open below the surface—a very useful feature when handling large prey in the water. Although highly adapted to life in water, most species are often surprisingly agile on land.

Crocodilians live in tropical regions throughout the world, although some species range into subtropical regions. With some notable exceptions, these aquatic carnivores are restricted to freshwater habitats, where they are at the top of the food chain and feed on a wide variety of animal prey. Small prey is swallowed whole, while large prey is sometimes held underwater until drowned, after which it is stored underwater for later consumption—when the cadaver starts to decompose, it is easier to dismember. Crocodilians have numerous sharp teeth, but because these teeth are all somewhat peglike, without a cutting edge, they are not useful for chewing or biting off pieces of flesh. Instead, crocodilians catch prey and hold it while they rotate their head fiercely around their body axis in order to tear off flesh. Since their heavy bodies are more agile when supported by water, crocodilians generally eat large prey in the water, although they are not usually submerged when eating. The diet of Costa Rican crocodilians mainly consists of small prey.

People all over the world fear crocodilians as ferocious man-eaters. Their thick, scaly body armor, their powerful jaws, and their vertically slit pupils do indeed present a threatening appearance. Only two species, however, the African Nile crocodile, *Crocodylus niloticus*, and the saltwater or Indo-Pacific crocodile, *Crocodylus porosus*, are known to include humans in their diet. Although casualties caused by other large species of crocodilians have been reported (including Costa Rican *Crocodylus acutus*), these are uncommon. Moreover, overexploitation of most crocodilians has reduced the average size of those species that, under ordinary conditions, would reach sizes capable of overpowering and devouring humans.

All crocodilians lay eggs, either in a moundlike nest they construct from vegetation and soil, or in a burrow they excavate, usually on the bank along a lake or river. Mating takes place shortly before egg-laying. During the mating season, some male crocodilians entice females to mate with them by raising their head out of the water, opening their mouth, and producing long, resounding roars that sound somewhat like the beating of a large drum. If a female enters the territory of a sexually active male, he performs an impressive courtship display in which he roars loudly and slaps the water surface with his head and tail. If the female is receptive to his advances, the pair swims away, and the male grabs hold of the female with his legs. Copulation invariably takes place in the water.

Juvenile **spectacled caiman** (*Caiman crocodilus*). *Photograph by Adrian Hepworth.*

During the development of the eggs, the female guards the nest and defends it persistently against intruders. When the young are ready to hatch, the female excavates the egg clutch to help the babies leave the nest. In some species, the young call from within the eggs to signal to their mother that the moment of hatching has arrived—hearing, and the sense of smell, are very well developed in crocodilians. Females of some species even participate in freeing their offspring from the egg, then pick up the baby crocodile with their mouth to carry it to the water.

Crocodilians are endangered worldwide. Massive habitat destruction and overexploitation, mainly to obtain hides and for the pet trade, have brought several species to the brink of extinction. The two Costa Rican crocodilians, *Caiman crocodilus* (in the alligator family) and *Crocodilus acutus* (in the crocodile family) have also been hunted relentlessly for their hides, and their numbers are seriously reduced.

How to identify Costa Rican crocodilians:

- Crocodilians are large, prehistoric-looking reptiles with four limbs; a long, muscular tail; and an elongate head with powerful jaws and many teeth. The teeth are visible even when the mouth is closed.
- Crocodilians are the only reptiles with only four toes on the hind limbs and five digits on the front limbs.

Literature

Behler & King 1979; Savage & Villa 1986; Zug 1993.

COLOR PLATES

Slender caecilian (*Dermophis parviceps*), p. 38.

Purple caecilian (*Gymnopis multiplicata*), p. 38.

Alvarado's salamander (*Bolitoglossa alvaradoi*), p. 45.

Ridge-headed salamander (*Bolitoglossa colonnea*), p. 45.

Bark-colored salamander (*Bolitoglossa lignicolor*), p. 45.
photograph by Willem Ferwerda

Ring-tailed salamander (*Bolitoglossa robusta*), p. 46.

Striated salamander (*Bolitoglossa striatula*), p. 46.

Mountain salamander (*Bolitoglossa subpalmata*), p. 46.
photograph by René Koller

Common worm salamander (*Oedipina uniformis*). This is one of the most commonly observed worm salamanders in Costa Rica, although it is difficult to distinguish from other members of its genus. See page 47 for a description of the genus *Oedipina*. *Photograph by René Krekels.*

Mexican burrowing toad (*Rhinophrynus dorsalis*), p. 54.
photograph by William Lamar

Chiriquí harlequin frog (*Atelopus chiriquiensis*), p. 58.
photograph by Peter Mudde

Variable harlequin frog (*Atelopus varius*), p. 58.
photograph by Peter Mudde

Dry forest toad (*Bufo coccifer*), p. 60.
photograph by René Koller

Green climbing toad (*Bufo coniferus*), p. 60. Young adult and pair in amplexus (photo insert).
main photograph by Tonnie Woeltjes

Smooth-skinned toad (*Bufo haematiticus*), p. 61.
photograph by Willem Ferwerda

Giant toad (*Bufo marinus*), p. 62.

Golden toad (*Bufo periglenes*), p. 63.
photograph by M. & P. Fogden courtesy of AUDIOVISE

Gulf Coast toad (*Bufo valliceps*), p. 64.

Ghost glass frog (*Centrolenella ilex*), p. 67.

Emerald glass frog (*Centrolenella prosoblepon*), p. 68. This is the only Costa Rican frog with a pointed spur on the upper arm.

Fleischmann's glass frog (*Hyalinobatrachium fleischmanni*), p. 68. Note transparent belly.

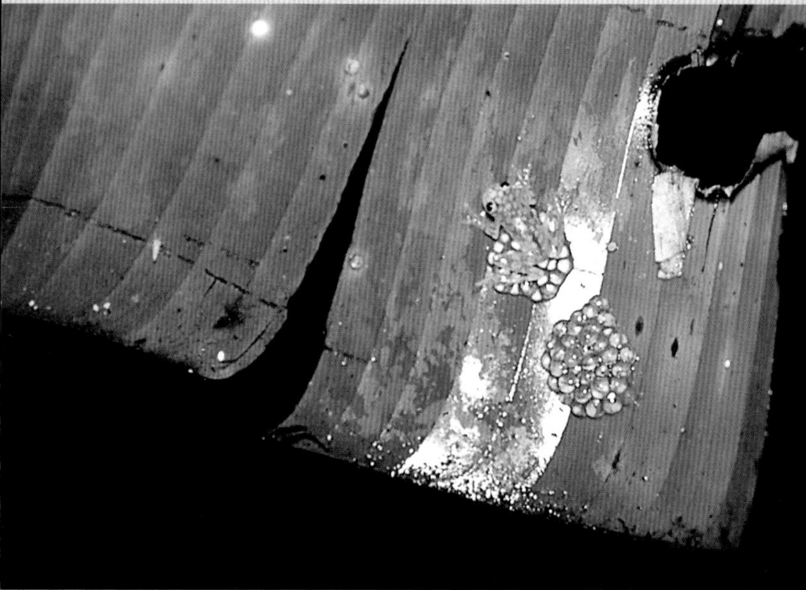

Reticulated glass frog (*Hyalinobatrachium valerioi*), p. 69. A male guarding two clutches of eggs located on the underside of a large banana leaf. The color pattern on his back closely resembles the eggs.
photograph by Peter Mudde

On left, **Talamanca rocket frog** (*Colostethus talamancae*), p. 72. Note similar appearance of related **striped rocket frog** (*Colostethus nubicola*), on right.
photograph on left by Tonnie Woeltjes; photograph on right by René Koller

Green and black poison-dart frog (*Dendrobates auratus*), p. 73.
photograph by Adrian Hepworth

Granular poison-dart frog (*Dendrobates granuliferus*), p. 74.
photograph by Tonnie Woeltjes

Strawberry poison-dart frog (*Dendrobates pumilio*), p. 75. Calling male.
photograph by Adrian Hepworth

Striped poison-dart frog (*Phyllobates lugubris*), p. 77.
photograph by Peter Mudde

Golfo Dulce poison-dart frog (*Phyllobates vittatus*), p. 77.
photograph by Tonnie Woeltjes

Red-eyed leaf frog (*Agalychnis callidryas*), p. 80.
photograph by Adrian Hepworth

Parachuting red-eyed leaf frog (*Agalychnis saltator*), p. 82.

Crowned tree frog (*Anotheca spinosa*), p. 83.
photograph by M. & P. Fogden

Red-eyed stream frog (*Duellmanohyla uranochroa*), p. 83.

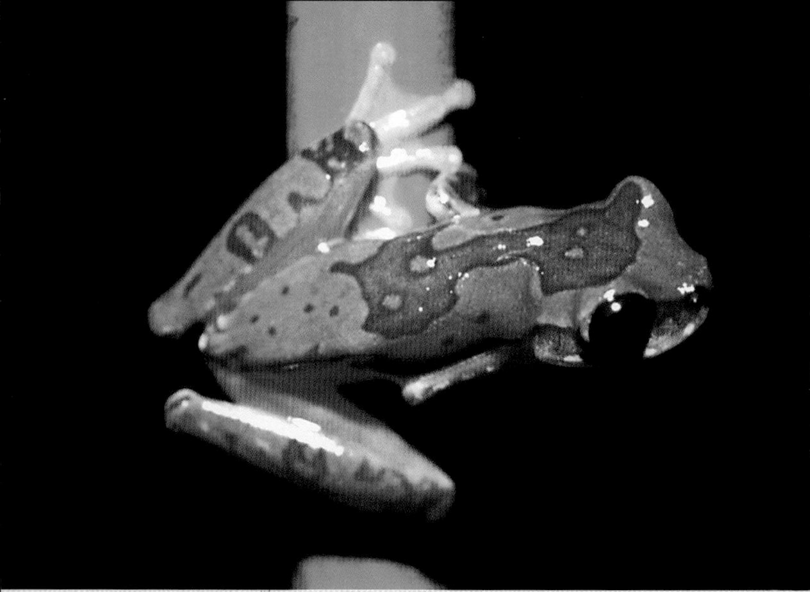

Hourglass tree frog (*Hyla ebraccata*), p. 84.

Loquacious tree frog (*Hyla loquax*), p. 86.

Small-headed tree frog (*Hyla microcephala*), p. 86.

Lowland fringe-limbed tree frog (*Hyla miliaria*), p. 86.
photograph by M. & P. Fogden

Veined tree frog (*Hyla phlebodes*), p. 87.

Gladiator tree frog (*Hyla rosenbergi*), p. 87.
photograph by René Krekels

Milk frog (*Phrynohyas venulosa*), p. 89.

Olive tree frog (*Scinax elaeochroa*), p. 90.

Stauffer's tree frog (*Scinax staufferi*), p. 91.
photograph by René Koller

Mexican tree frog (*Smilisca baudinii*), p. 91.

Masked tree frog (*Smilisca phaeota*), p. 92.

Drab tree frog (*Smilisca sordida*), p. 93.

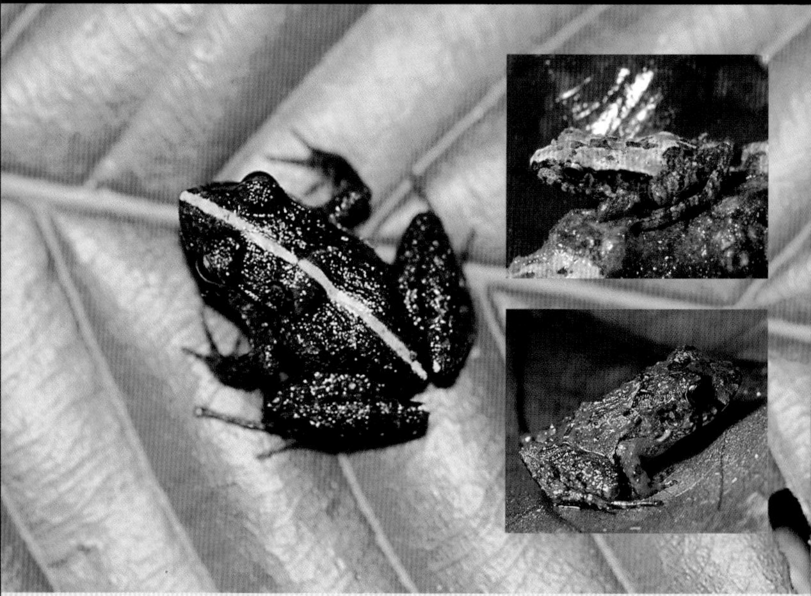

Bransford's litter frog (*Eleutherodactylus bransfordii*), p. 99. Note extreme variation within the species.

Clay-colored rain frog (*Eleutherodactylus cerasinus*), p. 101.

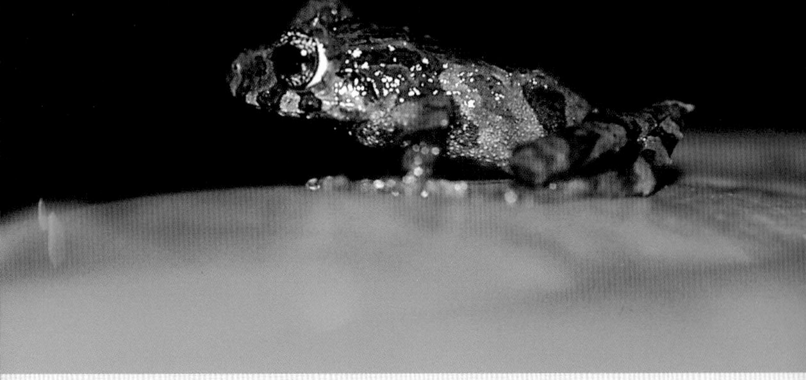

Golden-groined rain frog (*Eleutherodactylus cruentus*), p. 101.

Common tink frog (*Eleutherodactylus diastema*), p. 102.

Common rain frog (*Eleutherodactylus fitzingeri*), p. 103.

Broad-headed rain frog (*Eleutherodactylus megacephalus*), p. 104. Note ridges on head and back.

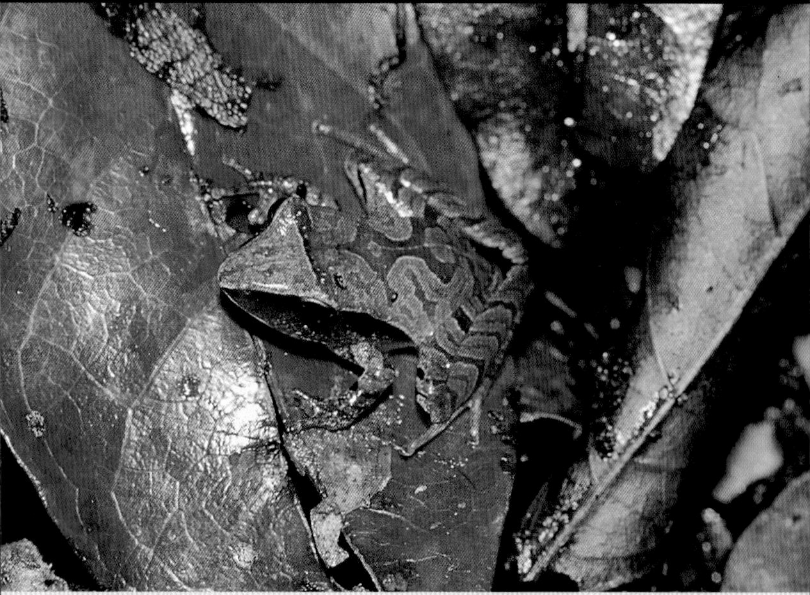

Mimicking rain frog (*Eleutherodactylus mimus*), p. 105.

Noble's rain frog (*Eleutherodacylus noblei*), p. 105.

Pygmy rain frog (*Eleutherodactylus ridens*), p. 106.

Black-backed frog (*Leptodactylus melanonotus*), p. 106.

Central American bullfrog (*Leptodactylus pentadactylus*), p. 107.

Tungara frog (*Physalaemus pustulosus*), p. 109.
photograph by René Koller

Sheep frog (*Hypopachus variolosus*), p. 111. This species uses spadelike tubercles on the hind feet to burrow into soil with surprising speed.

Black narrow-mouthed frog (*Nelsonophryne aterrima*), p. 112.

Vaillant's frog (*Rana vaillanti*), p. 114.
photograph by Paul Siffert

Green-eyed frog (*Rana vibicaria*), p. 115.
photograph by M. & P. Fogden

Brilliant forest frog (*Rana warszewitschii*), p. 115.

Spectacled caiman (*Caiman crocodilus*), p. 129.

American crocodile (*Crocodylus acutus*), p. 132.

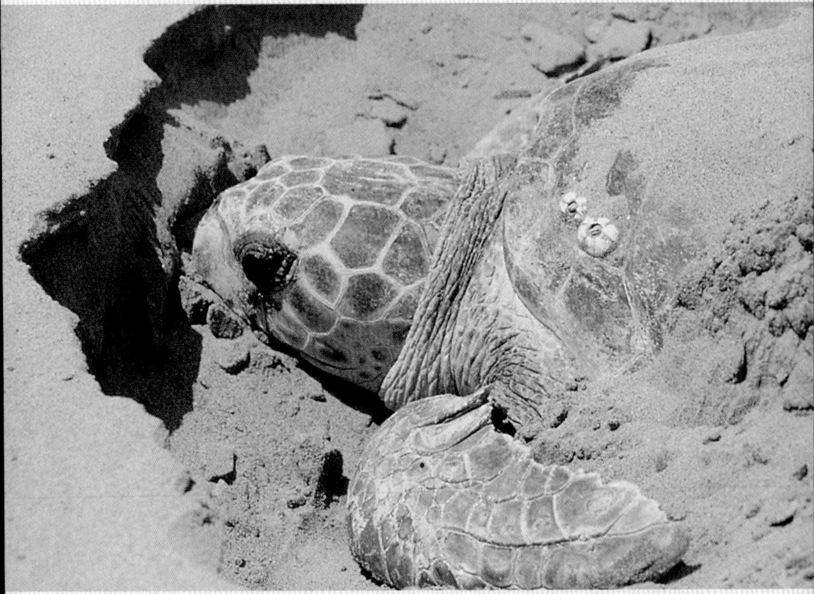

Loggerhead sea turtle (*Caretta caretta*), p. 139.
photograph by Koen Verhoeven

Green turtle (*Chelonia mydas*), p. 140.
photograph courtesy of CCC

Hawksbill sea turtle (*Eretmochelys imbricata*), p. 142.
photograph by Bob Thompson

Olive ridley (*Lepidochelys olivacea*), p. 144.
photograph by Adrian Hepworth

Leatherback turtle (*Dermochelys coriacea*), p. 146.
photograph by Tonnie Woeltjes

Brown wood turtle (*Rhinoclemmys annulata*), p. 148.

Black wood turtle (*Rhinoclemmys funerea*), p. 149.

Common slider (*Trachemys scripta*), p. 150.

White-lipped mud turtle (*Kinosternon leucostomum*), p. 153.
photograph by Willem Ferwerda

Red-cheeked mud turtle (*Kinosternon scorpioides*), p. 153.

Common snapping turtle (*Chelydra serpentina*), p. 155.

Central American banded gecko (*Coleonyx mitratus*), p. 160.
photograph by William Lamar

Yellow-headed gecko (*Gonatodes albigularis*), p. 163.
photograph by Willem Ferwerda

House gecko (*Hemidactylus frenatus*), p. 164. Geckos can adhere to almost any surface.
main photograph by René Koller

Litter gecko (*Lepidoblepharis xanthostigma*), p. 165. Note the difference in coloration between the adult (main photograph) and the juvenile (insert).

Spotted dwarf gecko (*Sphaerodactylus millepunctatus*), p. 165.

Turnip-tail gecko (*Thecadactylus rapicauda*), p. 166.
photograph by Paul Siffert

Common basilisk (*Basiliscus basiliscus*), p. 168.

Green basilisk (*Basiliscus plumifrons*), p. 169. Juveniles do not have prominent crests (insert photograph). Adult males (main photograph) have large crests; females have much smaller crests.
main photograph by Willem Ferwerda

Striped basilisk (*Basiliscus vittatus*), p. 170.

Helmeted iguana (*Corytophanes cristatus*), p. 171. This individual displays the typical defensive posture: the throat and neck fan are extended and the body is raised off the ground.
photograph by Adrian Hepworth

Five-keeled spiny-tailed iguana (*Ctenosaura quinquecarinata*), p. 173.

Black spiny-tailed iguana (*Ctenosaura similis*), p. 174. These prehistoric-looking giants are more carnivorous than their larger cousins, the green iguanas (*Iguana iguana*), as this crab-eating individual clearly shows.
photograph by Adrian Hepworth

Green iguana (*Iguana iguana*), p. 176.
photograph by Adrian Hepworth

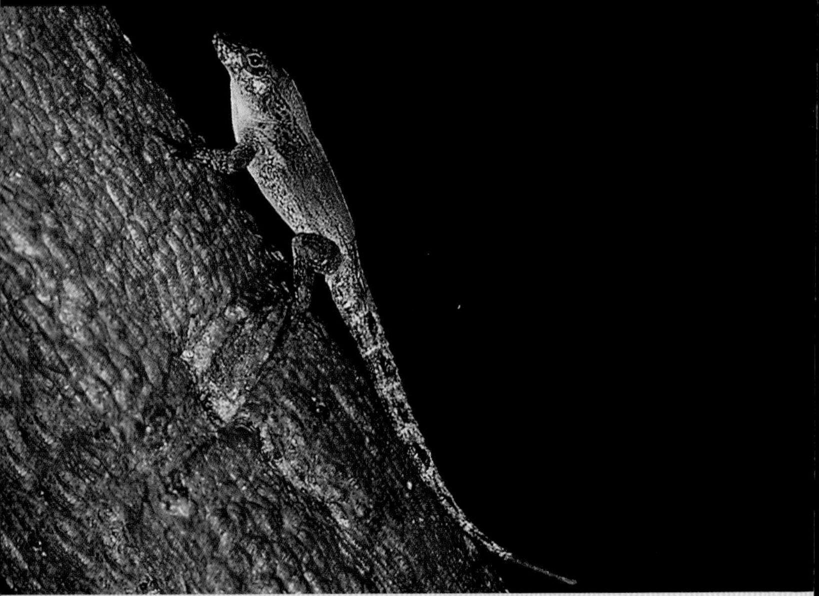

Puerto Rican crested anole (*Ctenonotus cristatellus*), p. 181.
photograph by Tonnie Woeltjes

Giant green anole (*Dactyloa frenata*), p. 181.
photograph by Leo Wijffels

Water anole (*Norops aquaticus*), p. 182.
photograph by Peter Mudde

Green tree anole (*Norops biporcatus*), p. 183.

Pug-nosed anole (*Norops capito*), p. 183.

Ground anole (*Norops humilis*), p. 184.

Canopy anole (*Norops lemurinus*), p. 185.

Slender anole (*Norops limifrons*), p. 185. Most anoles, like this individual, sleep exposed on leaves or on the tips of thin branches.

Stream anole (*Norops oxylophus*), p. 186. The color of the throat fan of male anoles often contrasts with the body.

Golfo Dulce anole (*Norops polylepis*), p. 187.
photograph by Chadwick Day

Indigo-throated anole (*Norops sericeus*), p. 188.

Canopy lizard (*Polychrus gutturosus*), p. 188.

Green spiny lizard (*Sceloporus malachiticus*), p. 190.

Rose-bellied spiny lizard (*Sceloporus variabilis*), p. 191.

Bronze-backed climbing skink (*Mabuya unimarginata*), p. 193.

Litter skink (*Sphenomorphus cherriei*), p. 194.

Bromeliad lizard (*Anadia ocellata*), p. 198.

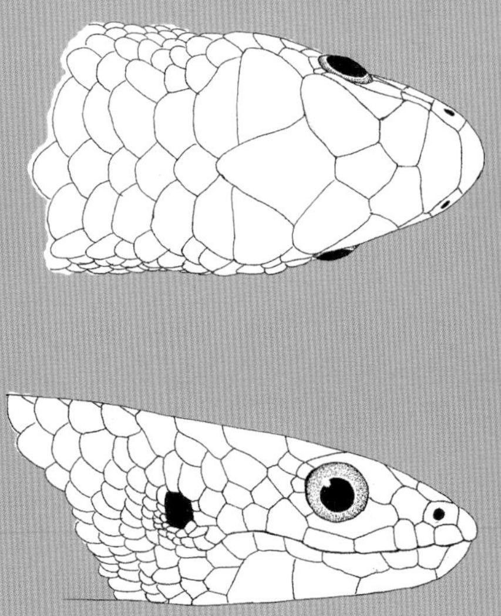

Golden spectacled lizard (*Gymnophthalmus speciosus*), p. 199. The head of this lizard is very snakelike in appearance. Each eye is covered with a transparent spectacle and lacks eyelids.

Water tegu (*Neusticurus apodemus*), p. 199.
photograph by Peter Mudde

Keeled leaf litter lizard (*Ptychoglossus plicatus*), p. 200.
photograph by Peter Mudde

Central American whip-tailed lizard (*Ameiva festiva*), p. 202.

Four-lined whip-tailed lizard (*Ameiva quadrilineata*), p. 203. Females (top photograph) are less colorful than males (bottom photograph). The head and throat of the male are blue, particulary so in the mating season.
both photographs by Tonnie Woeltjes

Deppe's whip-tailed lizard (*Cnemidophorus deppii*), p. 203.

Yellow-spotted night lizard (*Lepidophyma flavimaculatum*), p. 205.
photograph by Sandy Wiseman

Rainforest celestus (*Celestus hylaius*), p. 208.

Talamanca galliwasp (*Diploglossus bilobatus*), p. 208.
photograph by Peter Mudde

Galliwasp (*Diploglossus monotropis*), p. 208.

Highland alligator lizard (*Mesaspis monticola*), p. 209.

Neotropical slender blindsnake (*Leptotyphlops goudotii*), p. 216.
photograph by Wim van den Heuvel

Costa Rican blindsnake (*Typhlops costaricensis*), p. 218.
photograph by M. & P. Fogden

Neotropical sunbeam snake (*Loxocemus bicolor*), p. 219.
photograph by Willem Ferwerda

Boa constrictor (*Boa constrictor*), p. 222.

Annulated tree boa (*Corallus annulatus*) p. 224.

Common tree boa (*Corallus ruschenbergerii*), p. 224.
photograph by Willem Ferwerda

Ridge-nosed snake (*Amastridium veliferum*), p. 226.

Mussurana (*Clelia clelia*), p. 226. Juvenile *Clelia clelia* are red, adults are black.
main photograph by Koen Verhoeven

Roadguarder (*Conophis lineatus*), p. 227.

Barred forest racer (*Dendrophidion vinitor*), p. 228.

Speckled racer (*Drymobius margaritiferus*), p. 228.

Green frog-eater (*Drymobius melanotropis*), p. 229.

False coral snake (*Erythrolamprus mimus*), p. 229.

Juvenile **gray earth snake** (*Geophis brachycephalus*), p. 230. Juveniles are characterized by a white neck band.
photograph by Chadwick Day

Brown blunt-headed vine snake (*Imantodes cenchoa*), p. 231.

Yellow blunt-headed vine snake (*Imantodes inornatus*), p. 233.

Tropical king snake (*Lampropeltis triangulum*), p. 233.

Black and white cat-eyed snake (*Leptodeira nigrofasciata*), p. 233.

Black and red cat-eyed snake (*Leptodeira rubricata*), p. 233.
photograph by René Koller

Northern cat-eyed snake (*Leptodeira septentrionalis*), p. 234.

Satiny parrot snake (*Leptophis depressirostris*), p. 234.

Mexican parrot snake (*Leptophis mexicanus*), p. 235.

Fire-bellied snake (*Liophis epinephelus*), p. 236.

Spotted wood snake (*Ninia maculata*), p. 237.

Brown vine snake (*Oxybelis aeneus*), p. 237. Note the black interior of the snake's mouth (photo insert), revealed during this defensive display.

Short-nosed vine snake (*Oxybelis brevirostris*), p. 238.
photograph by Adrian Hepworth

Green vine snake (*Oxybelis fulgidus*), p. 239.
photograph by Wim van den Heuvel

Bird-eating snake (*Pseustes poecilonotus*), p. 240.

Green litter snake (*Rhadinaea calligaster*), p. 240.
photograph by M. & P. Fogden

Red-bellied litter snake (*Rhadinaea decorata*), p. 240.

Shovel-toothed snake (*Scaphiodontophis annulatus*), p. 241.

Neotropical rat snake (*Senticolis triaspis*), p. 242. True to form, this individual is eating a rat.
photograph by René Krekels

Lichen-colored snail-eater (*Sibon longifrenis*), p. 243.

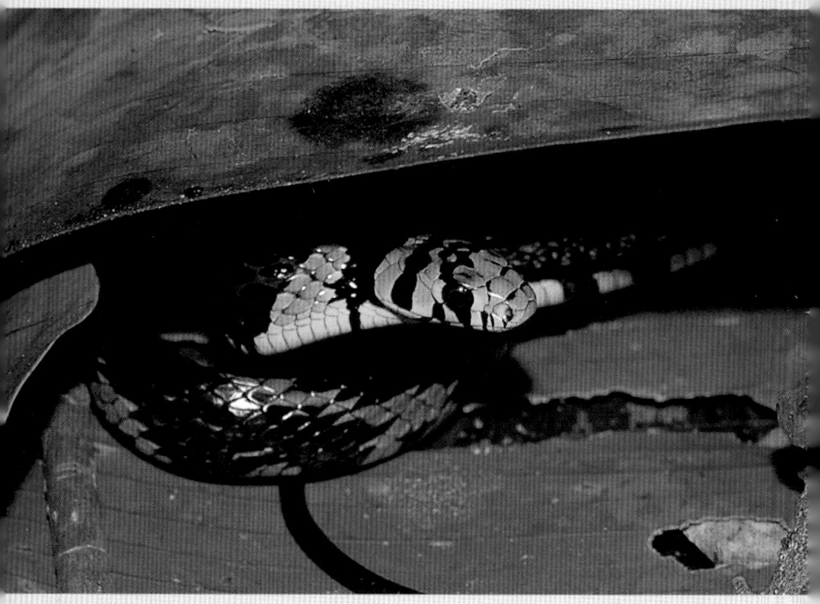

Tiger rat snake (*Spilotes pullatus*), p. 243.

Degenhardt's scorpion eater (*Stenorrhina degenhardtii*), p. 244.

Reticulated centipede snake (*Tantilla reticulata*), p. 244.

False fer-de-lance (*Xenodon rabdocephalus*), p. 245.

Allen's coral snake (*Micrurus alleni*), p. 248.
photograph by M. & P. Fogden

Bicolored coral snake (*Micrurus multifasciatus*), p. 249. This species normally has a pattern of orange or reddish body rings that alternate with black rings. The photo insert shows a variety with an extremely rare color pattern.

Central American coral snake (*Micrurus nigrocinctus*), p. 250.
photograph by Chadwick Day

Yellow-bellied sea snake (*Pelamis platurus*), p. 254. Individuals are occasionally found washed ashore on the Pacific coast, unable to crawl back into the water.
photograph by Adrian Hepworth

Cantil (*Agkistrodon bilineatus*), p. 263.

Jumping pit viper (*Atropoides nummifer*), p. 263.

Striped palm pit viper (*Bothriechis lateralis*), p. 264.

Eyelash pit viper (*Bothriechis schlegelii*), p. 265. The yellow variety (left photograph) is often referred to as *oropel*.

Fer-de-lance (*Bothrops asper*), p. 266.

Godman's montane pit viper (*Cerrophidion godmani*), p. 267.

Tropical rattlesnake (*Crotalus durissus*), p. 268.

Central American bushmaster (*Lachesis stenophrys*), p. 269.
photograph from Nature's Images

Hog-nosed pit viper (*Porthidium nasutum*), p. 270.
photograph by Chadwick Day

FAMILY: **Alligatoridae** (Alligator Family)
ORDER: Crocodylia (Crocodilians)

Alligatoridae is a small family within the order Crocodylia that includes the alligators and caimans; it is almost completely restricted to Central and South America.

All members of the alligator family live exclusively in freshwater habitats. They also lack a lingual salt gland, a feature present in all "true" crocodiles. This gland, located near the tongue, is necessary for regulating the animal's internal salt balance and facilitates life in saltwater. Alligators and caimans differ from all other crocodilians in that the two enlarged teeth on their lower jaw are not visible when the mouth is closed, since these teeth fit inside pockets in the upper jaw.

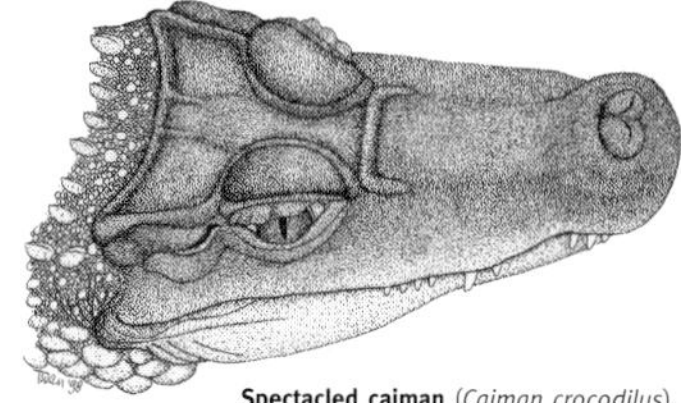
Spectacled caiman (*Caiman crocodilus*).

Only one representative of this family, the spectacled caiman (*Caiman crocodilus*), lives in Costa Rica.

SUMMARY

How to identify Costa Rican caimans:

- The alligator family only contains one Costa Rican species: the spectacled caiman, which typically has a curved, bony ridge in front of its eyes, much like the bridge on a pair of glasses.
- When the mouth is closed, no large fangs are exposed in the lower jaw.

SPECIES DESCRIPTION

Caiman crocodilus

Spectacled caiman (plate 31)

Caiman crocodilus is smaller than *Crocodylus acutus*, the American crocodile, which also occurs in Costa Rica. Most adult individuals have a total length of between 1.25 and 2.5 m (4 and 8 ft). They are unmistakably identified by the presence of a bony ridge in front of the eyes. This ridge resembles the bridge on a pair of glasses, thus the common name. The enlarged fourth tooth on each side of the lower jaw fits into a pocket in the upper jaw when the mouth is closed (in *Crocodylus acutus*, each fourth tooth on the lower jaw is visible even when the mouth is closed).

Caiman crocodilus generally has a light tan, yellowish, or brownish ground color, with obscure dark crossbands on the body and tail. The coloration of juveniles is much brighter; the crossband pattern, which is more distinct in young animals, fades with age.

Caiman crocodilus is a very widespread species, occurring from Mexico southward throughout Central America and ranging far into South America. It has also been introduced in southern Florida. This species is the most common crocodilian in Costa Rica. While it occurs in many marshes, rivers, canals, and lakes in both the Caribbean and the Pacific lowlands, it seems to prefer slow-moving rivers with a muddy bottom and soft sandbanks.

Although their numbers were drastically reduced in the last century, in Costa Rica these crocodilians are still common in some areas, such as the canals of Tortuguero, the Caño Negro Wildlife Refuge, or the Rio Frio area. They are more frequently observed during the dry season, when low water levels concentrate their numbers in the low reservoirs and receding rivers. During the day, *Caiman crocodilus* can be sighted basking on riverbanks, exposed logs, or sandbanks. At night, they are easily found by shining a powerful flashlight over the water surface; the reflection of light in their eyes can be seen from afar.

Because it is relatively small, *Caiman crocodilus* is not dangerous to humans. Its prey consists of all kinds of animals found in or near its watery habitat—adults eat fish, amphibians, and waterfowl; juveniles eat insects and snails. Other than humans, adult *Caiman crocodilus* have few predators. Baby caimans, on the other hand, fall prey to numerous animals. Their most common predators are birds of prey and large herons.

Costa Rican *Caiman crocodilus* reproduce in the rainy season, and mating seems to be initiated by the first heavy rains and the rising water level in its habitat. Like all other crocodilians, caimans are egg-layers. They invariably deposit their clutch of 15 to 40 elliptical, hard-shelled eggs in a mound-shaped nest. The nest is constructed on a high part of a riverbank, preferably in a forested environment but always within a few meters of the water. It is sometimes butted up against tree trunks or among vines. The nest consists of a low heap of vegetation and leaf litter, usually with a diameter of 1.5 m (5 ft). Parents clear several meters of vegetation from around the nest.

The main reason caimans choose to nest on top of high riverbanks is to minimize the risk from flooding, which would surely kill the embryos. In some populations of this species, the animals nest only after the water level has reached its peak; while in other populations, nesting occurs several weeks before this time. Even in the latter case, nests are constructed in high places.

The other main threat to caiman eggs is predation, and raccoons seem especially adept at locating and excavating nests. Frequently, one of the parents remains in the water near the nest site and attempts to deter trespassers that approach the nest by thrashing the water with its tail and head while growling or hissing.

Parental care in *Caiman crocodilus* is not restricted to guarding eggs. Once the young are ready to hatch, after an incubation period of 75 to 90 days, an adult opens up the nest by tunneling in, or sometimes even completely excavating the eggs. Hatching is possibly triggered by movement of the eggs, and the digging action of the parent may thus induce the babies to emerge. However, juvenile *Caiman crocodilus* are also known to vocalize from inside the egg to attract their mother and to prompt her to open the nest. On the rare occasion when there is no parent to help the hatchlings leave their nest, they tunnel out without assistance. Upon leaving the nest, hatchlings measure about 20 to 25 cm (8 to 10 inches) from the snout to the vent. The gender of the hatchling caimans is, as with many other crocodilians, determined by the incubation temperature of the eggs (see page 134 on temperature-dependent sex determination).

In one study, hatchlings were observed in a group in the immediate vicinity of the nest for about a week, during which time an adult caiman actively guarded them. Interestingly, both the adult and the group of juveniles disappeared, only to be seen again during the next dry season, about six months later. The juveniles still formed sibling groups, although several sibling groups were seen to join and form larger groups consisting of 20 to 60 individuals of different age classes. Adult caimans were still present attending their presumed offspring and defending the juveniles against potential predators. Whether the sibling groups spent the "missing" six months in hiding, or whether they temporarily left the immediate vicinity of the nest area is not known.

Until the early 1980s, the illegal trade in crocodile and caiman hides boomed, and thousands of caimans were killed for their skin. Additionally, large numbers of baby caimans were captured and sold for the pet trade or killed and mounted. At present, the hunting pressure on some populations of Costa Rican caimans has greatly decreased, and these animals can be quite abundant at some locations in the country.

Literature
Allsteadt 1994; Behler & King 1979; Lang & Andrews 1994; Mudde & van Dijk 1984a; Savage & Villa 1986; Zug 1993.

FAMILY: **Crocodylidae** (Crocodile Family)
ORDER: Crocodylia (Crocodilians)

True crocodiles of the family Crocodylidae occur in tropical and some subtropical regions around the globe. They are mostly freshwater species, but many species frequent coastal estuaries and swamps or live in the brackish tidal areas of rivers. Some crocodiles, such as the Indo-Pacific or saltwater crocodile (*Crocodylus porosus*), even occasionally venture into the ocean. All crocodiles possess special salt glands (lingual glands) that allow them to actively regulate their internal salt balance, making it possible for them to enter saltwater.

American crocodile (*Crocodylus acutus*).

The distinguishing feature of the crocodile family is the large, fourth tooth on each side of the lower jaw, which is clearly visible when the mouth is closed. Crocodiles are the most speciose family within the order Crocodilia, containing 14 species in three genera. A single species, the American crocodile (*Crocodylus acutus*), is found in Costa Rica.

SUMMARY

How to identify Costa Rican crocodiles:

- The crocodile family only has one Costa Rican species, the American crocodile. It lacks a curved, bony ridge in front of its eyes, but typically has a very elongate and slender snout.
- When the mouth is closed, a large, exposed fang is visible on each side of the lower jaw.

SPECIES DESCRIPTION

Crocodylus acutus
American crocodile (plate 32)

With a total length of 6 m (20 ft)—some unsubstantiated reports cite a maximum size of 7.2 m (24 ft)—this is one of the largest species of crocodile in the world. Today, however, because of excessive hunting of large individuals, most *Crocodylus acutus* average around 2.5 to 3 m (8 to 10 ft) in total length, and individuals over 4 m (13 ft) are rare.

The following characteristics clearly distinguish *Crocodylus acutus* from the only other Costa Rican crocodilian, the spectacled caiman (*Caiman crocodilus*): The animal has a massive body with a relatively narrow and elongate head and a slender snout; the upper jaw is indented on both sides, and an enlarged tooth on the lower jaw is completely exposed in an indentation in the upper jaw when the mouth is closed; and there is no spectacle-like bony ridge in front of the eyes.

Crocodylus acutus is a grayish-green, dark olive-green, or brownish-gray crocodile with dark crossbands on the back and the tail; it is white or cream below. The crossbands on the back are most obvious in juveniles and usually fade with age.

Crocodylus acutus can be found from extreme southern Florida through Mexico and Central America to

Colombia and Venezuela; it also occurs on several islands in the Caribbean and on some of the Antilles. In Costa Rica, this species inhabits rivers, swamps, lagoons, and estuaries in the lowlands along both coasts, although at present its distribution seems to be generally limited to a few regions—mostly national parks—where these crocodiles are fairly common. The best places to see American crocodiles in Costa Rica are probably the lagoons in Corcovado and Santa Rosa National Parks, the canals of Tortuguero, and the Tarcoles River near the Pacific coast.

Crocodiles are most frequently seen basking on shore or on sandbanks, where they may lie motionless for hours on end. When their body temperature gets too high, they either enter the water or open their mouth to cool down. American crocodiles are excellent swimmers, and large individuals are known to remain submerged for periods of more than one hour.

Usually toward the end of the dry season, female *Crocodylus acutus* deposit between 20 and 60 elliptical, china-like eggs in a shallow nest excavated near the water. After the eggs are laid, the female fills up the nest chamber with soil or plant material and conceals the nest. The female tends to stay near her nest, possibly to defend the eggs against predators. The eggs hatch roughly two to three months later, often coinciding with the beginning of the rainy season. Just prior to hatching, some of the hatchlings start calling from inside the nest to attract the attention of their mother. She opens the nest cavity using her front feet and gently helps her offspring leave the nest. If the nest is located a distance from the water, the mother will pick up the hatchlings in her mouth and carry them to the water, one by one. The sex of hatchlings of this species is not determined genetically, but instead is influenced by the temperature of the eggs during incubation (see page 134 on temperature-dependent sex determination).

Crocodiles used to be common in many lowland rivers throughout Central America, and until recently it was not always safe to go swimming in some areas. There have been occasional fatal attacks on humans, even in Costa Rica, but crocodiles sufficiently large to kill a human being are now very rare, having probably been exterminated. Generally, they feed on all kinds of aquatic animals, including crabs, amphibians and fish; infrequently they will consume water birds or small mammals.

Many populations of *Crocodylus acutus* are threatened by habitat destruction and by poachers involved in the hide trade. The future of the species as a whole is uncertain. This species is listed as endangered in the Red Data Book of the International Union for the Conservation of Nature (IUCN), and is listed on appendix I of the CITES lists (see Appendix 2, page 277, for information about CITES).

Literature

Behler & King 1979; Franzen 1988; Lee 1996; Mudde & van Dijk 1984a; Sasa & Solórzano 1995; Savage & Villa 1986; Schouten 1992; Zug 1993.

Temperature-Dependent Sex Determination

In nearly all vertebrates, the sex of offspring is determined genetically at the moment of fertilization. A fascinating exception to this rule is seen in some reptiles; in many species of crocodilians and turtles, and in some species of lizards, the sex of the young is determined by the temperature at which eggs are incubated. At a certain point during development of the embryo, the prevailing incubation temperature irrevocably determines whether the embryo continues its development as a female or a male. This phenomenon, which is known as temperature-dependent sex determination or TSD, is found only in nest-building, egg-laying species of reptiles.

The location and shape of the nest are of critical importance for the survival of any species whose sex is determined by temperature. An incubation temperature that is only slightly higher or lower than the pivotal incubation temperature (the temperature at which 50% of the offspring are males and 50% of the offspring are females), can result in either a sex ratio that is completely off-balance or the death of all embryos.

Two forms of TSD are found among Costa Rican reptiles. Turtles such as the green turtle (*Chelonia mydas*) and the common slider (*Trachemys scripta*) display a form of temperature-dependent sex determination called male-female TSD. In this form of TSD, eggs incubated at temperatures lower than the pivotal temperature produce predominantly (or exclusively) males, while eggs incubated at temperatures higher than the pivotal temperature produce mainly females. Both Costa Rican crocodilian species (*Caiman crocodylus* and *Crocodylus acutus*) exhibit female-male-female TSD, in which incubation below a certain temperature results in a brood of females only, incubation at that exact temperature value results in a brood of nearly all males, and incubation above that temperature value results in an increasing percentage of females.

Mating sea turtles. *Unknown photographer.*

Although the sex of hatchlings in several turtle species is genetically determined, in most species the sex ratio of the young is determined by the incubation temperature. The loggerhead turtle (*Caretta caretta*), for example, displays male-female TSD. At nesting beaches in the eastern United States, the pivotal temperature for a 50% female, 50% male clutch is 29°C (84.2°F). Incubation below this temperature yields proportionally more males, while a higher temperature results in more females.

In female-male-female TSD, the incubation temperature is even more critical. In the case of the spectacled caiman (*Caiman crocodylus*), for example, it is essential that the incubation temperature stay between 28.5 and 33.5°C (83.3 and 92.3°F); within this temperature range, more than 85% of the embryos successfully complete their development. The distribution of the number of males and females within a clutch at different incubation temperatures for this species is shown in table 4. This table also reveals that the pivotal temperature (34°C/93.2°F) is dangerously close to lethal temperatures at which the young fail to hatch and die within the egg.

Table 4: Female-male-female TSD in *Caiman crocodylus*

Incubation Temperature		*% of females in clutch*	*% of males in clutch*
< 31°C	(87.8°F)	100%	0%
32°C	(89.6°F)	5%	95%
32.5°C	(90.5°F)	10%	90%
33°C	(91.4°F)	15%	85%
33.5°C	(92.3°F)	25%	75%
34°C	(93.2°F)	50%	50%
> 34°C	(93.2°F)	all hatchlings die	all hatchlings die

There are so many factors that may influence incubation temperature—including shade created by surrounding vegetation, insulation, metabolic heat from the embryos, organic decomposition of nest materials, ambient temperature, and change in rainfall during incubation—that it seems improbable that species depending on TSD have been able to avoid extinction. However, one relatively new factor influencing the incubation temperature may soon become the downfall of some of those species. There are indications that, on some loggerhead turtle nesting beaches, global warming may be responsible for the hatching of many clutches that are nearly all female, a situation that eventually could lead to the extinction of these already-vulnerable sea turtles.

Literature

Aguilar 1994; Allsteadt 1994; Mrosovsky 1988; Mrosovsky & Provancha 1989; Mrosovsky & Yntema 1981.

ORDER: **Testudines** (Turtles)
CLASS: Reptiles

Costa Rica and the oceans off its two coasts are home to thirteen turtle species (see table 5). Five of those species are grouped into two families of sea turtles: the hard-shelled sea turtles of the family Cheloniidae, with four species, and the unique leatherback turtle, the sole member of the family Dermochelyidae. The remaining species, found on the mainland, spend a varying degree of time in or near freshwater. They are assigned to three families: the snapping turtles (family Chelydridae), the pond turtles (family Emydidae), and the mud turtles (family Kinosternidae).

Table 5: Taxonomy of Costa Rican Turtles

Family	*Common Name*	*Number of Species*
Cheloniidae	Hard-shelled sea turtle family	4
Dermochelyidae	Leatherback turtle family	1
Emydidae	Pond turtle family	4
Kinosternidae	Mud turtle family	3
Chelydridae	Snapping turtle family	1

Turtles, the most primitive surviving reptiles—at least 230 million years old—emerged long before the first dinosaurs lived. Their continued survival attests to the effectiveness of their most characteristic structure, the boxlike shell. This protective armor typically consists of a lower section, the plastron, which covers the belly, and an upper section, the carapace, which forms the actual shell. The carapace consists of bony plates, called scutes, which are fused to the vertebrae and ribs of the turtle; the plastron contains the breastbone, the clavicle, and the shoulder bones. The carapace and plastron are joined on the sides by bony bridges or ligaments. A turtle's shell is thus fused to its skeleton; cartoon images notwithstanding, no turtle is able to leave its shell.

Individuals in many species can withdraw their head, limbs, and tail inside the shell. This feat is performed with varying degrees of success. Some turtles can withdraw protruding body parts and even seal their shell; this is made possible by a hinged plastron. The white-lipped mud turtle (*Kinosternon leucostomum*) is a good example of this. Some turtles can even survive forest fires inside their closed shell. On the other hand, other turtles, such as the common snapping turtle (*Chelydra serpentina*), seem to have outgrown their shell; they cannot retract their head, limbs, and tail for lack of space inside. No marine turtles have the ability to withdraw their extremities within the shell.

Apart from their external body armor, turtles have developed several unique specializations over time. One of the more visible adaptations seen in all contemporary turtles is the absence of teeth; instead, their jaws are equipped with a hard, keratinous jaw sheath that grows with the developing skull.

Present-day turtles live in a wide range of climates and habitats and can be found worldwide throughout both temperate and tropical zones. Although some species are found in bone-dry deserts, as a group turtles are either predominantly aquatic or spend at least part of their life in or near water. Two families of sea turtles (Cheloniidae and Dermochelyidae) are strictly marine animals, and their encounters with dry land are restricted to a rapid crawl toward the sea after emerging from their nest on a tropical beach, and, in the case of females, an occasional return to that same beach to lay eggs.

Olive ridley (*Lepidochelys olivacea*) emerging from its egg. © *Nature's Images*

There are no live-bearing turtles—all species lay eggs. Some turtles simply deposit their eggs on the forest floor, but in general they deposit their eggs in a nest chamber that the female excavates using her hind feet. After laying her eggs, she fills the nest with sand or leaf litter. The eggs hatch after an incubation period that varies in length from species to species, and whose duration can be affected by environmental conditions. When the hatchling turtles tunnel their way out of the nest, they are immediately on their own. As soon as the female closes off the nest chamber, she abandons her offspring; no form of parental care is known among any species of turtle.

With their distinctive morphology, turtles appear strikingly different from other reptiles. However, they are similar to other reptiles in many respects. Their exposed skin is typically dry and scaly. Turtles are also ectothermous, since they rely on an external source of heat to increase their body temperature. Just like their reptilian relatives—the crocodilians, lizards, and snakes—turtles are most frequently seen basking in the sun.

The population numbers of several species of turtle are at an all time low. Many turtle species, including several found in Costa Rica, are on the brink of extinction due to excessive hunting, egg collecting, habitat destruction, and other threats from humans.

SUMMARY

How to identify Costa Rican turtles:

- All reptiles with a shell are turtles.

Literature

Behler & King 1979; Ernst & Barbour 1989; Savage & Villa 1986; Zug 1993.

FAMILY: **Cheloniidae** (Hard-shelled Sea Turtles)
ORDER: Testudines (Turtles)

Members of the family Cheloniidae are marine turtles with a hard, bony shell. The only other family of marine turtles, the family Dermochelyidae, consists of a single leathery-shelled species, *Dermochelys coriacea*. The family Cheloniidae includes six species of sea turtles, assigned to five genera. Most of these species are found at isolated locations around the world, and four of them, the loggerhead turtle (*Caretta caretta*), the green turtle (*Chelonia mydas*), the hawksbill turtle (*Eretmochelys imbricata*), and the olive ridley (*Lepidochelys olivacea*), periodically nest on Costa Rican beaches.

Loggerhead sea turtle (*Caretta caretta*). All marine turtles have paddle-like limbs.

With their streamlined heart- or shield-shaped shell and paddle-like limbs, sea turtles are well adapted to a life at sea. Chelonids usually live in tropical waters, although individuals of some species range into temperate seas in the summer for breeding, sometimes traveling great distances from the tropical waters in which they feed. When they reproduce, turtles return to the same beach on which they hatched, presumably guided by the stars and/or specific characteristics of ocean currents.

Sea turtles grow very slowly and may require up to 40 or 50 years before reaching sexual maturity and reproducing for the first time. Males and females congregate in shallow water near the nesting beach to mate. Copulating pairs often float at the water's surface, with the male atop the female. Males have enlarged, hooklike claws on the front flippers and a long, prehensile tail that provide a firm attachment. Females typically reproduce every 2 to 4 years. In breeding years, they lay from 2 to 5 egg clutches at intervals of several days. To lay her eggs, the female crawls ashore at night and digs a deep nest chamber with her hind flippers. The female lays over a hundred leathery-shelled eggs the size of a ping-pong ball inside the nest, carefully placing each one. After laying eggs, she fills the nest cavity with sand. She uses her flippers to sweep sand over the nest site, attempting to hide any trace of her digging from potential predators.

At sunrise, the nesting beach is empty; the nesting turtles have shuffled back into the water and swum off. A few weeks later, at night, the beach becomes alive again as hordes of sea-turtle hatchlings tunnel out of the nest and head for the water. Often, a wide variety of predators await the hatch, and many of the newly hatched turtles never reach the surf. Although much more agile in their marine environment, hatchling sea turtles still face many predators there. Few turtles survive their first year.

Although once numerous, all sea turtles are today endangered. Several centuries of relentless poaching of eggs and adult turtles (turtle meat is considered a delicacy), and hunting to obtain their skin, shells, or oil, as well as depredation by souvenir collectors, have drastically reduced the size of sea-turtle populations. Beach front developments continue to destroy nesting sites; commercial shrimp fishermen, who operate near shore, drown pregnant females in their nets; and global warming interferes with the incubation of the sea turtles' eggs. Although sea turtles are protected by international laws, limited funds and resources mean that these are often not strictly enforced. Most species may soon become extinct.

When visiting a nesting site, it is important to observe several rules. You should avoid making any kind of noise or sudden movements. And you should never use flashlights or cameras with flash, because these disturb nesting turtles. Eating sea turtle eggs or meat, or purchasing products made from their shells or skin, is illegal is many places. It is unethical everywhere.

SUMMARY

How to identify Costa Rican hard-shelled sea turtles:

- All marine turtles with a hard, bony shell are in the family Cheloniidae.

SPECIES DESCRIPTIONS

Caretta caretta

Loggerhead sea turtle (plate 32)

The largest hard-shelled marine turtle in the world, the loggerhead sea turtle (*Caretta caretta*) is surpassed in size only by the soft-shelled leatherback turtle (*Dermochelys coriacea*). The largest loggerhead on record, which had a shell measuring 2,300 mm (90½ inches), may have weighed up to 540 kg (1,190 lbs). Sadly, such marine giants are now gone, since many turtles are poached or drown in a fisherman's net before they reach such sizes. Most present-day *Caretta caretta* are considerably smaller, ranging from 800 to 1,200 mm (31½ to 47¼ inches).

This turtle's distinctive reddish-brown shell (carapace) has five or more large bony plates (costal scutes) bordering the center row on each side. When seen from above, a loggerhead shell is elongate and heart-shaped. The edges of the shell become slightly serrated as they taper toward the tail. The juvenile carapace bears three longitudinal keels that disappear with age; the adult shell is smooth. In this species, the bridge between the shell and the belly armor (plastron) typically consists of a series of three scutes on each side of the body. Two pairs of scales are invariably present between the eyes and the nostrils, one pair on each side of the head. The paddle-like limbs each bear a pair of claws.

Caretta caretta is a generally brown turtle; its carapace is reddish-brown to dark brown, and the upper surfaces of the head and limbs are chestnut or dark brown as well. The margins of the limbs and the underside of the body are light yellow to tan. The scales on the head often have a creamy yellow margin and a dark center.

The sexes can be differentiated based on the length of the tail; in males, it extends well beyond the margin of the shell, while in females it is much shorter.

Loggerhead sea turtles occur in most tropical and subtropical seas in the Atlantic, Indian, and Pacific Oceans, although they don't reach the Pacific coast of Costa Rica. During the summer, gravid females born in temperate zones return to those zones in order to breed. In Costa Rica, this turtle nests only on the Caribbean coast and is sporadically seen in Tortuguero National Park and on sandy beaches along the southern Caribbean coast. It frequents coral reefs and shipwrecks and is often encountered on diving and snorkeling trips.

Caretta caretta mate while in the water, near their nesting grounds. The male mounts the female and attaches himself with the aid of claws on each of his flippers. The couple may mate for more than three hours.

Females come ashore at night, usually at high tide, to lay their large clutches of round eggs. The clutch size for *Caretta caretta* ranges from 60 to 200 eggs, with an average of 125. During a breeding season, a female may nest several times at intervals of 12 to 15 days. The hatchlings emerge from their underground nest about 7 to 10 weeks after the eggs are laid, depending on the incubation temperature. Ambient temperature not only influences the length of the incubation period, it also affects the gender of the hatchlings (see page 134 on temperature-dependent sex determination).

Little is known about the natural history of juveniles when they reach the surf shortly after crawling out of their nest. Juvenile turtles that are more than a year old are sometimes seen in coastal waters, but sightings of younger turtles are extremely rare. In one instance, loggerhead babies were seen in a floating sargassum (seaweed) raft. Whether young loggerheads stay exclusively in sargassum rafts is unknown, although the food and protection they provide would seem to offer an ideal habitat.

Studies on the stomach contents of *Caretta caretta* indicate they are omnivores, yet their powerful jaws and their broad, muscular head suggest they are carnivorous. It is possible that the algae and other vegetation found in their stomachs may have been ingested incidentally while they fed on shrimp, crab, squid, mollusks, and jellyfish.

The meat of *Caretta caretta* is not valued as highly as that of most other marine turtles, although there is very high demand for their eggs. Unfortunately, poaching is only one of many threats they face. Development of nesting beaches for tourism and the use of shrimp nets, in which marine turtles drown, also take a toll. "Photo-pollution" is partly responsible for an increasing mortality rate of hatching marine turtles. When these turtles emerge from their nest, they move toward the lightest area on the horizon, which generally indicates the location of the ocean. Today, however, millions of hatchlings are misled by the glow of urban lights and head away from the ocean, toward land. The following day, they die from the heat of the sun.

Caretta caretta is listed as "vulnerable" in the Red Data Book of the International Union for Conservation of Nature (IUCN). Trade in these turtles is regulated by the rules of the Convention on International Trade in Endangered Species (CITES), which places *Caretta caretta* in appendix I, to which the strongest restrictions apply.

Chelonia mydas

Green turtle
Tortuga verde (plate 33)

Two forms of *Chelonia mydas* frequent Costa Rica: the Atlantic green turtle (*Chelonia mydas mydas*) and the Pacific green turtle (*Chelonia mydas agassizii*). These two forms are considered subspecies, although some authorities would elevate both to species status. Pacific green turtles are very similar in appearance to the Atlantic green turtles, but generally have a darker shell that is very dark brown to almost black. Additionally, the shell (carapace) of Pacific green turtles is often indented above the hind limbs.

Green turtles are mainly found in tropical oceans, but may occasionally wander into temperate seas. The Pacific green turtle is geographically isolated from its Atlantic counterpart and inhabits the warm waters of the Pacific and the Indian Ocean, whereas Atlantic green turtles migrate and nest along the east coast of the Americas. In Costa Rica, the Pacific green turtle is found on the Pacific coast; the Atlantic green turtle nests on Caribbean beaches.

Most of the information on *Chelonia mydas* is recorded from the famous population of Atlantic green turtles nesting at Tortuguero. However, since the two subspecies of the green turtle are so similar, the information in this section should apply to both.

The green turtle is the only marine turtle with four bony plates (costal scutes) on each side of a central row of scutes, and only a single pair of scales on top of the head, between the eyes. This is also the only marine turtle that comes to shore to bask in full sunlight. The green turtle, which is primarily herbivorous, has a diet deficient in vitamin D since plants do not provide that vitamin. The turtle's body can produce this important chemical compound, provided it receives direct sunlight.

These are very large animals; they may reach a shell length of over 150 cm (59 inches) and weigh almost 300 kg (660 lbs), although today individuals probably fall prey to humans or other predators before reaching such sizes. The broad, heart-shaped shell of most individuals measures about 1 m (40 inches) across. The surface of the shell is smooth, although in juveniles a keel may run down the middle of the carapace. This keel disappears with age. The bony plates on the shell do not overlap.

Green turtles are not green at all, but owe their common name to the greenish color of their fat. They have an olive to dark brown shell, sometimes with a mottled pattern. The protective armor (plastron) on their belly is white or cream. The head and limbs are dark brown above, and the scales on the head have a light margin with a dark brown center. The underside of the flippers, the chin, and the throat is white or yellowish.

As with all other marine turtles, the limbs are modified into flippers. Males have a single curved claw on each front flipper that is used to hold on to the female's shell during mating. Males and females can also be told apart by the male's long tail, which extends far beyond the margin of the shell and is tipped with a flattened nail, also used to grip the female during mating. When these turtles mate, the male's claws can cut into the female and sometimes cause significant bleeding.

Green turtles mate in the shallow waters off their nesting beaches, usually close to shore. In an aggressive attempt to mate, often more than one male simultaneously courts a single female; and occasionally, a second, or even a third, male climbs on top of a male who is already mounted on a female. During the mating frenzy, which takes place every year, one can see clumsy stacks of green turtles in awkward motion on the surface of the water.

Roughly between June and September, gravid females come ashore at Gandoca-Manzanillo and Tortuguero, the green turtle's two main nesting sites in Costa Rica. Under cover of darkness, a female lays 100 or so eggs in a cavity excavated with her hind flippers. After closing up the nest, the female returns to the sea, but may remain near the nesting beach in order to nest again. A female breeds only every 2 to 4 years, but during each reproductive season she produces several clutches of eggs at intervals of 12 to 15 days. The incubation period of the eggs is between 50 and 70 days, depending on ambient temperature, humidity, and other factors. Ambient temperature also determines the sex of the hatchlings (see page 134 on temperature-dependent sex determination).

Turtle nests are raided by a variety of predators; humans, dogs, and raccoons dig up and eat large numbers of eggs every year. Hatchling sea turtles also suffer a high mortality rate since they often come under attack as soon as they leave the nest. Vultures, gulls, and frigate birds, as well as crabs, attack the baby turtles as they plod toward the ocean, where many predatory fish await. According to some estimates, only 30% of the hatchlings reach the water.

Once they reach the relative safety of the sea, the hatchlings drift away on ocean currents, riding in large, floating mats of seaweed. The hatchlings mainly feed on small invertebrates; but as they mature they become increasingly vegetarian. Little is known about what happens to baby green turtles during the first year of life, or where they go. A year after leaving the nest, they reappear in shallow coastal waters, which have an abundance of the aquatic plants on which they graze until reaching maturity. These feeding grounds may be as far as 3,200 km (2,000 mi) from their birthplace. Green turtles may take 20 to 30 years to reach sexual maturity. As soon as they do, they travel great distances to return to the same beach where they hatched decades before, probably using the position of the stars and ocean currents to guide them.

In the 1997 breeding season in Tortuguero National Park, Costa Rica, biologists tagged 2,111 nesting green turtles. During the same period, at least 1,500 to 2,000 turtles were poached from the park. The Costa Rican Institute for Fishery and Aquaculture (INCOPESCA) licenses commercial fishermen to hunt 1,800 *Chelonia mydas* each year, but it restricts hunting to areas outside the park. Nevertheless, it is hard to find turtles outside the park, and fishermen regularly enter in order to poach. Likewise, the official turtle-hunting season, which lasts from June 1 to August 31, is another often-ignored restriction. Even if restrictions on hunting were complied with, the quota was fixed at 1,800 rather arbitrarily; this limit may also have dire effects on the population.

In addition to licensed fishermen, an even larger group of poachers enter the park in boats at night. Turtles are caught in various ways. Frequently, poachers tie a rope with a plastic float to every nesting female they encounter. When the turtle returns to sea, the float indicates its presence and it is caught by poachers in boats. The most frequently applied technique, however, especially when the sea is calm, is simply to walk the beach at night and flip over female turtles as soon as they emerge from the surf, which completely incapacitates them. The turtles are left until a sufficient number has been flipped over; they are then hauled aboard a waiting boat and taken away. Estimates on the number of turtles killed on any particular night are based on telltale signs—either turtle tracks that stop short of nesting sites or marks that indicate a turtle was dragged while upside down. Advancing waves can erase these clues, and the number of turtles killed every year on Costa Rican beaches is probably even higher than estimated.

Because of such exploitation, *Chelonia mydas* is highly endangered. On some beaches where they were once frequent and abundant visitors, these turtles are now rarely seen or no longer nest. If no drastic measures are taken, the future of these amazing animals is very uncertain. *Chelonia mydas* is listed as "endangered" in the IUCN Red Data Book and is also included in appendix I of the CITES convention.

Eretmochelys imbricata

Hawksbill sea turtle
Tortuga carey (plate 33)

Although one of the smaller species of marine turtle, *Eretmochelys imbricata* will defend itself aggressively if disturbed. It is recognized by its curved, beaklike upper jaw that somewhat resembles a hawk's beak and by the strongly overlapping bony plates (scutes) on its shell.

The hawksbill sea turtle has paddle-like limbs, and each of the front flippers bears two claws. Its shell is heart- or shield-shaped and is strongly serrated as it tapers toward the rear. Its maximum recorded length is slightly less than 100 cm (40 inches). A distinct keel runs down the middle of the shell. Important scalation characteristics that help identify this species are the presence of four bony plates on each side of the shell (costal scutes) and two pairs of large scales between the eyes, on top of the head. This is the only marine turtle with overlapping plates (scutes).

The sexes are distinguished by the long tail in males, which extends well beyond the rear margin of the shell, as well as by the shape of the belly armor (plastron). In females, the plastron is flat, while males have a concave plastron; this depression in the plastron makes it easier to rest on the female's domed shell during mating. The paired claws on each front flipper also help the male to hold on to the female.

The shell is normally some shade of brown, with a "tortoiseshell" pattern of light cream or yellowish markings. The plastron is yellow. The head and flippers are covered with yellow-margined scales with a reddish-brown or brown center.

The hawksbill sea turtle inhabits the warm tropical and subtropical regions of the Atlantic, Pacific, and Indian Oceans, as well as the Caribbean. It is mainly a species of shallow coastal waters, and is most often seen in rock formations underwater and in coral reefs. On occasion, hawksbills are also found in estuaries. In Costa Rica, they nest on both coasts on scattered beaches that they share with other species of marine turtles. Hawksbill sea turtles tend to nest individually, unlike green turtles and olive ridleys, which often nest in large numbers.

Mating and nesting generally take place between April and November, peaking around June or July. This species mates in shallow water off the nesting beach—after females return from having nested—thus fertilizing eggs that will be laid in future nesting attempts. Every three years, the female produces several clutches of eggs. At night, usually at high tide, she comes ashore and digs a nest chamber with her hind flippers approximately 60 cm (2 ft) deep. Between 50 and 200 spherical eggs are deposited inside the chamber, after which the female closes the nest and returns to the ocean. After an incubation period of about 8 or 9 weeks, the hatchlings emerge.

Eretmochelys imbricata is omnivorous, though it tends to become increasingly carnivorous with age. Its diet includes sponges and other nonmobile marine invertebrates such as mollusks, tunicates, and bryozoans. These turtles are also known to eat fish and jellyfish, including the highly toxic Portuguese man-of-war. Various toxic components of the jellyfish and sponges that the hawksbill eats are incorporated in its tissues; the meat of these turtles, therefore, is often toxic to humans.

The beautifully patterned, translucent shell of the hawksbill sea turtle is the primary source of tortoiseshell, which has long been used to make combs, frames for glasses, and jewelry. This species has suffered enormously from the harvesting of these shells. Today, cheap synthetic alternatives for tortoiseshell are readily available, but hunting continues. Both the turtle's meat—even though sometimes toxic—and eggs are prized. As a result, *Eretmochelys imbricata* is an endangered species, and its continued existence is uncertain. It is protected by international laws and is listed in the IUCN Red Data Book, as well as on appendix I of the Convention on International Trade in Endangered Species (CITES).

Eretmochelys imbricata has been divided into two subspecies based on differences in its shell morphology and coloration. In Costa Rica, both subspecies are found. *Eretmochelys imbricata imbricata* lives on the Caribbean coast, while *Eretmochelys imbricata bissa* nests on Pacific beaches. In Surinam, biologists have discovered hybrids of *Eretmochelys imbricata* and *Chelonia mydas* (green turtle). These animals display several traits of the green turtle, but also have the overlapping bony plates and serrated rear shell of the former species. These hybrids are handled at great risk, as they will defend themselves just as vigorously as true hawksbill turtles.

Lepidochelys olivacea
Olive ridley
Tortuga lora (plate 34)

Lepidochelys olivacea is the smallest of the marine turtles that visit Costa Rica. Its wide, heart-shaped shell (carapace) measures from 600 to 700 mm (23½ to 27½ inches). The carapace of this species has 6 to 8 bony plates (costal scutes) on each side of the row of scales that runs down the center of the back. On the top of the head, there are two pairs of scales between the eyes and the nostrils. Juveniles have three distinct longitudinal keels on their carapace; these become less obvious with age, but the central keel often remains visible. In this species, the bridgelike structure that connects the shell with the belly armor (plastron) consists of 8 bony plates (4 on each side of the body) with distinct musk-gland pores. As their common name indicates, these turtles are mainly olive-colored on their upper surfaces. Their undersurfaces are greenish-white.

The sexes can be distinguished by the shape of the plastron, which is flat in females but concave in males, and by the males' long tail, which extends far beyond the margin of shell; females have a short tail.

Lepidochelys olivacea inhabits the warm waters of tropical oceans around the globe. In Costa Rica, it nests on the Pacific coast, predominantly in Guanacaste. Two species of sea turtle are known to stage *arribadas*, or brief periods of synchronous nesting activity, during which more than 150,000 sea turtles may congregate and nest at the same time on the same beach. Kemp's ridley (*Lepidochelys kempi*), a highly endangered, perhaps nearly extinct turtle, nests solely along a short stretch of beach in the Gulf of Mexico. Its close relative, *Lepidochelys olivacea*, is known to have *arribadas* on only five beaches in the world, two of which are on the Pacific coast of northern Costa Rica: one at Playa Ostional, and the other 80 km (50 mi) north at Playa Nancite.

Arribadas of *Lepidochelys olivacea* on Playa Ostional take place throughout the rainy season (roughly June to December), and peak *arribadas* occur in September or October. On nights preceding the *arribada*, breeding females congregate in shallow water off the coast. At the appropriate time—generally at high tide—they start crawling ashore in massive numbers. Once the *arribada* is set in motion, nothing deters the turtles from nesting; the presence of humans or predators, or the arrival of daybreak, does not stop wave after wave of additional turtles from arriving on the beach. On peak nesting days, Playa Ostional has the appearance of an old cobblestoned boulevard paved with turtles.

In the 1990 and 1991 nesting seasons, during periods of extremely heavy rains, the olive ridleys postponed egg-laying and retained their eggs up to 63 days. Egg retention seems to be an adaptation that enables the turtles to delay laying eggs until nesting conditions are favorable. In this particular case, the breeding females simultaneously came ashore as soon as the inclement weather cleared.

Most *arribadas* last four days, and each high tide brings new hordes of turtles. Within those four days, between 150,000 and 200,000 *Lepidochelys olivacea* have visited Playa Ostional to lay their eggs. The *arribada* ends as suddenly as it begins, and on the fifth day the beach is again empty.

Because the number of nesting turtles can be enormous, and because Playa Ostional is a small beach, not much longer than 800 meters (0.5 mi), many turtles nest in places where earlier arrivals have already laid eggs. As a result 70% to 80% of those early eggs are dug up or destroyed. The Costa Rican Congress approved a management plan that legalizes the controlled harvesting of turtle eggs on Playa Ostional. Since 1987, the townspeople of Ostional have been allowed to harvest all eggs laid during the first 36 hours of an *arribada*, which amounts to roughly 3 million eggs, an estimated 10% of the yearly total. Many of these eggs find their way to bars in San José, where they are sold as appetizers.

Although the number of *Lepidochelys olivacea* surviving worldwide is probably greater than that of any other sea turtle species, their future is far from assured. They are protected by a number of endangered species laws and are included in the Red Data Book of the International Union for the Conservation of Nature (IUCN) and the appendices of the CITES convention.

Despite formal protection, the number of nesting females that come ashore to Costa Rica during *arribadas* is steadily declining. Even more frightening reports come from the Bhitara Kanika Sanctuary in India, where the world's largest population of olive ridleys nests. In 1997, no *arribada* took place there. The usual mating activity off the coast that precedes the *arribada* was observed to take place, but no females came ashore to lay eggs. Instead of the arrival of 200,000 to 600,000 gravid females, some 4,000 dead turtles washed ashore, having drowned in nets used by hundreds of trawlers that were illegally fishing offshore, trapping and killing thousands of turtles in the process.

Literature

Behler & King 1979; Bruemmer 1995; Das 1998; Ernst & Barbour 1989; Klemens & Thorbjarnarson 1995; Lee 1996; Lohmann 1991; Mrosovsky & Yntema 1981; Mudde & van Dijk 1984a; Opay 1998; Plotkin et al. 1997; Savage & Villa 1986; Schouten 1992; Smith 1968a; Troeng 1998; Wood et al. 1983; Zug 1993.

FAMILY: **Dermochelyidae** (Leatherback Turtles)
ORDER: Testudines (Turtles)

The leatherback turtle family consists of a single, extant species, the leatherback turtle (*Dermochelys coriacea*).

This species is unique among marine turtles in that it lacks the bony plates that make up the hard shell of all other marine species. Instead, the shell (carapace) and belly armor (plastron) consist of smooth, leathery skin, which is embedded with small platelets. The skin is supported by seven longitudinal bony ridges.

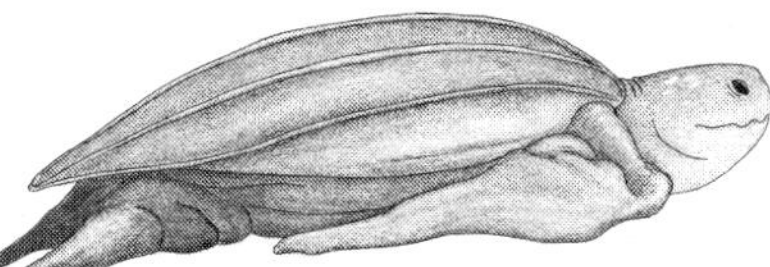

Leatherback turtle (*Dermochelys coriacea*).

Dermochelys coriacea, the largest living turtle, ranks among the largest reptiles in the world. The largest individual on record measured 244 cm (96 inches). Such large individuals may weigh in excess of 750 kg (1,650 lbs).

This large-flippered, streamlined giant occurs in all major oceans. Its main nesting beaches are restricted to tropical regions, but adult leatherback turtles regularly migrate into cold water. In Costa Rica, nesting females of this species can be found in small numbers on the beaches along both coasts. However, Playa Grande on the Pacific coast and the beaches in the Gandoca-Manzanillo wildlife refuge on the Atlantic coast are favored nesting sites for leatherbacks. During the nesting season, roughly from October to March, these beaches are frequented at night by gravid females.

SUMMARY

How to identify Costa Rican leatherback turtles:

- The only member of the leatherback turtle family is a giant marine turtle with long, paddlelike front limbs.
- Leatherback turtles have a leathery shell with distinct longitudinal ridges.

SPECIES DESCRIPTION

Dermochelys coriacea

Leatherback turtle
Siete filos (plate 34)

The two distinguishing characteristics of *Dermochelys coriacea* are its enormous size and ridged, leathery shell.

There are seven prominent longitudinal ridges on the shell (carapace), and five on the belly (plastron); these ridges are most distinct on juvenile turtles and become less distinct with age. The streamlined carapace is elongate, and roughly triangular when seen from above. *Dermochelys coriacea* has long, paddle-like limbs and lacks claws.

The sexes are distinguished by the shape of the belly armor, which is concave in males and flat in females. Also, males have a substantially longer tail than do females; their tail extends beyond the length of the hind limbs.

Leatherback turtles are usually a uniform dark color, either dark brown, slate gray, or blue-black; the undersurface is mostly white. In some cases, irregular light markings (white, cream, yellow, or pink) are present on the shell, head, and limbs. In juveniles, the colors tend to be more vivid than in adults.

This marine turtle prefers the open ocean. After individuals leave nesting beaches in tropical waters, they wander long distances across the Atlantic, Pacific, and Indian oceans. Along the coasts of the Americas, it is seen as far north as Newfoundland and British Columbia and as far south as Chile and Argentina. The leatherback turtle is a powerful swimmer, and with its streamlined body and large flippers, it may reach speeds in excess of 30 kph (18.5 mph). Besides being fast, it also has amazing endurance—one individual tagged in French Guiana arrived 128 days later in Newfoundland. The distance between the two points, as measured along a straight line, is 5,000 km (3,100 mi).

During their migrations, leatherback turtles range farther north and south than any of the other marine turtles. It is possible they follow their favorite prey, jellyfish, into these cold waters. *Dermochelys coriacea* can survive in these areas because of an ability to increase body temperature. Specific adaptations in the circulatory system and fatty insulation enable leatherbacks to maintain a body temperature of 25°C (77°F) in seawater that may be as much as 18°C (33°F) colder. Generation of body heat is unusual among reptiles, and *Dermochelys coriacea* is the only turtle known to do this.

Leatherback turtles mainly eat jellyfish, although they also feed on other marine invertebrates such as crustaceans and sea anemones. They are known to dive several hundred meters in pursuit of jellyfish. Long, spinelike projections on the upper jaws and in the esophagus help them snap up and swallow their slippery prey. The stingers and chemical defenses found in many jellyfish do not harm these turtles. Increasingly, however, dead leatherbacks are found with plastic bags in their stomachs. Apparently floating plastic is frequently mistaken for jellyfish; in one study, over 40% of the leatherback turtles examined had plastic in their intestines.

Like all marine turtles, *Dermochelys coriacea* mates in the open sea. Females do not nest every year; but in years when they do nest, they lay several egg clutches, at intervals of about 10 days. Gravid females crawl to shore after dark, usually on overcast nights, at high tide. After excavating the nest chamber, the female lays between 50 and 170 spherical eggs measuring between 50 and 65 mm (2 and 2½ inches). When a nesting female feels threatened, she emits loud sighs, groans, and belches. If harassed or approached too closely, she will flail at the assailant with her flippers.

On a dark night, approximately 8 to 10 weeks after nesting, hatchling turtles tunnel to the surface of the nest and head for the surf.

Dermochelys coriacea is a critically endangered species. Excessive hunting to obtain oils used to produce cosmetics, and overcollecting of the prized eggs, threaten this species with extinction. Although protected under the US Endangered Species Act, and also included in the IUCN Red Data Book and the Convention on the International Trade in Endangered Species, leatherback turtles face an uncertain future.

Literature

Behler & King 1979; Ernst & Barbour 1989; Goff et al. 1994; Lee 1996; Schouten 1992; Zug 1993.

FAMILY: **Emydidae** (Pond Turtles)
ORDER: Testudines (Turtles)

This family, which includes over 90 species, is the largest turtle family. Most emydids are found in the Americas; Costa Rica is home to 4 species in 2 genera: *Rhinoclemmys* and *Trachemys*. Pond turtles, which come in many different shapes and sizes, are also variable in their biology and habitat. Although the common name implies that they predominantly inhabit ponds, members of this family may live in terrestrial, semiaquatic, freshwater, or estuarine habitats.

Pond turtles are commonly seen basking on logs and mudflats along Costa Rican rivers.

There are no true terrestrial tortoises in Costa Rica, but 2 emydid species, *Rhinoclemmys annulata* and *Rhinoclemmys pulcherrima*, which live near small streams in forested areas, have at least partially adapted to life on land. The two other Costa Rican emydid turtles, *Rhinoclemmys funerea* and *Trachemys scripta*, spend most of their time in, or near, water and are often seen basking on logs protruding from water.

TURTLES

SUMMARY

How to identify Costa Rican pond turtles:

- Pond turtles are freshwater or terrestrial turtles, without paddle-shaped limbs but sometimes with skinlike webbing between the toes.
- All Costa Rican species lack moveable hinges on the belly armor (plastron), and also lack serrated keels on their shell (carapace).

SPECIES DESCRIPTIONS

Rhinoclemmys annulata

Brown wood turtle (plate 35)

Rhinoclemmys annulata has a high-domed shell with a single low keel down the middle and a serrated rear margin. The shell, which varies from uniform black to dark brown, may also display large yellowish or orange blotches. The growth rings at the edges of the scutes create a textured surface. The unhinged plastron is dark brown or black.

The brown wood turtle has a small head with a short, blunt snout. The upper jaw is slightly beaked. Exposed skin is yellowish to gray-brown, with a pattern of reddish or yellowish stripes on the head, and dark stripes on the forelegs.

This medium-sized turtle may reach slightly over 200 mm (8 inches) in total carapace length. Although not distinguishable by size, males and females differ in several ways. Males have a concave plastron; females have a flat plastron. The male's tail is longer than the female's tail. And, in males, the vent is located beyond the margin of the carapace; in females, it sits within the margin of the shell.

Rhinoclemmys annulata inhabits the Caribbean versant of southern Honduras, Belize, Nicaragua, Costa Rica, and Panama, and also ranges into Colombia and Ecuador. It inhabits rainforests and vegetation on the banks of rivers, from sea level to almost 1,500 m (4,900 ft).

Although generally seen on land, *Rhinoclemmys annulata* readily takes to the water when it needs to cool off. During periods of inactivity, it seeks refuge from the heat and predators in the leaf litter or beneath the root systems of trees.

Generally active during the early morning hours and after heavy rains, this turtle feeds on plants and fruits, seeming to prefer ferns, seedlings, and shoots. Its coloration allows it to blend in with the surroundings as it forages among the leaves and vegetation on the forest floor.

Little is known about the reproductive biology of this species, although it appears to mate on land.

Costa Rica is home to three species of *Rhinoclemmys*. The most commonly seen is *Rhinoclemmys funerea*, a semiaquatic species with extensively webbed feet. *Rhinoclemmys pulcherrima*, which within Costa Rica is restricted to the dry forests of Guanacaste, has a brown carapace with a gaudy pattern of red, yellow and black markings on each scute.

Rhinoclemmys funerea

Black wood turtle
Jicotea (plate 35)

Rhinoclemmys funerea is a large turtle—the largest in its genus—and may weigh over 4.5 kg (10 lbs). The shell (carapace), which may reach a size of 355 mm (14 inches), is highly domed and smooth, although the surface of individual scutes can sometimes be irregular. A faint keel runs along the center of the shell. As the shell tapers toward the tail, its edges are serrated. The belly armor lacks the hinges characteristic of mud turtles (family Kinosternidae). The head is moderately sized. A slightly protruding snout and a notched upper jaw are invariably present in this species.

Of the three species of this genus found in Costa Rica, *Rhinoclemmys funerea* is the most aquatic. Its toes are connected by skinlike webbing that almost reaches the tips. This webbing transforms the hind feet into paddles used for swimming. The margins of each foot also display a fleshy skin flap.

The sexes are distinguished by the shape of the belly armor (plastron) and by the size and shape of the tail. The plastron of females is flat; males have a concave plastron that makes it easier for the male to balance on top of the female's shell when copulating. Females have a shorter tail than males, and their vent is located within the margin of the shell; the opening of the male's cloaca is located beyond the margin of the shell, below the tail.

Adult black wood turtles have a uniform dark brown to black shell, hence the common name; in juveniles, the dark background may be tinged with yellow. The skin of these turtles is black with tiny yellow spots. A series of irregular yellow stripes runs from the corner of the mouth along each side of the neck. The lower jaw and the lower half of the neck are largely yellow, mottled with black.

Rhinoclemmys funerea occurs in the Caribbean lowlands of Nicaragua and Costa Rica, and in Panama up to the Canal Zone, below 1,050 m (3,450 ft). A second species of *Rhinoclemmys*, the brown wood turtle (*Rhinoclemmys annulata*), also inhabits the Costa Rican Caribbean lowlands, but is less aquatic than *Rhinoclemmys funerea*. This generally brown turtle further differs from the black wood turtle in having slightly webbed feet and a hooked upper jaw. The third Costa Rican species in this genus, the painted wood turtle (*Rhinoclemmys pulcherrima*), occurs only in the dry northwestern lowlands.

Although *Rhinoclemmys funerea* is very common at certain locations in Costa Rica, such as the canals of Tortuguero, where it is abundant, not much is known about its natural history. Black wood turtles are very shy, and when approached too closely they dive into the water and remain submerged for several minutes, surfacing in a different spot. This species is most frequently seen basking by day on sandbanks or logs in lowland rivers, sometimes accompanied by spectacled caimans (*Caiman crocodilus*) or common sliders (*Trachemys scripta*). Although juveniles often fall prey to spectacled caimans, adults, which are larger and have stronger shells, are generally safe from predation.

Sometimes, particularly at night, *Rhinoclemmys funerea* is encountered on land, where it actively searches for grasses, leaves, and fruits, the main components of its diet.

Both sexes reach sexual maturity when their shell length reaches approximately 200 mm (7⅞ inches). Mating is preceded by a courtship, during which a swimming female is chased by the male. At some point, the female slows down or stops, and the male comes alongside her, extending and rapidly vibrating his head and neck. This turtle reproduces at the end of the dry and the beginning of the rainy season, producing between one and four clutches, each containing three eggs on average. The eggs are placed on the ground and covered with leaves—no nest is dug. Juveniles hatch 3 to 3½ months after the eggs are laid.

Trachemys scripta
Common slider (plate 36)

Trachemys scripta is the only freshwater turtle in Costa Rica whose head and neck are greenish or gray and marked with prominent yellow or orange stripes.

The common slider is a large turtle, capable of reaching a shell length of up to 600 mm (23⅝ inches), although most individuals are substantially smaller. Many will recognize this species as the larger cousin of the diminutive baby turtles sold by the millions in pet stores worldwide.

The shell (carapace) of this turtle is oval in outline when seen from above. Unlike the highly domed shells of the wood turtles (genus *Rhinoclemmys*), *Trachemys scripta* has a low carapace that sometimes bears a weak keel. The belly armor is not hinged, as in the mud turtles (family Kinosternidae). *Trachemys scripta* has a large head; its snout is slightly protuberant and very short, and the distance between the tip of the snout and the eyes is about equal to the diameter of the eye. The undersurface of the chin is typically rounded. This species has powerful limbs and well-developed webs between the fingers and toes, an adaptation to its aquatic habitat.

The color of the shell is olive or brown, with a pattern of yellow or red stripes, reticulations, and eyelike spots. This pattern is most distinct in juveniles, but it darkens with age and may become hard to discern. The skin of this species is green or brown and marked with distinct yellow or orange lines.

Trachemys scripta has the largest geographical distribution of all turtles, excluding the marine turtles. Its range includes the central and eastern United States, Mexico, all of Central America, Colombia, and Venezuela. Isolated populations occur in Brazil, Uruguay, and Argentina. Within Costa Rica, this species is most often seen basking on logs in lowland rivers, streams, swamps, and ponds on both sides of the country.

Research on Panamanian common sliders showed that reproduction mainly takes place in the dry season (December to May). Courtship and mating take place in the water. Females excavate a flask-shaped nest chamber in a dry, sun-exposed area, into which 9 to 35 eggs measuring about 35 mm (1⅜ inches) in diameter are deposited. *Trachemys scripta* nests are not always located near water; they have been found as far as 1.6 km (1 mi) from the nearest river. Females may produce multiple clutches every year; the clutch size is positively correlated with the size of the female.

The eggs hatch after 2 to 2½ months, but the hatchling turtles stay inside the nest until the rainy season commences (usually May or June). Panamanian hatchlings are known to spend up to two months inside the nest chamber after hatching; their relatives from temperate regions, such as in the United States, sometimes spend the entire winter inside the nest and do not emerge until springtime. Juveniles require 5 to 7 years to reach sexual maturity.

The gender of hatchlings is determined by the incubation temperature of the eggs. High incubation temperatures will result in offspring that are all females, while lower temperatures predominantly produce males (see page 134 on temperature-dependent sex determination).

Juveniles are mainly carnivorous, eating a wide variety of animals, including water insects, crustaceans, mollusks, tadpoles, and fish. As they mature, the diet becomes increasingly vegetarian.

These turtles are frequently eaten by crocodiles. This is substantiated by the discovery in Mexico of a *Trachemys scripta* with crocodilian teeth-marks on its shell, and by frequent observation of adults with one or more missing limbs. In Caño Negro, in northern Costa Rica, raccoons are reported to prey extensively on the eggs.

Throughout their entire distribution range, common slider turtles suffer tremendously from hunting and collecting by humans. Eggs are collected for consumption, and adult turtles are hunted for their meat and shells. Many baby sliders end up in stores or markets to be sold as pets. Most Costa Rican populations, as well as those of other countries, have been greatly reduced in recent years.

It has been suggested that common sliders could be used as biological control agents to fight the aquatic plant *Eichhornia crassipes*. This plant has become a pest in parts of Costa Rica, locally growing in such abundance that entire waterways have become clogged. There is some disagreement as to the feasibility of such a project.

In older literature pertaining to this species, *Trachemys scripta* is also referred to as *Pseudemys scripta, Chrysemys scripta,* or *Chrysemys ornata.*

Literature

Acuña-Mesén 1998; Ernst 1980a,b, 1983a,b; Ernst & Barbour 1989; Himmelstein 1980, Lee 1996; Mudde & van Dijk 1984a; Savage & Villa 1986; Zug 1993.

FAMILY: **Kinosternidae** (Mud Turtles)
ORDER: Testudines (Turtles)

Members of the family Kinosternidae range widely throughout the Americas, from the United States through Mexico and Central America and into South America as far south as Bolivia and Argentina. Most mud turtles are small, usually with a carapace length between 150 and 200 mm (5⅞ and 7⅞ inches), and have a highly domed shell.

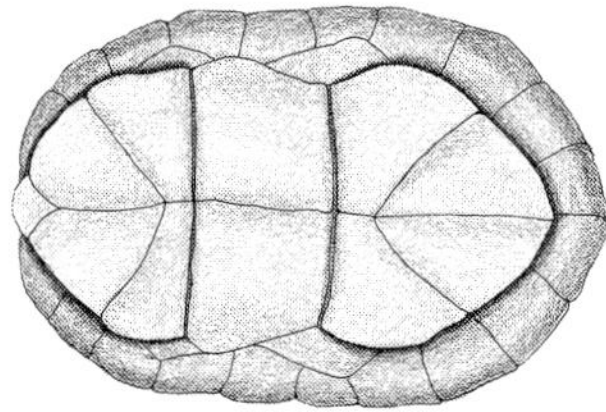
Ventral view of the **white-lipped mud turtle** (*Kinosternon leucostomum*) hiding within its closed shell.

Three species of mud turtle occur in Costa Rica: the narrow-bridged mud turtle (*Kinosternon angustipons*), the white-lipped mud turtle (*Kinosternon leucostomum*), and the red-cheeked mud turtle (*Kinosternon scorpioides*).

A distinguishing feature of all species in the genus *Kinosternon* is hinged belly armor (plastron). Costa Rican species either possess a single hinge (*Kinosternon leucostomum* and *Kinosternon scorpioides*) or two hinges (*Kinosternon angustipons*) on the plastron. These hinges allow the turtle to close its shell, although the degree to which the shell can be closed varies from species to species. For example, the white-lipped mud turtle (*Kinosternon leucostomum*) is capable of closing its shell completely, leaving no parts of the body exposed to predators, whereas the rare narrow-bridged mud turtle (*Kinosternon angustipons*) leaves large parts of its body exposed, even with the shell closed.

All kinosternids are aquatic to a varying degree and prefer calm water. Poor swimmers, they move around mostly by walking on the bottom of quiet streams, rivers, and ponds, feeding on small animals, carrion, and occasionally vegetable matter. The Costa Rican mud turtles are also frequently found on land, and some even spend considerable amounts of time in terrestrial hiding places.

SUMMARY

How to identify Costa Rican mud turtles:

- All Costa Rican mud turtles are small to medium-sized turtles with a highly domed shell. They have hinged belly armor (plastron).

SPECIES DESCRIPTIONS

Kinosternon leucostomum

White-lipped mud turtle
Tortuga amarilla (plate 36)

Kinosternon leucostomum has single-hinged belly armor (plastron) that can be closed completely, leaving no soft body parts exposed to predators. This is a medium-sized mud turtle, reaching 174 mm (6⅞ inches) in carapace length. The shell is dark brown or black. Older turtles have a smooth shell; juveniles and young adults have a single keel along the middle of the shell that disappears with age. Two features that distinguish this species from other Costa Rican turtles are the white to cream-colored jaws and the yellowish stripe behind the eyes.

White-lipped mud turtles can be found on both coasts below 1,050 m (3,450 ft), although they avoid the dry Guanacaste area. This species inhabits wet lowland forests and is usually seen in or near streams, marshes, or ponds. It is also known to enter brackish waters and is one of the very few turtles in the world that inhabits cascading mountain streams. *Kinosternon leucostomum* may be active both during the day and at night.

Juveniles of this species are sometimes offered for sale as pets in Costa Rican markets.

Kinosternon scorpioides

Red-cheeked mud turtle
Tortuga candado (plate 37)

Kinosternon scorpioides is a small- to medium-sized mud turtle; the carapace of most adults measures between 150 and 175 mm (5⅞ and 6⅞ inches). The highly domed shell bears two or three keels that run down the middle of the shell. As these animals age, the keels on the shell may become increasingly less visible, and even disappear entirely. The shell is usually a uniform shade of brown or tan; the plastron is usually orangish, though in rare cases it is yellowish. The single-hinged belly armor (plastron) is not always large enough to completely protect the soft body parts from predators.

The background color of the head, limbs, and tail is dark brown, while the jaw sheaths normally are of a slightly lighter shade of brown. The sides of the head are adorned with light brown markings, usually with bright orange or red spots as well. This combination of a keeled shell and bright orange or red spots on the sides of the head is unique among Costa Rican turtles.

Females are normally smaller than males, with a shorter tail and a less strongly hooked upper jaw. Males have a sharp, keratinized nail on the tip of their long and very muscular tail. This particular feature explains the scientific name *scorpioides*, which means "scorpionlike."

Kinosternon scorpioides has a vast distribution range, extending from Mexico through Central America and into South America as far south as central Brazil and northern Argentina. Within Costa Rica, this turtle is found at low elevations on the Pacific slope.

This species is probably the most commonly observed mud turtle in Costa Rica. It may inhabit marshes or almost any other stagnant body of water, but it also lives in slow-moving parts of large rivers or even in streams, sometimes in surprisingly high numbers. Occasionally, these animals wander onto land and are found at considerable distances from the nearest aquatic habitat.

In arid northwestern Costa Rica, where ponds and rivers may dry up completely during the dry season, *Kinosternon scorpioides* survives such unfavorable conditions by burying into the mud, awaiting the next rainy season. Even so, severe and prolonged droughts may result in death through dehydration, suffocation, or starvation. Both naturally caused brush fires and slash-and-burn agriculture are responsible for the loss of many turtles' lives. Of the 164 dead *Kinosternon scorpioides* examined within one year at Palo Verde, Guanacaste, 140 died during the course of a three-day fire, while the remaining 24 died of other causes during the rest of the year. Juveniles seem to be affected most by fires, and the annual burning of cultivated land in northwestern Costa Rica seriously endangers the replenishing of Costa Rican populations.

Red-cheeked mud turtles mainly feed on aquatic invertebrates, but an occasional fish or amphibian might be taken as well. They have also been observed to eat plants.

Females lay 5 to 10 somewhat elliptical eggs in a shallow, depressionlike nest excavated close to the water's edge. The incubation period of the eggs is about 3 months.

In some parts of Central America, the meat of *Kinosternon scorpioides* is thought to have medicinal properties and to cure heart conditions. In Costa Rica, however, people do not usually eat this species.

These turtles help reduce the populations of snails that are host to cercaria and metacercaria, parasites that cause severe lesions in cattle. And since they also feed on mosquito larvae, they may play a role in reducing malaria and dengue fever outbreaks.

Literature

Acuña Mesén 1990, 1998; Ernst & Barbour 1989; Lee 1996; Mudde & van Dijk 1984a; Savage & Villa 1986; Zug 1993.

FAMILY: **Chelydridae** (Snapping Turtles)
ORDER: Testudines (Turtles)

The only living representatives of this small, strictly American family are two species of large aquatic turtles, each placed in a separate genus. Among the largest freshwater turtles in the world, both species are aggressive and have an extremely nasty bite. These prehistoric-looking turtles are characterized by a flattened shell (carapace) with three rows of conspicuous pointed keels; the rear margin of the carapace is strongly serrated. Typically, the belly armor (plastron) is cross-shaped and very small. A very long tail, almost the same length as the shell, powerful legs, and a massive head protrude from the armor. These turtles appear to have outgrown their shell.

The **snapping turtle** (*Chelydra serpentina*) is the only representative of the family Chelydridae in Costa Rica.

Macroclemys temmincki, the alligator snapping turtle of southeastern and central United States, is the world's largest freshwater turtle, reaching a carapace length of over 700 mm (27½ inches) and a weight of up to 80 kg (176 lbs). The other member of this family, *Chelydra serpentina*, has an extensive range that includes Costa Rica. Although it is smaller than the alligator snapping turtle, large adults are a very impressive sight.

SUMMARY

How to identify Costa Rican snapping turtles:

- The only snapping turtle species in Costa Rica is a large turtle with a very long tail and neck. Its shell (carapace) bears three rows of conspicuous pointed keels and has a saw-toothed rear margin.

SPECIES DESCRIPTION

Chelydra serpentina

Common snapping turtle
Tortuga lagarto (plate 37)

Though its size alone can distinguish this species from all other Costa Rican freshwater turtles, its appearance is unique in other respects. *Chelydra serpentina* has a huge head with a pointed snout, and very strong, beaklike jaws. On first glance, the entire turtle gives a spiky impression; the shell (carapace) and the exposed skin of many body parts bear scattered pointed keels and tubercles, the carapace has three rows of saw-toothed keels, and the posterior margin of the shell is strongly serrated. The tail, which is surprisingly long, can be the same length as the shell, and bears two longitudinal rows of large protruding scales.

This aquatic giant may reach a carapace length of up to 50 cm (19⅝ inches) and weigh roughly 20 kg (44 lbs), although individuals more commonly measure between 20 and 30 cm (8 and 12 inches).

Chelydra serpentina is a more-or-less unicolored turtle, with a background color that can be olive, gray, or varying shades of brown, from tan to almost black. Algal growth and mud may give the animal a mottled appearance. The belly armor (plastron) is unpatterned and of a lighter color than the shell, usually yellowish or tan.

Chelydra serpentina ranges from southern Canada and most of the United States through Mexico and Central America and into South America as far as Ecuador. In Costa Rica, these turtles have been found in the lowlands of both the Atlantic and the Pacific slopes, to an elevation of at least 550 m (1,800 ft).

It is relatively uncommon to see a snapping turtle in Costa Rica, but they can be seen in stagnant bodies of water or in slow-moving rivers and forest streams. They prefer waters with a soft, muddy bottom and abundant aquatic vegetation, although they are also known to enter brackish water at times. This species prefers warm shallows, where it generally remains motionless, buried in mud, occasionally extending its long neck and snout out of the water to breathe.

Not much is known about tropical snapping turtles, although the biology of those in the northern part of the range is fairly well-studied. This highly aquatic turtle is an excellent swimmer; it rarely leaves the water, although in temperate zones females have been observed to travel considerable distances overland to find a suitable nest site. The nest consists of a flask-shaped cavity that is dug by the female; 20 to 40 ping-pong-ball eggs are usually deposited, but as many as 83 eggs have been reported from a single female. The female uses her hind feet to place the eggs inside the nest. In Costa Rica, snapping turtles start nesting around June. Incubation lasts between 55 and 125 days, depending on the ambient temperature. The ambient temperature not only determines the length of the incubation period, it also determines the gender of the hatchlings. At incubation temperatures below 20°C (68°F) and above 30°C (86°F) only females will hatch. At intermediate temperatures mostly males are produced (see page 134 on temperature-dependent sex determination). Female snapping turtles are capable of retaining viable sperm for many years, and they can produce several clutches of fertilized eggs after mating only once.

Chelydra serpentina is omnivorous; its prey includes aquatic invertebrates, fish, amphibians, reptiles, waterfowl, and small mammals, as well as aquatic plants. Snapping turtles are also good scavengers and consume a fair amount of carrion.

Man is doubtless the most significant hunter of these turtles, which have few predators. Hunters prize the meat, especially in the United States, where "snapper" meat is considered a delicacy in some regions. The eggs of this turtle are favored over those of marine turtles by some, and are collected for human consumption. Juveniles, sometimes labeled "living fossil turtles," are sold as pets or souvenirs.

Snapping turtles have a vicious temper and will readily defend themselves, especially when encountered out of the water. When harassed or handled, *Chelydra serpentina* will strike with such speed that the forepart of its body may be lifted off the ground. Since their powerful, hooked jaws can cause severe injuries, and since their surprisingly long neck gives them considerable reach (at least half the length of the shell), it is advisable to stay clear of these animals and treat them with great respect.

Costa Rican individuals are placed in the subspecies *Chelydra serpentina acutirostris*. Because of certain morphological traits, such as the low, rounded shape of the tubercles on the back of the neck, and its geographical isolation in lower Central America, some authors have suggested that this subspecies should be treated as a valid species, *Chelydra acutirostris*. However, this view is definitely not shared by all herpetologists.

Literature

Acuña Mesén 1998; Ernst 1988; Ernst & Barbour 1989; Lee 1996; Vogt & Flores-Villela 1992; Zug 1993.

ORDER: **Squamata** (Lizards and Snakes)
CLASS: Reptiles

Lizards, snakes, and a third group not found in Costa Rica, the Amphisbaenia, form the order Squamata. There are roughly 2,700 snake species and over 3,300 lizard species distributed throughout the world, except for on some islands and in colder latitudes (although some species do enter the polar circle). In Costa Rica, a dazzling variety of lizards and snakes is present virtually everywhere in the country.

It may seem strange that lizards and snakes are grouped together in a single order, but snakes have evolved from specific groups of living lizards, and they are very closely related. Evidence of this ancestry can be seen in some primitive snakes, such as *Boa constrictor*, that still bear vestigial remains of a pelvic girdle and hind limbs.

Lizards are a very successful group of reptiles that have adapted to a wide variety of habitats and climatic conditions. Some species are found within the polar circle, while others inhabit hot and humid tropical rainforests, bone-dry deserts, and even marine environments. Most species are terrestrial, but tree-climbing, burrowing, and even aquatic lizards exist.

Considering the variety of lifestyles and habitats, it is surprising that the general morphology of lizards is not more varied. Typically, lizards are four-legged and have elongated bodies and long tails.

Costa Rica is home to 73 species of lizards, divided into 11 families (see table 6).

Table 6: Taxonomy of Costa Rican Lizards

Family	*Common Name*	*Number of Species*
Eublepharidae	Banded geckos	1
Gekkonidae	Geckos	11
Corytophanidae	Casque-headed iguanas	4
Iguanidae	Iguanas	3
Polychrotidae	Anoles and allies	27
Phrynosomatidae	Spiny lizards and allies	3
Scincidae	Skinks	3
Gymnophthalmidae	Micro-teiid lizards	6
Teiidae	Whip-tailed lizards	6
Xantusidae	Night lizards	2
Anguidae	Anguid lizards	7

The size and shape of the scales on a lizard's body and head are keys to placing that individual in its proper family. Scalation characteristics also can indicate the habitat or lifestyle of a lizard. The body and head of skinks, which are covered with similarly-sized, small, very smooth scales, are perfectly adapted for slipping through small openings without creating much friction. This is ideal for a lizard that spends its time moving through dense leaf litter on the forest floor. Iguanas, on the other hand, have rough scales that help them grip the trees they climb.

Many lizards are capable of autotomy, a defense strategy in which a lizard volitionally breaks off its tail in order to escape predation. Often, the discarded tail wiggles vigorously, thus attracting the attention of the predator and allowing the lizard to escape. In time a new tail grows back; this replacement tail lacks the vertebrae of the original. Although autotomy is a useful defense mechanism, it does involve several disadvantages. Until the new tail grows back, the lizard is without its tail's balancing effect. It becomes less agile and thus less able to escape predators quickly. Second, the energy expended in creating the new tail is no longer available for other important activities such as searching for food or searching for mates. Third, some lizards, including several geckos, store energy reserves (in the form of fat) in their tails. When these lizards lose their tail they are less likely to survive when prey is not abundant.

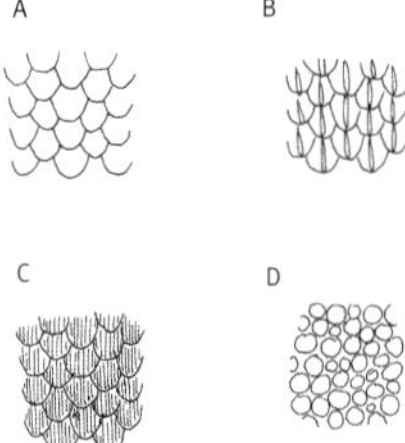

Scale types: (A) smooth cycloid, (B) keeled cycloid, (C) striated cycloid, and (D) granular.

Lizards, like snakes, shed their skin; juveniles shed more frequently than adults because they are growing. Lizards shed their skin in fragments, unlike snakes, which typically shed their entire skin in one piece. Some lizards eat their shed skin.

Certain species of lizards, such as geckos and night lizards, lack moveable eyelids. Their eyes are protected by a clear scale or spectacle that may become so scratched that vision is impaired. However, this clear scale is replaced by a new scale when the lizard sheds, and perfect vision is thus restored.

Contrary to popular belief, no Costa Rican lizard is venomous, nor do any sting with the tail. While some large iguanas whip their tail to defend themselves and all larger lizards deliver a painful bite, no Costa Rican lizard poses a serious threat to humans.

SUMMARY

How to identify Costa Rican lizards:

- Lizards are reptiles with four limbs and a long tail (although many lizards are capable of breaking off parts of their tail to escape predators, and in some animals part of the tail may be missing).

FAMILY: **Eublepharidae** (Banded Geckos)
SUBORDER: Lacertilia (Lizards)

Most members of the family Eublepharidae are found in the Old World. A single genus of banded geckos occurs in North and Central America, and its species range from the southwestern United States to northwestern Costa Rica.

Formerly, this family was considered a subfamily of the gecko family (family Gekkonidae). However, banded geckos differ from true geckos to such an extent that they are now placed in a separate family.

Central American banded gecko (*Coleonyx mitratus*).

The most obvious difference between banded geckos and true geckos is the presence of moveable eyelids in the former. This characteristic, along with fragile skin covered with small granular scales, should easily distinguish the only Costa Rican member of this family, the Central American banded gecko (*Coleonyx mitratus*), from all other lizards in the country.

SUMMARY

How to identify Costa Rican banded geckos:

- Only one species of banded gecko is found in Costa Rica. It is a night-active lizard whose body, head, and tail are covered with small, granular scales, and which has moveable eyelids.

SPECIES DESCRIPTION

Coleonyx mitratus
Central American banded gecko
Escorpión (plate 38)

Coleonyx mitratus is unique among Costa Rican lizards in having both moveable eyelids and skin covered with small, granular scales. All other Costa Rican lizards with small, granular scales on the body—all true geckos and the night lizards (family Xantusidae)—invariably have a spectacle-like, transparent scale that covers the eye and lack the moveable eyelids that characterize *Coleonyx mitratus*.

These are small to medium-sized lizards, measuring approximately 150 mm (5⅞ inches) in total length. They have narrow fingers and toes, without enlarged adhesive disks. The scales on the tips of their digits are formed into a sheath, which encloses the claws. Their large, protruding eyes have vertically elliptical pupils.

A pattern of wide, yellowish transverse crossbands on a dark brown background adorns the head, body, and tail of this species. This coloration is most evident in juveniles; with age, the pattern breaks up and the colors fade.

Coleonyx mitratus ranges from Guatemala and Honduras as far south as the lowlands of northwestern Costa Rica, where it is found strictly in the dry forests of Guanacaste Province. Unlike its North American cousins, which inhabit deserts or savannas, *Coleonyx mitratus* lives in the forest interior.

These lizards live on the forest floor, mostly hidden in leaf litter. They are predominantly active at night, but can sometimes be found during the day by removing the surface debris, logs, or rocks under which they hide. They have also been reported to live inside termite nests.

Very little is known about the biology of these shy and secretive lizards, but other *Coleonyx* species display behaviors that may also occur in *Coleonyx mitratus*. As a group, banded geckos are almost catlike in their graceful movements, a comparison that is reinforced by the observation that many banded geckos wave their tail like a prowling cat when stalking prey. Central American banded geckos feed on insects and spiders.

When alarmed, banded geckos raise their body off the round and assume a stiff-legged defensive posture; sometimes they inflate their throat, thus increasing the dramatic effect. Many species of the genus *Coleonyx* are also capable of emitting a high-pitched squeak when grabbed or otherwise provoked. Whether *Coleonyx mitratus* produces such calls is not known.

Female *Coleonyx mitratus* produce clutches of 2 eggs, each with a leathery shell that remains soft throughout incubation. The eggs are usually deposited beneath surface objects or in rock crevices. The lizard's main period of reproductive activity most likely takes place during the rainier months of the year.

Literature

Bustard 1968; Dixon 1970; Mudde & van Dijk 1984b; Sasa & Solórzano 1995; Savage & Villa 1986; Taylor 1956; Zug 1993.

FAMILY: **Gekkonidae** (Geckos)
SUBORDER: Lacertilia (Lizards)

This large family contains over 750 species worldwide. These small to medium-sized lizards can be characterized by their immovable eyelids; each eye is covered with a clear spectacle. Since these lizards are incapable of clearing irritating particles from their eyes by blinking, geckos use their tongue to lick their eyes clean. All geckos, including the banded geckos (family Eublepharidae), have delicate skin that is covered with small granular scales.

House gecko (*Hemidactylus frenatus*). This species has the lidless eyes and silky skin covered with small granular scales that characterize all true geckos.

The gecko family comprises species with a wide variety of body shapes, but most are adapted to life in trees and have a flattened body with a low center of gravity. Another commonly seen adaptation to life on vertical surfaces is the presence of enlarged overlapping adhesive disks under the tips of the toes and fingers. These disks allow them to cling to smooth upright surfaces, and geckos can be seen walking on the glass surface of windows or even running upside-down across a ceiling. In some of the more terrestrial geckos, the finger and toe tips are narrow and not as suitable for climbing; often such species also have a less-flattened body.

Although most gecko species are active at night, some commonly bask in the late afternoon; several tropical species are strictly diurnal. Nocturnal species generally have vertically elliptical pupils; diurnal species have round pupils.

Many geckos are capable of producing calls that play a role in territorial behavior and courtship. The house gecko, *Hemidactylus frenatus*, an Old World species that most likely arrived in Costa Rica as a stowaway on cargo ships, has become increasingly abundant in villages on both coasts and has recently reached San José. Its distinctive call—a barking "*chack-chack-chack*"—is frequently heard both in the daytime and at night.

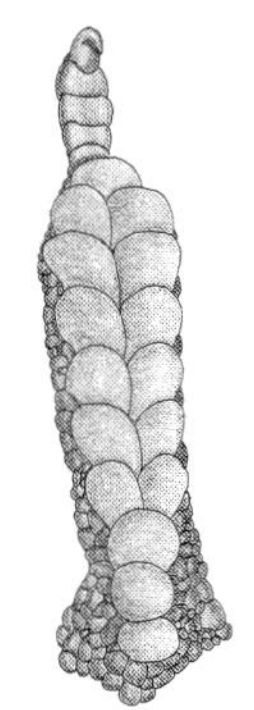

Adhesive disks on *Hemidactylus* toe.

Most gekkonids typically produce a clutch of two spherical eggs, although the dwarf geckos of the genus *Sphaerodactylus* and a few other small species produce a single egg per clutch. When deposited, a gecko egg has a sticky shell that adheres to the surface on which it is laid. As the shell dries, it hardens. In Costa Rica, gekkonids are the only lizards that produce spherical hard-shelled eggs; all other lizards lay elliptical eggs with a flexible leathery shell.

All geckos have a very fragile tail that breaks easily, and their velvety skin is so delicate that careless handling would tear it, harming the animal. You should not catch geckos by grabbing them with your hands; instead, attempt to make them run into a glass or other transparent container so that they can be observed without handling.

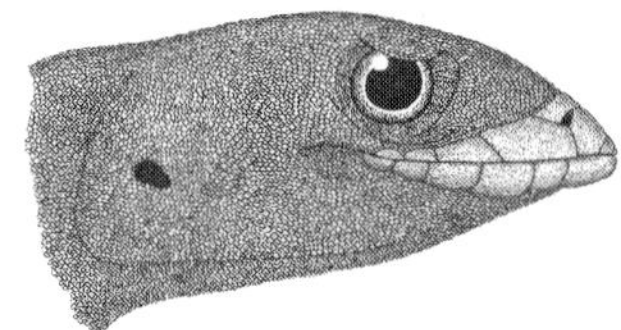

Leaf litter gecko *(Lepidoblepharis xanthostigma)*. This species' round pupils indicate that it is diurnal.

Currently, the Costa Rican gekkonids consist of 11 species in 7 genera. Three species of so-called wandering geckos (*Hemidactylus frenatus, Hemidactylus garnotii*, and *Lepidodactylus lugubris*) are non-native species that have migrated throughout the world on ships and floating driftwood. They are recent arrivals to Costa Rica, where they appear to be flourishing. The remaining, native gekkonids can be divided into two groups: the more typical geckos that are nocturnal and arboreal (*Phyllodactylus tuberculosus* and *Thecadactylus rapicauda*), and the diurnal, semiarboreal tiny geckos of the genera *Gonatodes, Lepidoblepharis*, and *Sphaerodactylus*.

SUMMARY

How to identify Costa Rican geckos:

- All geckos have delicate, velvety skin that is covered with small, granular scales; additionally, they all lack moveable eyelids—their eyes are covered with a clear spectacle.
- Some Costa Rican geckos have broadly expanded toes and fingers that enable them to walk on smooth, vertical surfaces. These lizards are usually nocturnal and have vertically elliptical pupils.
- Other Costa Rican geckos lack the expanded toes and fingers; these species are often active in the daytime and have round pupils.

SPECIES DESCRIPTION

Gonatodes albigularis
Yellow-headed gecko (plate 38)

Including tail length, these small geckos measure about 90 mm (3½ inches). *Gonatodes albigularis* is the only Costa Rican gecko that lacks expanded finger and toe tips and has a clearly visible, sharp claw on the tip of each digit.

Yellow-headed geckos have large eyes with round pupils. These round pupils, a feature generally uncommon in geckos, indicate that this species is mainly active during the day. All day long, yellow-headed geckos dart through shaded areas, chasing after crawling insects and spiders near their hiding place. In the early morning and late afternoon, they are often seen basking in the sun.

The male's coloration is particularly distinctive among Costa Rican lizards. The head, which ranges from bright yellow to orange, clearly stands out from the body and tail, which are dark brown to black. Often, a light-blue spot is present below the eye, and occasionally individuals have another light-blue spot above the point where the front legs join the body. The tail is white-tipped. The female's coloration differs distinctly from that of the male's. Her entire body is mottled with light brown, cream, and black; usually a light collar stripe is present. Juveniles resemble females in coloration. *Gonatodes albigularis* changes color at night. The male's head becomes darker; his body, which fades to blue-green, still remains distinct from the head. The female's coloration becomes gray.

Gonatodes albigularis ranges from Mexico south through Panama and into South America. This species has also been introduced into Florida. It is found at low elevations. In Costa Rica, yellow-headed geckos are commonly found in the lowlands along both coasts, but they are absent in the extreme southeastern part of the country. They are most frequently seen on tree trunks, walls, or fences, less than 2 to 3 m (7 to 10 ft) above the ground. They are also very common on the coconut palms that line most Costa Rican beaches.

Formerly, yellow-headed geckos could be seen on virtually every tree in the city park in Limón, a port city on the Caribbean coast. However, in early 1975, the Puerto Rican crested anole (*Ctenonotus cristatellus*) arrived as a stowaway and invaded the park, where it has now out-competed the geckos in that area.

Gonatodes albigularis reproduces continuously throughout the year, although reproductive activity occurs less frequently during the dry season and is at its peak in the rainy season. Each clutch the female produces consists of one small, spherical, hard-shelled egg. Eggs hatch about 4 months after being laid. Juveniles can reach sexual maturity at the age of 6 months, when they measure 40 mm (1⅝ inches).

Males are very territorial; when two males approach each other within 50 cm (20 inches), they assume a defensive posture, raising the body off the ground on outstretched legs and curling the tail over the back. While maintaining this posture, the males continue approaching each other in a jerky motion, until they are about 30 cm (12 inches) apart. At this point, the lizards have become highly agitated, and each begins shaking his head at the opponent. This will normally suffice to scare away one of the opponents, although sometimes one of the geckos will run toward the other and try to push him away, or even bite.

Gonatodes albigularis, like most geckos, has a fragile tail that breaks off easily when seized. Additionally, these lizards have very delicate skin that tears when they are handled roughly. Although both the tail and skin will eventually regenerate, these injuries may hinder the lizard's ability to survive. These fragile animals should never be caught or handled.

Hemidactylus frenatus

House gecko (plate 39)

Hemidactylus frenatus is one of the so-called wandering geckos; although originally from the Old World tropics, it now inhabits many tropical and subtropical areas around the world. It arrived in Costa Rica at least a decade ago, probably as a stowaway on a cargo ship, and has now successfully settled in large parts of the country.

This species is commonly found around human settlements and is often seen at night on walls of buildings, where it hunts for insects that are attracted by electric lights.

House geckos are small lizards that reach a snout-vent length of around 50 mm (2 inches). During the day, they are brownish, tan, or grayish, but at night their coloration is considerably lighter. A distinctive characteristic of this species is the whorls of enlarged pointed scales that encircle the tail at regular intervals. These large scales stand out from the otherwise small scales that cover the body and tail; it is the smaller scales that give this lizard a velvety appearance.

A second Costa Rican species, *Hemidactylus garnotii*, is virtually indistinguishable from the house gecko. Although each species displays minute differences in scalation characteristics, these are only visible on museum specimens with the aid of a microscope.

One reason that *Hemidactylus frenatus* is so successful at colonizing new areas is that the females can retain viable sperm for up to 8 months. A single female is capable of producing at least 10 clutches of fertilized eggs isolated from males. Interestingly, the closely related *Hemidactylus garnotii* is capable of reproducing without copulating, a capacity called parthenogenesis. All young lizards produced in this way are females.

Like many other geckos, *Hemidactylus frenatus* is capable of producing sound. In fact, this is the most "talkative" species of lizard in Costa Rica. It's call, a distinctive barking "*chack-chack-chack*," is frequently heard both in the daytime and at night. Although both males and females call, it is mostly the larger males that produce these sounds—either as a territorial marker or to attract females.

Lepidoblepharis xanthostigma

Litter gecko (plate 39)

Lepidoblepharis xanthostigma, like all true geckos, does not have moveable eyelids, although a small flap of skin that protrudes over the eyes does look like an eyelid.

Lepidoblepharis xanthostigma has round pupils; its fingers and toes are almost round in cross-section and bear claws that retract into a sheath. These features distinguish it from the nocturnal geckos, which have vertical pupils and expanded finger and toe tips.

This species is very similar in appearance and habits to the diurnal dwarf geckos of the genus *Sphaerodactylus*. However, species of the genus *Sphaerodactylus* bear a small spinelike scale above the eyes, a feature absent in the litter gecko.

Litter geckos reach a snout-vent length of approximately 45 mm (1¾ inches).

This brown to gray-brown lizard is adorned with two dorsolateral stripes. Each stripe is light with a dark border and starts behind the eye and runs along the side of the back to the tail. A chevron-shaped light mark connects both dorsolateral stripes on the back of the head. In adult litter geckos, the chevron mark and the dorsolateral stripes are gray to whitish, while in juveniles these are usually orange and more pronounced. The body of adults and juveniles is peppered with small, diffuse gray specks. Adult *Lepidoblepharis xanthostigma* often have a brick red tail.

This small diurnal gecko is a common inhabitant of the leaf litter of humid and wet forests along both coasts of Costa Rica. It ranges from sea level to at least 750 m (2,450 ft).

Lepidoblepharis xanthostigma feeds on small insects and is probably an ant-specialist. On several occasions, individuals have been found inside buildings in forested areas, apparently having followed ant trails into the house.

Sphaerodactylus millepunctatus

Spotted dwarf gecko (plate 40)

The dwarf geckos of the genus *Sphaerodactylus* reach their highest diversity in the West Indies. Most species are Caribbean Island forms, although approximately 10 species inhabit the Central American mainland. Four species have been reported for Costa Rica, one of which, *Sphaerodactylus pacificus*, occurs only on Cocos Island. The remaining three species (*Sphaerodactylus graptolaemus, Sphaerodactylus homolepis*, and *Sphaerodactylus millepunctatus*) occur in the lowlands of various parts of the country.

Adult *Sphaerodactylus millepunctatus* measure between 24 and 31 mm (1 and 1¼ inches); including tail length, they may reach a total length of about 55 mm (2⅛ inches). They have short, stocky legs, and their hands and feet lack broadly expanded, adhesive tips on the fingers and toes. The large eyes have a round pupil, indicating that these lizards are primarily active during the day (most night-active reptiles and amphibians, including nocturnal geckos, typically have vertically elliptical pupils).

Adults usually have a salt-and-pepper pattern of dark and light specks on a tan or brown background. Compared to the somewhat indistinct coloration of their parents, juvenile *Sphaerodactylus millepunctatus* are beautifully colored. Their body and tail are marked with dark crossbands outlined in pink, on a light gray background, while the head is gray with several longitudinal black stripes.

Sphaerodactylus millepunctatus is a lowland gecko that ranges from Mexico to northeastern Costa Rica on the Atlantic slope; it also inhabits the Pacific slope in Nicaragua and northwestern Costa Rica.

These lizards may be common throughout their range, but because of their small size and secretive habits, they are rarely seen. For the same reason, little is known about their natural history. *Sphaerodactylus millepunctatus* feeds on tiny invertebrates, and individuals have been seen sitting next to ant trails, eating insects as they pass by. These geckos appear to inhabit the leaf-litter layer on the forest floor; they have also been found under loose bark, or in the crevices in the trunks of large strangler fig trees. On several occasions, *Sphaerodactylus* species have been found in buildings in or near dense rainforests. Although all dwarf geckos have relatively narrow finger and toe tips compared to truly arboreal geckos, they nevertheless are fairly good climbers. One individual of another Costa Rican species, *Sphaerodactylus homolepis*, was observed walking up a tree trunk about 7 m (23 ft) above the ground.

Although it is commonly believed that the bite—and sting of the tail—of this species are lethally dangerous, all species of gecko are harmless animals.

Thecadactylus rapicauda

Turnip-tail gecko (plate 40)

Thecadactylus rapicauda is by far the largest gecko in Costa Rica. It may exceed 100 mm (4 inches), excluding the length of the fragile tail.

This nocturnal creature inhabits rainforest trees in the Caribbean and southwestern lowlands of the country. During the day, it hides underneath loose bark or in crevices in the trunk, and at night it leaves its hiding place to hunt for invertebrate prey. There are indications that its diet consists mainly of cockroaches.

Turnip-tail geckos are excellent climbers, and individuals have been seen in the rainforest canopy at heights over 30 m (100 ft).

Thecadactylus rapicauda lay a single large egg, which generally measures 15 mm (½ inch) in diameter. An egg of this species discovered buried between leaves and treeroots contained a young individual that measured 50 mm (2 inches) before hatching.

This lizard derives its common name from its turnip-shaped tail, which is strongly constricted at the base and may be greatly swollen toward the tip because of fat reserves stored there.

Literature

Behler & King 1979; Bustard 1968; Mudde & van Dijk 1984b,f; Sasa & Solórzano 1995; Savage & Villa 1986; Schwartz 1973; Taylor 1956; Villa et al. 1988; Zug 1993.

FAMILY: **Corytophanidae** (Casque-headed Iguanas)
SUBORDER: Lacertilia (Lizards)

Three genera of Central American and South American lizards (*Basiliscus, Corytophanes,* and *Laemanctus*) are assigned to the family Corytophanidae. These lizards were formerly included in the large and diverse iguana family (family Iguanidae), but in 1989 this group of closely related species was elevated to family status. Several species are still commonly referred to as iguanas, even though they are no longer considered members of that family.

Striped basilisk (*Basiliscus vittatus*). Note the helmet-like casque on the head.

One of the most characteristic features of this family is a bony casque, or sail-like crest, on the head and neck. Typically, all of the lizards in this group have a compressed body and long, slender limbs; the tail is very long and can measure up to three times the combined length of the body and head. Most of these morphological traits are adaptations to life in trees and bushes. All corytophanids are excellent climbers, and they are frequently found in trees or low bushes.

Costa Rica is home to four species of casque-headed iguanas, in two genera; three species of basilisks (*Basiliscus basiliscus, Basiliscus plumifrons,* and *Basiliscus vittatus*) and the strange-looking helmeted iguana (*Corytophanes cristatus*) inhabit the lowland regions of both slopes. *Corytophanes cristatus* is an infrequently observed rainforest lizard. The basilisks, on the other hand, are conspicuously present along almost any stream or river, where they are frequently seen darting across the water surface on their hind legs.

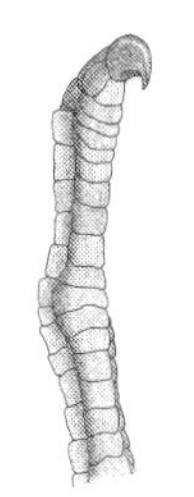
A seam of skin runs along the *Basiliscus* toe.

A narrow seam of skin, which runs around each basilisk toe, forms a moveable flap that is expanded when its foot is pressed onto the water, thus creating a larger surface area. The force that these lizards put into the downward movement of their feet produces an upward pressure that by itself creates almost a quarter of the total force required to keep the lizard from sinking. When the running basilisk presses its foot down onto the water, an air-filled pocket is formed around the foot. This pocket quickly fills with water, so the lizard must rapidly withdraw its foot to prevent from having to "plow" through the water. As the foot retracts, the moveable skin-flaps on the toes fold down against the sides of the toes to reduce friction against the air. The combined pressure that is produced during a single downward and upward stroke of the foot can be enough to provide 111% of the support required to allow an adult basilisk to run on water. Small juveniles, with a body weight of less than 2 g (0.07 oz), are capable of producing 225% of the upward pressure necessary for an animal of that weight. With the combination of speed and specially adapted toe fringes, these lizards can run considerable distances across the water surface, a trait that has given rise to the common name of "Jesus Christ lizard."

Apart from a few birds, no other animals have been able to copy this form of escape behavior. In order for a 80 kg (176 lbs) human to match a running basilisk's aquatic performance, he or she would have to run at almost 110 kph (69 mph) across the water and produce a muscle force 15 times greater than an average person is capable of.

Basilisks are named after the ancient Greek mythological figure Basiliskos. This monstrous creature had a crownlike crest on its head, fiery breath, and a deadly gaze.

SUMMARY

How to identify Costa Rican casque-headed iguanas:

- Casque-headed iguanas are fairly large lizards with a conspicuous, helmet-like crest on the head. The head, body, and tail are covered with numerous small scales; the head is never covered with large, symmetrical plates.
- These lizards typically have a compressed body, long slender limbs, and a very long tail. All species in this family are known to run on their hind limbs, and some even do so on water.

SPECIES DESCRIPTIONS

Basiliscus basiliscus

Common basilisk (plate 41)

The large common basilisk is the Pacific-slope counterpart of the green basilisk (*Basiliscus plumifrons*); the two species are very similar in biology and habitat choice. Males typically have high, sail-like crests on the head, back, and tail. These crests are weakly developed, or even absent, in females and juveniles.

A large lizard, *Basiliscus basiliscus* reaches a maximum length of 203 mm (8 inches); with the tail included, the maximum length is almost 800 mm (31½ inches).

Typically, *Basiliscus basiliscus* is brown or olive. A pair of white stripes—one on the upper lip and one along the side of the lizard—is present on each side of the animal. These stripes are distinct in juveniles, but fade with age. The brown background and white stripes are also found in the striped basilisk (*Basiliscus vittatus*), although that species is considerably smaller and the two species are separated geographically. *Basiliscus basiliscus* inhabits the Pacific lowlands, while *Basiliscus vittatus* is restricted to low elevations on the Caribbean slope.

Basiliscus basiliscus is found on the Pacific slope, from Nicaragua to northern Colombia. Like the other basilisks, it is found predominantly at low elevations, from sea level to at least 600 m (1,950 ft). This diurnal lizard is common along the edges of streams and lakes; basking adults are often seen on sandy stretches along watercourses.

When disturbed, *Basiliscus basiliscus* usually runs away on its hind legs, crossing water almost as readily as dry land. Because of the large surface area of the feet, created by moveable flaps of skin that line the toes, and the ability to run very quickly, these lizards are able to run across the surface of water some distance before finally sinking. In a study on the movement of these lizards, the average speed measured for a basilisk running on water was 8.4 kph (5.2 mph), only slightly less than their running speed on land. Both juveniles and adults appeared to run equally fast, but because juveniles weigh less, they manage to run on water a greater distance than adults. Large basilisks tend to run a short distance on the water surface before partially submerging, at which point they begin swimming.

Generally, basilisks escape into the water in order to avoid land-bound predators. The fact that they tend to minimize time in the water—even though they are good swimmers—suggests they may also be wary of aquatic predators.

Basiliscus basiliscus has an extremely varied diet and feeds on insects, scorpions, shrimp, and small vertebrates such as lizards, snakes, fish, mammals, and birds. Its diet is supplemented with vegetable matter such as flowers, fruits, and buds.

In the dry Guanacaste area, the reproductive season lasts for approximately 10 months of the year and comes to a pause during the driest months. Adult females reach sexual maturity about 1.5 years after they hatch. During the breeding season, they produce several clutches of between 2 and 18 eggs, with larger females laying more eggs per clutch than smaller females. The eggs hatch after about three months. On leaving the egg, juveniles must fend for themselves. Only about 60% of the hatchlings survive the first year since a wide variety of predators feeds on young basilisks.

Young males are sexually mature around the age of one year. However, because mating is generally the privilege of an old, dominant male, who actively defends the females within his territory against young competitors, these young males often do not reproduce until they are able to establish dominance themselves. This may not happen until the age of 3 or 4.

In nature, *Basiliscus basiliscus* reaches a maximum age of roughly 7 years, although a lifespan of 4 to 6 years is probably more usual.

Basiliscus plumifrons

Green basilisk (plate 42)

Adult males of this beautiful, large species are unmistakable: they are bright green and have sail-like crests on the head, back, and tail. Although females have smaller crests, their bright green coloration helps distinguish them from other Costa Rican lizards.

Basiliscus plumifrons reaches a maximum size of approximately 200 mm (7⅞ inches) and a combined body-tail length of almost 800 mm (31½ inches). It is the only basilisk whose adult males have two crests on the head as well as prominent crests on the back and tail; females and juveniles have weakly developed crests or none at all.

A distinguishing feature of *Basiliscus plumifrons* is its brilliant green coloration, adorned with blue and white spots on the sides. In the mating season, males have a blue throat. Juveniles, which display a less conspicuous coloration, are brownish or olive, with a green head; a pattern of dark transverse bands is often present on the back and tail. The juvenile pattern disappears gradually after individuals reach a snout-vent length of approximately 80 mm (3¼ inches). These lizards typically have bright yellow eyes.

Basiliscus plumifrons inhabits the Caribbean lowlands in southern Honduras, Nicaragua, Costa Rica, and possibly adjacent Panama. In Costa Rica, it has been reported at elevations of 1,200 m (3,950 ft), but it is most common at elevations below 500 m (1,650 ft).

Throughout much of its range, *Basiliscus plumifrons* co-occurs with the smaller, brown striped basilisk (*Basiliscus vittatus*), though its color, size, and larger crests distinguish it from the latter.

Basiliscus plumifrons is more arboreal and relatively less dependent on water than either of the other Costa Rican basilisks (*Basiliscus basiliscus* and *Basiliscus vittatus*); individuals are frequently found in trees or bushes at a considerable distance from any body of water.

Nevertheless, *Basiliscus plumifrons* is frequently seen on the banks of almost every river in the Caribbean lowlands and along the canals of Tortuguero. These lizards generally perch on logs, rocks, bushes, and even the sloping banks of rivers; they seem to prefer spots shaded by trees and bushes so that they are somewhat hidden from view. This contrasts with the behavior of the striped basilisks (*Basiliscus vittatus*), which almost invariably sit in full view. Because they are easier to see, it is sometimes mistakenly believed that *Basiliscus vittatus* is more common than *Basiliscus plumifrons*. Juveniles of *Basiliscus plumifrons* are less averse to open places than adults and are seen regularly on sunny days, basking on rocks or logs.

When approached, these lizards initially remain motionless; but when approached too closely, they launch themselves into water, or sometimes into dense vegetation. Like all basilisks, *Basiliscus plumifrons* can run a considerable distance across the surface of water on its hind legs. Moveable flaps of skin on the sides of each toe increase the surface area of the feet. This special foot structure, combined with the lizard's fast running speed, allow them to cross small bodies of water without sinking. Basilisks are also excellent swimmers, and often they simply escape by swimming away. Juveniles observed basking on large boulders in a forest stream escaped by diving into the water and clinging to the underside of rocks, hiding in air pockets. One individual remained in its submerged hiding spot for more than two hours before emerging again.

Like its relatives, green basilisks mainly feed on insects and other arthropods, although they occasionally eat small vertebrates. *Basiliscus plumifrons* has been observed to eat small lizards and even fish. In captivity, individuals have lived over ten years, although their maximum age in nature is probably considerably lower.

Basiliscus vittatus

Striped basilisk (page 42)

Basiliscus vittatus is the only lizard in the Caribbean lowlands with low crests on the head, back, and tail and a pattern of white stripes on the side of a brown body and head. It is also the smallest of the Costa Rican basilisks, with an average size of about 130 mm (5⅛ inches); including the tail, it measures nearly 550 mm (21⅝ inches). *Basiliscus vittatus* has a pointed, almost triangular crest on its head, as opposed to the more rounded helmet-shaped crests of *Basiliscus basiliscus* and *Basiliscus plumifrons*.

In Costa Rica, *Basiliscus vittatus* and the closely related green basilisk, *Basiliscus plumifrons*, both inhabit the Caribbean lowlands, but *Basiliscus vittatus* lacks the brilliant green coloration of the latter. Although *Basiliscus vittatus* is similar in appearance to the common basilisk (*Basiliscus basiliscus*), distinguishing between the two poses no problems since they live in different parts of the country. *Basiliscus vittatus* inhabits the Caribbean slope, while *Basiliscus basiliscus* is restricted to the Pacific lowlands.

This species is abundant throughout most of its range, which extends from Mexico south through the Atlantic lowlands of Central America and terminates in northern South America. It is known to occur from sea level to almost 1,200 m (3,950 ft), but individuals are mostly seen below 200 m (650 ft).

The biology of *Basiliscus vittatus* is very similar to that of the other two Costa Rican basilisks. Individuals are frequently seen near rivers, streams, and ponds, where during the day they scamper noisily through vegetation on the forest floor. When alarmed, they run on their hind legs toward water and skip across its surface.

As do all basilisks, this species lays eggs. During each annual breeding season, females are reported to produce at least 4 clutches of eggs. Each clutch contains, on average, 4 eggs. Most reproductive activity starts during the second half of the dry season; the majority of juveniles hatch at the beginning of the rainy season, which coincides with the period of highest insect density. Consequently, juveniles are assured a generous supply of invertebrate prey.

Basilisks are active hunters, and juveniles especially are often seen chasing insects. Although *Basiliscus vittatus* is mostly seen in exposed locations—more so than the other two species in Costa Rica—they are not easily approached and remain alert throughout the day. At night, they climb into low bushes and trees and sleep exposed on leaves or branches that overhang water. When the vegetation is disturbed by an approaching predator, they escape into the water.

Corytophanes cristatus

Helmeted iguana
Perro zompopo (plate *43*)

This is the only Costa Rican lizard that has both a large, serrated crest on the head (extending onto the neck and back) and a serrated, extendable throat fan.

Helmeted iguanas owe their common name to the prominent helmet-like crest on the head, which extends onto the back as a serrated skin flap. This crest is well-developed in both males and females, in contrast to the basilisks (genus *Basiliscus*), whose females have less-developed crests, or none at all. The crest continues down the middle of the back as a series of enlarged scales, forming a low, spiky ridge that ends at the base of the tail. The top of the head has a diamond-shaped depression bordered by bony ridges. These ridges start on the tip of the snout, pass over the eyes, and converge at a point halfway up the "helmet." A large, extendable throat fan with a saw-toothed edge extends from the throat to a point level with the insertion of the front limbs.

Corytophanes cristatus is a medium-sized lizard with a combined snout-vent length of at least 130 mm (5⅛ inches). The long, slightly compressed tail measures approximately 2 to 2.5 times the length of the head and body, and adults of this species usually have a total length of approximately 350 mm (13¾ inches).

Helmeted iguanas have long, slender limbs and very long toes, which lack the moveable fringes that allow *Basiliscus* species to run on water. The limbs and the undersides of the head, body, and tail are covered with very strongly keeled scales. Their large eyes have a round pupil and a coppery-red to orange iris.

These lizards can change their color rapidly, and individuals may be a reddish-brown, brown, tan, olive, or black color, sometimes with irregular blotches and spots. The limbs and the tail are often marked with dark or white spots; the belly is cream or white. When this lizard sits motionless in its natural environment, it looks very much like a dry branch spotted with lichens.

Corytophanes cristatus ranges from Mexico to northern Colombia. In Costa Rica, it is found at low and intermediate elevations along both coasts, in habitats ranging from dry forest in Guanacaste to the very wet Braulio Carillo National Park. Individuals have also been seen in secondary forests.

Field observations of these lizards are rare, both because population densities are apparently low and because the body shape and coloration of motionless individuals very much resembles the branches of a tree, making them difficult to see. Helmeted iguanas can remain still for hours perched on a branch or trunk, with their body pressed flat against the surface and their tail hanging down. Albeit rarely, *Corytophanes cristatus* is sometimes seen on the forest floor, where it runs in sudden short spurts; if pursued, individuals run on their hind legs only. In the trees, they move from branch to branch by jumping sideways, usually with several short hops in succession.

A Mexican specimen of *Corytophanes cristatus* was discovered with a liverwort, a mosslike plant, growing on its head. This piece of vegetation was found amidst a mass of green filamentous algae that almost completely covered the top of the lizard's head. The somewhat depressed area on top of the head of a helmeted iguana may retain some moisture when the lizard clings motionless to a branch. The humid area this creates seems perfect for the settlement and germination of liverworts; the spores necessary to initiate this colonization are ubiquitous in the lizard's habitat. The lifespan of the vegetation on top of the lizard's head is not long—the miniature garden disappears as soon as the lizard sheds its skin.

Corytophanes cristatus is a sit-and-wait predator; it sits, waiting to ambush any suitable prey that may pass, then it jumps toward the prey and grabs it in rapid motion. These lizards eat a wide variety of insects and spiders, but seem to prefer very large katydids, grasshoppers, and caterpillars. They are also known to occasionally eat small anole lizards.

Normally, stealth and camouflage render these lizards invisible to their predators. When they do find themselves threatened, however, individuals display a repertoire of defensive actions. They may play dead by freezing their position. This sometimes leaves them in very awkward looking postures, which they are capable of maintaining for hours. When confronted with a snake, these lizards have been observed to expand the skin that connects the crest to the back by elevating their helmet and extending their throat fan. Simultaneously, they compress their body and raise it off the ground, stretching out their legs. These actions are an attempt to appear larger in the eyes of the predator. Individuals sometimes lunge forward with their mouth open; this is generally to feign an attack, but sometimes to bite ferociously.

Perhaps because of these defensive displays, some Costa Rican *campesinos* mistakenly believe these lizards are extremely aggressive and venomous. *Corytophanes cristatus* is in fact a harmless animal.

Corytophanes cristatus lays eggs (of the three known species of *Corytophanes*, two lay eggs and one is live-bearing). There are indications that reproduction takes place year-round and that females are capable of retaining sperm for a prolonged period of time after mating. Because of their low population density and stationary lifestyle, male and female encounters are probably infrequent. Sperm storage is a fairly common survival strategy in reptiles and in some amphibians; it enables the female to lay her eggs whenever specific environmental or bodily conditions are ideal, regardless of whether an appropriate mate is at hand.

Females lay their eggs in a nest that is excavated in the forest floor. Nests are between 50 and 100 mm (2 and 4 inches) in diameter. In one observation, a female who had just laid her eggs vigorously defended her nest against intruders by expanding her throat fan and crest, and by gaping and lunging at researchers who attempted to examine the nest. This particular lizard, like females observed on other occasions, had soil on the depressed top of her head, suggesting that the ridged top of the head is used to construct nests.

Five or six eggs, with a length of about 20 mm (¾ inch) are laid inside the nest chamber and covered with soil afterwards. In captivity, eggs hatched roughly 6 months after they were laid; the incubation time in nature probably depends strongly on the ambient temperature.

Literature

Andrews 1979; Bock 1987; Boonman 1998; Davis 1953; Ferwerda 1993; Frost & Etheridge 1989; Glasheen & McMahon 1996, 1997; Gradstein & Equihua 1995; Hayes et al. 1989; Lee 1996; Leenders 1995a; Mudde & van Dijk 1984c; Rand & Marx 1967; Savage & Villa 1986; Zug 1993.

FAMILY: **Iguanidae** (Iguanas)
SUBORDER: Lacertilia (Lizards)

Members of the family Iguanidae are generally large, prehistoric-looking lizards with powerful limbs and a long tail. All species have a spiky appearance due to the comblike, pointed crests on the head, back, and tail and the spines on the tail.

In spite of their often intimidating appearance, iguanas are harmless creatures when left undisturbed. Some species are strictly vegetarian, while others consume varying quantities of plant and animal food throughout their lives.

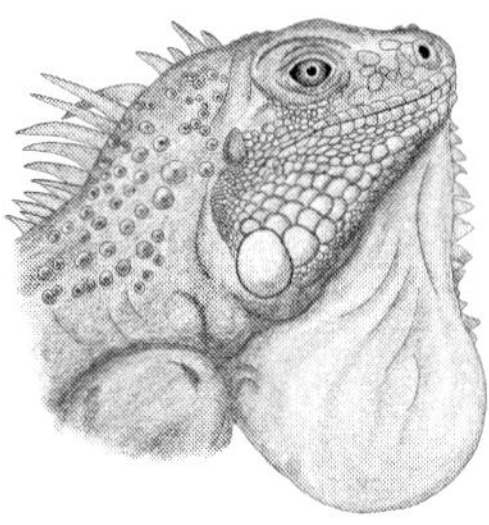
Green iguana (*Iguana iguana*).

Three species of iguanas are found in Costa Rica: the green iguana (*Iguana iguana*) and two species of spiny-tailed iguanas, the black spiny-tailed iguana (*Ctenosaura similis*) and the five-keeled spiny-tailed iguana (*Ctenosaura quinquecarinata*). The first two species are very large lizards; the latter species is substantially smaller. The green iguana is common in the lowlands of both coasts, but the black spiny-tailed iguana is found only in the lowlands of the Pacific coast. The third species is restricted to a few isolated areas in Santa Rosa National Park in northwestern Guanacaste Province.

SUMMARY

How to identify Costa Rican iguanas:

- Iguanas are large to very large lizards with a conspicuous comblike spiny crest on the head, back, and tail. Their head, body, and tail are covered with numerous small scales; the head is never covered with large, symmetrical plates.
- While all iguanas have spiky tails, only spiny-tailed iguanas (genus *Ctenosaura*) have whorls of large spines that encircle the tail at regular intervals.

SPECIES DESCRIPTIONS

Ctenosaura quinquecarinata
Five-keeled spiny-tailed iguana
(plate 43)

This species of spiny-tailed iguana has a very low crest on its head, back, and tail. The skin has pointed, enlarged scales. While the crest is continuous on the back and tail of the black spiny-tailed iguana (*Ctenosaura similis*), it is interrupted at the base of the tail in *Ctenosaura quinquecarinata*.

Ctenosaura quinquecarinata, which ranks among the smaller spiny-tailed iguanas, is significantly smaller than the black spiny-tailed iguana (*Ctenosaura similis*). It reaches a maximum snout to vent length of 185 mm (7¼ inches), and its total length, including tail, does not exceed 50 cm (20 inches). Five-keeled spiny-tailed iguanas have whorls of pointed scales encircling their tail; the middle row and two rows on each side are heavily keeled, forming five longitudinal keels that run the entire length of the tail, hence their common name.

Adults are usually olive-green to gray, with a pattern of dark transverse bands that may be fused on the middle of the back. An irregular pattern of green is present between these crossbands. The limbs are either uniform olive-green or marked with a pattern of spots or bands. On the underside, these lizards are grayish-white with black spots; this coloration extends onto the throat, where the black spots may form a pattern of diffuse streaks. Like its relative, *Ctenosaura similis*, the juveniles of this species are bright green.

Ctenosaura quinquecarinata has a discontinuous range, with isolated populations occurring in relatively small areas in Mexico, Nicaragua, and Costa Rica. In Costa Rica, it is only found in a few spots in Santa Rosa National Park, at elevations below 600 m (1,950 ft).

These lizards are exclusively found in dry subtropical forests and arid bushy savannas, where they live in and around a preferred burrow. Their hole is usually located in tree stumps, or underneath large rocks or logs. A steeply sloping terrain and the presence of many potential hiding places seem to be required for these extremely shy animals to feel at home. Each burrow typically contains only a single individual.

Ctenosaura quinquecarinata are mostly seen when basking, usually during the hottest time of the day, exposed on a branch or rock. They are never far from the entrance of their refuge, however; at the least sign of disturbance, they retreat hurriedly.

All adult spiny-tailed iguanas are predominantly vegetarians, and this is also true for *Ctenosaura quinquecarinata*. Examination of their stomach contents has revealed mainly fruits and leaves, but occasionally invertebrates are also eaten.

This species was formerly known as *Enyaliosaurus quinquecarinatus*.

Ctenosaura similis

Black spiny-tailed iguana
Iguana negra (plate 44)

In Costa Rica, *Ctenosaura similis* is surpassed in size only by the green iguana (*Iguana iguana*). The largest *Ctenosaura similis* known is an adult male, measuring 489 mm (19¼ inches) from snout to vent. However, males normally measure around 350 mm (13¾ inches), and females 275 mm (10⅞ inches). The tail in adults may be 1.5 to 2 times the length of the head and body combined, and the total length of these lizards often surpasses 100 cm (40 inches).

Ctenosaura similis is impressive not only because of its size. Adult males appear extremely powerful with their massive elongate head, muscular body and limbs, and long tail. The spiky crest that adorns the back and the rings of enlarged, spiny scales on the tail complete the dinosaur-like look of these lizards. Females are smaller and less robust in their proportions; they have a more delicate head and a lower crest.

Despite its name, the black spiny-tailed iguana is not generally black, although adults are capable of making their coloration darker or lighter and may sometimes be nearly black. Generally, this iguana's color pattern consists of broad, black transverse bands on a background of tan, olive-brown, or bluish-gray. The tail is marked with a series of dark rings, as are the limbs. The head may be a slightly different color than the body—orange, yellow, and bluish hues have been recorded. Hatchlings are either greenish or tan, but they change to a bright yellowish-green/leaf-green color soon after leaving the egg. Juveniles retain this color until about six months of age, when they measure about 120 mm (4¾ inches) from snout to vent, after which they gradually take on adult coloration.

In addition to having a completely different coloration than adults, the juveniles' crests are also poorly developed. Although they very much resemble juvenile green iguanas (*Iguana*

iguana), they are distinguished from the latter by conspicuous rings of spiny scales on their tail. Adult *Ctenosaura similis* are distinguished from *Iguana iguana* in that they lack the conspicuous large circular scale on each side of the head, just below the ear, that is characteristic of the latter species.

Ctenosaura similis ranges from Mexico to Panama and is found throughout Central America. In Costa Rica, it lives in the Pacific lowlands, from the dry deciduous forests of Guanacaste to the extremely wet Osa Peninsula. It is a very common inhabitant of the vegetation lining the beaches of the entire Pacific coast.

These iguanas bask on bright sunny days and can tolerate very high temperatures. Individuals have been observed on sun-exposed corrugated-iron roofs at midday, when the air temperature was over 30°C (86°F). On overcast rainy days, they stay inside their burrows, emerging when the skies clear and the sun begins to shine.

Adults are excellent climbers and are often seen perched on branches high in the crowns of large trees. Many individuals spend the night sleeping inside hollow branches. Juveniles, on the other hand, are mostly active on the ground, although they often sleep exposed on twigs and leaves in low vegetation.

The daily activities of individual *Ctenosaura similis* are centered around a hiding place, which is usually a burrow in the ground but may also be a hollow branch or tree trunk. The lizards excavate holes in the ground by digging with their strong legs and sharp claws. These holes are usually made beneath rocks or logs to keep predators from digging through the roof of the burrow. Their tunnels, which sometimes branch and wind, are usually not much more than 1 meter (40 inches) deep.

Another type of burrow is excavated by females prior to laying their eggs. In an open, sunny area, the female constructs a long 11- to 22-m (36- to 72-ft) winding tunnel, with several branches, dead ends, and chambers. These breeding burrows are usually close to the surface, only about 30 cm (1 ft) deep. Though shallow, the sand on the bottom of the chamber retains sufficient humidity to incubate the eggs. Several females may use the same tunnel system, but each deposits her eggs in a separate chamber.

Compared to most lizards, females of this species are prolific egg layers. All females lay eggs once a year, starting when they reach sexual maturity at the end of their second year. As the female continues to grow, the number of eggs per clutch increases. Clutch sizes ranging from 12 to 88 eggs have been reported, but the typical number of eggs laid per clutch seems to be from 40 to 45. The eggs are laid just before the end of the dry season (around March), and the first hatchlings appear starting in April. Most juveniles emerge between May and August, at the beginning of the rainy season, a time that parallels the period when the maximum amount of the lizards' prey is available. Furthermore, the bright green juveniles match the young, new vegetation that springs up after the first heavy rains, which may increase their chances of survival.

During the early rainy season, the population density of *Ctenosaura similis* may be very high. Juveniles are sometimes aggressive toward each other, but they do not evoke defensive behavior in adults. Adults, on the other hand, especially older males, are extremely territorial and vigorously stand their ground when defending their burrow and perches against intruders. A single dominant male inhabits an area in which only females and juvenile males are allowed. If a potential competitor enters the male's domain, a ritualized defensive behavior follows. The resident male performs a head-bobbing display in which the head is jerked upward and lowered again in a bouncing motion. The intruder will answer this display by imitating the head-bobbing pattern of the first male. Normally, territorial disputes are settled solely by head-bobbing, but sometimes encounters end in fighting. Head-bobbing is widespread among iguanas, although each species uses slightly different routines and motions to communicate.

These iguanas are true omnivores. Juveniles predominantly eat insects and other arthropods, but become increasingly vegetarian as they mature. The diet of large adults consists mainly of leaves, buds, and fruits. Though predominantly vegetarian, adults occasionally eat relatively large vertebrate prey, such as lizards, frogs, rodents, bird chicks and adult birds, eggs of other lizards, and even their own species. One individual was seen with a bat in its mouth.

Juveniles of this species have many predators and are eaten in large numbers by various species of snakes, birds of prey, and some mammals (raccoons, for example). The most significant predator of adult *Ctenosaura similis* is man. The meat of black spiny-tailed iguanas is prized throughout Central America, and they are often caught and eaten by local *campesinos*. One of their Spanish common names, *gallina de palo* (tree chicken), attests to the flavor of their flesh. Apart from being edible, the flesh is also accredited with several medicinal properties; a supposed cure for impotence appears to be the most widely accepted.

Although they may appear abundant locally, black spiny-tailed iguanas suffer from overhunting throughout much of their range, and their numbers are declining steadily. Management plans for several populations, as well as captive breeding programs, are being developed to ensure the prolonged existence of this species.

Iguana iguana

Green iguana
Iguana verde (plate 44)

This is the largest species of lizard in Costa Rica, and its sheer size is often sufficient to distinguish it from other lizards. Other characteristic features are a conspicuous crest of comblike spines down the neck, back, and tail and a large circular scale below each ear opening.

Measured from the snout to the base of the tail, adults reach an average size of approximately 300 to 350 mm (11¾ to 13¾ inches); adult males sometimes greatly exceed these average sizes, and when the tail is included may reach a total length of almost 2 meters (78 inches). Female *Iguana iguana* are considerably smaller.

These dinosaur-like lizards have a robust, somewhat compressed body with muscular limbs that bear long, sharp claws; the tail is very long and whiplike. They have a short-snouted head that is equipped with a large flap of skin underneath the chin and throat. This throat fan, which bears a serrated edge, is especially well-developed in large males. A distinct, large circular scale is invariably present on each side of the head below the eardrum. This feature helps distinguish this species, particularly in the case of juveniles, whose crests and throat fan are not strongly developed. In most individuals, a series of pyramid-shaped, enlarged scales is present on each side of the neck.

The relatively small eyes of *Iguana iguana* typically have vertically elliptical pupils. A few projecting, spinelike scales may be present on top of the snout; the presence of these "rhinoceros" scales has been used to argue that individuals exhibiting this trait belong in a separate subspecies, *Iguana iguana rhinolopha*. However, this division is controversial and not generally accepted by the herpetological community.

Iguana iguana is bright green when young, but changes to gray, brown, greenish-gray, or even almost black as it grows older. Normally, a pattern of wide black transverse bars on the back and tail is present. During the breeding season, the male's head sometimes becomes patterned with splashes of orange or yellow.

Native to Central and South America, *Iguana iguana* occurs from southern Mexico to Brazil and Bolivia. This species also occurs on several Caribbean Islands. Within Costa Rica, it is distributed along both coasts, mainly at low elevations. These iguanas are commonly seen in trees lining the canals of Tortuguero or any other lowland river with forested banks.

Adults are agile climbers that descend to the ground only to lay eggs or to move to a part of the forest that they cannot reach via the canopy. Their preferred perches are on branches overhanging water, and large adult iguanas will not hesitate to dive into the water from great heights to escape danger. They will sometimes hide on the bottom of the river and swim away when the coast is clear, using their long tail for propulsion. When threatened or seized, these iguanas are formidable opponents and will not hesitate to bite; their lashing tail and sharp claws can cause serious damage.

Small juveniles of *Iguana iguana* spend most of their time on the ground, often forming large groups. They spend much of their time basking in the sun and hunting for insects and other invertebrates. As they get older, their food preference changes to a predominantly vegetarian diet.

Like most herbivorous vertebrates, *Iguana iguana* is unable to digest plant matter through direct action of the physical processes of its body. Cellulose, the main component of plant fibers, is degraded by microorganisms that live in the digestive tract of the herbivore. These microbes need a specific optimum temperature to function properly. In mammals, this usually approaches the normal body temperature of the host, but little is known of the temperature requirements or responses of these microbe populations in reptiles, whose body temperatures may fluctuate considerably depending on the ambient temperature. *Iguana iguana* appears to maintain a relatively constant body temperature of 36 to 37°C (96.8 to 98.6°F) during active daytime periods, when solar heat is available. Experiments have shown that when an iguana's body temperature dropped below this temperature, the efficiency of digestion decreased and required more time than at the optimal temperature.

The reproductive behavior of this species changes according to where it lives; in general, mating takes place during September, October, and November. Gravid females start excavating a nest burrow during the dry season, just before the eggs are laid. Up to 70 eggs have been reported from a single clutch, but the number of eggs differs according to geographic location and perhaps also with the size of the female. Juveniles hatch about three months after eggs are laid, just before the beginning of the rainy season, when prey becomes increasingly abundant. Black vultures (*Coragyps atratus*) have been reported to prey on the eggs of *Iguana iguana*. The attacks occurred while eggs were being laid or shortly thereafter, when the female was attempting to close the nest chamber.

Like the other large Costa Rican iguanid, the black spiny-tailed iguana (*Ctenosaura similis*), *Iguana iguana* are heavily hunted for their meat. Around human settlements, this species has suffered tremendously, and its numbers are declining throughout its entire distribution range. Additionally, thousands of these iguanas are caught annually to be sold as pets. For this reason, the import and export of *Iguana iguana* is now regulated by the Convention on International Trade in Endangered Species (CITES), and special permits are required to export these lizards from Costa Rica. In many places in Central America, special breeding projects have been initiated to restock natural populations of green iguanas that have been seriously reduced.

Literature

Behler & King 1979; Bock 1987; Boonman 1993; Dugan 1982; Frost & Etheridge 1989; Köhler 1995a,b; Lee 1996; Leenders 1996; Mudde & van Dijk 1984c; Rand & Myers 1990; Sasa & Solórzano 1995; Savage & Villa 1986; Schouten 1992; Sexton 1975; Troyer 1987; Villa & Scott 1967.

FAMILY: **Polychrotidae** (Anoles and allies)
SUBORDER: Lacertilia (Lizards)

The family Polychrotidae contains over 650 species of slender-bodied lizards. Formerly included in the iguana family (Iguanidae), species in this group were granted family status in 1989. More than half the species in this family are in the genus *Norops*, one of the largest and most diverse of all vertebrate genera.

Costa Rica is home to 27 species of Polychrotidae in four genera: *Ctenonotus, Dactyloa, Norops*, and *Polychrus*. In Costa Rica, species formerly assigned to the genus *Anolis* are currently assigned to three genera, *Ctenonotus, Dactyloa*, and *Norops*. Members of the genus *Anolis* are now thought to occur mainly on Caribbean islands—there are no species of *Anolis* in Costa Rica.

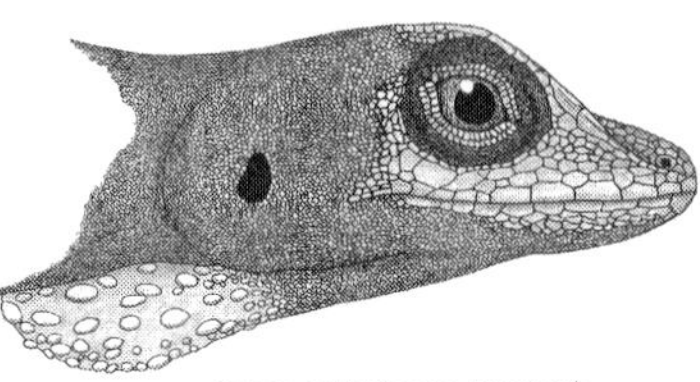

Canopy anole (*Norops lemurinus*). Most anoles have small scales that cover the head, body, and tail.

The introduced Puerto Rican anole, *Ctenonotus cristatellus*, is the only member of its genus in the country. Similarly, the chameleon-like canopy lizard, *Polychrus gutturosus*, is the only member of its genus in the country. A group of four giant anoles in the genus *Dactyloa* are rarely observed inhabitants of the rainforest's treetops. The remaining 21 species of anoles in the country are assigned to the genus *Norops*.

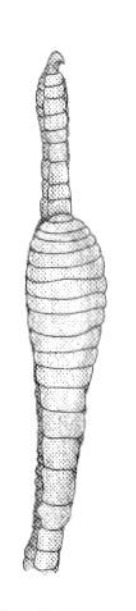

Anole toe.

All members of this family are small to medium-sized and have long limbs, a slender body, and a long tail. Anoles have broadly expanded toes and fingers that end in a narrow tip with a long claw. Most species are arboreal and inhabit various kinds of vegetation, from the twigs of low bushes to the trunks and canopy of some of the rainforest's largest trees. All species lay eggs; in most cases, one egg is produced every few weeks, year-round.

Generally, males are larger than females. The sexes are also distinguished by the swollen appearance of the tail base in males, marking the location of the reproductive organs. And the males of all Costa Rican species have an extendable throat fan, called a dewlap, that is usually brightly colored.

The dewlap is used by males in territorial conflicts with other males and in courtship rituals. Individual stream anoles (*Norops oxylophus*) have been observed trying to appear bigger during aggressive encounters with other males by turning the side of the body toward the opponent, raising the low crest on the back of the head, and slowly extending the dewlap. The colors of the dewlap are also used to attract potential mates. The dewlap of each male anole has a unique combination of size, color, and pattern.

Stream anole (*Norops oxylophus*) displaying dewlap.

Males also use head-bobbing displays during territorial conflicts, and both males and females display head-bobbing behavior to communicate in courtship rituals. The pattern of the head-bobbing display is species-specific.

Anoles are among the hardest lizards to identify. Not only is the variation in color pattern extreme in most species, but these lizards are also capable of considerable color change individually as a response to environmental stimuli. However, one part of the body always has the same coloration, the male's dewlap. Table 7 lists the dewlap colors of all Costa Rican anoles; this trait may be helpful in identifying an anonymous anole.

Table 7: Dewlap Colors for Most Adult Male Costa Rican Anoles

Species	***Dewlap Color***	***Remarks***
Norops woodi	dark olive-green to black	blue eyes
Norops capito	greenish-gray	very small dewlap
Ctenonotus cristatellus	greenish-yellow, sometimes with an orange margin	males with crests
Norops biporcatus	red with a pale-blue center	large lizard
Norops intermedius	bone white	
Dactyloa frenata	cream white	very large lizard
Norops limifrons	white with orange or yellow basal spot	very small dewlap
Norops townsendi	amber	only on Cocos Island
Norops sericeus	yellow or orange with a blue spot	
Dactyloa chocorum	pale orange with series of faint green longitudinal stripes, white margin	large lizard
Norops altae	orange	
Norops polylepis	orange	large dewlap
Norops oxylophus	uniform yellow-orange	large dewlap
Norops cupreus	orange-red to red with a light margin and a large white spot	large dewlap
Norops carpenteri	bright orange	
Norops pachypus	red-orange	highlands only
Norops aquaticus	red-orange with oblique yellow spots	
Norops humilis	red with a yellow margin	
Norops fungosus	red with a few white scales	
Norops vociferans	red with white scales	high Talamanca only
Norops lemurinus	dark red	small dewlap
Dactyloa insignis	dark red	very large lizard
Dactyloa microtus	pink with white scales	very large lizard
Norops pentaprion	purplish-red	
Norops tropidolepis	plum red to purple	highlands only
Polychrus gutturosus	green	

SUMMARY

How to identify Costa Rican anoles:

- Anoles are lizards with a slender body, a long tail, and long limbs. All male anoles, and some females, have a unique extendable throat fan that is often conspicuously colored.
- Anoles—including the canopy lizard—are small to medium-sized lizards with broadly expanded toes and fingers that end in a narrow tip with a long claw. Their head, body, and tail are covered with numerous small scales; the head is never covered with large, symmetrical plates.

SPECIES DESCRIPTIONS

Ctenonotus cristatellus

Puerto Rican crested anole (plate 45)

Ctenonotus cristatellus originally inhabited the Virgin Islands and Puerto Rico, but has been introduced to Central America. In Costa Rica, it inhabits the Caribbean coast near the port city of Limón.

This is the only anole in the country whose males have a low crest on the tail; females of this species also have a crest on the tail, but it is barely visible. The male and female of this species also have a crest on the back, as do many other species of anoles. In most other species, however, the crest on the back is generally not visible, except when displayed during territorial combat and courtship rituals.

There is a striking sexual dimorphism in this species. Males may reach a snout-vent length of up to 75 mm (3 inches), while females are up to 30% smaller. Furthermore, the crests on the tail and back of these lizards are considerably lower in females than in males. Mature males also have an additional crest on the neck that is only erected during aggressive and courtship displays.

Puerto Rican crested anoles are among the few reptiles known that are able to perceive ultraviolet (UV) radiation, which stimulates special cells in the retina of the eyes. Upon exposure to direct sunlight, their otherwise rather drab throat fan (unusual for anoles, which normally have brightly colored dewlaps) appeared very bright when photographed with UV-sensitive film, much brighter than the rest of the body. The UV-sensitive film also revealed a bright spot at the corner of the mouth that is only exposed when the mouth is opened, a pose characteristically assumed during aggressive encounters. Since *Ctenonotus cristatellus* spends most of its time in areas exposed to sun, it is invariably exposed to high doses of UV radiation. These facts suggest that, rather than relying on bright colors, Puerto Rican crested anoles use body surfaces with a bright UV-reflection factor as a means of communication with members of their own species.

Dactyloa frenata

Giant green anole (plate 45)

The distinctive, very large arboreal lizards of the genus *Dactyloa* were formerly placed in the genus *Anolis*. Costa Rica is home to four species of *Dactyloa*.

The giant green anole, *Dactyloa frenata*, may reach a snout-vent length of 137 mm (5½ inches); its tail is sometimes more than twice as long as its snout-vent length. *Dactyloa frenata* has a distinctively raised protuberance on top of its snout, which bears elevated nostrils. Although some species of *Dactyloa* have distinctive crests on the neck, *Dactyloa frenata* does not, and thus appears relatively slender.

The upper surfaces of these lizards are green with a pattern of dark reticulated crossbands. The limbs and tail are similarly marked. Its head is adorned with alternating dark and light stripes that appear to radiate from the eyes. The belly and throat are white, cream, or yellowish. Males have a large, cream-colored dewlap that extends along the belly to a point that may measure one-third of the snout-vent length. Females have a small dewlap. In general, juveniles are the same color as adults. Some very small juveniles display very dark coloration, so that they appear to be a black-and-white version of their parents. Like most anoles, *Dactyloa frenata* is capable of considerable color change—during stressful situations or even in response to changing light conditions, the lizard may become darker or lighter.

Dactyloa frenata occurs from Costa Rica to northern Colombia, in lowland and premontane evergreen forests, between sea level and 850 m (2,800 ft). Within Costa Rica, this rare species occurs along the Atlantic versant; it may also occur in the Golfo Dulce area in the southwest.

Giant green anoles are highly arboreal. They often perch in a head-down position, at a considerable height on the trunks of large rainforest trees. This species seems to occur in low numbers in the rainforest canopy, where it is sometimes seen on larger branches, sitting motionless for hours. Presumably, these lizards are sit-and-wait predators that eat large insects and possibly small vertebrates.

Norops aquaticus
Water anole (plate 46)

This little-known species is similar in behavior to the stream anole, *Norops oxylophus. Norops aquaticus* is a fairly large species; males may have a snout-vent length up to 80 mm (3⅛ inches), females are generally a few millimeters smaller. The scales on the back are distinctly larger than those on the sides of the body.

The color of the body and tail is olive-green; each side of the body has a dark stripe and a pattern of dark crossbands. The head is usually a shade of brown or olive, slightly lighter than the color of the body. The head is marked with a light stripe that runs from eye to eye across the nape; another light line, usually cream or yellow, runs below the dark stripe on the side of the body. Juveniles have the same markings as do adults, but they are more intensely colored and usually have traces of blue in their coloration.

Norops aquaticus is a relatively rare species that inhabits humid premontane forests in southwestern Costa Rica; it is also found in the Chiriquí highlands in adjacent Panama.

Within its limited distribution range, *Norops aquaticus* gravitates to fast-flowing streams in densely forested valleys. These lizards tend to shy away from direct exposure to sunlight and do not tolerate high temperatures. A lizard that is held in the hand may go into shock after only a few minutes. They live near and in the water, usually perched on rocks or logs within a few yards of the water's edge. Upon discovery, they sometimes hide by moving to the back of a branch or stem, away from the source of threat, a tactic used by many anoles. If this strategy does not work, the lizard may run away along the stream bank and retreat into a crevice or hole. On many occasions, individuals were observed to dive into the water and hide in depressions in the stream bed, or inside holes in the river bank.

Many species of anoles detect prey on the basis of movement. In the case of stream-dwelling anoles such as *Norops aquaticus* and *Norops oxylophus*, however, whose habitat (the stream) is in constant motion, the lizards must be capable of distinguishing between the movements of an insect and the movements of other objects in the water. Adult stream anoles (*Norops oxylophus*) have been observed feeding on dead insects floating by on the water surface. In addition, experiments with *Norops aquaticus* indicate they can recognize immobile as well as mobile insects as potential prey. It is not known what kind of cues—visual, scent, or a combination of both—these anoles use to distinguish between edible and nonedible immobile objects, but this adaptation is advantageous.

Norops biporcatus

Green tree anole (plate 46)

Distinctive characteristics of this lizard are its size and its bright green coloration. The rare giant green anole, *Dactyloa frenata*, which is also large and has similar coloration, differs from *Norops biporcatus* in having smooth belly scales. Both lizards are green, but *Dactyloa frenata* has a pattern of four dark, transverse bands between the front and hind limbs.

Males and females reach an average size of about 85 mm (3⅜ inches); the maximum known length of the head and body is 106 mm (4⅛ inches). The long, slender tail may measure up to twice the length of the head and body. *Norops biporcatus*, which ranks among the largest anoles in Costa Rica, commonly reaches a total length of about 300 mm (11¾ inches).

Norops biporcatus has a long, pointed head with powerful jaws. The limbs are short and stocky. The tips of all fingers and toes are expanded. A small fleshy crest on the neck and the back of the head is present in some individuals.

Norops biporcatus has a uniform leaf-green color, occasionally with darkly-outlined pale blue spots. This anole, which is capable of considerable color change, may change to a mottled dark brown with white and black spots. The throat and belly are white with a bluish cast. The dewlap of adult males is small and red, with a pale blue center. The iris can be orange or gold.

Norops biporcatus is found at low and intermediate elevations in Mexico, Central America, and northern South America. In Costa Rica, it occurs on both the Pacific and Caribbean coasts, from near sea level to about 1,200 m (3,950 ft).

A solitary species, individuals are infrequently encountered in their preferred habitat, evergreen lowland forests. They usually perch on branches or in a vertical, head-up position on the trunk of a tree. Though generally observed perching at 1 to 3 m (3 to 10 ft) above the ground, these lizards are excellent climbers and have been found in the canopy of rainforest trees at heights of 35 m (115 ft). During the daytime, they usually bask in spots that are not exposed to direct sunlight; at night, individuals can be discovered sleeping on exposed branches or on the top of palm fronds.

Norops biporcatus uses strong jaws to overpower prey, which may weigh as much as 20% of their own body weight. Their diet consists mainly of invertebrates—insects and spiders—but also includes small anoles. When threatened, *Norops biporcatus* may bite to defend themselves. Their jaws have a sturdy, persistent grip, and their numerous short, sharp teeth may draw blood.

Females produce multiple clutches, though each clutch typically consists of a single egg. A cream-colored, oval egg, measuring 11 x 20 mm (⅜ x ¾ inch) was found in the layer of moss covering the branch of a recently fallen tree, although it is not known whether the lizard laid the egg before or after the tree fell. Also, it is not known whether females generally lay their eggs close to the ground or high in the forest canopy. A captive female was reported to lay two eggs within 7 hours. Although the clutch size in this species is generally one, the time between producing two consecutive eggs can be very short.

Some species of anoles are known to vocalize; individuals of *Norops biporcatus* have been reported to produce a squeak when seized.

Norops capito

Pug-nosed anole (plate 47)

This large anole may reach a snout-vent length of over 90 mm (3½ inches). It is fairly easily recognized by its large size and blunt pug nose. The coloration of this species is highly variable, but many female individuals are marked with a broad light or tan stripe that runs from the back of the head down the middle of the back and tail.

Although most frequently observed on the ground or perched low on a trunk, these lizards climb well and have been found at heights of over 15 m (50 ft).

Norops capito are very well camouflaged and have the habit of pressing their body against a trunk; they are easily overlooked.

This is a powerful species, capable of overpowering relatively large insects and other invertebrates; individuals are also known to eat other, smaller anoles.

In Costa Rica, *Norops capito* lives on the Caribbean slope and in the southwestern lowlands, where it inhabits deeply shaded forest interiors.

Norops humilis

Ground anole (plate 48)

Norops humilis is the only ground-dwelling anole in Costa Rica that has a small, tubelike axillary pocket in the armpit of each front limb. The function of these pockets is still a mystery. In almost every individual examined, the cavity contained several parasitic mites, but it is not known what effect these mites have on their lizard host.

This is a small anole with an average adult size of about 40 mm (1⅝ inches). It has a relatively short tail. Its body is covered with small granular scales of similar size, and it typically has 7 to 12 rows of conspicuously enlarged scales on the middle of the back. There are no crests on the back or tail.

Norops humilis is a chocolate-brown lizard; the band of enlarged scale rows on the back is often a coppery or bronze hue. In some individuals, a pattern of chevron- or diamond-shaped spots is superimposed on this light stripe. The extendable throat fan (dewlap) of males is deep red to red-orange with a bright yellow margin, a unique coloration among the Costa Rican anoles.

Norops humilis ranges from extreme southern Honduras south into eastern Panama. In Costa Rica, this forest-floor species is commonly found in lowland rainforests; it is also found in mountainous regions north of San José and in the Monteverde Cloud Forest Preserve. It is absent from the arid northwestern lowlands.

These lizards live in the layer of fallen leaves that covers the ground in habitats ranging from virgin rainforest to plantations. Although they are predominantly ground-dwelling, individuals frequently ascend low perches up to 60 cm (2 ft) above the ground. Generally, males utilize low perches during the day, while females and juveniles tend to remain in the leaf litter. *Norops humilis* has a strong preference for deeply shaded areas; it is often associated with buttresses of large trees, where it inhabits the leaf litter that collects between the roots. The buttresses are used as perches.

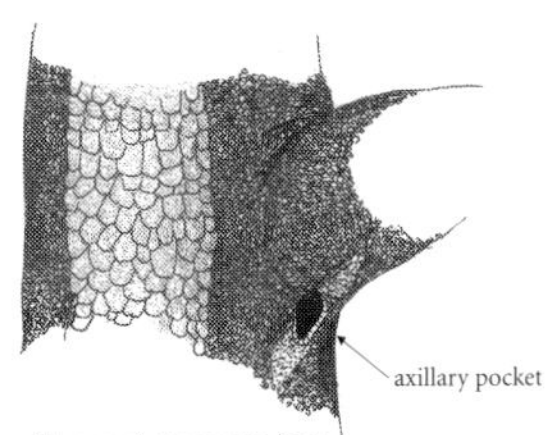

The axillary pocket appears here as a dark spot in the armpit.

Most lizards bask in the sun to raise their body temperature above the temperature of the surrounding air. Since *Norops humilis* lives in a deeply shaded habitat, it does not bask and is able to function at a body temperature equaling that of the surrounding air. They have been observed active at ambient temperatures as low as 16°C (61°F).

This is one of the few Costa Rican herpetofauna species that has been studied by biologists, mainly because it is abundant and easy to observe. Findings from some of the studies are summarized here.

Examination of stomach contents revealed that they eat a wide variety of invertebrates. Spiders, caterpillars, beetle larvae, cicadas, and many crickets were found. Several stomachs also contained soil and plant matter that was probably ingested along with prey.

The smallest sexually mature male of this species measured 26 mm (1 inch). Females become sexually active when they reach 32 mm (1¼ inches). Both sexes appear to be sexually active continuously once maturity is reached, which is approximately 6 months after hatching. Reproduction and egg-laying occur year-round, although the number of hatchlings that emerge during the dry season is lower than at other times of the year. It is not known whether this is caused by a decrease in the number of eggs produced in the dry season, or if the dry climate hinders egg development or lowers the successful hatching-rate. Hatchlings are tiny lizards with a combined snout-vent length of 17 mm (⅝ inch).

When active, *Norops humilis* spends its time foraging. Most prey (79%) is caught in leaf litter; the remaining 21% is seized above the ground on trunks or roots. Generally, these lizards scan their surroundings from an elevated foraging perch and run short distances to grab invertebrates that come within reach. Juveniles, less experienced at catching prey, may forage the entire day.

Males devote a substantial amount of their time to social interactions, more than do females. They typically start their day by flashing their brightly colored dewlap and bobbing their head, both signals used to communicate with other *Norops humilis*. A male spends several hours advertising his presence in his territory, usually without receiving a response from other individuals. This activity is comparable to birds singing at dawn.

If a female enters a male's territory during this advertisement period, the male will court her by doing a short sequence of dewlap flashing, followed by a chase over the surface of the leaf litter. If the female is receptive to the male's wooing, mating may follow. Both males and females of this species have a restricted area in which most of their activities take place. This so-called home range includes suitable sites for egg-laying, sleeping, and foraging, as well as ideal escape routes.

Norops lemurinus

Canopy anole (plate 48)

Norops lemurinus is a moderately slender anole with a maximum known snout-vent length of 68 mm (2⅝ inches). These lizards typically have a W-shaped bony protuberance on the back of the head.

Canopy anoles have a uniform or mottled brown to gray coloration. Some females have a dark-outlined cream or tan stripe down the middle of the back, although this color pattern is shared by the females of several other species. Males have a small dark-red dewlap that extends to a point between the front limbs. Some females may have a tiny, poorly developed white dewlap. The belly, throat, and underside of the head are whitish to cream in color.

Norops lemurinus is distributed along the Atlantic versant of Central America. In Costa Rica, it has also been found in the southwestern area of the country. It inhabits forested lowland regions, from sea level to at least 800 m (2,600 ft).

Canopy anoles rarely venture out of the canopy to the forest floor. The crown of a large rainforest tree may harbor a substantial population of these agile anoles, which travel nimbly through the maze of branches by jumping from limb to limb. This species often exposes itself when basking on tree trunks, branches, or leaves, where it sometimes falls prey to raptors such as the American swallow-tailed kite (*Elanoides forficatus*).

Norops limifrons

Slender anole (plate 49)

Norops limifrons is a small lizard with a snout-vent length measuring between 35 and 40 mm (1⅜ and 1⅝ inches). It is very slender and has a long, delicate tail.

The color of the upper surfaces is tan, gray-brown, olive-brown, or sometimes rather reddish-brown. Most individuals have a banded tail. A pair of thin black lines often runs from the neck down the middle of the back. The lips, chin, and throat are white, and the belly is cream or yellowish. The extendable throat fan (dewlap) of the males is very small and white, bearing an orange or yellow spot at the base.

Norops limifrons is a widespread species, occurring from Mexico to Panama at elevations from sea level to at least 1,200 m (3,650 ft). In Costa Rica it is abundant in lowland deciduous and evergreen forests, but it is also found in disturbed habitats along both slopes. Slender anoles are tolerant of different environmental conditions, but seem to prefer shaded forest interiors. They are mostly seen perched on low vegetation or on a tree trunk between 0.5 and 2 m (2 and 7 ft) above the ground, but they frequently visit the leaf litter as well.

Individuals tend to avoid direct exposure to bright sunlight and thus are only seen exposed in areas with filtered light or on overcast days. During the dry season or on hot days, they bask in the early morning and late afternoon; during the warmest part of the day, they retreat into the deeply shaded parts of the forests. Just before dark, individuals start looking for a suitable spot to spend the night, invariably on a twig or on the upper surface of a leaf in low vegetation.

Observations of *Norops limifrons* indicate that a male and female often stay close to each other, generally only a few yards apart. It appears that males spend the majority of their life with a single mate, and that this bond is lifelong. Pairs have been observed to travel considerable distances together, pausing frequently to perform head-bobbing displays, each to the other. This form of communication, which is repeated at regular intervals, about once every hour, may serve to reinforce the pair-bond. Instead of investing time in territorial interactions with other males, males spend "social time" maintaining a loose pair-bond with one particular female, a trait highly unusual for any lizard.

These anoles spend most of the day searching for invertebrate prey, 80% of which is captured on tree trunks and branches; the remaining 20% is caught in leaf litter. On many occasions, adults were observed to jump or run from 2 to 3 m (7 to 10 ft) in order to catch prey.

Although snakes, birds, and mammals are probably the main predators of these abundant lizards, they are also preyed on by spiders. A juvenile slender anole was found caught in the web of a golden orb spider (*Nephila clavipes*). And in one observation, a hunting spider (*Cupiennius* species) attacked and ate an adult *Norops limifrons*.

These lizards try to escape predation by moving to the back of a branch and flattening themselves against the surface, making themselves inconspicuous. If this technique fails, they either run up into the canopy or jump down and disappear in the leaf litter.

Like other species of *Norops, Norops limifrons* produces clutches of one egg every few weeks. Hatchlings are tiny, measuring a mere 15 mm (½ inch), about 40 mm (1⅝ inches) with the tail included. After about 58 to 60 days, they reach sexual maturity; their life-expectancy ranges between 4 and 6 months.

Norops oxylophus
Stream anole (plate 50)

This beautiful, medium-sized anole differs from all other Costa Rican anoles in having a dark brown to olive color on the back and sides and a distinct white stripe on each side of the body, starting at the neck and extending to at least mid-body. The white underside of the body, throat, and chin may incorporate parts of the white side-stripe on the throat and underside of the head. In some individuals, the white coloration is heavily mottled with dark pigment. A series of tiny, white eye-spots, with dark outlines, may be present on each side of the body, between the limbs; these spots are situated above the white stripe. The limbs are brown and irregularly patterned with dark bands. The large dewlap of males is a uniform yellow-orange.

This long-legged anole reaches a maximum snout-vent size of 85 mm (3⅜ inches) in males; females generally do not grow larger than 68 mm (2⅝ inches). The tail measures approximately 1.5 times the length of the head and body, so these lizards usually have a total length of 15 to 20 cm (5⅞ to 7⅞ inches).

Besides being larger, males are differentiated from females by a large, distended tail base, which is the location of the hemipenes, or paired copulatory organs. A low crest on the neck and on the tail may be present in large males; all adult males have a large extendable throat fan (dewlap).

Norops oxylophus occurs in Nicaragua, Costa Rica, and Panama, from sea level to 1,150 m (3,500 ft). In Costa Rica, it is mainly found on the Caribbean side of the country; it also occurs on the Pacific slope, but is less common there.

This semiaquatic anole is almost invariably found by rivers or streams, where it is seen perched on rocks, logs, or plants during the day. It eats a variety of insects and, occasionally, small fish. *Norops oxylophus* swims and dives very well, and when approached too closely it seeks refuge in the water. To avoid detection, it sometimes hides submerged, clinging to the underside of a rock or log. Often it manages to find air bubbles trapped underneath large objects and is able to stay there, breathing the underwater oxygen supply. During periods of inactivity—at night or when the air temperature is very low—it retreats into rock crevices.

Norops oxylophus often live in dark, shadowy areas of dense forests, but always in or near streams. They are often active at temperatures that are too low for other species of lizards to emerge from hiding places. Juveniles have been seen basking on overcast days with air temperatures of 16°C (61°F).

When seized, individuals of this species sometimes hold their body rigid, in a sticklike fashion. However, when they are held for more than a few minutes, they show signs of overheating. The lizard changes color to a nearly black hue and goes limp; this may be caused by the high temperature of the human hand.

Reproduction in this species takes place year-round. Eggs are deposited in moist places, possibly in leaf litter. In captivity, juveniles reached sexual maturity 101 to 118 days after hatching.

The taxonomic status of this species and the extremely similar *Norops lionotus* is under question. *Norops lionotus* occurs in Panama, near the Costa Rican border, and its range may extend across the border. Perhaps both species should be treated as members of a single, variable species. Further research is needed to resolve this matter; until then, the Costa Rican individuals will continue to be referred to as *Norops oxylophus*.

Norops polylepis

Golfo Dulce anole (plate 50)

Norops polylepis is endemic to the Golfo Dulce area in southwestern Costa Rica, where it lives at low elevations. It is easy to observe, since it is abundant and lives on the ground or on low vegetation less than 2 m (7 ft) above the ground. Males are often seen signaling with their large, bright orange dewlap as they are perched on low branches.

This species usually has a uniform or mottled brown coloration. Some females display a light cream or tan stripe down the middle of the back, or have a middorsal row of dark diamond-shaped markings.

Norops polylepis is a small to medium-sized species with a maximum known snout-vent length for males of 55 mm (2⅛ inches). Females remain somewhat smaller at a maximum size of 48 mm (1⅞ inches).

Norops polylepis is a very territorial lizard. Males defend an area between 30 and 65 m^2 (275 and 600 sq ft) that provides them with exclusive access to a number of females and sufficient food. A female's territory is strictly for feeding and is smaller than that of males (7 m^2, or 65 sq ft, on average). Males vigorously defend their home range against intruders, initially by flashing their dewlap and bobbing their head. If this does not deter the intruding male, he will resort to physical combat.

Females lay a single leathery-shelled egg almost every week. After an incubation period of about 50 days, a tiny hatchling emerges with a snout-vent length of approximately 20 mm (¾ inch). Juvenile *Norops polylepis* reach sexual maturity after three to four months. Most individuals probably do not live for more than one year.

Like other anoles, this species feeds predominantly on insects, which are caught in the leaf litter.

Norops polylepis can be confused with the more widespread but co-occuring *Norops cupreus*; the two species are similar in size and habits. However, they can be distinguished by the dewlap, which in *Norops polylepis* is orange and in *Norops cupreus* is orange-red to red with a light margin and a large white spot.

Norops sericeus
Indigo-throated anole (plate 51)

Norops sericeus is one of the smaller anole species in Costa Rica, with a maximum snout-vent length of 45 mm (1¾ inches). This species is also known as the silky anole, a name which derives from the silky sheen of its scales.

Like other Costa Rican anoles, the coloration of this species is variable. It is generally a uniform gray to brownish-bronze. Indistinct darker markings may be present, especially on the legs. The belly is usually white to cream, but may be yellowish. Females of this species, and of many other anole species, often have a dark-edged cream to tan stripe that runs the length of the back.

The most distinctive feature of male *Norops sericeus* is the dewlap, which is yellow to orange with an indigo-blue round spot in the center. Females have a very small, rudimentary dewlap that is often the same color as the throat.

Both male and female indigo-throated anoles have a low, sail-like crest on the back of the neck, which is erected during courtship and territorial battles. Males also have a crest on the back that is displayed for the same purposes.

Norops sericeus is distributed from northeastern Mexico to Costa Rica, where it lives in the northwestern region of the country. Throughout its range, it seems to prefer dry lowland forest, but has also been reported in humid foothills at elevations above 1,300 m (4,250 ft). It appears to be extremely tolerant to a range of habitats and environmental conditions.

Polychrus gutturosus
Canopy lizard
Cameleón (plate 51)

This rarely observed species of lizard is the only Costa Rican lizard that has cone-shaped eyes.

Polychrus gutturosus is a relatively large lizard; excluding the tail, it can measure 170 mm (6⅝ inches). Its very long tail, which has a round cross-section, is 2.5 to 3 times the combined length of the head and body—the total length of a large adult may exceed 550 mm (21⅝ inches).

Polychrus gutturosus has a strongly compressed body without crests on the back, head, or tail. It has an extendable throat fan in the same leaf-green color as the rest of the body. Its long limbs bear five fingers and toes, all of which lack the widely expanded adhesive disk present in other anoles.

The tiny eyes of this species, which are positioned on a cone-shaped elevation, can be moved independently of one another; the eyes are further characterized by a round pupil and a coppery iris.

These well-camouflaged lizards are nearly leaf-green with a pattern of darker transverse bands on the body and tail. In some individuals, a reddish-brown stripe runs the length of the back. Often a pattern of dark stripes on the sides of the head radiates from the eyes. This species displays remarkably fast color changes, so individuals may not fit this description.

Polychrus gutturosus is known from a few scattered locations in Honduras, in Nicaragua, and in Costa Rica, where it has been found at low and intermediate elevations on the Pacific and Caribbean slopes, from near sea level to at least 1,000 m (3,300 ft). It is absent from very dry areas like Guanacaste Province. South of Costa Rica, this species occurs in Panama and possibly ranges into northern South America.

Polychrus gutturosus is a slow-moving lizard that spends most, if not all, of its life in trees. Sometimes it is found relatively close to the ground, but it predominantly inhabits the crowns of rainforest trees, as its common name indicates. Since these elusive animals live out of sight of terrestrial observers (including biologists), information on their natural history is scarce.

Even at close range, *Polychrus gutturosus* manages to escape detection; it is perfectly camouflaged. Its body coloration matches its direct environment, and it further escapes detection by remaining motionless for hours, sometimes freezing in what seem to be highly uncomfortable positions.

When it moves, this lizard superimposes a rocking motion on its forward locomotion, appearing to mimic windblown vegetation. This may mask its movements from the view of potential predators and prey. When threatened, these lizards defend themselves fiercely; they gape at the source of the threat and will inflict a painful bite.

The body shape of *Polychrus gutturosus* and its ability to change color rapidly is highly reminiscent of Old World chameleons. The two are not closely related, however, and the similarities between these lizards are more likely rooted in comparable adaptations to a similar way of life (convergent evolution). The telescopic eyes, long claws, and long tail, which is not prehensile but most likely functions as a counterbalance, are all adaptations to life in trees.

Most individuals of this species have been found in edge situations in densely forested areas. For example, one adult male was found exposed on top of the outermost leaves of a tree, overhanging a river; the lizard was perched at midday at a height of approximately 28 m (92 ft) above the water. Another individual was seen at night on the edge of a road, sleeping inside a dense clump of vines, branches, and leaves at a height of 1.5 m (5 ft).

Polychrus gutturosus are omnivores and are known to eat insects as well as leaves, fruits, and seeds. The main predators of these lizards are birds of prey. One such raptor, an American swallow-tailed kite (*Elanoides forficatus*), was seen to pluck a juvenile canopy lizard from its elevated perch.

Literature

Andrews 1971, 1983; Avila-Pires 1995; Ballinger et al. 1970; Bock & Quintero 1987; Dugan 1982; Fitch 1973, 1975; Fitch & Hackforth-Jones 1983; Fitch & Seigel 1984; Fitch et al. 1976; Fleischman et al. 1993; Frost & Etheridge 1989; Goodman 1971; Guyer 1986, 1994; Hayes et al. 1989; Henderson 1972; Jungfer 1987b; Koller 1996; Lee 1996; Leenders 1995a, 1996; Mudde 1989; Mudde & van Dijk 1984f; Myers 1971; Savage & Villa 1986; Talbot 1979.

FAMILY: **Phrynosomatidae** (Spiny Lizards and allies)
SUBORDER: Lacertilia (Lizards)

This small family of North and Central American lizards was formerly included within the family Iguanidae. Although the taxonomic position of the family Phrynosomatidae and other former iguanids remains under debate, in this book Phrynosomatidae is treated as a distinct family.

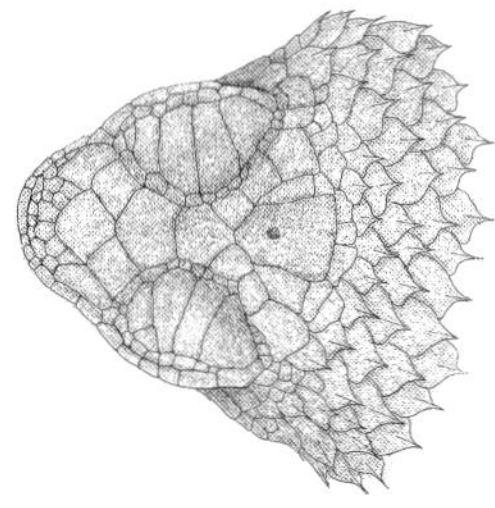
Head of a **green spiny lizard** (*Sceloporus malachiticus*).

The range of this family extends from southern Canada through much of the United States and Mexico and terminates in Panama. Most species are small or medium-sized terrestrial lizards that are found mainly in dry and rocky areas with sparse vegetation. All species are day-active.

Costa Rica has three species of spiny lizards, all in the genus *Sceloporus*. The green spiny lizard (*Sceloporus malachiticus*) inhabits the Central Valley and the surrounding mountain ranges. The brown spiny lizard (*Sceloporus squamosus*) and the rose-bellied spiny lizard (*Sceloporus variabilis*) are restricted to the arid lowlands of Guanacaste Province in the northwest.

All *Sceloporus*, including the three Costa Rican species, are easily distinguished from other lizards in lower Central America by the scales with a spine-tipped keel that cover the body and tail. This spiky, hedgehog-like appearance accounts for the common name, spiny lizard.

LIZARDS

SUMMARY

How to identify Costa Rican spiny lizards:

- Spiny lizards typically have the head, body, and tail covered with keeled, spine-tipped scales. They have a robust body and a blunt, short-snouted head.

SPECIES DESCRIPTIONS

Sceloporus malachiticus
Green spiny lizard (plate 52)

Sceloporus malachiticus are beautiful lizards that are bright emerald green, yellowish green, olive, or brown. Most individuals are capable of color change and may darken considerably until almost completely black. Irregular blue markings may be present on the body and, especially in males, the tail is often bright blue. Additionally, males have a black collar on the sides of the neck, and the white throat and belly are adorned with large patches of azure outlined in black.

This is a medium-sized lizard with a maximum adult size of 91 mm (3½ inches). With tail included, it measures about 200 mm (7⅞ inches). Like other spiny lizards, *Sceloporus malachiticus* has a robust body and a blunt, short-snouted head. Its scales are keeled and spine-tipped, lending a spiky appearance. Males have a swollen tail base, indicating the location of the paired copulatory organs (hemipenes).

The other Costa Rican species of the genus *Sceloporus* (*Sceloporus squamosus* and *Sceloporus variabilis*) may be brown or tan like some *Sceloporus malachiticus*, but they differ in having light longitudinal stripes. Both are also geographically isolated from *Sceloporus malachiticus*; within Costa Rica they are only found in the dry northwestern lowlands of Guanacaste.

Sceloporus malachiticus lives at intermediate and high elevations in the highlands and mountain ranges of Central America, from Guatemala to Panama. In Costa Rica, this species is found in the Tilarán, Central, and Talamanca mountain ranges at elevations over 600 m (1,950 ft). This is one of the few Costa Rican lizards still commonly seen at elevations as high as 2,500 m (8,200 ft). *Sceloporus malachiticus* is visibly abundant in the Central Valley and the surrounding mountains; it can even be seen in the streets and city parks of downtown San José.

In the Central Valley and at lower elevations, males and females are mostly bright emerald green in coloration. At higher elevations, these lizards tend to be smaller in size, with different coloration; males are more yellowish green, while females have a grayish-brown background color that is marked with black and white spots. At lower elevations, *Sceloporus malachiticus* is primarily seen on trees, buildings, and other high perches, whereas, with increasing elevation, it seems to become increasingly terrestrial.

Many places where this species lives have a relatively cool and humid climate; for example, on Mount Chirripó it may freeze at night. In areas with such a cold climate, *Sceloporus malachiticus* lives in the driest and warmest spots it can find. Rocky outcrops, fallen logs, and stumps of dead trees warm up quickly and retain heat for a long time, and individuals are most frequently seen basking on such surfaces. When the sun comes out, these lizards position themselves in such a manner that they receive the most solar radiation possible. They increase their own body surface by flattening and widening their body. The dark coloration of the highland populations of this species may speed up heat absorption, since dark, rough surfaces absorb heat better than bright, smooth surfaces.

As opposed to most lizards in the genus *Sceloporus*, which lay small clutches of eggs, *Sceloporus malachiticus* is live-bearing. Such ovoviviparity is an adaptation frequently seen in lizards living in cold climates; eggs deposited in the highly variable ambient temperature of the Costa Rican highlands would be subject to temperature changes that could be fatal to a developing lizard embryo. In live-bearing species, the eggs are basically incubated inside the female's body; by thermoregulating to keep her own body temperature at an acceptable level, the female regulates the incubation temperature for her developing offspring at the same time. Reproduction in this species seems to be dependent on the season, and 4 to 6 young are born in the first part of the dry season (late November through February). Mating activity has been observed in June and July, so the gestation period probably lasts from 5 to 7 months.

Sceloporus variabilis

Rose-bellied spiny lizard (plate 52)

This spiny lizard has a vast distribution range and can be found from Texas in the United States to northwestern Costa Rica, where it is only found in the arid lowlands of Guanacaste Province. Rose-bellied spiny lizards live on the ground and on trunks and rocks. They are active strictly during the day, when they can be seen foraging for insect prey.

These lizards can be distinguished from the co-occurring brown spiny lizard, *Sceloporus squamosus*, by the presence of a pocket-like pit behind each hind leg. They also have a pattern of two light dorsolateral stripes, with two rows of paired black spots that run down the middle of the back between the light stripes.

Literature

Behler & King 1979; Frost & Etheridge 1989; Hayes et al. 1989; Mudde & van Dijk 1984c; Robinson 1983b; Savage and Villa 1986.

FAMILY: **Scincidae** (Skinks)
SUBORDER: Lacertilia (Lizards)

Skinks are a highly successful group, with over a thousand species occurring worldwide in a wide variety of habitats. In many parts of the world, skinks are the most prevalent of the local lizard species. In Latin America, however, the situation is different; in Costa Rica, for example, only three of the more than 70 lizard species are skinks.

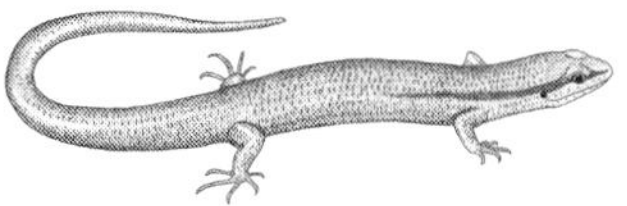

Litter skink (*Sphenomorphus cherriei*).

Although there may not be many true skinks in Costa Rica, several lizards in other families (e.g., Anguidae, Gymnophthalmidae) have evolved into very skinklike animals, suggesting that it may be advantageous to resemble one.

Skinks have an elongate cylindrical body, a robust medium-length tail, and a conical head that is scarcely wider than the neck. In Costa Rican species, the small but powerful limbs bear five digits. Typically, skinks have several rows of uniform cycloid scales completely encircling the body, and enlarged plates covering the head. The scales on the body are smooth and often very shiny.

The three species of skinks that occur in Costa Rica are each in a different genus. Two of these, *Mabuya unimarginata* and *Sphenomorphus cherriei*, are abundant and widespread inhabitants of the lowlands throughout both slopes. The third, *Eumeces managuae*, is a rare species that—within Costa Rica—is found only in the dry northern Pacific lowlands. All Costa Rican skinks have moveable eyelids.

LIZARDS

SUMMARY

How to identify Costa Rican skinks:

- Skinks are lizards with a cylindrical body and tail and a small, conical head that is scarcely wider than the neck. Typically, their body and tail are covered with very smooth, similarly shaped scales. The head bears large, symmetrical plates.
- Costa Rican skinks all have moveable eyelids. Their relatively small limbs each bear five slender digits.

SPECIES DESCRIPTIONS

Mabuya unimarginata

Bronze-backed climbing skink
(plate 53)

Mabuya unimarginata is the only Costa Rican lizard with a skinklike body that has a bronze ground color and a wide, dark band, bordered above and below by a light stripe, that runs along each side of the body.

Mabuya unimarginata is considerably larger than *Sphenomorphus cherriei*, the other common skink species in Costa Rica. It has an average snout-vent length of approximately 62 mm (2½ inches) in males and 72 mm (2⅞ inches) in females. A long tail measures 1.5 to 2 times the snout-vent length.

These skinks have a cylindrical and streamlined body and tail, and a small head that seems to flawlessly blend into the attenuate shape of the body. The eyes have a round pupil, a dark iris, and moveable eyelids, with a transparent window in the lower eyelid that enables the lizard to see with its eyes closed. The limbs are well developed, but fairly short, and bear five digits. The entire body has a very glossy appearance because of the smoothly polished body scales and head plates.

The color of the back is bronze-brown to reddish-brown. On each side of the body, a wide, dark brown band runs from the tip of the snout through the eye and the ear to the base of the tail. This dark band is bordered above and below by an indistinct light stripe, cream to white in color. The undersurfaces of the body are usually immaculate white, sometimes with a bluish or greenish hue.

The genus *Mabuya* is widespread, but most of its species live in the Old World. *Mabuya unimarginata* is the only species from this genus that inhabits mainland Central America; it ranges from central Mexico to Panama. In Costa Rica, this species inhabits a variety of habitats in the lowlands and ranges up to 1,500 m (4,950 ft) on the Pacific slope of the Tilarán mountains.

Unlike most skinks, which have a mainly terrestrial life, *Mabuya unimarginata* spends much of its time in trees. Individuals are frequently found in relatively open and dry areas: roadsides, forest clearings, and regions around human settlements. These skinks feed on small insects.

Generally, this is a very shy species that does not venture far from its hiding place; often, when basking, it does not even expose its entire body, extending only part of it from hollow trunks or rocky crevices.

Apart from its arboreal habits, *Mabuya unimarginata* is also somewhat unusual among skinks in that it is viviparous, giving birth to four to seven young. The young are most likely born during the rainy season.

Sphenomorphus cherriei

Litter skink (plate 53)

Sphenomorphus cherriei is the smallest of the three Costa Rican skinks. The snout-vent length is between 48 and 66 mm (1⅞ and 2⅝ inches). The tail is normally about 1½ times the combined length of the head and body, but may be slightly longer.

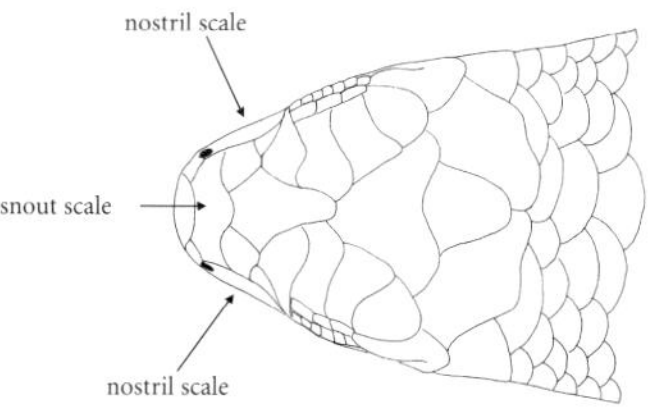

Litter skink (*Sphenomorphus cherriei*). Note the snout scale that connects the two nostril scales.

Among Costa Rican skinks and skinklike lizards in this size range, *Sphenomorphus cherriei* is the only lizard with a single large scale that connects the nostril scales on each side of the snout.

Sphenomorphus cherriei has moveable eyelids (without the transparent disk in the lower eyelid found in *Mabuya unimarginata*). The eye has a black iris and a round pupil. The head is short, bluntly rounded, and only slightly wider than the neck. The elongate body and tail, both round in cross-section, as well as the short limbs, are covered with extremely smooth, shiny scales. The tail is relatively fat.

Sphenomorphus cherriei always has five fingers and toes. This differentiates it from the golden spectacled lizard (*Gymnophtalmus speciosus*), a small lizard in the family Gymnophthalmidae that closely resembles *Sphenomorphus cherriei*, but which has four fingers and five toes.

These lizards are inconspicuously colored, either tan, brown, or gray.

They normally have a black masklike eye stripe that continues on both sides of the body, where it gradually disappears at a point somewhere between the front and the hind limbs. Often, a pattern of yellow or cream spots is present on the body, the lower half of the head, and the throat, blending into the yellowish-gray of the belly. The tail, if unbroken, is often reddish or orange.

This skink ranges from Mexico southward into northern South America. It occurs at low and intermediate elevations throughout Central America. In Costa Rica, *Sphenomorphus cherriei* is commonly seen in the lowland regions on both sides of the country in areas with dense ground cover.

Rarely seen, these lizards can be heard darting through the thick layer of fallen leaves on the forest floor. They infrequently bask in sun-exposed spots, and much of their activity occurs out of sight, beneath the safe cover of the leaf litter.

Apart from being slippery and difficult to grasp, these lizards also carry hidden body armor; underneath each body scale is a minute, bony platelet, called an osteoderm, that provides additional protection. Although its armorlike protection is effective against some smaller predators, many large predators (birds, mammals, snakes, lizards, and large frogs and toads) are capable of eating *Sphenomorphus cherriei* once they have it in their grasp. The shovel-toothed snake (*Scaphiodontophis annulatus*), whose diet consists mainly of litter skinks, has developed special teeth with shock absorbers to ensure a better grip on the slick, hard body of these lizards.

Frequently, *Sphenomorphus cherriei* escapes predation by purposely breaking off a section of its tail, an ability called autotomy. Like many other lizard species, it has multiple fracture planes on the vertebrae of the tail that allow the tail to be broken off when the animal is threatened. The broken-off part of the tail usually falls to the ground, where it wriggles vigorously and distracts the predator for a few seconds, allowing the lizard to escape.

A secondary, or regenerated, tail grows back from the remaining stump in a short period of time. Lizards have no trouble surviving without a tail. However, the loss of such a large part of the body does have implications for growth and development. In *Sphenomorphus cherriei*, the tail is used to store energy in the form of fat. Tail-breakage not only results in the loss of fat reserves, but it also requires the lizard to expend energy to regenerate a secondary tail, energy that could otherwise have been invested in reproduction, for example. Also, the tail is used for balance; running individuals of this species have been seen to avoid predators by flipping their entire body around 180 degrees using the heavy tail for leverage. Thus, individuals who have lost their tail also lose a certain amount of agility.

Normally, when these lizards move at high speed, they use their entire body in a snakelike, undulating fashion, bracing themselves against available surfaces and hardly using their short limbs. The limbs are used during slow walking movements, when they are looking for food, for instance.

Sphenomorphus cherriei is an active forager of invertebrate prey. With the aid of chemical cues, it locates insect larvae, spiders, and cockroaches and other arthropods. It is known to eat relatively large prey, which sometimes includes hatchlings of its own species. The bulk of foraging activity occurs in the mid-morning hours, when the ambient temperature has reached about 25°C (77°F). During the midday heat, they retreat to a cool part of the forest floor. A second bout of foraging may follow at mid-afternoon.

These lizards remain within a small area—called the home range—when searching for food or trying to locate mates. The reproductive habits of *Sphenomorphus cherriei* are not very well known, but in the Atlantic lowlands mating and egg-laying appears to occur year-round. Between 1 and 3 eggs (usually 2) are laid on the forest floor. It appears that the female does not attempt to bury her eggs or construct a nest, but simply drops them in the leaf litter. Recently hatched juveniles, which measure about 22 mm (⅞ inch), can reach sexual maturity 7 months after hatching.

Literature

Fitch 1983; Guyer 1994; Hayes et al. 1989; Henderson 1984; Lee 1996; Mudde & van Dijk 1984d; Savage & Villa 1986; Zug 1993.

FAMILY: **Gymnophthalmidae** (Microteiids)
SUBORDER: Lacertilia (Lizards)

The members of this family of slender, elongate lizards were formerly included in the family Teiidae (whip-tailed lizards). For this reason, and because of their small size, gymnophthalmid lizards are also referred to as microteiids. Although microteiids are closely related to members of the family Teiidae, they differ in many ways.

The family Gymnophthalmidae is principally a South American family, but six species range as far north as Costa Rica. Each of these species is in a different genus; some appear to have a very localized distribution, although their elusiveness makes it difficult to define their range of occurrence.

Our knowledge of Costa Rican gymnophthalmids is very limited. Some species are nocturnal, some diurnal, and other species may be active both during the day and at night.

Lizards of this family inhabit a wide variety of habitats; individuals have been found in leaf litter, in rotting logs, under fallen trees or rocks, or in burrows in loose soil. Some species inhabit treetop bromeliads in the rainforest canopy, while others live a semiaquatic life in small cascading streams.

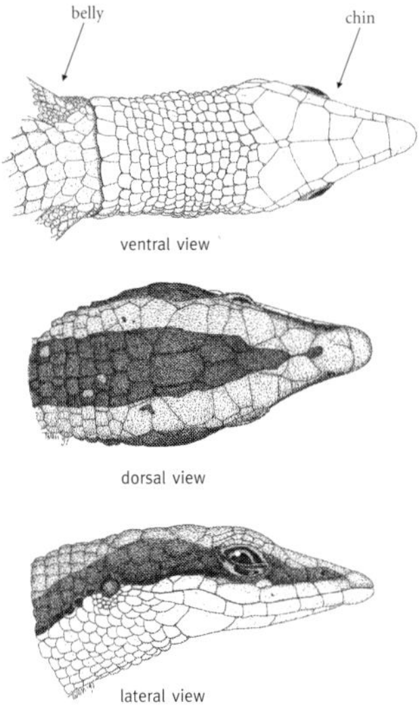

belly
chin
ventral view
dorsal view
lateral view

Bromeliad lizard (*Anadia ocellata*). Costa Rican members of this family have squarish scales on the belly (ventral view), side, and back. Large plates adorn the chin (ventral view) and the head (dorsal and lateral views).

The Costa Rican species in the family Gymnophthalmidae have variable body sizes and shapes, although all species have an attenuate body and short, sometimes highly reduced limbs. The members of this family can be distinguished from all other Costa Rican lizards by their scalation. The belly is covered by large squarish or rectangular plates, and the back is covered with keratinized square or rounded scales (rather than the small granular scales found in members of the family Teiidae); large plates cover the head. Moveable eyelids are present in all but one Costa Rican species, *Gymnophthalmus speciosus*.

SUMMARY

How to identify Costa Rican gymnophthalmids:

- Costa Rican gymnophthalmids are very diverse. However, all have enlarged, symmetrical plates on the head, squarish plates on the belly, and square or rounded scales on the rest of the body.
- These lizards never have small granular scales on the upper surfaces of the body and tail.

SPECIES DESCRIPTIONS

Anadia ocellata

Bromeliad lizard (plate 54)

These slender, elongate lizards have a narrow, pointed head and tiny limbs, each of which bear 5 digits. The tail is very long—it may be almost 3 times the length of the head and body combined. In Costa Rica, no other lizard has a body with similar proportions and shape.

Anadia ocellata is small, with a maximum snout-vent length of about 75 mm (3 inches); because the tail is so long, the total length may exceed 210 mm (8¼ inches).

The elongate head of *Anadia ocellata* has distinctly visible ear openings; the eyes are covered with moveable eyelids, of which the lower lid bears a clear transparent disk.

The body and tail are covered with many rows of smooth squarish scales that encircle the body. There is a distinct skin fold across the throat.

These lizards have a light brown to golden background color, with a pattern of dark brown stripes. A broad dark stripe runs from the top of the head down the middle of the back to the tip of the tail. On each side of the body, another dark stripe passes through the eye onto the side of the body and tail. On the body, these three stripes are more or less straight with irregular edges, but on the tail they become conspicuously zigzagged. The throat, chin, and lower half of the head are immaculately white, but the undersurfaces of these lizards gradually become cream-colored below the body and tail. In some individuals, the dark stripes are weakly developed, and instead the light brown background color is marked with a row of widely spaced light dots, some of which may have dark borders, between the front and hind limbs. The smooth scales of these lizards have a brilliant oil-like reflection that, in the proper light, appears iridescent red, green, or blue.

This rarely observed lizard has been seen in scattered locations throughout the low montane regions of both slopes of Costa Rica and adjacent Panama. Its elevational distribution ranges at least from 500 to 1,450 m (1,650 to 4,250 ft).

Anadia ocellata inhabits the crowns of rainforest trees and is only occasionally found on the forest floor. As its common name indicates, this lizard is often found in bromeliads. It has been suggested that the distribution of this species is strongly correlated with the distribution of tank bromeliads (*Guzmania* species), large arboreal plants that collect and retain water and form an ideal habitat for a wide selection of animals and plants. However, recent observations indicate that theses elongate lizards prefer small to very small bromeliads, including species such as Medusa's head airplant (*Tillandsia caput-medusae*) that would appear too small to harbor any animals.

Anadia ocellata has a prehensile tail, a unique trait among Costa Rican lizards. One individual was observed dangling by its tail from the core of a bromeliad. Individuals have been observed to lose their grip occasionally and plummet to the forest floor. Perhaps the individuals sometimes found on the forest floor have just fallen there and are on their way back up. Because they weigh little, and because their landing is often cushioned by low vegetation, these lizards can most likely survive a fall from the canopy without sustaining permanent damage.

The short limbs of *Anadia ocellata* appear to be inadequate to carry its long body and tail; these lizards move slowly, in a salamander-like, undulating fashion. Although their limbs may make horizontal motion slow and awkward, they climb trees very well.

Little is known about the reproductive behavior of *Anadia ocellata*. They are oviparous and produce small clutches of one or two eggs. A tiny individual, possibly a hatchling, was measured at 26 mm (1 inch); with tail included it measured 70 mm (2¾ inches).

Gymnophthalmus speciosus
Golden spectacled lizard (plate 54)

Gymnophthalmus speciosus is very skinklike in appearance and superficially resembles the litter skink (*Sphenomorphus cherriei*). However, there are a number of striking differences between these two species. First, *Gymnophthalmus speciosus* has only 4 digits on each hand, a unique characteristic among Costa Rican lizards. Second, it lacks moveable eyelids, and its eyes are covered with transparent spectacles.

Golden spectacled lizards are small, reaching a snout-vent length of about 45 mm (1¾ inches). Their cylindrical body is covered with smooth, shiny scales and bears relatively short limbs.

This species, the northernmost representative of the family Gymnophthalmidae, occurs from Mexico and Guatemala south to northern South America. These secretive, diurnal leaf-litter inhabitants live in forested areas, where they hunt for small insects.

Gymnophthalmus speciosus is oviparous and produces several small clutches of eggs each year.

Neusticurus apodemus
Water tegu (plate 55)

A flattened body and rows of strongly keeled scales on the back and tail lend this unique, tiny lizard a crocodile-like appearance.

Neusticurus apodemus is a delicate, attractive lizard, with an elongate, flattened body, a long neck, and a tapered head that is slightly wider than the neck.

These are small lizards; the largest recorded male had a snout-vent length of 47 mm (1⅞ inches). The tail of *Neusticurus apodemus*, which is slightly compressed, measures from 1.5 to 1.7 times the length of the body and head.

Four rows of large keeled scales form weak keels that run the length of the back and neck. Irregular rows of smaller keeled scales are visible on the sides and the tail. The scales on the belly are smooth and squarish.

The eardrums of many species of lizards are situated in pocketlike depressions on the head, but in the water tegus, the eardrums are clearly visible on the surface. A transparent area present in the lower eyelids permits these lizards to see even when the eyes are closed.

Neusticurus apodemus is a light brown lizard. The two outer rows of large keels on the back often have a somewhat lighter hue than the background, thus forming two irregular light bands. On each side of the body, between the front limbs and hind limbs, is a series of indistinct, dark-bordered spots with a light center. The arms and legs are dark brown, but the upper arms are distinctly marked with large yellowish white blotches. The dark brown head is often marked with two light vertical bars between the eye and the mouth. A prominent white patch is situated below the eardrum. The belly is dark brown on the side, usually with a light stripe in the middle; the throat is mottled with white and dark brown. One adult male with an orange-red chin was observed, as was a large female with a pale orange belly.

Neusticurus apodemus belongs to a South American genus; the only species of its genus in Central America, it lives in a small area in Costa Rica. Its nearest relative lives in southern Colombia, roughly 1,200 km (750 mi) to the southeast. Their isolated existence gives rise to the species name *apodemus*, Greek for "away from home."

These lizards have a limited distribution at intermediate elevations between San Isidro del General and Dominical, on Costa Rica's Pacific slope. Individuals have also been found in the San Vito region. They inhabit hilly areas with relatively dry and low forests, generally in places where small cascading streams come down from the overgrown slopes.

The South American relatives of the water tegu live in holes in the banks of jungle streams and rivers. The limited observations of the water tegu indicate that it commonly enters the water at night, when it has been seen wading and swimming in small streams. Most Costa Rican individuals have been observed under rocks or driftwood at the edge of streams, or in the leaf litter that accumulates at the edge of pools or streams. Sometimes individuals are found half submerged; when picked out of the water, they keep their body completely rigid.

South American *Neusticurus* species are known to eat tadpoles, fish, and water beetles; what comprises the diet of *Neusticurus apodemus* is not known. The reproductive behavior of *Neusticurus apodemus* also remains unstudied.

Ptychoglossus plicatus

Keeled leaf litter lizard (plate 55)

Until recently, this rarely seen lizard was thought to live exclusively in Costa Rica, but in recent years a few individuals have been found in adjacent Panama.

In Costa Rica, *Ptychoglossus plicatus* is found on the Caribbean slope up to 700 m (2,300 ft) and in the southwest to 1,200 m (3,950 ft).

These small brown lizards have an average total length of about 115 mm (4½ inches). *Ptychoglossus plicatus* has a slightly flattened head and body; the cross-section of the tail is round. Its most characteristic feature is the heavily keeled appearance of the scales on the body and tail; these contrast sharply with the shiny, smooth head plates. A very similar-looking gymnophthalmid lizard, *Leposoma southi*, also has strongly keeled scales on the back, but it differs in having keeled head plates, a characteristic not found in any other Costa Rican lizard. The squarish belly scales of *Ptychoglossus plicatus* are cream or bluish-white with a pattern of black spots. A distinctly visible transverse skin fold is present across the throat.

Nothing substantial is known about the biology of this small lizard, except that individuals are invariably found in the leaf litter layer that covers the ground in dense rainforests. South American species in the genus *Ptychoglossus* are known to lay small clutches of eggs, so it is likely that this is also the case with *Ptychoglossus plicatus*.

Literature

Avila-Pires 1995; Guyer 1994; Hayes et al. 1989; Heyer 1967; Lee 1996; Mudde & van Dijk 1984d; Oftedal 1974; Taylor 1949, 1955; Savage & Villa 1986; Uzzell 1966; Zug 1993.

FAMILY: **Teiidae** (Whip-tailed Lizards)
SUBORDER: Lacertilia (Lizards)

This large family of active, terrestrial lizards is restricted to the Americas, ranging from Canada and the northern United States southward through Central America and far into South America.

Teiid lizards are generally elongate, streamlined lizards. They have a tapered head, a drawn-out body and neck, a long tail, and powerful limbs.

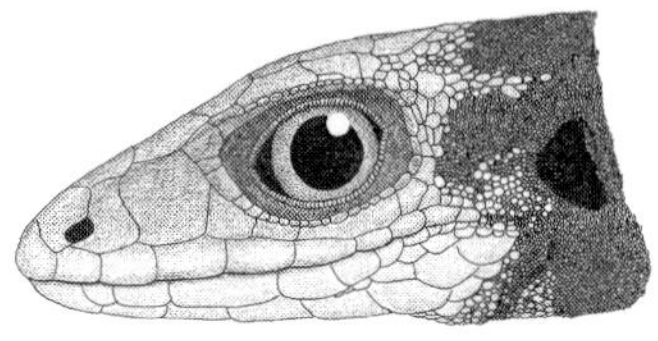

Central American whip-tailed lizard (*Ameiva festiva*). Note the large plates on the head and the granular scales on the sides and top of the neck.

These lizards are predominantly day-active insect feeders; they only emerge from their hiding places to search out prey when the temperatures are high. Teiids are frequently seen basking on Costa Rican beaches when the temperature of the sand is almost unbearably hot for our bare feet. As a result of their preference for warm temperatures, teiid lizards in Costa Rica are found mostly in relatively dry and hot areas, although some species can be found in wet rainforest habitats.

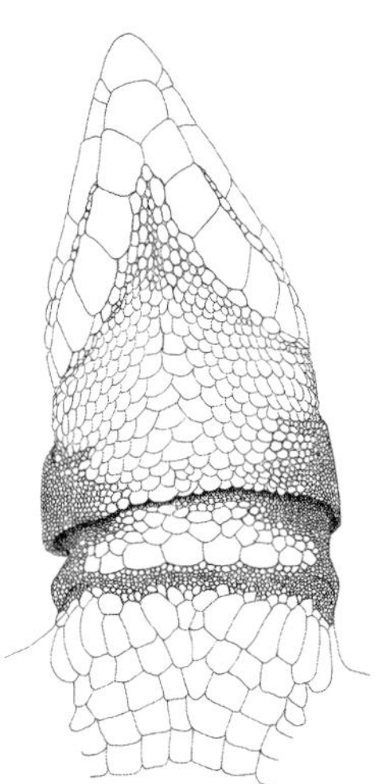

Ventral (belly) view of **four-lined whip-tailed lizard** (*Ameiva quadrilineata*). The transverse skin fold that separates the belly and the throat is clearly visible.

Representatives of the family Teiidae have minute granular scales covering the upper surfaces of the body and large plates on the head. The belly scales are large and rectangular, and a distinct, transverse skin fold separates the belly from the throat region. These scalation characteristics, combined with the presence of moveable eyelids, separate teiid lizards from all other Costa Rican lizards.

The whip-tailed lizards are represented by 2 genera and 6 species in Costa Rica, all found mainly in lowland regions. Five species are in the genus *Ameiva*: the South American whip-tailed lizard (*Ameiva ameiva*), the Central American whip-tailed lizard (*Ameiva festiva*), the Pacific whip-tailed lizard (*Ameiva leptophrys*), the four-lined whip-tailed lizard (*Ameiva quadrilineata*), and the barred whip-tailed lizard (*Ameiva undulata*). *Ameiva festiva* and *Ameiva quadrilineata* are widespread and common along both slopes. *Ameiva quadrilineata* is replaced by *Ameiva undulata* in the arid northwestern parts of the country. In Costa Rica, *Ameiva ameiva* and *Ameiva leptophrys* are restricted to the southern Pacific lowlands. The sixth species, Deppe's whip-tailed lizard (*Cnemidophorus deppii*), occurs in the dry areas of Guanacaste Province.

SUMMARY

How to identify Costa Rican whip-tailed lizards:

- Whip-tailed lizards are medium-sized lizards with a streamlined body, a pointed head, and a long, whiplike tail.
- All Costa Rican species have large, symmetrical plates on the head, square plates on the belly, and very small, granular scales on the upper surfaces of the body and tail.

SPECIES DESCRIPTIONS

Ameiva festiva

Central American whip-tailed lizard
Chisbala (plate 56)

This beautiful, attractively colored lizard is the only whip-tailed lizard in Costa Rica that is marked with a light stripe running from the tip of the snout to the base of the tail. This stripe is distinctly visible in all but the oldest individuals. Hatchlings and juveniles with a snout-vent length less than 60 mm (2⅜ inches) characteristically have a bright blue tail.

There is a pronounced difference in size between adult males and females. Males attain a maximum snout-vent length of 120 mm (4¾ inches); females have a maximum snout-vent length of 94 mm (3¾ inches). Males generally have a heavier build than females, and a more robust head.

These agile lizards seem to be designed for speed; their body is elongate and streamlined, with a narrow head and a pointed snout. The tail is long and slender, and if undamaged, it may be about twice the length of the head and body combined.

The background color in this species is olive, dark gray, brown, or almost black; juveniles often have a reddish tinge. A dark stripe on each side of the body starts behind the head and runs to the insertion of the hind limbs. Several series of irregular yellow, orangish, or cream spots or dashes adorn each side of the body and neck. The belly is a uniform cream, gray, or bluish. During periods of sexual activity, males have a bright blue head and throat.

Ameiva festiva ranges from Mexico to Colombia. In Costa Rica, it inhabits the Caribbean and Pacific slopes, from sea level to an elevation of approximately 1,000 m (3,300 ft).

Among Costa Rican species of whip-tailed lizards, *Ameiva festiva* is the species most frequently found in the deep forest interior. However, within this habitat they are mostly seen in disturbed areas, such as in tree-fall gaps or other areas where the sun reaches the forest floor.

Ameiva festiva is generally seen either basking in a sun-exposed spot or scanning the forest floor for food. When in search of insect prey, it runs short distances, moving jerkily, and then stops to dig in the leaf litter using its front paws. Grasshoppers and spiders constitute the main part of the diet. In one study, small amphibians were found in the stomach of nearly 10% of the individuals examined.

In Costa Rica, *Ameiva festiva* appears to reproduce throughout the year. Females produce egg clutches of 2 or 3 eggs, three or more times a year. The size of each clutch does not vary with the size of the lizard; both small and large females produce an average of 2.2 eggs per clutch. However, the number of clutches produced per year may increase with increasing body size.

The leathery-shelled eggs of this species are elliptical in shape and measure about 12 x 24 mm (½ x 1 inch). The eggs are laid in a hole in the ground. After an incubation period that changes according to the environmental temperature, the eggs hatch and small hatchlings emerge with an average size of 37 mm (1½ inches).

Ameiva festiva are wary lizards that do not leave the holes they inhabit until assured they are free from danger. When the weather conditions are not optimal (sunny and dry), these lizards are reluctant to surface; on cold, rainy days they remain inactive. Early in the morning, they are usually seen basking in sunlit spots; as soon as their body temperature reaches the level required for activity, they start foraging.

A basking *Ameiva festiva* actively regulates its body temperature. By flattening its body, it increases the surface area that is exposed to sunlight and is thus able to heat up more quickly. This posture is mostly seen when the lizards first emerge from their burrows or on days when there is little sunshine. Once the internal temperature approaches its optimum, the body becomes less flattened to prevent overheating. After these lizards begin moving about, they keep their body temperature at a relatively constant level by moving in and out of the sun.

Ameiva quadrilineata

Four-lined whip-tailed lizard (plate 57)

Ameiva quadrilineata is one of the lizards most commonly seen amidst roadside vegetation and in open areas in forested regions. It is particularly abundant in the vegetation lining many Costa Rican beaches. Along the entire Caribbean coast, and from near Quepos southward along the Pacific coast, large numbers of these lizards can be seen busily foraging during the day. *Ameiva quadrilineata* seems to prefer sun-exposed, hot, dry "oases" in otherwise humid habitats.

Relatively small, reaching a snout-vent length of about 80 mm (3¼ inches), these beautiful lizards are dark-hued with four longitudinal light stripes on the back and sides, but never down the middle of the back (compare *Ameiva festiva*, p. 202). There is a striking difference in pattern and color between males and females of this species. In particular, when males are sexually active, their head turns bright blue, contrasting sharply with the less conspicuously colored females.

Reproduction in this species is thought to occur year-round, but it peaks in the early part of the rainy season (June, July). Mating usually takes place under the cover of low vegetation. As with many species of lizards, the male holds on to the female during copulation by biting her in the neck. Females lay small clutches of eggs—generally 2 or 3 per clutch—which are buried in sand or humus.

Cnemidophorus deppii

Deppe's whip-tailed lizard (plate 57)

The distinguishing feature of Deppe's whip-tailed lizard is its dark brown to black coloration, interrupted by seven narrow cream-colored stripes that run longitudinally. The top of the head is a uniform dark color; the throat is a light cream to white color. Juveniles have a striking bright blue tail.

The maximum snout-vent length of this species is approximately 80 mm (3⅛ inches).

Cnemidophorus deppii is widespread throughout Central America, inhabiting lowland areas from Mexico to northwestern Costa Rica. In Costa Rica, it inhabits sparsely vegetated open areas such as the sand dunes along the coast of the Pacific Ocean. This fast-moving lizard moves with a darting motion across the sand.

These lizards are active only on hot, sunny days. When the ambient temperature drops or when a cloud obscures the sun, they retreat into their burrows. The body temperature of this species can reach 42°C (108°F). One study recorded body temperatures 9 to 12°C (16 to 22°F) higher than the ambient air temperature.

In Costa Rica, *Cnemidophorus deppii* shares its habitat with *Ameiva festiva* and *Ameiva undulata*, although *Cnemidophorus* seems to have a greater preference for open, sun-exposed areas than do the *Ameiva* species.

Literature
Echternacht 1983; Fitch 1973; Hillman 1969; Lee 1996; Mudde 1992b; Mudde & van Dijk 1984d; Savage & Villa 1986; Smith 1968b; Zug 1993.

FAMILY: **Xantusidae** (Night Lizards)
SUBORDER: Lacertilia (Lizards)

Night lizards are strictly diurnal, contrary to what their name suggests. This misnomer is one indication of the poor state of our knowledge of members of this family.

The family Xantusidae is small—it includes about 20 species—and is found exclusively in the New World. Most species inhabit the southwestern United States and Mexico. Only two species, *Lepidophyma flavimaculatum* and *Lepidophyma reticulatum*, range into Costa Rica.

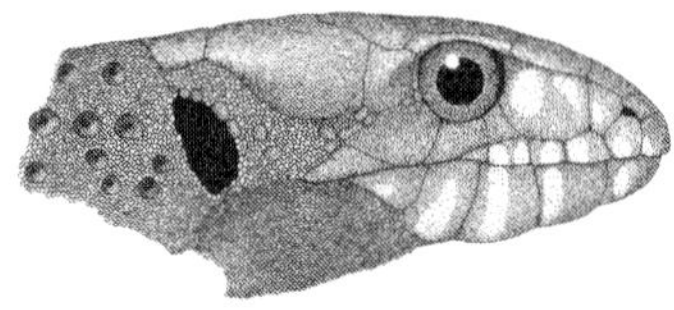
Yellow-spotted night lizard (*Lepidophyma flavimaculatum*).

Xantusid lizards resemble geckos in that they lack moveable eyelids and their eyes are covered with a spectacle-like transparent scale. Another feature they have in common with geckos is that their limbs and back are covered with soft granular scales instead of the keratinized roundish scales seen in most lizards. However, night lizards are unlike geckos in that they have large plates covering the top of the head and squarish scales on the belly.

Night lizards have an elongate and cylindrical body with a long, fragile tail; the head is robust with a bluntly rounded snout.

SUMMARY

How to identify Costa Rican night lizards:

- Costa Rican night lizards have large symmetrical plates on the head, square plates on the belly, and very small granular scales on the upper surfaces of the body. They also have large pointed scales scattered between the small granular scales on the body and tail. They lack moveable eyelids; instead, their eyes are covered with a transparent spectacle.
- These are medium-sized lizards with a cylindrical body, a long tail, and a bluntly rounded head.
- The limbs each bear five digits; neither toes nor fingers are expanded into adhesive pads.

SPECIES DESCRIPTION

Lepidophyma flavimaculatum
Yellow-spotted night lizard (plate 58)

Distinguishing features of this lizard are a combination of immovable eyelids, enlarged plates on the head, and tiny granular scales on the back and tail. These granular scales are not of uniform size, but are interspersed with larger, pointed scales that form irregular rows.

Lepidophyma flavimaculatum is a medium-sized species. It reaches a maximum snout-vent length of 110 mm (4⅜ inches); with the tail included, it measures at least 240 mm (9½ inches). Large individuals are often missing a part of the tail.

The body is elongate with relatively short limbs. The head is bluntly rounded in profile and almost triangular when viewed from above. The immovable eyelids have a transparent spectacle that covers the eye, which has a round pupil and a dark, dull-copper to reddish-brown iris. A large ear opening located in a deep depression is clearly visible behind each eye. From the ear openings downward, a skin fold runs underneath the neck.

The scale arrangement in night lizards is extraordinary among lizards. Large conical, pointed scales, scattered between smaller granular ones, form longitudinal rows along the back and transverse rows on the sides of the body and on the tail. The scales on the belly, which are squarish or rectangular in shape, are arranged in longitudinal rows.

Lepidophyma flavimaculatum characteristically has a dark gray, dark brown, or black dorsal ground color with a pattern of distinct yellow, cream, or white rosettelike spots. The belly is usually of a uniformly dark coloration, although each belly scale may have a lighter center. The chin and throat are whitish, sometimes with a few tiny scattered brown specks. A pattern of alternating dark and light bars adorns the upper and lower lips.

Lepidophyma flavimaculatum occurs in the lowlands from Mexico to the Canal Zone in Panama. In Costa Rica—where it is widespread, but rarely seen—it is found on the Caribbean slopes. This lizard probably does not inhabit elevations over 1,000 m (3,300 ft).

This night lizard species is very reclusive. Despite its common name, it is mostly active during the day, slowly moving through leaf litter or in dense vegetation on the darkly shaded rainforest floor. These lizards are sometimes uncovered when moving rocks or logs; they may also be seen in rock crevices or under loose bark on dead trees.

Lepidophyma flavimaculatum may spend most of its life in a home range that is not bigger than a few meters across. It feeds primarily on invertebrates, sometimes consuming some plant matter as well. Some Guatemalan individuals were reported to mainly eat termites.

These lizards do not have moveable eyelids and therefore cannot remove dirt from their eyes by blinking. Instead, they wipe their spectacles and face with their flat, broad tongue, much like geckos.

The females of this species are capable of producing offspring from an unfertilized egg (parthenogenesis). All young lizards produced in this way are females. The advantage of parthenogenesis is that females that have become isolated from males can continue to produce offspring. In some areas of Panama, and possibly also in Costa Rica, isolated populations consist solely of females. Of course, if a male were to reach one of these populations, the females can still reproduce with him. In such a case, there is a 50% chance of either male or female offspring. Like all other Xantusidae, *Lepidophyma flavimaculatum* is live-bearing. Each year, or possibly every other year, it gives birth to 1 to 5 young. Births seem to coincide with the rainy season.

A second Costa Rican species of night lizard, *Lepidophyma reticulatum*, occurs in the Pacific lowlands. Although very similar in appearance to *Lepidophyma flavimaculatum*, it differs in scalation and in the pattern on the throat. The chin and throat of *Lepidophyma reticulatum* display a cream background that is boldy marked with a dark brown or black reticulated pattern. The chin and throat of *Lepidophyma flavimaculatum* also have a cream background, but the markings, when present, consist of tiny scattered dark specks.

Literature

Bezy 1984; Hayes et al. 1989; Lee 1996; Savage & Villa 1986; Taylor 1939, 1955; Telford & Campbell 1970; Zug 1993.

FAMILY: **Anguidae** (Anguid Lizards)
SUBORDER: Lacertilia (Lizards)

All anguids have a small, bony plate called an osteoderm underlying each body scale. These plates form a kind of chain-link armor, a somewhat rigid structure that limits the expansion of the body when the lizard eats and breathes. Many anguid lizards have a skin fold that separates the armor on the back and the armor on the belly, a groove that runs along the body from the insertion of the front limbs to the groin that allows the lizard to increase the girth of its body when eating. Costa Rican anguids can be divided into two morphological subgroups based on the presence or absence of a skin fold: the gerrhonotines, which have a skin fold, and the diploglossines, which do not.

Highland alligator lizard (*Mesaspis monticola*).

Costa Rica has 7 species in 4 genera (*Celestus* and *Diploglossus* in the diploglossine subgroup; *Mesaspis* and *Coloptychon* in the gerrhonotine subgroup). The status of the genus *Celestus* is under debate; some herpetologists prefer to include *Celestus* species in the genus *Diploglossus*. Here they are treated as distinct genera. Although anguid lizards in other parts of the world are sometimes legless, all Costa Rican species have front and hind limbs, each with five digits.

All Costa Rican anguids have moveable eyelids, a clearly visible ear opening, and a fragile tail. Information on the life history of most species is lacking, although all appear to be predominantly terrestrial or semifossorial. Anguids can be either oviparous or ovoviviparous.

SUMMARY

How to identify Costa Rican anguids:
The members of this family can be divided into two groups:

- The Costa Rican anguid lizards of the genera *Coloptychon* and *Mesaspis* typically have a distinct skin fold between the front limbs and hind limbs that looks like a deep longitudinal groove.
- Costa Rican anguids in the genera *Celestus* and *Diploglossus* lack this groove, but typically have ridged or keeled scales on their body and tail, as opposed to smooth scales.
- The lizards in these two genera otherwise closely resemble skinks (family Scincidae) in their scalation and body shape. Like skinks, their head is covered with large symmetrical plates, and both the body and tail bear similarly shaped, rounded scales. The body and tail of both is cylindrical, but anguids usually have a more robust head than skinks.

Celestus hylaius
Rainforest celestus (plate 58)

Described in 1993, this species is a recent addition to the Costa Rican herpetofauna.

Celestus hylaius has a snout-vent length of 107 mm (4¼ inches), and a total length of 210 mm (8¼ inches).

Celestus hylaius is a skinklike lizard with short limbs, each bearing five digits that end in a clearly visible claw. The body scales do not have keels, but have multiple ridges instead. An external ear opening is present on each side of the head.

The background color of the dorsal surfaces is coppery brown, with a pattern of cream-tipped black scales scattered over the lizard's back, sides, and tail. These marked scales form a cross-banded pattern on the posterior half of the body. The throat and the lower parts of the head (including upper and lower lips) are yellowish-green, grading to light green on the belly. A dark irregular stripe extends from the eye to the front limbs and along the sides of the body to the groin.

Celestus hylaius occurs in the Caribbean lowlands and in the Tilarán mountain range, at elevations up to 700 m (2,300 ft). The other two species recorded in Costa Rica live exclusively at elevations above 1,200 m (3,950 ft). *Celestus cyanochloris* inhabits the Tilarán mountain range; *Celestus orobius* inhabits the Talamanca mountain range.

The short limbs of *Celestus hylaius* are relatively strong and well-developed. Nevertheless, when attempting to escape, these lizards move rapidly by coiling the body in a snakelike fashion and do not use the hands or feet.

Individuals of this species were observed in the leaf litter of dense primary forest. Its habits, diet, and life history are unknown.

Lizards of the genus *Celestus* are closely related to the galliwasps of the genus *Diploglossus*. *Celestus* species can be distinguished from members of the latter genus by their exposed, clearly visible claws on the digits; the claws of *Diploglossus* are covered by a sheath, leaving only the tip of the claw visible.

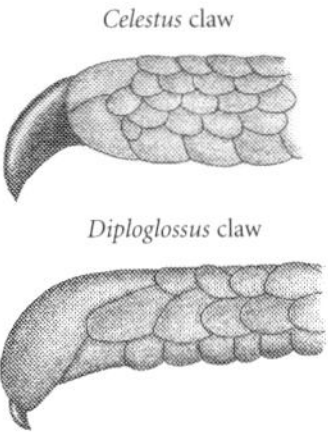

The three Costa Rican species of *Celestus* are rarely sighted; each species is known from less than a dozen individuals. *Celestus orobius* is known only from a single specimen.

Diploglossus bilobatus
Talamanca galliwasp (plate 59)

The Talamanca galliwasp, *Diploglossus bilobatus*, inhabits the southwestern lowlands of Costa Rica, but it can also be found at low and intermediate elevations on the Caribbean slope. In the latter region, both galliwasps (*Diploglossus bilobatus* and *Diploglossus monotropis*) may co-occur. *Diploglossus bilobatus* is of similar build as *Diploglossus monotropis*, but much smaller—less than 100 mm (4 inches) without the tail—and with a very different color pattern. A wide dark brown to black band that runs the entire length of the back is separated from the lighter sides of the body by a black stripe that is often bordered by a light dashed line on each side of the body. There is a pattern of conspicuous light spots on the side of the neck. All other Costa Rican lizards with a similar body shape (e.g., genera *Celestus* and *Mabuya*) do not have sheath-covered claws with only the tips visible; instead, their claws are uncovered and clearly visible.

Diploglossus monotropis
Galliwasp
Escorpión coral (plate 59)

Diploglossus monotropis is a large, skinklike lizard with an elongate, fairly cylindrical body and tail.

LIZARDS

Among the Costa Rican lizards with a similar body shape—anguid lizards, skinks, and some gymnophthalmids—only the extremely rare *Coloptychon rhombifer* reaches the impressive size of an adult *Diploglossus monotropis*, which, with the tail included, may measure nearly 450 mm (17¾ inches).

The most striking feature of this beautiful species is the bright orange to red coloration on the sides of the body and head. This coloration extends onto the lower surfaces of the body, tail, and throat. The dorsal background color of the body and tail is usually a uniform brown, dark brown, or black interrupted by a series of black-edged white, gray, or yellowish-green cross-bands. Light bands on the tail are wider than the narrow stripes that break up the dark dorsal coloration, creating a pattern of alternating, similarly sized, dark and light bands. The light stripes are very distinct in juveniles, but may occasionally fade with age. The top and sides of the head are often suffused with yellow or yellowish olive, as is the chin. The iris of the eye is orange or brown.

The many rows of small, uniform cycloid scales that completely encircle the body form a shiny and effective body armor. The bony osteoderms that underlie each scale are strong, and one author reported that, in a large individual, the scales can sometimes even deflect a .22 caliber bullet. The dorsal body scales have a pronounced median keel and are textured with several additional small ridges. There is no skin fold between the front and hind limbs. The head is covered with enlarged plates. Moveable eyelids and a clearly visible ear opening are present. The limbs are small but powerful, with five fingers and five toes. The claws are mostly covered by a compressed claw sheath around the base of the claw, leaving only the claw tip visible.

In Latin America, practically any elongate animal with a considerable amount of red in its coloration is associated with the venomous coral snakes (*Micrurus* species). Many people believe, incorrectly, that *Diploglossus monotropis* is also venomous, and this belief is reflected in some of its local names: *madre de culebra* (mother of serpents), *madre coral* (mother of coral snakes), and *escorpión coral* (coral scorpion). In fact, no venomous lizards exist in Costa Rica.

Diploglossus monotropis is an uncommon but geographically dispersed species. On the Caribbean coast, it ranges from southern Nicaragua to western Panama; on the Pacific coast, it ranges from eastern Panama to Colombia and Ecuador. Within Costa Rica, it is restricted to the rainforests of the Caribbean lowlands, from sea level to approximately 1,000 m (3,300 ft), although unsubstantiated records report that this species also occurs at elevations above 2,000 m (6,600 ft).

Like other Costa Rican anguids, *Diploglossus monotropis* is predominantly diurnal. It is also a terrestrial or fossorial species that seems to prefer forest edges, disturbed situations, and even secondary forest. It is most frequently observed moving about in leaf litter. When discovered, it flees with surprisingly rapid movements.

Diploglossus monotropis is thought to be a specialized predator of land crabs.

Mesaspis monticola

Highland alligator lizard

Dragón (plate 60)

This medium-sized, diurnal lizard is restricted to the highland regions of the Central Valley and the Talamanca mountain range. It is the only lizard found on the highest peaks of Costa Rica, at elevations over 3,300 m (10,800 ft). Among these peaks are Cerro de la Muerte and Mount Chirripó.

A well-developed skin fold between the front and hind limbs separates the lateral scales from the large rectangular plates that cover the belly. This feature, combined with the lizard's geographic occurrence, distinguishes *Mesaspis monticola* from other Costa Rican lizards.

Mesaspis monticola (often referred to as *Gerrhonotus monticola*) is a broad-headed, heavy-bodied, and heavy-tailed lizard with short, strong limbs. It displays a striking sexual dimorphism: males have a vivid yellowish-green ground color heavily speckled with black, while females have a greenish-brown to gold-brown body, also speckled with black, and with a greenish or yellow venter. Males are larger than females, and have a proportionately larger and more massive head. These animals do not generally exceed 200 mm (7⅞ inches) in total length.

The head is covered with large plates, the belly scales are enlarged rectangular plates, and the dorsal scales all bear a heavy well-developed keel. These keeled scales create a series of continuous ridges that run along the lizard's entire back, flanks, and tail. The skin fold, which encloses a series of small, granular scales, is often infected with ectoparasites such as mites and ticks.

The only other Costa Rican lizard with a distinct skin fold is *Coloptychon rhombifer*, a member of the same family. However, these two lizards do not coincide geographically. The extremely rare *Coloptychon rhombifer* is found only in southwestern lowland Costa Rica, near the Panamanian border. An individual discovered near Golfito in September 2000 represented only the fourth individual of this species ever found, making it one of the rarest lizards in Costa Rica.

Alligator lizards owe their common name to the heavily keeled ridges that run along the upper surfaces and somewhat resemble the keels on a crocodilian tail and back. This feature also most likely explains the local common name *dragón* or *dragoncillo*, meaning "dragon" or "little dragon."

This lizard is seen basking on the low vegetation that characterizes the *paramó* vegetation of the Latin American highlands. Old logs are another preferred microhabitat; decaying wood retains heat very well, and these lizards seek out logs to regulate their body temperature.

One trait that allows ectothermous animals like lizards to survive in such a cold climate is ovoviviparity. The eggs are produced and retained inside the female's body, where they complete their development and hatch. The main advantage this form of reproduction has over placing an egg clutch in a fixed location is that the female can actively influence the incubation temperature by carrying her eggs to places with a favorable temperature. This means that the eggs can be incubated at temperatures substantially higher and much more constant than the ambient temperature.

These creatures are sometimes thought, incorrectly, to be highly venomous.

Literature

Hayes et al. 1989; Mudde & van Dijk 1984d; Myers 1973; Savage & Lips 1993; Savage & Villa 1986; Scott & Limerick 1983; Tihen 1949; Zug 1993.

Snakes are essentially lizards that lost limbs, moveable eyelids, and external ear openings during the course of evolution. This successful group of vertebrates, which includes almost 2,700 species, occupies a great variety of habitats and climates; snakes are found in deserts, in tropical rainforests, and even in habitats within the polar circle. They live at elevations above the tree line in the Himalayas, at sea level, and anywhere in between. One group of snakes, the sea snakes, even inhabits tropical seas and oceans.

Each of the 133 snake species that live in Costa Rica may immediately be recognized as a snake, but identifying the specific species may pose challenges. Costa Rican snakes are currently placed within 8 families (see table 8). However, the taxonomic placement of several species is still under investigation, and the general state of taxonomic understanding is more confused for snakes than for the other Costa Rican reptiles.

Table 8: Taxonomy of Costa Rican Snakes

Order	*Common Name*	*Number of Species*
Anomalepididae	Neotropical blindsnake family	3
Leptotyphlopidae	Slender blindsnake family	1
Typhlopidae	True blindsnake family	1
Loxocemidae	Neotropical sunbeam snake family	1
Boidae	Boa family	5
Colubridae	Colubrid snake family	103
Elapidae	Coral snake family	5
Viperidae	Viper family	14

Three families of wormlike snakes (Anomalepididae, Leptotyphlopidae, and Typhlopidae) are grouped together in a kind of suprafamily known as the Scolecophidia, the blindsnakes.

The boa family (Boidae) has witnessed a number of taxonomic changes in recent years. One Costa Rican species, the neotropical sunbeam snake (*Loxocemus bicolor*) was formerly considered a member of the boa family; but at present, this snake is family-less, and its relation to other groups is poorly understood. This book follows the convention established by some writers and assigns the neotropical sunbeam snake to the family Loxocemidae.

The three remaining families, collectively called advanced snakes, comprise the bulk of the Costa Rican snakes. The word *advanced* denotes the fact that these snakes evolved more recently than the older, more "primitive" snakes. The nonvenomous colubrid snakes form the largest family within the reptiles, and 103 species inhabit Costa Rica. This family is sometimes referred to as the trash can of the snake families since every advanced snake that is not obviously a coral snake or a viper is automatically placed in it. Biologists recognize that not all species in this family are closely related, and it is likely that future classification efforts will reassign current colubrids to other families or subfamilies.

The other two groups of advanced snakes are the coral snakes (Elapidae) and the vipers (Viperidae). The Costa Rican elapids include brightly colored, terrestrial coral snakes and one sea snake. The latter is placed in a sea snake subfamily of the Elapidae called Hydrophiinae. All Costa Rican members of the viper family are assigned to the subfamily Crotalinae, commonly called pit vipers.

The snakes in these two families are venomous, and their classification is based in part on the structure of the venom delivery system. In general, coral snakes possess short, permanently erect fangs on the upper jaw, at the front of the mouth. The fangs are connected to venom glands that contain a nerve toxin. Vipers, on the other hand, have hinged fangs, also located on the upper jaw at the front of the mouth. These fangs are folded back when the snake's mouth is closed and erected during a strike. The venom glands of vipers mainly contain tissue-destructive venom, although some species also have neurotoxic components in their venom.

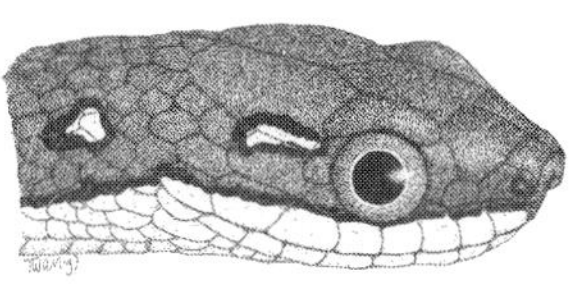

The **red-bellied litter snake** (*Rhadinaea decorata*) is one of many colubrid snakes found in Costa Rica.

Some colubrid snakes possess enlarged teeth at the back of the mouth that may be connected to a venom gland (Duvernoy's gland). Although colubrid snakes are not considered venomous, some species do produce a mild toxin. At least two African species, the boomslang (*Dispholidus typus*) and the savanna twig snake (*Thelotornis capensis*), have caused human fatalities, but bites of most colubrids do not pose a serious threat to humans.

Several Costa Rican snakes are rear-fanged; and some, such as the road guarder (*Conophis lineatus*) or some of the false coral snakes (*Urotheca euryzona, Erythrolamprus* spp.), may deliver a painful bite. No information exists on bites of some of the larger rear-fanged species, such as the mussurana (*Clelia clelia*), but a bite from those species could cause serious discomfort. Since the effects of snake venom may vary from person to person, it is impossible to say generally which species are potentially dangerous. As a rule, it is better to avoid being bitten, and rear-fanged colubrids should always be treated with great care.

Snakes, like lizards, shed their skin frequently, although juveniles shed more often than adults. The skin is shed in a single piece that includes the transparent scales that normally cover the snake's eyes. An opaque liquid is secreted between the outer, dead layer of skin and the new layer of skin a few days before shedding. During this period, when the eyes appear milky and the vision is obstructed, snakes normally retire to a hiding place, since they are more vulnerable to predation. Just before shedding, the eyes uncloud and the new skin becomes vividly visible through the soon to be removed old layer. The snake rubs its head against a rough surface to rupture the skin, and then crawls out of its old skin. The shed skin, which can often be found, represents an inside out copy of the regular scalation and color patterns. In fact, it is possible to identify a snake solely by its shed skin.

S U M M A R Y

How to identify Costa Rican snakes:

- Snakes are limbless reptiles with an elongate body that is covered with scales. They invariably lack moveable eyelids and an externally visible ear opening.

Literature

Greene 1997; Zug 1993.

SUPRAFAMILY: **Scolecophidia** (Blindsnakes)
SUBORDER: Serpentes (Snakes)

Scolecophidia, or blindsnakes, includes three families of the most primitive snakes: Anomalepididae, Leptotyphlopidae, and Typhlopidae.

Members of all three families are recognized by the polished, rounded, equal-sized scales that cover a small, cylindrical body. All blindsnakes have a spinelike tip on the otherwise blunt tail. Unlike all other terrestrial snakes in Costa Rica, the belly scales are not enlarged.

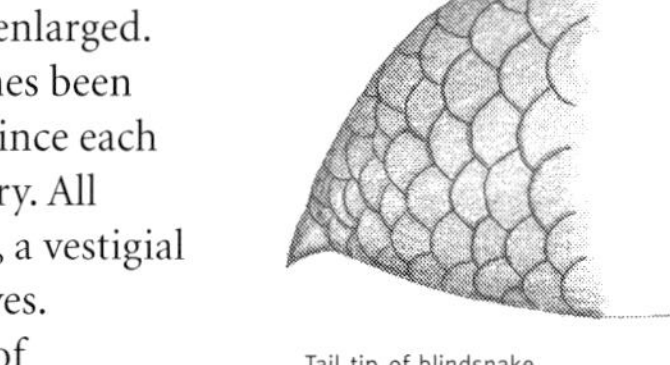
Tail tip of blindsnake.

These tiny snakes have sometimes been dubbed "degenerate degenerates," since each body part appears to be rudimentary. All species have highly modified skulls, a vestigial pelvic girdle, and highly reduced eyes.

A distinguishing characteristic of blindsnakes is a rounded head with an enlarged plate on the tip of the snout. This large plate sometimes covers most of the front of the head. The eyes of blindsnakes are vestigial, and all species have poor vision. In some species, the eyes are only barely visible through skin and scales as vague dark spots. Blindsnakes depend mainly on chemosensory signals for feeding, reproduction, and defense, and their perception of chemical cues is highly developed.

Blindsnakes are burrowers and are rarely seen on the surface. Hardly anything is known about their biology or distribution. The five blindsnakes found in Costa Rica are briefly discussed in the following three family descriptions.

SUMMARY

How to identify Costa Rican blindsnakes:
It is very hard to distinguish the various groups of Costa Rican blindsnakes without the aid of a microscope. However, as a group, these tiny snakes share a number of characteristics.

- All Costa Rican blindsnakes are very small to small snakes with a cylindrical body that is covered entirely with smooth, similarly sized scales. No enlarged belly scales are present.
- The eyes of blindsnakes are covered with scales, and are only visible as dark spots on the sides of the head. The tail of blindsnakes typically is bluntly rounded and carries a pointed, spinelike tip.

FAMILY: **Anomalepididae** (Neotropical Blindsnakes)
SUBORDER: Serpentes (Snakes)

The small snakes of this family occur in lower Central America and South America. Three species in three genera, all of them rare, are reported to occur in Costa Rica: *Anomalepis mexicanus*, *Helmintophis frontalis*, and *Liotyphlops albirostris*. Biologists have collected fewer than five individuals of each species in Costa Rica; individuals have been collected in other countries, but also in very small numbers. In the case of *Liotyphlops albirostris*, a single individual has been collected in Costa Rica—the collector, who found this snake in the 1800s, failed to note its location.

While anomalepidids are poorly understood, biologists do know that all species are wormlike and small, with a total length usually less than 30 cm (12 inches). All anomalepidid blindsnakes discovered thus far have smooth, round, equal-sized scales covering a cylindrical body. They have a burrowing lifestyle, vestigial eyes covered by skin and scales, and a skull highly modified for digging and for eating termites, their preferred prey.

The snakes in this family differ from the other Costa Rican blindsnakes (families Leptotyphlopidae and Typhlopidae) in having teeth on both jaws.

All anomalepidids are thought to be egg-laying, with clutches of 2 to 13 eggs. In the genera *Anomalepis* and *Helmintophis*, the left oviduct is absent or vestigial, probably as an adaptation to the extremely small and thin body; all other snakes have two oviducts.

Anomalepis mexicanus has been reported from Nicaragua, Costa Rica, Panama, and northwestern Peru. It probably also occurs in the intermediate countries of Colombia and Ecuador, but has not yet been found there. The few individuals that have been collected measure between 82 and 164 mm (3¼ and 6½ inches). In Costa Rica, this species has been found in forested areas of Guanacaste Province.

Helmintophis frontalis, commonly called the pink-headed blindsnake, is a dark brown snake with a somewhat lighter belly. The pink head and tail tip are patterned with red lines that, on close inspection, appear to be blood vessels that are visible through the pigmentless skin. An individual of this species measured 158 mm (6¼ inches). *Helmintophis frontalis* inhabits the Caribbean slope and Central Valley of Costa Rica, and is also found in Panama.

Liotyphlops albirostris is a tiny snake with a narrow and somewhat flattened head. Its eyes, which are covered by head scales, are vaguely distinguishable. The coloration of *Liotyphlops albirostris* is reported to be blackish or dark brown, with each scale having a reddish border.

No photographs were available for any of these three species at the time of publication.

Literature

Greene 1997; Kofron 1988; Taylor 1951, 1954b.

FAMILY: **Leptotyphlopidae** (Slender Blindsnakes)
SUBORDER: Serpentes (Snakes)

The largest known member of this family measures less than 500 mm (19⅝ inches) in total length, while most species are between 200 and 300 mm (7⅞ and 11¾ inches) in total length.

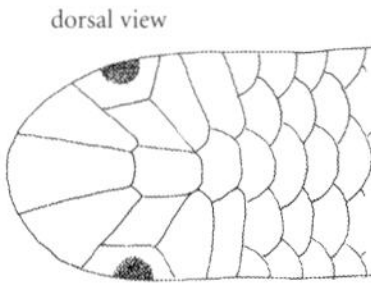

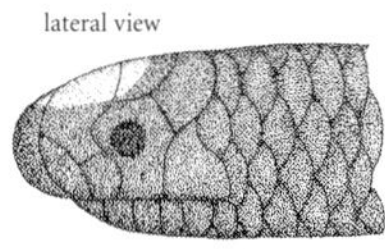

Neotropical slender blindsnake (*Leptotyphlops goudotii*). This sole representative of the slender blindsnake family in Costa Rica has large, platelike scales on the head and small, cycloid scales on the body.

Members of this family are unique among snakes in having teeth on the lower jaw only; most snakes have teeth on both upper and lower jaws.

Most leptotyphlopids are egg-laying, producing small clutches of tiny, highly elongate eggs. A North American species, *Leptotyphlops dulcis*, is known to remain coiled around the eggs during incubation and has also been reported to nest communally. It is not known whether these facts are true for the Costa Rican species.

Slender blindsnakes prey exclusively on invertebrates, with ants and termites comprising the bulk of the diet. When entering an ant or termite nest, the snake excretes a chemical substance that makes the ants or termites accept it as a nest mate; this allows the snake to remain inside the nest without being attacked by the soldier ants or termites.

In Costa Rica the family Leptotyphlopidae is represented by one species, *Leptotyphlops goudotii*.

SPECIES DESCRIPTION

Leptotyphlops goudotii

Neotropical slender blindsnake
(plate 60)

Leptotyphlops goudotii is a very slender, small snake. While it can measure up to 275 mm (10⅞ inches) in total length, it is usually smaller and can easily be mistaken for a worm. The body is of a uniform diameter throughout, and the head and the neck are not discernible. The 14 scale rows around the body are all of the same size; a single scale covers the vent. A cream or yellow spot is present on top of the head and on the spine-tipped tail. The head is rounded, and the eyes are covered by large scales that are in contact with the lip.

The snake's body is dark brown. Usually each scale has a dark center and light edges; collectively, the scales form indistinct longitudinal stripes. In some individuals, these stripes are hard to see, giving the snake a uniformly dark appearance.

Leptotyphlops goudotii is widespread in the drier areas of the neotropics, ranging from Mexico to Colombia and Venezuela, from sea level to at least 700 m (2,300 ft). In Costa Rica, it is found, albeit infrequently, in the northwestern part of the country.

These secretive snakes are active both by day and by night. Mainly fossorial, they are sometimes found by digging in soil or in termite nests, or by looking under logs or rocks. On one occasion, an individual was seen climbing up a tree trunk, in broad daylight, toward a termite nest that was at a height of approximately 1 m (3 ft). Occasionally, observers have stumbled across small aggregations of *Leptotyphlops goudotii*; the function of these aggregations still remains unknown.

Blindsnakes' loss of functional eyes is most likely an evolutionary result of a subterranean lifestyle, where eyes are more a burden than a benefit. For information on its environment, a blindsnake relies primarily on chemosensory cues. Some species are known to follow the pheromone trails of the ants they prey on. *Leptotyphlops goudotii* feeds on termites, which it grabs by the abdomen. It bites through the insect's armor, and eats the intestines.

In Mexico, *Leptotyphlops goudotii* have been reported to produce clutches consisting of 8 to 12 eggs that were laid in June and July. It is likely they display similar behavior in Costa Rica.

Some authorities argue that Costa Rican members of the species *Leptotyphlops goudotii* should be assigned to the species *Leptotyphlops ater*.

Literature
Alvarez del Toro 1983; Greene 1997; Sasa & Solórzano 1995; Scott 1983h; Taylor 1951; Wilson & Meyer 1985.

FAMILY: **Typhlopidae** (True Blindsnakes)
SUBORDER: Serpentes (Snakes)

Costa Rican blindsnake
(*Typhlops costaricensis*).

Another family of similar-looking, wormlike snakes is the true blindsnake family, Typhlopidae. Members of this relatively small family are found in tropical regions worldwide, and in temperate zones of Asia and Australia.

True blindsnakes have more scale rows around the body than do the slender blindsnakes (family Leptotyphlopidae). In addition, true blind snakes have teeth on the upper jaw only, while slender blindsnakes have teeth on the lower jaw only; all other snakes have teeth on both jaws.

In Costa Rica, this family is represented by a single species, *Typhlops costaricensis.*

SPECIES DESCRIPTION

Typhlops costaricensis
Costa Rican blindsnake (plate 61)

Typhlops costaricensis looks like a large, blunt-headed, blunt-tailed worm. Its size, shape, and color are somewhat reminiscent of the caecilians; those amphibians, however, have glandular skin that lacks scales and that is creased into folds.

The Costa Rican blindsnake's slightly flattened head and short spine on the tail are the only features that are discernible from the otherwise featureless, cylindrical body. More than 14 rows of smooth, equally sized, shiny scales encircle the body completely. The eyes, which are tiny and covered by scales, are still clearly visible as little black dots placed fairly high on the head.

The dorsal ground color of this snake is a uniform brownish-gray to lavender-gray. The color of the snout and belly is usually of a slightly lighter hue than the rest of the body.

Typhlops costaricensis is currently known from just five definite locations in Central America: one in Honduras, two in Nicaragua, and two in Costa Rica (Poco Sol in Alajuela Province, and the Monteverde Cloud Forest Preserve in Puntarenas Province). All locations are between 1,100 and 1,500 m (3,600 and 4,900 ft).

Literature
Hayes et al. 1989; Villa 1988.

FAMILY: **Loxocemidae** (Neotropical Sunbeam Snakes)
SUBORDER: Serpentes (Snakes)

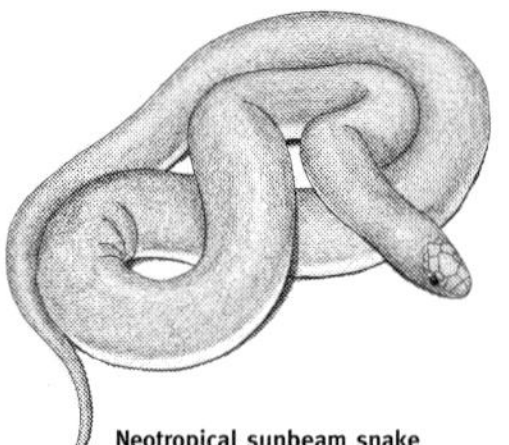
Neotropical sunbeam snake (*Loxocemus bicolor*).

Until recently, *Loxocemus bicolor*, which is the single species in this family, was included in the boa family (Boidae). Presently, it is thought to be even more primitive than all contemporary boas and has thus been removed from that family.

Although the unique features of *Loxocemus bicolor* seem to justify its placement in a separate family, its taxonomic status is still under investigation, and several alternative views on its taxonomic placement exist. Such questions are beyond the scope of this book, and the author has adopted the assignment of this species to the family Loxocemidae, of which it is the only member.

SUMMARY

How to identify Costa Rican neotropical sunbeam snakes:

- This family contains a single species, which, in Costa Rica can be found in the Guanacaste area only. It is immediately recognized by its prominently upturned snout and the distinctive two-toned coloration (light belly and dark upper surfaces).
- Although some venomous pit vipers also have a few upturned scales on the tip of their snout, the neotropical sunbeam snake lacks the heat-sensitive pits, one on each side of the head, characteristic of pit vipers.

SPECIES DESCRIPTION

Loxocemus bicolor
Neotropical sunbeam snake (plate 61)

The combination of dark upper surfaces and a light belly, a prominently upturned snout, and parietal head scales completely separated from one another are features that distinguish this species from all other Costa Rican snakes. *Loxocemus bicolor* is a medium-sized snake; most adults reach a total length of approximately 1 m (3 ft).

The species name *bicolor* refers to the contrast between the color of the upper surfaces and the color of the belly. The upper surfaces are dark lavender, grayish, bluish, or brown. This coloration contrasts sharply with the cream or white-colored belly. The scales on the back are smooth and highly iridescent. In some individuals small irregular light blotches may be scattered throughout the dark colors of the upper surfaces.

Loxocemus bicolor ranges from Mexico southward, reaching its southern limit in the dry forests of Guanacaste Province, in northwestern Costa Rica.

Little is known about the natural history of the secretive *Loxocemus bicolor*. Although it sometimes burrows, it is a terrestrial snake that is frequently found hidden in leaf litter. It is primarily active at night, but individuals also have been seen foraging during the day. These snakes feed on small mammals and lizards, but have also been known to prey on the eggs of sea turtles and lizards; included among the species of lizards whose eggs they eat are the spiny lizards (genus *Sceloporus*) and the spiny-tailed iguanas (genus

Ctenosaura). The snake uses its upturned snout to dig up the eggs from their nests.

Although it is known to lay eggs, the reproductive behavior of *Loxocemus bicolor* is still undescribed.

Literature

Greene 1997; Taylor 1954b; Trutnau 1988; Wilson & Meyer 1985; Zug 1993.

FAMILY: **Boidae** (Boa Family)
SUBORDER: Serpentes (Snakes)

Until a few years ago, the family Boidae was a taxonomic hodgepodge. At present, about 27 species of former boids are included in the python family (Pythonidae). A few obscure primitive snakes have been removed from the boa family and placed in separate families. The remaining 5 genera and 35 species of Old and New World boas comprise the new, and considerably smaller, boa family.

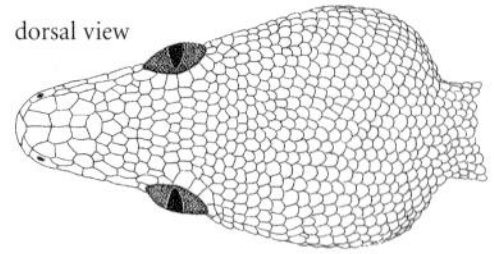

Common tree boa (*Corallus ruschenbergerii*). The snakes in the boa family have small smooth scales on the head, which is triangular shaped.

Although this family includes some of the largest snakes on Earth—including the giant anaconda (*Eunectus murinus*) of South America—most species are medium-sized or even small snakes.

Boids are adapted to life in a variety of habitats, ranging from arboreal species that inhabit jungle treetops to semi-aquatic species that live in swamps and rivers. Some species spend most of their lives buried in desert sand.

All boas are nonvenomous constrictors, but large boas, which have numerous large, curved teeth and great constricting power, should be treated with care.

Boas are primarily sit-and-wait predators; rather than moving through vegetation in active search of prey, they wait to ambush it.

The living representatives of the family Boidae are primitive snakes, as attested to by the presence of a vestigial pelvis and hind limbs. These rudimentary limbs are visible as nail-like spurs, one on each side of the vent. These "anal spurs" are usually better developed in males than in females and are used during courtship behavior to stimulate the female. As far as is known, all boids are live-bearing.

Anal spurs in *Boa constrictor*.

Members of the family Boidae share several characteristics with the pit vipers. Boas and pit vipers are heavy-bodied snakes with a triangular head; both also have a high number of scale rows that surround the body and numerous small scales on the top of the head. Boas, however, lack the two pitlike heat-sensitive organs that characterizes the pit vipers. While some boids, such as *Corallus annulatus* and *Corallus ruschenbergerii*, do have a series of heat-sensitive organs, these appear as small slits in the lip shields, never as a deep hole between the eye and nostril.

Costa Rica is home to 5 species of boids. The most commonly seen, and the most familiar to popular consciousness, is *Boa constrictor*, which occurs in lowland regions country-wide. Two species of tree boa, the common tree boa (*Corallus ruschenbergerii*) and the annulated tree boa (*Corallus annulatus*), are also described in the following section. The rainbow boa (*Epicrates cenchria*) is a medium-sized snake that is found, infrequently, in the drier parts of Costa Rica. The Central American dwarf boa (*Ungaliophis panamensis*) is a very rare species. A few individuals have been found in dense rainforests, where this species probably inhabits the treetops.

SUMMARY

How to identify Costa Rican boids:

- Snakes in the boa family have a very large number of scale rows that encircle the body. All Costa Rican individuals have at least 21 such scale rows, but most individuals have more than 50 scale rows.
- Numerous small scales cover the head.
- Some boids have nail-like anal spurs on the base of the tail, one on each side of the vent.
- While boas share many characteristics with pit vipers, they never have the deep, pitlike heat-sensitive organ (one on each side of the head) found in pit vipers.

SPECIES DESCRIPTIONS

Boa constrictor

Boa constrictor
Bequer (plate 62)

Boa constrictor is the largest and heaviest snake in Costa Rica, and it is often recognized on the basis of its size alone. The maximum known size for this species is about 550 cm (216 inches), but individuals that exceed 350 cm (138 inches) are a rarity in nature.

Boas are somewhat pit viper–like in appearance, with a heavy-set body and a head that is distinctly wider than the neck. The many small scales covering the top of the head—as opposed to the large symmetrical plates characteristic of most harmless snakes—and the high number of scale rows that encircle the body are also characteristics of the dangerously venomous pit vipers. *Boa constrictor* does not have the deep heat-sensitive pit between the eye and nostril that gives the pit viper its common name, but it does have heat-sensitive organs. A concentration of extremely sensitive nerve endings is located inside the lip scales, and these allow *Boa constrictor* to register the slightest changes in temperature.

The horny spur that is located on each side of the vent is a visible remainder of the vestigial hind limbs and pelvis that are present inside the body of *Boa constrictor*. These anal spurs, which are better-developed in males than they are in females, are used during courtship to stimulate the female.

Boa constrictor has a tan, gray, or yellowish brown background color patterned with spots, bars, and diamonds of chocolate brown, black, and white. The most distinctive aspect of the snake's markings is a series of light elliptical spots outlined in dark pigment that runs down the middle of the back. Toward the tail, this pattern gradually changes into a row of large, rounded dark brown spots outlined with light rings; on the tail itself, the dark spots are reddish brown. The head has the same light shade of brown or gray as the body and is marked with a broad, dark stripe that passes through the eye. Often a thin dark stripe is present on top of the head, running from the snout to the neck. Juvenile *Boa constrictor* have a lavender-gray body with a faint version of the adult pattern.

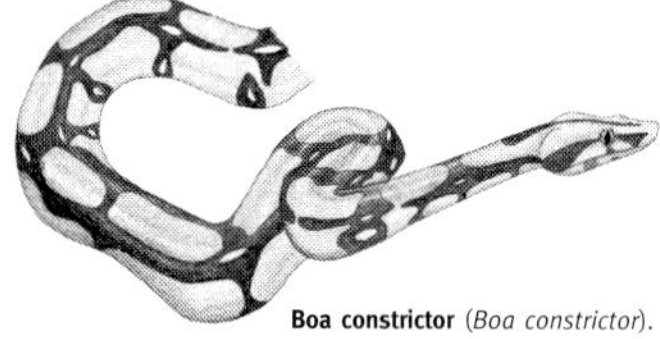
Boa constrictor (*Boa constrictor*).

Boas have highly iridescent scales, and individuals that have recently shed display a particularly beautiful radiance.

The eyes of a boa have vertically elliptical pupils; the iris is beige.

Boa constrictor has a huge distribution range, from Mexico southward along both coasts of Central America into South America, where it reaches as far south as Peru, Bolivia, and Argentina. In Costa Rica, this species lives in a wide variety of habitats, from areas close to human settlements in arid Guanacaste to the wet rainforests of the Caribbean slope. It inhabits altitudes from sea level to at least 900 m (2,600 ft).

Boa constrictor is primarily a nocturnal snake, although it is occasionally seen active during the day. It lives both on the ground and in trees, and several individuals have been observed in animal burrows.

Even the largest boa can be difficult to spot because of its exquisite camouflage. Except when they move, these snakes do not stand out against the background of dead leaves, a trait that aids them when hunting. Boas are typical ambush hunters; they select a spot where prey may pass—near the entrance to a mammal burrow, for example—and wait. Individuals will sometimes sit in the same strategic spot for two or more days before moving to the next ambush point, which is usually within several dozen meters of the previous point.

Prey includes iguanas and other lizards, a variety of birds, and mammals. The size of the mammal targeted will depend on the size of the boa; common mammal prey include rats, coatimundis, monkeys, and vested anteaters. Large individuals have been seen eating ocelots and white-tailed deer.

Large *Boa constrictor* are formidable predators that are at the top of the food chain. As such, these individuals are very rare since their direct environment would not sustain a large population of such carnivores. An encounter with this snake is comparable to spotting a jaguar or a harpy eagle, animals that have a similar position in the intricate web of interactions in nature.

These live-bearing snakes give birth to litters of up to 60 young, but in nature very few of these will reach maturity. Before they reach a massive size, boas are as often prey as predator, and those who prey on them are numerous. Even fairly large individuals are taken by predators, as indicated by the discovery of a 168 cm (66 inches) *Boa constrictor* in the stomach of a 295 cm (116 inches) indigo snake (*Drymarchon corais*).

Boas are generally rather docile snakes, moving majestically through their habitat. Even when approached, they are not inclined to defend themselves. However, some individuals have a more irascible disposition and will hiss loudly, coil their neck in an S-shaped curve, and sometimes even strike. Since *Boa constrictor* is a nonvenomous snake, a bite by these snakes is not dangerous, although it can definitely be painful; large individuals may cause deep lacerations. Boas have numerous curved, needlelike teeth that frequently break off and may remain embedded in a bite wound.

The genus *Boa* is currently thought to consist of four species. *Boa constrictor* is found in Central and South America; all three remaining species, Dumeril's boa (*Boa dumerili*), the Madagascar ground boa (*Boa madagascariensis*), and the Madagascar tree boa (*Boa mandrita*) live on the island of Madagascar. The origin of this genus and the dynamics that so widely separated these closely related species are still unknown.

Corallus annulatus

Annulated tree boa (plate 62)

The rare annulated tree boa (*Corallus annulatus*) occurs in the humid rainforests of the Caribbean lowlands of Costa Rica. This species, which appears to prefer living in the tops of tall trees, is mainly active at night. It is thus rarely seen by earthbound observers. One juvenile, which was spotted on a low shrub, was reddish-orange. In Central America, this species changes coloration during its life. The vivid coloration of juveniles is gradually replaced by a less conspicuous brown color, often with irregular, dark ring-shaped markings on the body and tail.

Corallus ruschenbergerii

Common tree boa (plate 63)

Corallus ruschenbergerii is a recently recognized species that is often referred to as *Corallus enydris*. It was formerly identified as *Corallus hortulanus*. Before recent studies, *Corallus hortulanus*, whose enormous distribution range seemed to include large parts of the South American mainland, southern Central America, and several islands in the Caribbean and along the coast of South America, displayed a very diverse ecology and morphology. A recent study compared individuals from the entire distribution range and concluded that the individuals formerly identified as *Corallus hortulanus* actually form a complex of four different species. The name *Corallus hortulanus* now only applies to Amazonian tree boas. Common tree boas, found in Costa Rica, Panama, and northern South American, are now called *Corallus ruschenbergerii*. This species reaches the northern limit of its distribution along the Pacific coast of Costa Rica, where it occurs at least as far north as Dominical.

Corallus ruschenbergerii characteristically has a relatively slender compressed body, a long prehensile tail, and a large head. This body shape is an adaptation to life in trees; the species rarely descends to the ground. *Corallus ruschenbergerii* is frequently seen coiled on a low branch, anchored by its tail, waiting for prey to pass within striking distance. Birds were long assumed to be the preferred prey because the snake's long, needlelike teeth in the front of the mouth seemed ideal for gripping through a thick layer of feathers. Observations on the feeding behavior of these snakes, however, revealed that they actually mainly prey on lizards, mouse opossums, and other small mammals.

Like *Boa constrictor, Corallus ruschenbergerii* have heat-sensitive receptors in their lips that are employed to locate prey. These receptors are visible as deep slitlike pits between the scales that form the snake's lips, while in *Boa constrictor* the receptors are not externally visible. Once located, prey is caught with a lightning strike and then constricted.

Corallus ruschenbergerii has an irritable temper, and when approached too closely it coils the neck and the front of the body into an S-shaped curve. If further perturbed, it may strike at the intruder. Because of the large size of these snakes, which may exceed 200 cm (79 inches), and the long, sharp teeth, it is advisable to keep a safe distance when encountering one. Their powerful bite, which is often aimed at the face, may cause deep, painful lacerations.

Corallus ruschenbergerii is live-bearing. The gestation period in captivity varies between 200 and 250 days. The mother produces litters of up to 20 live young. Females have been observed to eat the unfertilized, undeveloped eggs that sometimes emerge with the young.

Literature

Eerden, van der 1986; Greene 1997; Henderson 1993a,b, 1997; Kluge 1991; McDiarmid et al. 1996; Trutnau 1988, Zug 1993.

FAMILY: **Colubridae** (Colubrid snakes)
SUBORDER: Serpentes (Snakes)

About 80% of all living snakes—or some 2,200 species—are assembled in this enormous family, which includes species with a diversity of shapes, sizes, feeding habits, habitat preferences, and activity patterns. At present, 103 species of Costa Rican snakes are assigned to the family Colubridae.

All colubrid snakes have 9 enlarged symmetrical plates on the top of the head. These plates are arranged in a pattern that is also found in the coral snakes (Elapidae), but colubrids differ from coral snakes in lacking the permanently erect fangs at the front of the mouth.

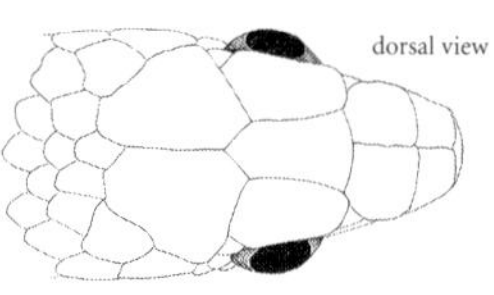

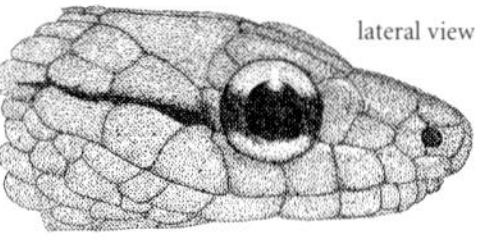

Satiny parrot snake (*Leptophis depressirostris*). Note the 9 enlarged plates on the top of the head.

Interestingly, some colubrids have enlarged teeth on the back of the upper jaw that are sometimes grooved to form a crude canal. Although technically nonvenomous, many such rear-fanged colubrids produce a mild venom that can be chewed into prey by means of these enlarged teeth, with the grooves in the teeth serving to channel the venom. The main functions of such secretions are to paralyze struggling prey and to aid in digestion. Usually, the venom consists of anticoagulants and digestive enzymes. In humans, the bite of some rear-fanged snakes may produce such local symptoms as swelling, discoloration at the location of the bite, itching, and pain. Large rear-fanged snakes should always be dealt with very carefully.

Small Costa Rican colubrid snakes include the centipede snakes (genus *Tantilla*) and other miniscule insect-eating genera (genera *Geophis, Trimetopon*, etc.) that may not even reach 300 mm (11¾ inches) in total length. At the other end of the spectrum, individuals of some species—such as the tiger rat snake (*Spilotes pullatus*), tropical king snake (*Lampropeltis triangulum*), or indigo snake (*Drymarchon corais*)—may exceed 250 cm (98 inches) in total length.

Costa Rican colubrids show equal diversity in food preferences. The Middle American swamp snake (*Tretanorhinus nigroluteus*) feeds on fish; the scorpion-eating snakes (genus *Stenorrhina*) eat scorpions and spiders; and species of the genera *Dipsas* and *Sibon* are snail eaters.

Colubrid snakes can be found underground, in leaf litter, in water, or even in the rainforest treetops. Although some species are more flexible in their requirements than others, every species of snake in Costa Rica displays a specific combination of habitat preference, diet, and activity pattern. This niche differentiation makes possible the high number of co-occurring snake species that are found almost everywhere in the country. For example, the Mexican parrot snake (*Leptophis mexicanus*) hunts for tree frogs in low vegetation. Cat-eyed snakes (genus *Leptodeira*), which inhabit the same range as the Mexican parrot snake, have a similar diet and also live in low vegetation. However, cat-eyed snakes are active only at night, while Mexican parrot snakes are diurnal.

Thus the many Costa Rican species in this family are extremely diverse, a fact reflected in the following set of guidelines for identifying Costa Rican colubrid snakes. In essence, these guidelines state that any snake that does not display characteristics of the other less diverse families of snakes found in Costa Rica may be a colubrid.

SUMMARY

How to identify Costa Rican colubrid snakes:

- The colubrid snake family is a large group of very diverse snakes. Colubrids are small to very large snakes with a relatively slender body. All have 9 enlarged symmetrical plates covering the top of the head. Colubrid snakes never have a heat-sensitive pit on each side of the head.
- Venomous coral snakes (genus *Micrurus*) also have 9 enlarged symmetrical plates on the top of the head, but can be distinguished from colubrid snakes by their distinctive coloration and their small, black eyes, which are often hard to see (most colubrid snakes have large eyes).

SPECIES DESCRIPTIONS

Amastridium veliferum

Ridge-nosed snake (plate 63)

Amastridium veliferum owes its common name to the sharp-edged ridge between the eyes and the tip of the snout. This feature, along with a slightly protruding scale above each eye, lend the snake a somewhat menacing, viperlike appearance. Nonetheless, it is a harmless nonvenomous snake, and lucky observers may see it probing through leaf litter hunting for lizards and their eggs.

Amastridium veliferum is a small snake. The maximum recorded total length is 724 mm (29 inches), although most individuals are much smaller. Its long tail may be 30% of the total length.

On the Atlantic versant, *Amastridium veliferum* occurs from Mexico to Panama; on the Pacific versant, it occurs only in Chiapas, Mexico and in southwestern Costa Rica. It inhabits wet forests from sea level to about 1,500 m (4,900 ft).

This snake initially appears to have a solid black body and a rust-brown head; on closer inspection, it reveals a delicate color pattern. The dorsal coloration is a dark slate gray with five thin black longitudinal stripes. A series of tiny cream or white dots, spaced every four to five scales, forms two indistinct rows, one on each side of the spine. The belly is dark gray to black with a beautiful oily sheen. The rust-brown head has an intricate pattern of dark undulating markings.

Clelia clelia

Mussurana

Zopilota (plate 64)

Adult *Clelia clelia* are large, blue-black to dark gray snakes with a pale belly. They have a muscular body that is roundish in cross-section and covered with smooth, shiny scales. The short head is scarcely wider than the neck; the eyes are small and dark. This is a very long snake, with a maximum known total length of 247 cm (97 inches).

Except for the center of the belly and the underside of the head and throat, which are creamy white, adults of this species are a uniform blue-black color. The upper lips are normally somewhat lighter in color than the rest of the body, and medium-sized individuals sometimes display a pale band across the neck. Juveniles smaller than about 700 mm (27½ inches) are a uniform bright red; they have a black head and a distinct broad yellow band across the back of the head and the neck. With age, the red is gradually replaced by black or slate-gray until the snake reaches the uniform black pattern of maturity.

This species, which has a very large distribution range, is found at sea level to 1,200 m (3,950 ft) from Mexico and Guatemala south to Uruguay and Argentina. In Costa Rica, it lives in both the Pacific and the Caribbean lowlands.

Clelia clelia is one of the few snakes people in Latin America consider useful. This is due to the fact that its diet consists primarily of other snakes, including the venomous pit vipers. In the 1930s, a Brazilian plan to raise and release large numbers of these snakes as pit viper–control agents faded out because of several impracticalities. Still, the Instituto Butantan in Brazil, which produces antivenoms, has erected a statue of *Clelia clelia* as a tribute to its fellow-combatants against venomous snakebites.

Although not considered dangerous to man, *Clelia clelia* is a rear-fanged snake and does have toxin-producing glands. This snake uses venom and constriction to overpower its prey. With a lightning strike, *Clelia clelia* grabs another snake behind the head, immediately wrapping its entire body around the victim. The snake is killed by constriction; but the venom, which is administered through grooved fangs in the back of the mouth, is used to paralyze the prey. *Clelia clelia* appears to be immune to the venom of Costa Rican pit vipers.

These large, powerful snakes are almost lethargic when seized, and do not attempt to bite. However, since the effects of their venom on humans remain unstudied, large individuals should be treated with care.

Clelia clelia lay eggs. In captivity, females have produced clutches of between 10 and 42 eggs. A Costa Rican individual produced a clutch of 10 large eggs, averaging 61 x 35 mm (2⅜ x 1⅜ inches) in size. The eggs were deposited 47 days after mating and hatched four months later.

A second, less common species of the genus *Clelia*, the montane mussurana (*Clelia scytalina*), is known to occur in Costa Rica. This snake reportedly occurs at higher elevations than does *Clelia clelia*, although it has been reported from low elevations in Mexico and Belize. Little is known about its biology.

Both species of *Clelia* closely resemble one another and display the same dramatic change in coloration during their development. They can be distinguished based on the number of scale rows that encircle the body—19 in *Clelia clelia*, 17 in *Clelia scytalina*.

Conophis lineatus

Roadguarder (plate 64)

Conophis lineatus is a fast-moving diurnal snake. It has a distinct cone-shaped head that is scarcely wider than the neck. The body generally displays a cream to tan coloration with a bold pattern of dark longitudinal stripes on the back, although uniform dark individuals have also been observed.

This medium-sized snake reaches a maximum length of 130 cm (52 inches).

Conophis lineatus occurs from Mexico to northwestern Costa Rica, from sea level to 1,000 m (3,300 ft). It prefers dry or semi-dry open habitats with low vegetation, and is often found in vegetation along the side of roads (hence its common name).

The roadguarder is an active predator that prefers lizards—generally the whip-tailed lizards of the genera

Ameiva and *Cnemidophorus*—but also eats frogs, toads, snakes, small mammals, and bird eggs. When hunting, this species may inject a venom that is strong enough to paralyze or kill its prey. In one observation, an individual punctured the skin of a Mexican tree frog (*Smilisca baudinii*) with its rear fangs. After a few minutes, the frog stopped moving and the snake swallowed it.

Within Costa Rica, *Conophis lineatus* is the most venomous of the "nonvenomous" snakes. In humans, its venom can cause pain, local swelling, headache, vomiting, and a general feeling of discomfort. Bite wounds often bleed profusely for an hour or more, most likely due to anticoagulating components in the venom. The effects of the venom have been known to persist for two days.

Dendrophidion vinitor
Barred forest racer (plate 65)

Dendrophidion vinitor is a brown to gray snake with a pattern of crossbands that are either light gray or blue with a dark outline. On the neck, the crossbands have a center stripe that is often orange or reddish. These neck crossbands are always more than one scale row wide, a feature which distinguishes this species from the closely related *Dendrophidion nuchale*, whose neck crossbands are always *less* than one scale row wide. Toward the tail, the crossbands gradually change into light spots or longitudinal stripes. The dorsal scales of *Dendrophidion vinitor* are all distinctly keeled. Its large eyes have a gold iris and a round pupil.

This medium-sized snake reaches a maximum total length of slightly less than 100 cm (40 inches).

Dendrophidion vinitor has a scattered distribution: there are isolated populations in southern Mexico, northern Guatemala, Nicaragua, Costa Rica, Panama, and western Colombia. It inhabits lowland and premontane rainforests from near sea level to at least 1,300 m (4,250 ft). This is one of the most commonly observed snakes in the Caribbean and southwestern lowlands of Costa Rica.

The barred and striped pattern of this snake effectively breaks up the outline of its body against the mosaic pattern of the forest floor. And, as the snake crawls, the motion of the alternating dark and light crossbands produces a stroboscopic effect that makes it difficult for predators to judge the direction in which the animal is headed. This effect is further enhanced under the low light conditions of the rainforest understory or when only a segment of the snake's body is visible through an opening in the foliage.

These active diurnal snakes are frequently seen crawling on the forest floor, using their head to probe the leaf litter in search of small lizards and, possibly, frogs.

Drymobius margaritiferus
Speckled racer (plate 65)

Drymobius margaritiferus has a very distinctive coloration. The upper surface of these snakes is dark green to black; the center of each scale is marked by an orange or yellow spot. The belly and underside of the tail are cream, and each scale on the underside is marked with a black edge. The head is greenish-brown to black, with a distinct Y-shaped yellow marking. The large eyes have a round pupil and a rust brown iris. A black stripe is often present behind each eye, and the upper lips are suffused with cream pigment. Juveniles and adults less than roughly 600 mm (23⅝ inches) have a pattern that consists of irregular yellow transverse bands on a dark background.

Drymobius margaritiferus is a medium-sized species with a maximum known size of 1,340 mm (53 inches); most adults, however, average around 800 mm (31½ inches). The tail comprises about one-fourth of its total length. It is a relatively slender snake. The scales on the back, sides, and tail are weakly keeled.

Drymobius margaritiferus lives between sea level and 1,450 m (4,750 ft), from the southern United States to Colombia. Costa Rican individuals have been found along both coasts.

This active ground-dwelling species is found in a variety of habitats, ranging from humid tropical rainforests and arid scrub savannas in the lowlands to cloudforests at higher elevations. It is also sometimes found near human settlements. In dry areas like Santa Rosa National Park, speckled racers seem to prefer cooler, more humid sections of the forest because their main prey, frogs, inhabits these areas.

Within any given habitat, these snakes are found predominantly near bodies of water where anurans breed. This fast-moving, diurnal snake feeds on different species of frogs and toads; it seeks out sleeping frogs and toads during daytime foraging trips.

In turn, these snakes are hunted mainly by large birds of prey.

All species of *Drymobius* have greatly enlarged fangs in the back of the mouth, but none have venom glands. Although they are not venomous, the profuse bleeding caused by *Drymobius* bites suggests that the saliva contains anticoagulants.

Costa Rican individuals lay clutches of 4 to 5 eggs in the second half of the dry season. After an incubation period of slightly over two months, the juveniles emerge at the onset of the rainy season, when the abundance of their prey is highest.

Drymobius melanotropis

Green frog-eater (plate 66)

Adult green frog-eaters have a leaf green dorsal coloration and a rust-brown to orange snout. The belly, throat, and chin are yellow. Typically, the three vertebral scale rows have black keels; all other scale rows have green keels. Another characteristic, one that is more noticeable in juveniles than in adults, is the distinctive pattern of alternating black and white transverse bands on the skin between the scales.

Green frog-eaters are medium-sized snakes that can reach a total length of 132 cm (53 inches).

Drymobius melanotropis has been found at elevations from near sea level to 700 m (2,300 ft), at scattered locations in Honduras, Nicaragua, and Costa Rica. It inhabits moist and wet forests in the Atlantic lowlands and foothills. Although this species is very rare in most of its range, in Costa Rica it is common in the Peñas Blancas Valley and the Rara Avis Reserve.

These fast-moving diurnal snakes feed predominantly on frogs.

The eggs of *Drymobius melanotropis* appear to hatch when the rainy season begins, a period that also coincides with the peak in frog reproduction. The hatchling snakes thus begin to hunt when the supply of potential prey is at its highest.

Drymobius melanotropis is capable of breaking off a part of its tail if that part is restrained by a predator. This antipredator technique is called pseudoautotomy. The severed tail tip continues to wriggle for several minutes, thus distracting potential predators from the trail of the escaping snake.

Erythrolamprus mimus

False coral snake (plate 67)

Of the many Costa Rican snakes that resemble venomous coral snakes (genus *Micrurus*), this is probably the most convincing mimic. *Erythrolamprus mimus* has a color pattern similar to that of true coral snakes, and also has a comparable lifestyle and diet. Both types of snakes are secretive, forest floor inhabitants that are most active under low light conditions, and both hunt for the same type of prey—other snakes and occasionally lizards. The false coral snake has also adopted the characteristic defensive behavior of true coral snakes; when threatened, it flattens its body, hides its head under a body coil, and performs sham attacks with its curled tail tip.

This colubrid snake has enlarged teeth at the back of the mouth that are connected to a Duvernoy's gland, which contains digestive enzymes. These glands may also contain other substances, since in several cases people bitten by a false coral snake experienced local pain and swelling and a general feeling of discomfort.

Although *Erythrolamprus mimus* resembles a coral snake, it has a few characteristics that distinguish it from the true coral snakes. Most easily observed are the imperfections in the "coral snake" color pattern. In coral snakes, the black bands are uniformly black, have clearly marked edges, and completely encircle the body; in *Erythrolamprus mimus*, these black bands are usually marked with a white center, have edges that are never clearly defined, and never completely encircle the body. Additionally, *Erythrolamprus mimus* has large clearly visible eyes, as opposed to the hard-to-see beady eyes of coral snakes.

In Costa Rica, *Erythrolamprus mimus* inhabits forested areas at low and middle elevations of the Caribbean slope. On the Pacific slope it is replaced by a second species of *Erythrolamprus*, *Erythrolamprus bizonus*, which also resembles a coral snake.

Geophis brachycephalus

Gray earth snake (plate 67)

The little snakes of the genus *Geophis* have a long, bullet-shaped snout, small beady eyes, and reduced head scales. Costa Rica is home to seven species of *Geophis*. All are very similar in size, shape, and coloration, and it may be difficult to establish unequivocally the identity of an anonymous *Geophis*.

The coloration of Costa Rican *Geophis brachycephalus* is highly variable, and at least three distinct color patterns exist. One pattern is a uniform gray coloration with a pale belly. A second consists of a gray body color marked with a reddish longitudinal stripe on each side of the body. Third, individuals may have a black body and tail, with a pattern of bright red blotches toward the tail end of the snake's body. These blotches are sometimes fused to form red crossbands. The belly of this species is white, marked with gray spots and blotches. Other distinguishing features are tiny shields above the eyes and distinctly keeled scales on most of the neck and body. Juveniles have a distinct white collar on the back of the head and neck that disappears with age and is replaced with black pigment. The small black eyes have a round pupil that is not easily distinguishable.

The maximum known total length for females of this species is 460 mm (18⅛ inches); the maximum recorded total length for males is 418 mm (16½ inches).

The head scalation typical of colubrids is reduced in these snakes to form a smooth helmet-like head that is suited for digging. In this species, the preocular scales (small scales in front of the eyes) have disappeared, and the supraocular scales (directly above the eyes) are extremely small.

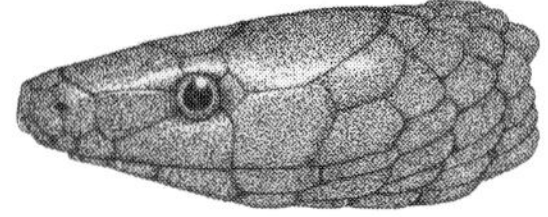

Gray earth snake
(*Geophis brachycephalus*).

Geophis brachycephalus occurs from the central mountain ranges of Costa Rica south to the Chocó region in northern Colombia, at elevations between 250 and 2,000 m (800 and 6,600 ft). In Costa Rica *Geophis brachycephalus* is chiefly found at intermediate and high elevations in the Central Valley and its surrounding mountains, the Tilarán and Talamanca mountain ranges. In some areas on the Caribbean slope, this species descends to elevations below 1,000 m (3,300 ft).

While preferring dense rainforest, individuals are occasionally found in disturbed areas. This predominantly burrowing snake has been found in insect burrows in rotting logs, under piles of debris, or, on wet nights, crawling on the forest floor.

One individual was found in a mound of sand containing a nest of leaf-cutter ants (*Acromyrmex octospinosus*), approximately 50 cm (19½ inches) below ground. The snake was uncovered during ground work in the early morning, and was crawling in a tunnel that had probably been made by insects. Interestingly, the individual was followed at a few centimeters distance by a Central American coral snake (*Micrurus nigrocinctus*). Whether the *Geophis* was looking for insect prey is not known, although it is possible. It is very likely that the coral snake was attempting to prey on the earth snake, since *Micrurus* seems to have a liking for this species. The coral snakes kept in the collection of the antivenom producing Instituto Clodomiro Picado are fed *Geophis brachycephalus* almost exclusively.

The food preferences of *Geophis brachycephalus* are not known. Individuals of other *Geophis* species have been found with insect larvae in their stomach, and earthworms, slugs, and leeches have also been cited in studies. An interesting observation was made concerning the co-occurrence of individual *Geophis brachycephalus* and large, similar-looking leeches. Underneath several logs, a snake was uncovered accompanied by one or more large leeches, each with a black body and a pattern of red spots. The leeches were of similar size, or even larger, than the snakes. Both the leeches and the snakes were coiled tightly, almost into a ball. There were no indications that the leeches preyed on the snakes or vice versa.

All earth snakes are egg-layers, and *Geophis brachycephalus* is known to produce clutches consisting of 3 to 6 eggs that are buried under smooth soil. In captivity, eggs hatched after 109 days of incubation. The tiny hatchlings measured between 136 and 143 mm (5⅜ and 5⅝ inches) in total length. This species has a prolonged breeding season and possibly produces multiple clutches every year.

Imantodes cenchoa

Brown blunt-headed vine snake
(plate 68)

Imantodes cenchoa is a very distinctive snake. The head is at least 2 or 3 times as wide as the extremely slender neck. It has large, bulging eyes that are accentuated by the small head. The snout is very short and blunt. Including the length of the tail, this unusually elongate and thin-bodied snake may reach a maximum size of 111 cm (43½ inches). A row of conspicuously enlarged scales adorns the middle of the back; these squarish scales are 3 or 4 times the width of the adjoining scale rows. The body and tail are covered with smooth scales.

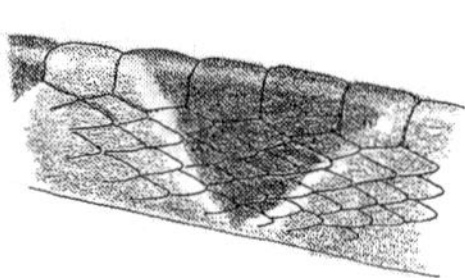

Enlarged scales cover the vertebrae of the **brown blunt-headed vine snake** (*Imantodes cenchoa*).

The color pattern of *Imantodes cenchoa* consists of a series of dark saddle-like blotches (reddish-brown to chocolate-brown) on a silvery-gray, tan, or pale brown background. Often, the dark blotches are outlined in dark brown or black. The top of the head is marked with an irregular blotched pattern, which has the same color as the saddle-like spots. The underside of the head, chin, and throat are off-white, gradually changing into the cream or tan color of this species' underside. The belly is normally speckled with tiny dark spots. The eyes have a golden iris; as with most other night-active snakes, the pupils are vertically elliptical.

Imantodes cenchoa, whose range extends from Mexico to Argentina, is widespread and abundant throughout Central American and much of South America. Costa Rican individuals are found from sea level to about 1,500 m (4,900 ft), although generally below 1,000 m (3,300 ft), on both the Caribbean and Pacific sides of the country. *Imantodes cenchoa* is strictly found in areas with dense evergreen forest; it is absent from the dry deciduous forests of Guanacaste. In such habitats, it is replaced by a closely related species, the dry forest blunt-headed vine-snake, *Imantodes gemmistratus*.

During the day, this gentle snake spends most of its time coiled in a bromeliad, or under loose bark. At dusk, it emerges from its hideout and starts moving around with great deliberation. It can be found in low vegetation but also in the tops of rainforest trees, over 30 m (100 ft) above the ground. This species is highly arboreal; only rarely do individuals descend to the ground.

The elongated body and long, prehensile tail are both adaptations to arboreal life, as is the ability to cast the eyes downward, which is not a common ability in snakes. In cross-section, the compressed body of a brown blunt-headed vine-snake has the shape of an I-beam. Specially structured vertebrae have long spines for the attachment of strong body muscles, and this feature, combined with the typical body shape, allows this snake to extend up to half of its entire body horizontally in order to bridge gaps between branches. Because of its very low body weight, individuals are able to move on the very ends of slender twigs without breaking them.

The main advantage of these morphological adaptations is that *Imantodes* can go where few other snakes can. The thin twigs and the leaves on the outside of a bush or a tree's crown are perfect places to find sleeping anoles (genus *Norops*), the favored prey of brown blunt-headed vine snakes. Its slender body enables *Imantodes cenchoa* to approach a sleeping lizard without shaking the branch it is on and thus waking up the lizard. These very active snakes cover large distances to locate potential prey. Once a lizard is located, it is caught with a quick strike and moved to the back of the mouth, where the small rear fangs administer a weak paralyzing venom. After the struggling lizard is immobilized, it is swallowed headfirst. This snake is able to swallow lizards that may be ten times wider than its own neck. After eating a lizard, it is not unusual for *Imantodes cenchoa* to retreat into a safe hiding place and remain inactive for a few weeks.

This snake obtains water in several interesting ways. Individuals have been observed drinking from water-filled bromeliads as well as swallowing drops of water on leaf surfaces or beads of water on the snake's own body. One snake was even seen drinking out of a large pond while dangling from an overhanging branch.

Although rear-fanged, brown blunt-headed vine snakes are not dangerous to humans. These peaceful snakes are extremely passive and never attempt to bite. Instead of biting defensively, they rely mainly on camouflage to escape predators.

In addition to *Imantodes cenchoa*, two other species of this genus live in Costa Rica. *Imantodes inornatus*, the yellow blunt-headed vine snake, is described in the next entry. *Imantodes gemmistratus*, the dry forest blunt-headed vine snake, was once thought to be a variant form of *Imantodes cenchoa*. Although these species are very similar in appearance, they can be distinguished by the width of the middorsal scale relative to the width of the adjoining body scales. In *Imantodes cenchoa*, the middorsal scales are 3 to 4 times wider than the adjoining body scales; in *Imantodes gemmistratus*, the middorsal scales are 1.5 to 2 times wider than the adjoining body scales.

Imantodes gemmistratus employs an unusual approach to escaping predators. Individuals were seen to plunge from their arboreal perch when disturbed. They fell distances of at least 2 m (7 ft) and successfully landed on branches below that barely moved when impacted by the very slight weight of the snake's body.

Imantodes gemmistratus is commonly seen in the deciduous dry forests on the Pacific slope of Costa Rica. It also inhabits the Central Valley. It has been found in scattered locations in the Caribbean lowlands, where it may live together with the other two species of blunt-headed vine snake.

Imantodes inornatus

Yellow blunt-headed vine snake (plate 68)

Imantodes inornatus is similar in body-shape, size, and other features to the other two species of *Imantodes* found in Costa Rica, but its coloration is distinctly different. Its body is gold to tan and is marked with black specks and numerous vague, dark, narrow crossbands.

Like the brown blunt-headed vine snake (*Imantodes cenchoa*), this species lives in dense evergreen forests. In Costa Rica, it is found at low and intermediate elevations—below 1,450 m (4,750 ft)—along the entire Caribbean slope and in the uplands of the Tilarán mountain range; it also occurs in the southwest Pacific lowlands.

Imantodes inornatus also differs from its two relatives in that it predominantly feeds on frogs and frog eggs, rather than lizards.

Lampropeltis triangulum

Tropical king snake (plate 69)

Lampropeltis triangulum has a pattern of red, yellow, and black rings encircling its body, similar to that of the venomous tricolor coral snakes of the genus *Micrurus*. In this species, however, red rings are bordered on each side by a black ring; in all tricolor coral snakes, red rings are bordered on each side by a yellow ring.

This is a very large snake—some individuals measure more than 200 cm (80 inches) in total length.

Lampropeltis triangulum has a large distribution range, occurring in many parts of the United States, Mexico, and Central America, and ranging into northern South America. In Costa Rica, it lives at elevations below 2,000 m (6,600 ft), and can be found everywhere except for the southern Caribbean slope. Apparently a habitat generalist, *Lampropeltis triangulum* has been found in dry scrub forests as well as cool cloudforests.

This species varies in size and pattern throughout its range, and several subspecies have been described. While various forms live in Costa Rica, it is not certain if these represent subspecies. Individuals from the Pacific lowlands of Costa Rica tend to be larger and more brightly colored than those living on the Atlantic slope or at higher elevations. Interestingly, some individuals from the Sarapiquí region display red and yellow bands heavily suffused with black pigment. These individuals appear almost solid black.

Tropical king snakes are powerful constrictors. They feed on a variety of prey, including mammals, birds, reptiles, and the eggs of birds and reptiles. This species is high on the food chain, and, therefore, generally occurs in small numbers within any given area. At La Selva Biological Station in Costa Rica, one of the most intensively researched rainforests in the world, these snakes escaped detection for over twenty years.

Leptodeira nigrofasciata

Black and white cat-eyed snake (plate 69)

In Costa Rica, this species is found only in the dry lowlands of Guanacaste Province. Like the other cat-eyed snakes, *Leptodeira nigrofasciata* predominantly eats frogs and, occasionally, lizards. It hunts at night and, during the day, hides in tree holes or under loose bark.

Leptodeira rubricata

Black and red cat-eyed snake (plate 70)

The rare *Leptodeira rubricata* seems to be more earthbound than its tree-dwelling relatives, though little is known about the biology of this species. In Costa Rica, *Leptodeira rubricata* has been reported in Tarcoles and the Osa Peninsula. This medium-sized snake reaches at least 660 mm (26 inches) in total length.

Leptodeira septentrionalis

Northern cat-eyed snake (plate 70)

Leptodeira septentrionalis is a slender-bodied night-active snake with large eyes and vertically elliptical pupils. Although surprisingly similar to some of the blunt-headed vine snakes (genus *Imantodes*) in appearance and behavior, this species is not as slender as those snakes; it also lacks their short, blunt snout.

Leptodeira septentrionalis is a moderate-sized snake with a maximum total length of about 900 mm (35⅜ inches). In cross-section, its body and tail are slightly compressed, though nearly round; this cross-section shape further distinguishes *Leptodeira septentrionalis* from *Imantodes* species, which have cross-sections with an I-beam shape.

The head is broad and distinctly wider than the neck, often appearing somewhat triangular. Because of the shape of its head, this species may be mistaken for a venomous pit viper, but the characteristic heat-sensitive pits on each side of the head are never present in cat-eyed snakes. These inoffensive snakes are rear-fanged, but they rarely attempt to bite.

Leptodeira septentrionalis is a light brown, reddish brown, or gray snake with a series of dark brown or black blotches or bars down the middle of the back. In some individuals, these blotches are fused and form a zigzag band. The bulging eyes have a tan or brown iris. Usually a dark spot or band is present on each side of the head, starting behind the eyes. The color of the belly and the underside of the tail is an immaculate white, beige, or tan. Juveniles sometimes have a distinct white band across the neck and back of the head; this band disappears with age.

This species is widely distributed from southern Texas to Peru. In Costa Rica, it is commonly seen in the lowlands on both the Caribbean and the Pacific slopes.

Throughout its extensive range, *Leptodeira septentrionalis* is found in diverse habitat types, ranging from semidesert to wet rainforest. Costa Rican individuals are mostly found at night on low vegetation in humid forested areas, especially around ponds where frogs breed.

Although these snakes have been reported to eat lizards and even snakes, they seem to prefer the eggs of the leaf-breeding red-eyed leaf frogs (*Agalychnis callidryas*). The snake drills its head into the sticky egg mass and consumes the eggs. *Leptodeira septentrionalis* also eats adult tree frogs. Because large individuals are often hard to subdue, the snake waits until the frog succumbs to the mild venom that is administered by prolonged chewing.

Leptodeira septentrionalis lays clutches of between 6 and 13 eggs. A captive solitary female produced clutches of fertilized eggs at irregular intervals up to four years after having had an opportunity to mate. This suggests that the species is capable of long-term sperm storage and delayed fertilization. Such an adaptation may be beneficial for tropical snakes that occur in such low densities that it may be impossible to encounter a potential mate during every period of reproductive activity.

Leptophis depressirostris

Satiny parrot snake
Lora falsa (plate 71)

Costa Rica is home to five species of the genus *Leptophis*. All are big-eyed, racerlike snakes with bright green coloration.

Leptophis depressirostris has a uniformly green body with two rows of heavily keeled scales on the middle of the back. These keels are often outlined in black, creating a pair of thin black lines that run from the snake's neck onto the tail. In most individuals, a short black stripe is present behind each eye.

Leptophis depressirostris is also one of two Costa Rican *Leptophis* with a loreal scale, a scale that separates the eye and the nostril. The second species, the Mexican parrot snake (*Leptophis mexicanus*), is described in the following entry.

These slender-bodied serpents usually measure between 100 and 120 cm (40 and 47½ inches) in total length.

This species, which is distributed from Nicaragua to Ecuador, may also live in Peru. In Costa Rica, *Leptophis depressirostris* inhabits very wet forests along the Caribbean slope, from sea level to at least 750 m (2,450 ft).

Satiny parrot snakes are primarily active during the day, but on a few occasions they have been seen moving about at night. During periods of rain, these snakes often seek cover beneath large leaves; under conditions of prolonged rain and cool weather, the snakes retreat into hiding places and remain inactive for longer periods of time. Individual snakes that had been equipped with a radio transmitter for tracking movement were observed to climb in vegetation to considerable heights, up to almost 5 m (16 ft), foraging for amphibian or reptilian prey.

A biologist walking through a rainforest in Costa Rica observed an anole (genus *Norops*) that landed in front of him, clearly coming from an overhead perch. The slightly stunned lizard paused for a split second and then ran away, instantly followed by a plummeting adult *Leptophis*. The snake landed on the exact spot where the lizard had been shortly before, and proceeded to chase the lizard. Presumably the snake, in pursuit of potential prey, had launched itself from the same branch as the lizard.

Leptophis depressirostris is not venomous, but it does have enlarged fangs at the rear of the mouth. Puncture wounds from its bite often bleed for a surprisingly long time, and a slight tingling of the skin around the bite area has been noticed on a few occasions. The saliva of these snakes may contain anticoagulants and other substances that normally play a role in the digestion of prey, but which may also affect potential predators.

All members of this genus are thought to lay eggs. An egg clutch of *Leptophis depressirostris*, consisting of 3 eggs, was discovered concealed in a terrestrial bromeliad. Hatchlings of this species measure about 250 mm (9⅞ inches) in total length.

Another *Leptophis* species, the widespread green parrot snake, *Leptophis ahaetulla*, which occurs throughout the Costa Rican lowlands, is sometimes found in areas where *Leptophis depressirostris* lives. Superficially, these two bright green snakes appear very similar, but on closer inspection it becomes clear that *Leptophis ahaetulla* lacks the two ridges found on the back of *Leptophis depressirostris*, as well as a loreal scale on each side of the head. Size alone often distinguishes the two snakes, since the green parrot snake reaches a far greater total length than does any other Costa Rican parrot snake; individuals may exceed 220 cm (87 inches).

Leptophis mexicanus

Mexican parrot snake
Ranera bronceada (plate 71)

*Leptophis mexica*nus is the only *Leptophis* that has both a loreal scale between the eye and the nostril and an ivory white belly. The only other *Leptophis* with a loreal scale is the satiny parrot snake (*Leptophis depressirostris*); that species, however, has a leaf-green belly of the same color as the almost uniform head, body, and tail. *Leptophis mexicanus* has an elongated head that bears a pair of large eyes with round pupils. The scales on the middle of the back and tail are keeled; those on the sides may be very weakly keeled or smooth.

Leptophis mexicanus is a slender medium-sized snake, reaching an average size of between 900 and 1,100 mm (35⅜ and 43¼ inches).

This elegant snake has a dark green to bluish green color. A narrow black stripe along the side of the head passes through the eyes and continues down the sides of the body and tail. The black stripe is bordered below by the ivory white of the belly, throat, and lower half of the head. A broad bronze or brown stripe runs down the middle of the back and tail.

The distribution of *Leptophis mexicanus* in Costa Rica is limited to the dry Guanacaste area. This is the southernmost occurrence of this species, which is found at low and intermediate elevations from Mexico to northwestern Costa Rica.

This agile snake appears to have a preference for relatively dry, open areas. Both a ground-dweller and a tree-climber, it is invariably active during the day. *Leptophis mexicanus* prefers bushes and low trees, where it actively searches for sleeping frogs. Although the prey recorded for this species includes tadpoles, lizards, small snakes, and even bird eggs, it feeds mainly on semiarboreal and arboreal tree frogs (family Hylidae). At night, when parrot snakes are not active, this ecological niche is filled by such species as blunt-headed vine snakes (genus *Imantodes*) and cat-eyed snakes (genus *Leptodeira*).

Leptophis mexicanus are even known to eat milk frogs (*Phrynohyas venulosa*), which have a very sticky, toxic secretion in their skin.

These snakes are not venomous, although they do have ungrooved fangs in the back of the mouth. Puncture wounds caused by the bite of this snake sometimes swell up, and continued bleeding may occur for a surprisingly long time. This indicates that the saliva of Mexican parrot snakes contains anti-coagulants.

In the Caribbean lowlands and at low elevations in southwestern Costa Rica, a species of *Leptophis* occurs whose color pattern is very similar to *Leptophis mexicanus*. This species, the bronze-backed parrot snake (*Leptophis nebulosus*), is an uncommon snake that inhabits humid rainforests. Apart from being completely separated geographically, the species can also be differentiated by the absence of a loreal scale in *Leptophis nebulosus*.

Liophis epinephelus

Fire-bellied snake (plate 72)

This medium-sized, rear-fanged snake is easily distinguished from all other Costa Rican snakes by its unique color pattern. The general coloration of this snake is dark olive to gray. During defensive displays, these snakes spread their neck in a hoodlike fashion, much like cobras do. In doing so, bright orange skin with black transverse bands suddenly becomes visible between the dark gray scales. The top of the head is dark gray, with yellow lips; the underside of the head, chin, and throat are creamy white, gradually changing into orange or red on the belly and underside of the tail. Most of the undersurface of this snake is checkered with large, squarish black spots.

Usually individuals do not exceed 500 mm (19⅝ inches) in total length, but this species may reach 800 mm (31½ inches).

Liophis epinephelus is known to occur from Costa Rica southward to Colombia and Ecuador. In Costa Rica, it has been found at elevations higher than 1,500 m (4,900 ft) in the Tilarán, Central, and Talamanca mountain ranges. In the northeast and southwest of the country, this species descends to near sea level. The unusual distribution range of this snake includes a wide diversity of habitats; it is reported to live in areas with an average annual temperature that ranges from 12.5 to 30°C (54.5 to 86°F).

Liophis epinephelus has an array of strategies to deter potential predators. When threatened, it flattens its body and exposes the bright orange and black pattern on the skin between its scales that is largely concealed when the body is not distended. Flattening the body makes the snake look bigger, and thus more intimidating and harder to eat. The sudden exposure of brightly colored surfaces (the flash color effect) often confuses predators. The pattern of alternating red and black bands is also reminiscent of the bicolored coral snake (*Micrurus multifasciatus*) and

Liophis epinephelus possibly mimics this dangerously venomous coral snake. Other means of defense include a vibrating tail tip, which produces an audible rattlesnake-like buzz, and the presence of paired glands close to the vent. When the snake is grabbed, it empties these glands, which contain an extremely foul-smelling substance. If all else fails, this snake will attack aggressively.

Liophis epinephelus is a predator of amphibians. It has been observed eating unidentified rain frogs (genus *Eleutherodactylus*), a brilliant forest frog (*Rana warszewitschii*), and tadpoles of green climbing toads (*Bufo coniferus*). This snake is famous for eating extremely toxic species of amphibians such as the variable harlequin frog (*Atelopus varius*) and poison-dart frogs (family Dendrobatidae). The mechanism by which *Liophis epinephelus* overcomes the toxicity of these anurans is not known, but its enlarged adrenal gland possibly plays a role.

Fire-bellied snakes lay eggs, and females are known to produce clutches of 8 or 9 eggs.

Ninia maculata

Spotted wood snake (plate 72)

Ninia maculata is common in Costa Rica, where it lives in the Central Valley and at low and intermediate elevations on both coasts.

Ninia maculata is a variable species, with a dorsal ground color of tan, reddish brown, brown, gray, or black. The back and head are marked with a pattern of narrow black crossbands and/or square black spots. This pattern shows most markedly in lighter individuals, whose light background contrasts with the darker crossbands and spots. Generally, the belly is light, either white or cream, with a pattern of dark markings that align to form either one or two longitudinal stripes or a checkerboard pattern. Its small round head is not noticeably wider than its neck.

This small species can reach a total length of 352 mm (13⅞ inches).

Ninia maculata hunts strictly for insects, which it finds in the leaf litter on the forest floor.

This docile species displays a remarkable defensive behavior. When disturbed, *Ninia maculata* spreads its ribs and flattens the body while remaining completely rigid and motionless. The flattening of the body is sometimes so extreme that the snake can resemble a ribbon.

Oxybelis aeneus

Brown vine snake (plate 73)

Oxybelis aeneus is one of three species of the genus *Oxybelis* that reside in Costa Rica. It is the only vine snake in Costa Rica that combines all of these characteristics: a brown body and tail, a narrow elongate head, and large eyes with a round pupil.

Oxybelis aeneus

Oxybelis brevirostris

Oxybelis fulgidus

The shape of the head distinguishes the three Costa Rican *Oxybelis*.

This medium-sized to large species—the maximum known total length is a little over 150 cm (59 inches)—has the characteristic slender, elongate build of the diurnal vine snakes that comprise the genus *Oxybelis*. The head is sharply pointed and very elongate, with a snout 3 to 3.5 times the diameter of the eye.

Oxybelis aeneus has a highly variable color pattern. Its dorsal ground color is usually grayish-brown, becoming tan or yellowish-brown toward the head. Its color pattern can be uniform, peppered with tiny black and white spots, or marked with a pattern of large, dark brown or black spots. Its upper lip, the underside of the head and the throat are white or cream. The belly color gradually changes toward the tail into the same color as the upper body surfaces. A dark line runs from the nostril through the eye to the side of the neck, separating the white upper lip from the brown top of the head. The large eyes have a bronze or yellow iris and a round pupil.

This is one of the five snake species with the largest distribution range in the world; it occurs from extreme southern Arizona to southern Brazil and occupies habitats ranging from arid scrub forest to tropical rainforest, from sea level to 1,500 m (4,900 ft).

The characteristic elongation and narrowing of the head and attenuation of the snout in *Oxybelis*, which aids in binocular vision, is typical for snakes that feed on mobile prey. *Oxybelis aeneus* is an energetic day-active hunter that invariably inhabits areas of dense vegetation. It hunts for prey in bushes or small trees, but also descends to the forest floor where it crawls around with its head held erect. This snake feeds mainly on lizards, but it also captures frogs, insects, and small birds and mammals. Prey is immobilized with a mild venom that is administered through enlarged, grooved fangs in the back of the mouth. In humans, this venom has caused local swelling and blistering.

Two similarly sized adult males were observed crawling over the forest floor in a Caribbean rainforest location with their bodies wrapped around each other, biting each other in the head and neck region. This action is reminiscent of a type of ritualized fight reported for other snake species, except for the fact that biting is unusual in such encounters. The fight ended in an even more unusual fashion—one snake overpowered the other one while biting it in the head. The subdued snake died shortly after with signs of muscular paralysis. Whether predation was the reason for this casualty is unknown, but it seems unlikely since *Oxybelis aeneus* is not known to feed on snakes. Although it is not unlikely that a brown vine snake would occasionally feed on other snakes, the size of this subdued individual seems to preclude this option.

When threatened, *Oxybelis aeneus* assumes a rather impressive defense posture in which the neck is coiled in an S-shape and the mouth is opened, showing its purple-black lining. Aroused snakes sometimes strike with the mouth closed; at other times they strike with the mouth open, although they don't actually bite. Generally, these snakes depend on camouflage for protection. When seeking to escape detection, they remain immobile, typically with the tongue extended. This tongue extension is thought to improve the snake's camouflage and disrupt its body outline, although it may also allow the animal to continue monitoring chemosensory information from the surrounding environment. Interestingly, on windy days, *Oxybelis aeneus* displays a rocking motion superimposed on its normal method of locomotion; with this oscillating motion, the snake appears to mimic the movement of wind-blown twigs.

An egg clutch of *Oxybelis aeneus* consists of 3 to 5 eggs, each measuring roughly 50 mm (2 inches) in length. The eggs hatch after approximately 2½ months, during the rainy season. Hatchlings are about 225 mm (8⅞ inches), not counting the tail.

Oxybelis brevirostris

Short-nosed vine snake (plate 73)

This is a medium-sized green vine snake with a black eye stripe. While it resembles many other species of Costa Rican snakes that are green, the most easily observed difference is the shape of the head, which is elongate and relatively pointed in *Oxybelis brevirostris* and rounded in most other species.

Oxybelis brevirostris has a maximum total length of approximately 120 cm (47½ inches). It has a slightly compressed body and a long tail. All dorsal scales are entirely or almost entirely smooth, and the vertebral scale row is somewhat enlarged.

This species is similar in appearance to some of the parrot snakes (genus *Leptophis*). It can be distinguished from these by the anal scale—the large plate covering a snake's vent—which is undivided; it is divided in *Leptophis*. *Oxybelis brevirostris* owes its common name to the uncharacteristically short snout for this genus, a feature that immediately distinguishes it from the closely related *Oxybelis fulgidus*, which has a snout that is approximately 3 times the diameter of the eye.

Adults are a uniformly dark green to olive green; the undersurfaces are a paler green to yellowish green. Juveniles with a total length less than 600 mm (23⅝ inches) sometimes have weakly marked pale bands. A short, black line on the side of the head runs through the gold colored eye. This species has a bluish-green tongue.

The range of *Oxybelis brevirostris* extends from Honduras to Ecuador; it lives at elevations from sea level to 800 m (2,600 ft). In Costa Rica, it is reported from the Caribbean slope, and from some areas in the northwestern part of the country. This species is one of the most commonly observed diurnal snakes in some locations on the Caribbean slope. It inhabits areas with dense vegetation and is most frequently seen in disturbed edges in rainforest habitats.

Upon discovery, *Oxybelis brevirostris* will remain motionless, like *Oxybelis aeneus* and *Oxybelis fulgidus*, relying on its excellent camouflage. It has been observed to freeze its movements, trusting its cryptic coloration completely, while sitting in the middle of a road, even though it is extremely visible there. Compared to its close relatives, this species spends a relatively large amount of time on the forest floor.

There are some indications that juveniles of this snake are nocturnal. Adults normally sleep at night on the tips of thin branches, from 1 to 3 meters (3 to 10 ft) above the ground. Sleeping *Oxybelis* assume a typical loose-coiled, head-down posture.

Oxybelis brevirostris ambushes lizards and possibly frogs on low vegetation and on the ground. When a potential prey moves within reach, the snake moves toward the animal, moving only when the prey moves and freezing when the prey stops moving. The prey is finally caught with one fast, rushing strike and held in the snake's mouth until the venom does its immobilizing work.

The defensive display of *Oxybelis brevirostris* is possibly even more impressive than that of the brown vine snake (*Oxybelis aeneus*). When threatened, this snake lifts the front half of its body off the ground in an S-curve and spreads and compresses its neck region, opening its mouth in a huge gape. The author has observed individuals maintaining this defensive posture for several hours, long after the source of the threat has left.

This species is not generally inclined to bite, but when bitten, human subjects have reported localized effects of the mild venom similar to those caused by the venom of *Oxybelis aeneus*.

Oxybelis fulgidus

Green vine snake (plate 74)

No other Costa Rican snake has a head more elongated—the snout in front of the eyes is at least three times the diameter of eye. Its bright green coloration, of an almost Day-Glo intensity, and the presence of a white line along each side of the belly, are also distinguishing features. This is a large, slender species, with individuals exceeding 150 cm (59 inches) in total length.

Within Costa Rica, this snake appears to be restricted to lowland regions below 1,500 m (4,950 ft) on both coasts in the northern half of the country. It is found in disturbed habitats, in secondary forest, and in edge situations in primary forest, usually perched in small trees and on scrub vegetation.

Oxybelis fulgidus is an ambush hunter, and it commonly stays motionless in the same tree or bush for up to several days. It escapes detection by predators and prey by virtue of its vine-like appearance and excellent camouflage. Its diet consists mainly of different species of lizards, but small and medium-sized birds and small mammals are also eaten. Prey is killed with a mild venom that has caused localized pain and swelling in humans.

Oxybelis fulgidus is oviparous; egg clutches of up to 10 eggs have been reported. In captivity, hatchlings with a mean body length of 235 mm (9¼ inches) hatched after an incubation time of approximately 3 months.

Pseustes poecilonotus

Bird-eating snake (plate 74)

Pseustes poecilonotus is similar in size and behavior to the tiger rat snake (*Spilotes pullatus*). Active during the day, it spends at least part of its time foraging for prey in trees and bushes. It reaches a total length of at least 200 cm (79 inches).

The diet of *Pseustes poecilonotus*, which is more limited than that of *Spilotes pullatus*, appears to consist of birds and their eggs, and occasionally bats. A large adult *Pseustes poecilonotus* was discovered raiding a nesting colony of white-collared swifts (*Streptoprocne zonaris*) located in a cliff behind a waterfall. The snake was perched in one of the holes that the birds use for nesting, with the front third of its body protruding from the cavity, and was busy swallowing one of the swifts. It appeared that the snake was waiting for the swifts to return to their nests, hidden from the bird's view until the last moment by the waterfall. This technique seemed very successful, as was indicated by the large bulges that became visible in the snake's body after it left the rock cavity.

These snakes are harmless creatures, but they often try to discourage potential predators with an impressive defensive display that includes flattening the head, puffing up the neck and the front of the body, and gaping and striking at the source of the threat.

Pseustes poecilonotus undergoes a very noticeable change of color and pattern during its life. Juveniles and young adults have a pattern of brown, gray, or blue-gray irregular crossbands on a cream or yellowish background. Normally, these transverse blotches are arranged in a V shape or crescent shape. Large adults tend to be uniformly dark brown, olive, or blue-black above, with a yellowish to cream belly, although some adult individuals appear to retain their juvenile pattern.

Rhadinaea calligaster

Green litter snake (plate 75)

The green litter snake is one of the few snakes that can be found at very high elevations in the Costa Rican mountains. It generally does not occur at an elevation lower than 1,500 m (4,900 ft) and may be found even near the summit of Cerro de la Muerte, one of the highest peaks in the country.

As its common name implies, *Rhadinaea calligaster* is generally some shade of green—a uniform olive to dark green—although brown individuals are sometimes found. A pattern of five longitudinal dark stripes is usually present, but, in animals with an already dark background color, this is not always obvious. Several light markings are normally present below the eye. Another distinctive characteristic is the appearance of the scales that cover the belly: the center of each scale is marked with a triangular, crescent-shaped, or squarish blotch. These markings form a row along the middle of the belly and may or may not be fused.

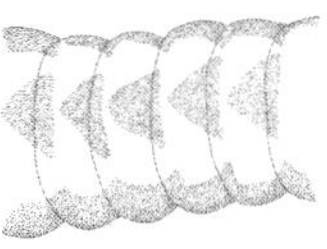
Distinctive pattern on belly of *Rhadinaea calligaster*.

Rhadinaea decorata

Red-bellied litter snake (plate 75)

Rhadinaea decorata is a relatively common but inconspicuous inhabitant of the leaf litter layer in humid forests throughout the Costa Rican lowlands. The dark brown coloration of its back, head, and tail is hardly distinctive, although it has a conspicuous dark-rimmed white spot behind each eye and a pattern of light longitudinal stripes. The most striking color characteristic of this species is seen on the underside of its body: the chin and throat are white or cream, but the color of the belly gradually changes into a bright red hue. Interestingly, individuals observed on the Pacific coast, in Dominical, had a cream-colored belly instead of the characteristic red belly.

This small, slender-bodied snake has a total length usually less than 350 mm (13¾ inches). Its tail, which is extraordinarily long, may comprise up to 40% of the combined length of the head and body. A proportionally large number of individuals has been found with a part of the tail missing, and it is believed that this species can break off the tail when it is restrained. Although this predator escape strategy is uncommon among snakes, it is displayed by a few other Costa Rican species, and has been perfected by the shovel-toothed snake (*Scaphiodontophis annulatus*).

In observations, *Rhadinaea decorata* foraged by day and ate tadpoles, frogs, and a small ground anole (*Norops humilis*). Its prey is immobilized by a mild venom that poses no threat to humans. These snakes also feed on the terrestrial eggs of rain frogs (genus *Eleutherodactylus*).

Scaphiodontophis annulatus

Shovel-toothed snake (plate 76)

This interesting snake has an extremely variable and peculiar color pattern. Generally, the body is marked with a tricolor coral snake pattern of red, yellow, and black rings, often interrupted by a series of longitudinal black stripes on a uniform grayish-brown background. Since this coloration is similar to that of the Costa Rican tricolored coral snakes (*Micrurus alleni, Micrurus clarki,* and *Micrurus nigrocinctus*), *Scaphiodontophis annulatus* is considered a coral snake mimic and is thought to gain protection by closely resembling these dangerously venomous reptiles. Those parts of the body not marked with a coral snake pattern—usually the back half of the body and the tail—have a grayish or brownish color, often with a pattern of dark spots that form longitudinal stripes. Across the neck, immediately behind the eyes, is a broad yellow crossband. The throat and belly are cream or yellowish and may be flecked with darker pigment.

In the Caribbean lowlands, small juveniles—those with a body length less than 200 mm (7⅞ inches)—differ strikingly in coloration from larger individuals. In these juveniles, the red bands are often completely suffused by black pigment, creating the impression of a two-colored snake that is black with narrow white rings. A distinct white band is also present on the back of the head and the neck. As these juveniles grow larger, the black pigment gradually becomes more concentrated on the tips of the red scales, and the red pigment becomes increasingly prominent. Simultaneously, the white mark on the head is replaced by the adult head pattern.

Shovel-toothed snakes are moderately sized, slender snakes with a maximum known body length of 480 mm (18⅞ inches). The extremely long tail is relatively thick and very fragile. An intact tail may measure almost half of the snake's total length, but in most individuals at least a part of the tail is missing. The estimated maximum total length of this species—with an intact tail—is about 920 mm (36¼ inches). The head is slightly wider than the neck, and the large eyes have round pupils. The body and tail scales are smooth.

This snake ranges from Mexico to northern Colombia. In Costa Rica, it occurs in the wet lowlands of both slopes from about sea level to 1,300 m (4,250 ft). *Scaphiodontophis annulatus* is primarily an inhabitant of the leaf litter in rainforest habitats, but it has also been found in cut-over areas and on plantations. There are indications that this snake spends at least part of its life in underground burrows.

The common name of this species derives from its short teeth, which are blunt and shovel-like. The teeth are attached to the jawbone by a functional hinge that allows the teeth to be folded backwards when the snake's prey moves toward the esophagus; but the teeth lock into place if the prey attempts to struggle out of the snake's mouth. These highly specialized jaw and tooth structures are adaptations for catching and handling slippery and hard-bodied prey. In Costa Rica, the diet of shovel-toothed snakes consists almost exclusively of litter skinks (*Sphenomorphus cherriei*), although elsewhere in its range it also eats other skinks and gymnophtalmid lizards.

Individual *Scaphiodontophis annulatus* are typically found hidden underneath the leaf litter, with the coral-ringed portion of the neck and the head exposed, elevated and motionless. In this position, they wait for a skink to pass within range. The prey is grabbed with a lightning strike and swallowed alive with astonishing speed. Observations on the prey-handling behavior of this species revealed that the average time between capture of a litter skink and the disappearance of the lizard's tail tip down the snake's throat is 7.7 seconds, with the fastest feeding lasting only 2.8 seconds.

Scaphiodontophis annulatus is a fast-moving, nervous snake. It never attempts to bite, but when seized by a predator, or merely touched, it thrashes its tail and body. This snake can deliberately break off a portion of the tail if the tail is restrained, a mechanism called pseudoautotomy that is very unusual among snakes. Some species are known to break off their tail tip by rotating their body in one direction when they are picked up by the tail. However, the presence of multiple fracture planes in the long tail of *Scaphiodontophis annulatus*, which allow for several breaks, is a highly specialized adaptation that is only seen in a small assemblage of leaf litter snakes. Costa Rican snakes of the genera *Rhadinaea, Urotheca*, and *Enulius* also have long and fragile tails and may have evolved a similar strategy to avoid predation.

There is no regeneration of a broken off tail in snakes, unlike lizards and salamanders, whose lost tails are completely replaced by a new one. The separated piece of the shovel-toothed snake's tail will continue to wriggle and move for a few minutes, distracting the predator that grabbed it and granting the snake valuable time to escape.

Scaphiodontophis annulatus has been observed to lay small clutches of 3 to 4 eggs in decomposing leaf litter, under rotten logs, or in depressions in the forest floor. Hatchlings of this species measured between 114 and 152 mm (4½ and 6 inches).

The extreme variability of these snakes throughout their entire distribution range has led to a long history of taxonomic confusion. For several years, Costa Rican individuals were assigned to a different species, *Scaphiodontophis venustissimus*, and several additional species have been thought to exist. A recent study demonstrated that all color and pattern varieties in these snakes can be regarded as traits of a single, extremely variable species.

Senticolis triaspis

Neotropical rat snake
Ratonera (plate 76)

Costa Rican *Senticolis triaspis* are characterized by a brownish, orange-brown, or dark grayish-green color, marked with 58 to 78 indistinct saddle-like blotches on the body and tail. Juveniles usually have a more vivid color and pattern, whereas large adults may appear of a uniform color. This medium-sized snake reaches about 1,300 mm (51⅛ inches) in total length.

This species ranges from the extreme southern United States, where it is known as the green rat snake, to northwestern Costa Rica. It is seen infrequently in the dry forests of Guanacaste Province, predominantly at dusk or during the night, depending on the weather.

Senticolis triaspis mainly eat small rodents, which they kill by constriction. They are nervous animals and are quick to escape. When cornered, they coil the front of the body in an S-shaped curve slightly above the ground and lunge at the source of the threat with a lightning strike. Like many other colubrid snakes, *Senticolis triaspis* vibrate the tip of their tail when threatened, much as rattlesnakes do.

Neotropical rat snakes are egg-layers; they produce small clutches consisting of about 4 eggs.

Senticolis triaspis was formerly known as *Elaphe triaspis.*

Sibon longifrenis

Lichen-colored snaileater (plate 77)

Sibon longifrenis is a small, slender snake with a prehensile tail, a chunky head, and large, bulging eyes. The pupils are vertically elliptical, and the iris is brown or greenish. The bluntly rounded snout is short; the distance between the eye and the nostril is less than the diameter of the eye.

The maximum size known for this species is 624 mm (24⅝ inches) in total length, but most individuals are considerably smaller.

Sibon longifrenis is a well-camouflaged snake. The body, head, and tail are an olive or grayish green color. A series of reddish-brown spots, each outlined in black, runs down the middle of the back. A series of similar spots is present on the lower scale rows on each side of the body, between the greenish color on the upper surfaces and the light belly. The underside of the body is usually white, cream, or yellowish, dusted with a fine black speckling.

This uncommon snake is known from the Caribbean slope of Costa Rica and adjacent western Panama. Individuals have been found from near sea level to at least 750 m (2,450 ft).

Sibon longifrenis is mostly seen at night in dense, humid rainforest habitats. Individuals are usually perched on a large leaf or a branch, from 1 to 2 m (3 to 7 ft) above the ground. When approached, these inoffensive snakes often coil the neck in an S-curve, flatten the head, and spread the jaws. The resulting triangular-looking head and the lichenous color-pattern—features also found in some individuals of the eyelash pit viper (*Bothriechis schlegelii*)—make them look surprisingly like a dangerous pit viper.

In reality, *Sibon* species are harmless snakes that are specialized predators of snails and slugs. The snake rapidly seizes a snail with its needlelike teeth; and when the snail withdraws inside its shell, the snake pulls it out using its lower jaw, which is especially adapted for this purpose. The snail eater then bites into the snail's body with its upper jaw and, while holding the shell in its coils, extracts the mollusk little by little. Once the connection between the snail's body and its protective housing is broken, the gooey meal is swallowed. Slugs are probably tracked by their mucus trail.

In Costa Rica, no less than 6 species of *Sibon*, and another 3 species in the genus *Dipsas*, are specialized eaters of slugs and snails. All these snakes have a slender but chunk-headed body shape, and all have special jaw adaptations for extracting snails from their shell.

Spilotes pullatus

Tiger rat snake
Mica (plate 77)

This is one of the larger Costa Rican species of the family Colubridae—its total length occasionally exceeds 250 cm (98½ inches). *Spilotes pullatus* is a fairly slender snake with a long whiplike tail that may comprise up to ⅓ of the snake's total length. The body is somewhat compressed and covered with large, keeled scales. Its large eyes have a round pupil and a dark brown to blackish iris.

Tiger rat snakes owe their common name to a tiger-striped color pattern. Adults usually display a pattern of cream to yellow transverse streaks, bars, or spots on a black background, often with the tail and the rear part of the body being completely blue-black. However, yellowish individuals with scarce black streaks are known as well, and the extent and shape of the markings is extremely variable. The tiger rat snake's belly is also patterned with alternating yellow and black, with the underside of the tail and the rear part of the body often being solid black. The skin, which is often visible between the large scales, is jet-black.

There seems to be a gradual change in coloration as the snakes age; juveniles typically have a well-defined pattern of crossbands, but these become increasingly broken up and diffuse with age.

Spilotes pullatus has a huge distribution range that extends from Mexico to Bolivia, Peru, and Argentina. In Costa Rica, it inhabits low and moderate elevations of both the Caribbean and Pacific slope.

Spilotes pullatus is active during the day. It is a common species in a variety of habitats, including dense rainforest, swamps, and dry savannas. It seems to prefer environmental edges, open areas such as stream banks, trails, or forest edges, where the vegetation cover is broken. This preference for open areas is probably due to thermoregulation behavior; *Spilotes pullatus* regulates its body temperature by moving into and out of the sunlight.

Spilotes pullatus is not only found on the forest floor; it is also an astonishingly agile climber and has been encountered several dozens of meters above the ground. One individual, equipped with a radio transmitter to track movement, was reported hiding in an underground burrow during heavy rains. Either underground, on the forest floor, or in the treetops, these snakes hunt for a variety of prey, including birds, mammals, and reptiles.

The reticulated pattern of this snake perfectly breaks up its body outline, and even the largest individuals are sometimes only noticed when in motion. The snake is capable of reaching such an impressive speed that it sometimes appears to be flying, giving rise to its Mexican common name *voladora*. Occasionally, individuals stand their ground when approached closely and employ an impressive threat display. The neck and the front of the body are compressed and sometimes lifted off the ground; the tail tip is rattled simultaneously, creating an audible buzz. When further threatened, the snake will strike repeatedly; although it is nonvenomous, a bite by a large individual may be painful.

Stenorrhina degenhardtii

Degenhardt's scorpion eater (plate 78)

Stenorrhina degenhardtii lives at low and intermediate elevations in the northeast and southwest of Costa Rica. It is a robust, medium-sized snake with a maximum known total length of 1,000 mm (40 inches).

Degenhardt's scorpion eater may be boldly patterned with dark saddle-like blotches, but uniformly colored individuals, with or without a broad stripe down the middle of their back and tail, are also known. The tail is short and tipped with a horny spine. These harmless snakes cannot even be induced to bite; when handled, they will wriggle vigorously, using their tail tip to brace themselves.

Little is known about the biology of *Stenorrhina degenhardtii,* except for the fact that they generally eat large spiders and scorpions. A second species of scorpion eater, *Stenorrhina freminvillii*, is found in northwestern Costa Rica.

Tantilla reticulata

Reticulated centipede snake (plate 78)

The genus name *Tantilla* is derived from the Latin *tantillum*, "so small a thing." Seven species of this genus live in Costa Rica, all of which are ground-dwelling or burrowing snakes, and all of which are infrequently seen.

With a total length of less than 300 mm (11¾ inches) and a girth of only 5 mm (¼ inch), these snakes are easily overlooked as they crawl through leaf litter on the shadowy forest floor.

Tantilla reticulata is the only Costa Rican *Tantilla* with a light stripe running down the middle of the back. Additional light and dark longitudinal stripes are present on a background of light brown or tan. A darkly colored head cap is present, and the sides of the neck are marked with a wide cream or yellow band that is interrupted on the back of the head by a dark extension of the head pattern. The upper lips are white or cream, sometimes with dark brown spots. A distinct black spot is usually present below each eye. In this species, the belly is unpatterned and of a yellow or whitish color.

Tantilla reticulata can be found throughout the Caribbean slopes of Nicaragua and northern Costa Rica. Its distribution is continued on the Pacific slope from southwestern Costa Rica through Panama and into northwestern Colombia, from sea level to at least 750 m (2,450 ft).

With almost 50 species, the genus *Tantilla* is one of the largest colubrid genera in the world, but little is known about the habits of any of the species.

Tantilla reticulata generally inhabits the leaf litter of the rainforest floor, although an individual was also seen crawling on a branch in the rainforest canopy. Most individuals have been encountered in the early morning or late afternoon. It seems these snakes have bouts of activity that are restricted to a few consecutive days, though observations of this species are too scarce to even suggest a pattern or function for these periods of increased visibility.

Although all species of *Tantilla* have grooved fangs in the back of their mouth and a functional venom gland (Duvernoy's gland), their small size and inoffensive behavior make them absolutely harmless to humans. North American species of *Tantilla* quickly immobilize and kill large centipedes with their venom. These centipedes are often highly venomous themselves, and some species even eat small snakes. During the capture of a centipede, the snake often receives bites from its prey, but it appears to be immune to the venom of these dangerous invertebrates.

Xenodon rabdocephalus

False fer-de-lance (plate 79)

Adult *Xenodon rabdocephalus* are heavy-bodied snakes with a maximum total length of approximately 900 mm (35⅜ inches). Their body shape, color pattern, and defensive behavior make them look surprisingly like the dangerously venomous fer-de-lance (*Bothrops asper*). However, the former species lacks the heat-sensitive pits, has round pupils, and has smooth scales covering its body, all signs that *Xenodon rabdocephalus* is a colubrid.

Xenodon rabdocephalus is a somewhat nervous species. When cornered, it will flatten its head and body, gape, and strike. Although not venomous, the enlarged teeth in the back of its mouth are of almost fanglike proportions and may cause painful lacerations.

False fer-de-lances are dietary specialists that only feed on frogs and toads. When facing predators, many frogs and toads inflate their body, attempting to increase their body size beyond the gape of their potential predator. *Xenodon rabdocephalus* uses it long rear fangs to pierce the amphibian's body and deflate it so that it can be more easily ingested. These snakes appear to be immune to amphibian skin toxins.

Literature

Behler & King 1979; Campbell & Lamar 1989; Connors 1989; Crimmins 1937; Dowling & Fries 1987; Downs 1967; Dunn 1937; Fleischman 1985; Greene 1997; Hayes et al. 1989; Henderson 1984; Henderson & Nickerson 1976; Henderson et al. 1977; Koller 1996; Lee 1996; Leenders

1995a, 1996; Myers 1974, 1982; Myers et al. 1978; Nickerson et al. 1978; Pérez-Santos & Moreno 1988; Pounds 2000; Sasa 1993; Sasa & Solórzano 1995; Savage & McDiarmid 1992; Savage & Scott 1985; Savage and Slowinsky 1992, 1996; Savage & Villa 1986; Savitzky 1981; Schulz 1992a,b; Scott 1983d,e; Taylor 1951, 1954b; Verhoeven 1995; Wilson 1974; Wilson & Meyer 1985; Zug 1993.

FAMILY: **Elapidae** (Coral snakes)
SUBORDER: Serpentes (Snakes)

Worldwide, this family includes the dangerously venomous cobras, mambas, kraits, and sea snakes. The only elapids occurring in the Americas are approximately 50 species of coral snakes and one species of sea snake. Although sea snakes have sometimes been assigned to a separate family, they currently are placed in the sea snake subfamily, Hydrophiinae.

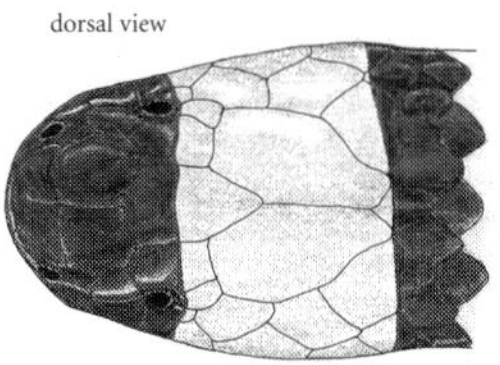

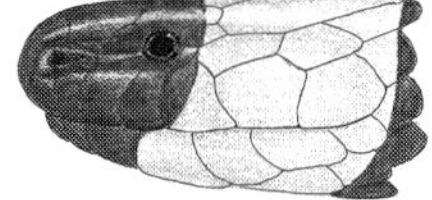

Central American coral snake (*Micrurus nigrocinctus*). The scale pattern on the top of the head resembles that of colubrid snakes. The dark eyes are very small.

Costa Rica is inhabited by one species of sea snake and four species of coral snakes. The Yellow-bellied sea snake (*Pelamis platurus*) is sometimes found stranded on Pacific beaches; it is easily recognized by its flat, oarlike tail and its distinct yellow and black coloration. Three of the Costa Rican coral snakes, Allen's coral snake (*Micrurus alleni*), Clark's coral snake (*Micrurus clarki*), and the Central American coral snake (*Micrurus nigrocinctus)*, have a typical coral snake pattern consisting of red, yellow, and black rings that completely encircle the body. The red rings of these tricolor coral snakes are invariably bordered on both sides by yellow rings, never by black. The tricolor species can be distinguished from each other by the color pattern on the top of the head. The fourth coral snake species in the Costa Rica is the bicolored coral snake (*Micrurus multifasciatus*), which has a bicolor pattern of black rings alternating with either red, orange, or white rings.

Technically, elapids differ from all other snakes in the New World in having a short, hollow, erect fang near the front of each upper jaw. These fangs are permanently erect, as opposed to the fangs in vipers, which are folded back when not in use. When the mouth is closed, the elapids' fangs fit into grooved slots. Each fang contains an enclosed passage that extends the length of the tooth and is connected with a venom gland. There are two venom glands, one located behind each eye. Coral snakes and sea snakes all have potent neurotoxic venom, and each Costa Rican elapid snake is capable of inflicting a potentially lethal bite.

Coral snakes look very similar to their colubrid relatives; snakes of both groups have a slender body; enlarged, symmetrical head plates; and large, overlapping scales on the body and tail. To further complicate matters, several nonvenomous and back-fanged colubrids in Costa Rica, such as *Erythrolamprus mimus* and *Scaphiodontophis annulatus*, have a color pattern very similar to that of venomous coral snakes.

Snakes of the genus *Micrurus*, to which all Costa Rican coral snakes belong, typically lack the loreal scale that is normally situated between the eye and the nostril, and they invariably have 15 scale rows encircling the body. Such characteristics, however, are hard to discern and not very useful in the field. Better distinguishing features are the shape of the head and the size and color of the eyes. Venomous coral snakes have a bluntly rounded head that is scarcely wider than the neck. The eyes are small, with a round pupil and an iris that is not discernible when standing at a safe distance. Most colubrid coral snake mimics have a more angular head and relatively large eyes with either round or vertically elliptical pupils. Frequently, the mimic's iris is distinctly visible, and has a brown, copper, or gold color.

One should never attempt to handle or catch coral snakes, or any snake resembling one; the bite of any Costa Rican coral snake is potentially life-threatening.

Three of the four species of coral snakes found in Costa Rica are described in the following pages. The fourth species, *Micrurus clarki*, occurs in southern Costa Rica, on the border with Panama, and rarely has been observed in Costa Rica.

SUMMARY

How to identify Costa Rican elapids:
Costa Rican elapids can be divided into two groups: coral snakes and sea snakes.

- Costa Rican coral snakes either have a pattern of red, yellow, and black rings that completely encircle the body, or a pattern of alternating black and orange rings, or black and white rings. Coral snakes closely resemble colubrid snakes in having 9 symmetrical plates on the top of the head.
- Coral snakes are most easily recognized by the combination of their color pattern and the presence of small, black eyes, which are often hard to see.
- The one sea snake species that frequents Costa Rica is only found in the Pacific Ocean or on west coast beaches. It has a distinctly compressed, oarlike tail and yellow and black (or sometimes all-yellow) coloration.

SPECIES DESCRIPTIONS

Micrurus alleni
Allen's coral snake
Coralillo (plate 79)

Micrurus alleni is a long, slender snake. It differs from the other two tricolor species of *Micrurus* in Costa Rica by the shape of its black head cap, which extends toward the neck and follows the suture between the paired large parietal scales on top of the head.

This species was previously considered a subspecies of *Micrurus nigrocinctus*, which it closely resembles. It also possesses the typical coral snake pattern of red, yellow, and black rings, although often the yellow is not very bright and may be faded to cream or even a dirty white.

Micrurus alleni occurs on the Caribbean slope of Nicaragua and Costa Rica. A geographically isolated population of this species exists in southwestern Costa Rica and adjacent Panama. This species is mainly found in lowland rainforests, but it occasionally occurs at intermediate elevations; its vertical distribution range extends from sea level to at least 1,200 m (3,950 ft).

Micrurus multifasciatus
Bicolored coral snake
Gargantilla (plate 80)

This is the only coral snake in Costa Rica that lacks the typical red, yellow, and black coral snake pattern. Instead, it has a pattern of either orange, red, pink, or white rings on a black background. Some individuals have a pattern of alternating bluish-white and black rings; individuals with this coloration have a head and tail marked with bright red pigment.

Micrurus multifasciatus is a slender snake with a maximum total length of 120 cm (47 inches), but most individuals are considerably smaller. The head is rather flat and scarcely wider than the neck; it bears diminutive eyes with round pupils.

The pattern of *Micrurus multifasciatus* consists of 40 to 65 black body rings alternating with contrastingly colored rings. In some individuals of the tricolored Allen's coral snake (*Micrurus alleni*) and the Central American coral snake (*Micrurus nigrocinctus*), the yellow body rings are suffused with black pigment, giving the impression of a bicolored red and black snake. However, the original color pattern of these other species is never obscured on the belly, which is invariably patterned with red-yellow-black-yellow rings.

There are a number of harmless colubrid snakes in Costa Rica that are thought to mimic the color pattern of *Micrurus multifasciatus*. These include fire-bellied snakes (*Liophis epinephelus*), calico snakes (*Oxyrhopus petolarius*), Halloween snakes (*Urotheca euryzona*), and harlequin snakes (*Scolecophis atrocinctus*).

Micrurus multifasciatus is an uncommonly encountered snake on the Caribbean slope of Nicaragua, Costa Rica, and Panama. Its vertical distribution ranges from near sea level to approximately 1,200 m (3,950 ft).

Bicolored coral snakes are most frequently seen crawling in and on top of the leaf litter in deeply shaded parts of the rainforest, in particular during low-light conditions of the early morning and late afternoon.

Like other coral snakes, this species predominantly eats other snakes, and individuals spend a considerable amount of time actively searching for potential prey.

Compared to the other Costa Rican coral snakes, *Micrurus multifasciatus* is a somewhat nervous species. Unlike *Micrurus nigrocinctus*, which hides its head underneath its body coils when threatened, bicolored coral snakes stand their ground and may even strike at the source of the threat when approached too closely. The venom of these snakes contains very strong nerve toxins, and a bite may have very severe consequences. The polyvalent antivenom produced by the Instituto Clodomiro Picado to counteract the effects of Costa Rican coral snake venoms seems to be ineffective in the case of a bite of *Micrurus multifasciatus*.

The most commonly encountered color variety of the bicolored coral snake appears to be the black and orange form. Although this species is known to be variable in coloration, all other color varieties are infrequently seen. An unusual situation is found in the Rara Avis Nature Reserve, near Las Horquetas de Sarapiquí, where bicolored coral snakes with three different pattern types are known to co-occur: the common black and orange variety, a rare form with only black and white rings, and a third intermediate type. The latter snake, known only from a single individual, was a juvenile patterned with black and pinkish-orange rings bordered on both sides by a narrow white ring, creating a tricolor pattern of orange-white-black-white. In addition, its head and tail rings were bright orange, contrasting sharply with the much paler body rings.

The advantages or disadvantages of having a contrastingly ringed color pattern are poorly understood, but the extreme local variation within *Micrurus multifasciatus* suggests that there is an evolutionary pressure to have a particular color pattern. It has been suggested that this coral snake species may have developed different color patterns to escape from the confusion created by the presence of too many "false" coral snakes. Dangerously venomous bicolored coral snakes may no longer be shunned by predators if those predators attack and eat nonvenomous snakes with a pattern of black and orange rings without experiencing any negative effects. Once snake eaters learn that the bright warning coloration is very often not backed up by any sort of bad experience, real coral snakes may be regarded harmless as well, and the frequency of attacks on them may increase.

The taxonomy of this snake has been under debate for many years. Until recently, Costa Rican two-toned coral snakes were referred to as *Micrurus mipartitus*, but the latter species is now thought to occur not farther north than Panama.

Micrurus nigrocinctus

Central American coral snake
Coral macho (plate 80)

The Central American coral snake is the most commonly encountered coral snake in Costa Rica. This species is characterized by a pattern of red, yellow, and black body rings—the red rings bordered on both sides by yellow—and the presence of a bright yellow band across the head.

Micrurus nigrocinctus is a medium-sized coral snake with a maximum total size of 114 cm (45 inches). The head, which is bluntly rounded when seen from above, bears very small eyes with a round pupil. The scales on the body and tail are smooth.

Central American coral snakes have a typical coral snake pattern of black-yellow-red-yellow-black body rings that completely encircle the body. The head and tail of these snakes are marked with alternating black and yellow rings. The completely black snout usually incorporates the darkly colored eyes, often making them hard to see.

This coral snake ranges from Mexico to Panama and into northern South America. In Costa Rica, Central American coral snakes are common almost anywhere below 1,500 m (4,900 ft).

Coral snakes are secretive, burrowing animals that spend most of their time in soil, leaf litter, logs, stumps, or rock crevices. Although they are infrequently encountered, these snakes are in fact quite common; they can be found in a variety of habitats ranging from dry, rocky areas to marshes, rainforests, and even cultivated fields. Central American coral snakes are even found in the outskirts of San José.

The widespread assumption that coral snakes are strictly nocturnal animals is incorrect; individuals of this species have been seen foraging, eating, and mating during the daytime.

The coral snakes' diet consists mainly of other snakes, but occasionally caecilians and lizards such as skinks are also eaten. Central American coral snakes also prey on members of their own species. Prey is detected with the aid of chemical cues, and approached carefully. A sudden movement on the part of prey usually results in a rapid attack by the coral snake, but because of its relatively poor eyesight, this is often not successful.

Coral snakes usually seize their prey and hold on in order to chew in the venom. The neurotoxic components of the venom quickly paralyze the prey. As soon as the victim stops moving, it is eaten headfirst. Coral snakes identify the head of the killed snake by following the arrangement of the overlapping scales on the victim's body.

Micrurus nigrocinctus is not immune to its own venom; on two occasions, individuals were observed succumbing to the venom's effects. Once a hatchling bit itself and was found dead with its own fangs imbedded in its body. A second individual was still alive when it was discovered halfway down the throat of a second *Micrurus nigrocinctus*. The victim was released from its awkward position, but it had been bitten in the head and neck several times by its captor. The liberated snake was still alive, but appeared to have lost the ability to control its movements, and although it tried to crawl away, its motions became increasingly weak and erratic. After approximately 15 minutes, the snake was completely limp, but still breathing. Several minutes later it died. Species of venomous snakes appear to have different responses to their own venom. Individuals of the Mexican coral snake (*Micrurus fulvius tenere*), for example, have been reported to bite and vigorously chew themselves without any noticeable effect.

A common but erroneous belief among some people in Central America is that only males of this species are venomous, hence the local common name *coral macho*.

Coral snakes deposit a small clutch of elongated eggs in leaf litter or in the soil of the forest floor. The eggs hatch after an incubation period of approximately 2 to 3 months. Hatchling *Micrurus nigrocinctus* have been observed from the beginning of the rainy season on both slopes, suggesting that the eggs of this species are deposited at the end of the dry season.

Some authors assign the Costa Rican individuals of this species to two subspecies, *Micrurus nigrocinctus nigrocinctus* on the Pacific slope and the Central Valley, and *Micrurus nigrocinctus mosquitensis* on the Caribbean slope. The Caribbean subspecies *Micrurus nigrocinctus mosquitensis* has wide yellow bands, which are 3 to 4 scales wide, and a relatively low number of red body rings (9 to 13). Pacific Central American coral snakes, *Micrurus nigrocinctus nigrocinctus*, have narrow pale-yellow bands that are 2 scales wide, and the number of orangish-red body rings varies between 11 and 24 (most frequently there are 15 or 16 rings). Whether Costa Rican *Micrurus nigrocinctus* belong to one species, two subspecies, or even two separate species (as some biologists suggest), is still a matter of debate.

Literature

Campbell 1973; Campbell & Lamar 1989; Greene 1997; Gutiérrez & Bolaños 1981; Leenders 1994; Leenders et al. 1996; Peterson 1990; Sasa & Solórzano 1995; Savage & Vial 1974; Savage & Villa 1986; Taylor et al. 1974; Villa 1972; Zug 1993.

Coral Snakes and Their Look-Alikes

All "true" coral snakes in the New World are venomous and have brightly colored bands that encircle the body. Interestingly, numerous other snakes of the family Colubridae resemble the coral snakes to varying degrees. Why?

Mimicry is an evolutionary process in which a harmless species develops physical features and/or behaviors that resemble those of a harmful species. According to the classic version of the theory, the mimic avoids being eaten because it so closely resembles a harmful species that predators naturally avoid. In Costa Rica, several nonvenomous snakes display the brightly colored bands characteristic of the venomous coral snakes, even though these snakes are not closely related to coral snakes. These snakes, sometimes referred to as "false" coral snakes, supposedly gain protection from looking like venomous coral snakes of the genus *Micrurus*.

Theories of mimicry rest on a critical assumption that predators avoid eating the animal being mimicked. Otherwise the mimic would gain no advantage by resembling the model animal. Field observations of interactions between true or false coral snakes and their predators are too rare to indicate whether these snakes are even avoided. In fact, a recent study in which wild coatimundis (*Nasua narica*) were confronted with snakes suggested that these snake predators did not avoid the brightly colored venomous coral snakes, let alone the harmless mimics. On the other hand, one individual coatimundi reacted with fright to a venomous hog-nosed pit viper (*Porthidium nasutum*), indicating that these animals are capable of recognizing dangerous snakes.

If coral snakes are not avoided by predators, and if, therefore, mimicry is not at play, what other theory might explain the resemblance between true coral snakes and false coral snakes? Perhaps, in certain habitats, brightly colored bands provide some advantage or set of advantages to the snake. If so, then selective pressure over time would favor snakes with colored bands, regardless of whether they are venomous or not.

When uncovering a brightly colored snake from underneath a surface object, predators may be startled for a split second by its conspicuous coloration. This effect, known as the flash color effect, may give the snake just enough time to escape. Flash coloration is an avoidance technique employed by a wide variety of animals, including butterflies, frogs, and birds. In this case, the brightly colored bands are advantageous only in combination with a certain set of behaviors; unless the snake is hidden initially, and unless it is initially motionless, the bright coloration will not startle the potential predator.

While the nonspecialist might assume that any brightly colored animal would be particularly conspicuous to potential predators, in fact the bright rings on snakes effectively break up the serpentine outline of the body, making them harder to recognize as snakes. Thus, while the bright rings may indicate to a potential predator that an organism is present, they make it more difficult for the predator to identify the organism as a snake.

When coral snakes are cornered, they typically hide their head under a coil of the body and wave their tail at the attacker. The tail, though it has the same coloration as the head, is patterned differently from the rest of the body. The tail is curled up in order to approximate the bulk of the head more closely. The snake thus tries to direct the attention away from the real head. In this case, the function of the brightly colored rings is to *attract* the attention of the potential predator. Interestingly, some false coral snakes of the genus *Erythrolamprus* display similar defensive behavior.

Another behavior frequently observed in both true and false coral snakes is a sudden erratic movement of the body. Coral snakes usually remain still when discovered and then explode in a burst of very fast wriggling, twitching, and crawling. During such rapid movement, the snake's brightly colored rings move too fast to be perceived independently, and the impression one gets from looking at an excited coral snake is a uniform brown blur. This apparent change in color and pattern renders the snake momentarily invisible against a background of dead leaves, and it may escape without notice.

The **false coral snake** (*Erythrolamprus mimus*) mimics the defensive behavior of coral snakes by flattening the body, hiding the head, and performing sham attacks with the coiled tail.

While textbooks tend to treat coral snake mimicry as an established fact, rather than theory, new research suggests other explanations for the occurrence of brightly colored bands among snakes in unrelated species. The coral snake mimicry problem has occupied biologists for over a century, and current research centers on collecting data to support the theory. In search of such proof, some biologists have found examples of coral snake mimicry in some rather surprising candidates, including the large *Boa constrictor* (because of the reddish blotches on its tail), several brightly banded caterpillars, and even a turtle (*Rhinoclemmys pulcherrima*)!

Literature

Beckers & Leenders 1994; Beckers et al. 1996; Brodie 1993; Greene & McDiarmid 1981; Jackson et al. 1976; Janzen 1980; Pough 1976; Smith 1975, 1977; Taylor 1951.

SUBFAMILY: **Hydrophiinae** (Sea snakes)
FAMILY: Elapidae (Coral snakes)

Some authors regard the sea snakes as members of a distinct family. However, recent findings suggest that these marine serpents are closely related to the elapids and should be included in that family.

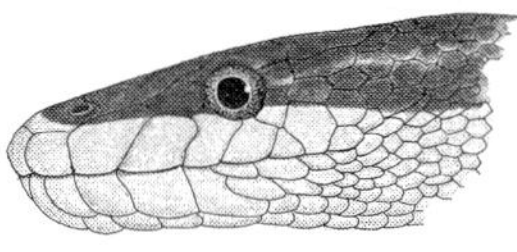

Yellow-bellied sea snake (*Pelamis platurus*).

Sea snakes are basically tropical in their wide distribution, although they are not found in the Atlantic. They range from the east coast of Africa to the west coast of tropical America and reach their highest diversity in the Indo-Pacific region.

Along the American west coast, only one species, the yellow-bellied sea snake (*Pelamis platurus*), has been positively identified. This species is fairly common in the Pacific Ocean off the coast of Costa Rica, and individuals frequently wash up on shore. Like their terrestrial relatives, the coral snakes, yellow-bellied sea snakes posses a strong nerve toxin that is potentially life-threatening to humans.

SPECIES DESCRIPTION

Pelamis platurus

Yellow-bellied sea snake
Serpiente marina (plate 81)

Pelamis platurus, which lives in the Pacific Ocean, is the only sea snake in Costa Rica. Beached individuals are easily recognized by the oarlike, compressed tail. This sea snake occurs from the east coast of Africa throughout the Indian and Pacific oceans to the west coast of the Americas. On the American Pacific coast, it is found from Ecuador in the south to the Gulf of California in the north. The southern and northern limits of its distribution seem to be constrained mainly by the presence of cold surface waters (below 20°C/68°F).

Apart from blindsnakes, *Pelamis platurus* is the only snake in Costa Rica with rows of similarly sized scales completely encircling the body. All other snakes have enlarged plates on the belly and sometimes underneath the tail. Moray eels or other eels are sometimes mistaken for sea snakes. Eels have smooth skin and visible gills, however, and the body is never covered with the knoblike, hexagonal scales typical of *Pelamis platurus*.

Yellow-bellied sea snakes have an elongate, compressed head. The valved nostrils are placed on top of the head. The eyes are on the side of the head for sighting nearby fish, which are caught with a sideways strike. The mouth is tightly sealed by special overlapping scales that also allow for extending the tongue without opening the mouth and letting in saltwater. The vent has a special valvelike arrangement for the same

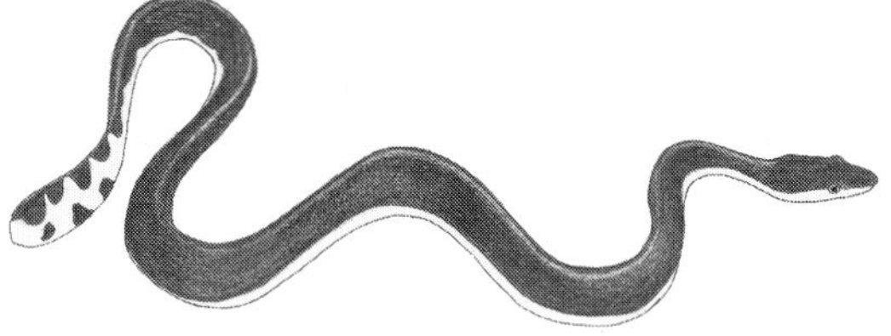

The **yellow-bellied sea snake** uses its flattened, oarlike tail to swim.

purpose. The head is covered with enlarged scales.

These unusual snakes do not grow very large; they measure 500 to 550 mm (19⅝ to 21⅝ inches) in total length. The largest recorded *Pelamis platurus* was a female that had a total length of 833 mm (32¾ inches).

The color pattern of yellow-bellied sea snakes is highly variable, but generally a broad black band covers the top of the head, the entire back and the top of the tail, while the belly is a bright yellow. Just before a snake sheds its skin, all yellow parts of the body may be brown. The tail is usually yellow with a pattern of bold black spots. In some individuals, a brown band is present along the belly. An all-yellow color variety of this species has infrequently been found in the gulf of Panama and in Golfo Dulce in southwestern Costa Rica.

Pelamis platurus is particularly abundant off the coast of southwestern Costa Rica. On windless days during the dry season, these sea snakes can be found in large numbers floating amidst flotsam in slicks, which are narrow strips of calm water where two ocean currents meet. The crew of a research vessel reported catching almost 300 *Pelamis platurus* within two hours from a 3.2 km (2 mi) slick in the mouth of Costa Rica's Golfo Dulce.

Pelamis platurus is sometimes called the pelagic sea snake because it spends its entire life drifting on ocean currents. When the direction of the current changes, it is completely helpless, and individuals that get stranded on a beach perish because they lack the muscle power to crawl back to the water. Like all snakes, yellow-bellied sea snakes have lungs; they die on the beach, however, not because they cannot breathe, but because they overheat when exposed to direct sunlight all day. Besides breathing through lungs, these marine snakes are capable of absorbing a substantial part of their oxygen requirements through skin respiration. The small hexagonal scales do not overlap, and a well-developed web of blood vessels passes underneath the skin, between the scales. Dissolved oxygen from the water passes through the thin skin and is absorbed by the snake's blood. Normally, active *Pelamis platurus* surface every 10 to 20 minutes to breathe. Resting animals have been observed to remain submerged for up to 90 minutes; and under experimental conditions, individual yellow-bellied sea snakes tolerated submergence for over five hours.

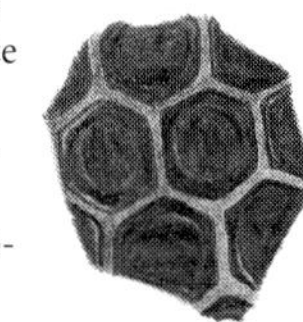
Hexagonal scales.

Reproduction in this species takes place at sea. The snakes mate while floating near the water surface. After a gestation period of at least five months, 5 or 6 live young are born in the water, each measuring 220 to 260 mm (8⅝ to 10¼ inches). Both adults and juveniles feed on small fish that congregate at the debris that accumulates in slicks. The feeding response is usually triggered by schools of small fish, which are attracted to the snake's floating body. Individual snakes showed no response when confronted with immobile or solitary fish. Prey is caught with a swift strike and killed with an extremely toxic venom.

It is generally thought that the black-and-yellow coloration serves as warning display. Besides being venomous, the skin and meat of this species also appears to be distasteful. In experiments, predatory fish were able to recognize individual *Pelamis platurus*, and pieces of snake meat were instantly rejected when tasted, even when completely hidden inside a piece of squid. As far as is currently known, yellow-bellied sea snakes have no natural predators, and the only cause of early mortality is the whim of ocean currents that may carry them onto shore or into lethally cold water.

Pelamis platurus is not an aggressive snake, but is reported to bite and lock onto nets or its own body when restrained. The symptoms of yellow-bellied sea snake bites in man are normally very mild, and bites are rare. Still, human fatalities have been associated with bites of this species, and individuals caught in nets or found on a beach should be treated with great care since sea snake venom is a very potent nerve toxin. Since this species normally does not frequent shallow waters, it poses no substantial threat to swimmers.

Literature

Ernst 1992; Greene 1997; Kropach 1975; Solórzano 1995; Zug 1993.

Venomous Snakes and Snake Venoms

Worldwide, several hundred thousand humans each year are bitten by venomous snakes, and perhaps some 20,000 of those die. The bulk of these bites and fatalities are mainly from about 50 species of snakes in two families, the Elapidae (cobras, mambas, kraits, coral snakes, sea snakes, etc.) and the Viperidae (vipers and pit vipers).

Snake venoms probably evolved when snakes started eating prey animals that were too big, strong, and/or dangerous, to otherwise subdue. Snake venoms arose as a means of aiding in the capture of prey and digestion, but they also bestowed snakes with defensive weapons against animals that feed on them. Different snakes have different toxin "cocktails," depending on the preferred prey. Although snake venom did not evolve to kill humans—since humans have never been preyed on by snakes—snakes will bite humans when defending against a perceived threat.

Venomous snakes of the families Elapidae and Viperidae all have fangs at the front of the mouth. Some rear-fanged colubrid snakes, though technically not considered venomous because they lack the means of *actively* injecting venom, are nevertheless capable of envenomating humans and prey. The term rear-fanged refers to the enlarged teeth located in the rear of the upper jaw, which are often grooved to form a crude channel for "dripping" venom into the bite wound. This feature has evolved independently in a number of unrelated genera of colubrid snakes around the world.

Some rear-fanged colubrids have venom glands, but even those who don't may still have saliva that contains anticoagulants. When these snakes bite, the anticoagulants can enter the puncture wound and cause profuse bleeding and, in some cases, itching.

In rear-fanged colubrids that do have venom glands, these glands usually contain digestive enzymes, anticoagulants, and sometimes a neurotoxic component. During the process of eating its prey, the snake "chews in" its venom. This contrasts with venomous, front-fanged snakes, which actively inject venom into prey. While the main purpose of colubrid venom is to aid digestion, species that feed on large or dangerous animals usually posses a more potent venom that also helps to immobilize prey.

In most cases, a bite from a rear-fanged snake has no serious consequences for humans. The position of the fangs makes it unlikely that venom would be injected during a quick bite, and the fangs are often too short to pierce the human skin. However, if the snake has the opportunity to bite and chew venom into the bite wound, the possibility of envenomation exists. No Costa Rican colubrid snake is known to cause severe envenomation in humans, but some produce a painful bite. In most cases, the effects are local and limited to pain, swelling, and prolonged bleeding from the wound. More severe reactions, including nausea, headache, and general discomfort, have been reported after bites from the roadguarder (*Conophis lineatus*), which is probably among the Costa Rican "harmless" snakes most likely to have a bite with unpleasant effects.

Rear-fanged **Roadguarder** (*Conophis lineatus*).

In other parts of the world, bites from rear-fanged snakes can prove lethal. Two well-known examples of such snakes are the African boomslang (*Dispholidus typus*) and the savanna twig snake (*Thelotornis capensis*) both of which have caused a number of fatalities, including those of two world-famous herpetologists.

The Costa Rican members of the family Elapidae, the coral snakes and the yellow-bellied sea snake, are typical examples of snakes with the more sophisticated venom delivery system found in this family. These snakes have enlarged but fairly short (a few millimeters) immobile fangs in the front of their mouth on the upper jawbone. When the mouth is closed, the fangs fit into a small pocket in the gums of the lower jaw. The teeth, shaped like small hypodermic syringes, are connected through a duct with the venom glands. A part of the snake's jaw musculature is connected to the venom glands and expels venom through the duct and fangs during a bite. Costa Rican elapids typically bite and hold on to their prey until it is immobilized. This is achieved chiefly by the nerve toxins (neurotoxins) in the venom, which cause paralysis of the prey animal's muscles. Victims of severe coral snake bites, including humans, may eventually die from respiratory difficulties or cardiac arrest.

A different venom-delivery system and a different type of venom are found in the family Viperidae. Costa Rican pit vipers, like all other viperids, have very long, hinged fangs located on the front of the upper jaw. These hypodermic needlelike teeth are so long that the snake can only close its mouth when the fangs are folded back against the roof of the mouth. During a bite, the fangs rotate forward into a stabbing position, and the powerful toxins are usually injected deep into the prey's body. Although vipers generally strike and release the victim—slowly following the scent trail it leaves until they reach the dead or dying animal—they usually continue to hold on to birds, frogs, and many lizards, since these animals are hard to follow or do not leave a scent trail.

The venoms of vipers and pit vipers usually contain a high proportion of tissue-destructive components (hemotoxins) and digestive enzymes. Viper venoms may cause massive tissue damage and swelling. When humans are bitten, up to one third of the body's blood volume may leave the circulatory system and accumulate in an extremity or in the intestines. Death usually occurs because the blood pressure in the veins drops to a level that is too low for the heart to function. Because of the extensive damage to tissues, nonlethal bites may still have a devastating and permanent effect on the kidneys and lungs, or may result in the loss of a limb.

The tissue-destructive properties of hemotoxic venoms aid in the digestion of bulky prey. Snakes need to swallow prey animals whole, and vipers are specialized in eating large prey. After a heavy meal, the snake is left with an incapacitating bulge in its body that would leave the reptile much more vulnerable to predators. The injection of digestive enzymes and hemotoxins is a form of predigestion outside of the snake's stomach that speeds up the digestion process and enables the snake to crawl around soon after a meal.

The difference between neurotoxins in Elapidae and hemotoxins in Viperidae was long thought to be very distinct. However, some pit viper bites (from the tropical rattlesnake, *Crotalus durissus*, for example) have strong neurotoxic side-effects; and severe tissue damage can occur from some elapid bites, particularly certain cobra bites. Many snake venoms have both neurotoxic and tissue-destructive properties that may vary between species, populations, and individuals, and may even change during the life of a single snake. Such variations are often explained by the snake's biology, by different diets between populations, or by changes in diet during an animal's life.

Venom is of critical importance to the survival of every venomous snake, and most snakes are careful to conserve it. Although empty venom glands are refilled with a new supply of toxins within weeks, absence of venom prevents venomous snakes from eating or properly digesting prey. Laboratory tests with Palestine vipers (*Daboia palaestinae*) showed that in about 20% of bites to mice, no venom was injected. Several reports of venomous snakebites in humans in which no venom was injected lend credence to the notion that when a snake bites defensively, or when hunting, the amount of venom injected is carefully metered by the snake. On the other hand, there are also numerous reports of defensive bites that led to very serious envenomation, and it is therefore not advisable to assume that a venomous snake biting out of defense will not inject venom.

An interesting morphological study showed that when solar energy (light) penetrates venom glands, it can damage venom production and detoxify stored venom. Deposits of melanin, a black pigment, concentrated on the top and sides of the venom glands are often visible in the form of dark stripes or spots on the heads of snakes in different families. This suggests that these black markings shield the venom glands from light. Especially in vipers, a dark stripe is often present behind the eye, and lab tests revealed a high concentration of melanin in these markings. New World coral snakes (genus *Micrurus*), which are among those with the lowest melanin deposits, are secretive and inhabit areas infrequently exposed to direct sunlight, even though elapid venoms appear less susceptible to detoxification by light. The exception among the elapids is the yellow-bellied sea snake (*Pelamis platurus*), a species that spends most of its life floating on the ocean surface. These snakes were found to have the highest melanin score of all species tested. Some of the "venomous" colubrids have pigment over the venom glands that is as dense as the pigment of some vipers.

Literature

Ernst 1992; Greene 1997; Pough et al. 1978.

FAMILY: **Viperidae** (Viper Family)
SUBORDER: Serpentes (Snakes)

The viper family occurs worldwide, except for Australia and some oceanic islands. All vipers possess long, hinged fangs that can penetrate thick fur or several layers of feathers and inject a strong venom deep into a prey animal's body. When not in use, the fangs rest against the roof of the mouth. Vipers are heavy-bodied, short-tailed snakes, with a head that appears triangular when seen from above. The head of vipers is generally covered with numerous small scales, in contrast to the large head plates of colubrids and coral snakes. Most scales on the viper's head, body, and tail are heavily keeled.

SUBFAMILY: **Crotalinae** (Pit Vipers)
FAMILY: Viperidae (Viper Family)

All viper species in the New World are assigned to the subfamily Crotalinae, or pit vipers. In addition to the features that all vipers have, the snakes in this subfamily have a distinct additional feature, a deep, pitlike hole on each side of the head between the eye and the nostril. These so-called loreal pits are sophisticated infrared receptors that allow the snake to locate and track prey whose body temperature differs from background temperatures.

Because they have highly developed senses and extremely potent venom, pit vipers are efficient hunters. For the most part, these snakes are sit-and-wait predators; they stay in the same spot for a varying amount of time, ranging from a few hours to several weeks, waiting for prey to pass within striking distance. Their excellent camouflage makes them nearly invisible to both prey and predators.

dorsal view

lateral view

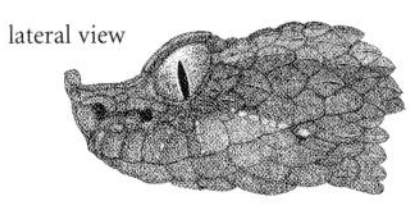

Hog-nosed pit viper (*Porthidium nasutum*). The triangular head is covered with small irregular scales. All pit vipers have a heat-sensitive pit between the eye and the nostril.

Most snakebite incidents in the New World tropics are caused by snakes of the subfamily Crotalinae; only a fraction is caused by coral snakes. The venom of pit vipers usually contains hemotoxins, which cause destruction of blood cells and tissues. However, the venom of some species (e.g., the tropical rattlesnake, *Crotalus durissus*) also appears to contain neurotoxic elements that affect the nervous system. Pit viper venom is usually injected in relatively large quantities in comparison with the amount injected by coral snakes, although sometimes pit vipers bite without injecting venom.

Costa Rica has 14 species of pit vipers in 8 different genera, ranging from small, slender snakes that live in trees in cool mountainous regions (*Bothriechis lateralis* and *Bothriechis nigroviridis*) to very large, thick-bodied, terrestrial pit vipers that inhabit the hot lowlands (*Bothrops asper, Crotalus durissus, Lachesis melanocephala, Lachesis stenophrys*). Almost any combination of body size and shape, preferred habitat, and distribution can be found in the remaining Costa Rican species.

SUMMARY

How to identify Costa Rican pit vipers:

- Pit vipers are the only snakes in Costa Rica with a distinct heat-sensitive pit located between the eye and the nostril on each side of the head.
- These small to very large snakes have a thick, heavy body; a short, slender tail; and a roughly triangular head that is distinctly wider than the neck.
- Most pit vipers have numerous small scales, which are often heavily keeled, on the top of the head.

Agkistrodon bilineatus

Cantil
Castellana (plate 82)

A combination of three features distinguishes this species from all other Costa Rican snakes: a heat-sensitive pit on each side of the head between the eye and the nostril, a distinct white stripe on each side of the head, and enlarged head plates. *Agkistrodon bilineatus* is the only Costa Rican pit viper that has enlarged head plates—colubrid snakes, which share this feature, lack the heat-sensitive pits.

This is a heavy-bodied pit viper with a maximum known total length of 138 cm (54½ inches). Most individuals do not exceed 1,000 mm (40 inches), including the relatively long nonprehensile tail.

The eyes have a vertically elliptical pupil; the lower half of the iris is orangish or brown, the top half is lighter.

The upper surface of *Agkistrodon bilineatus* is tan, chestnut, or reddish-brown with a series of broad, dark crossbands, irregularly outlined with a paler border or series of spots. The belly is pale gray to dark reddish-brown. The head is dark, with two distinct white or cream stripes on each side of it. The upper stripe starts at the tip of the snout and passes over the eye to a point on the side of the neck, while the lower stripe starts at the snout, but runs along the upper lip. The tip of the tail is gray or greenish in adults, but bright yellow in juveniles.

This species occurs from southern Sonora, Mexico, to the Pacific coast of northwestern Costa Rica. Populations of *Agkistrodon bilineatus* also occur on the Atlantic side of Central America in Mexico and Belize. Predominantly found at low elevations, this snake can be found from sea level to 1,500 m (4,900 ft). Within Costa Rica, its distribution is limited to the seasonally dry forests in Guanacaste Province, where it has been reported at Santa Rosa National Park. *Agkistrodon bilineatus* is a relatively rare snake in Costa Rica; its presence in the country was not noted until 1970.

Agkistrodon bilineatus is closely related to the more familiar copperheads (*Agkistrodon contortix*) and cottonmouths (*Agkistrodon piscivorus*) of the United States. In contrast with the cottonmouth, which is semiaquatic, *Agkistrodon bilineatus* inhabits dry savannas, grasslands, and dry tropical forests.

In Santa Rosa National Park, this species synchronizes the birth of its live young with the beginning of the rainy season, when the preferred prey of juvenile snakes—lizards, frogs, and small mammals—is most abundant. These animals are lured to within striking distance by the brightly colored tail tip of juveniles. This snake's prey is killed with a relatively strong venom that is more potent than that of its North American cousins. Bites of this species can be very dangerous for humans, and fatalities have been reported—in some cases within a few hours after the bite.

Atropoides nummifer

Jumping pit viper
Mano de piedra (plate 82)

The pit vipers of the genus *Atropoides* have an extremely robust body and a short nonprehensile tail. The head is broad, distinctly wider than the neck, and has a bluntly rounded snout. The top of the head is covered with numerous more or less similarly sized scales that are all heavily keeled. Two species, the jumping pit viper (*Atropoides nummifer*) and the closely related Picado's jumping pit viper (*Atropoides picadoi*), are found in Costa Rica.

The most distinctive characteristic of this species is the marked ridge on the back formed by three adjoining scale rows that are all extremely heavily keeled. This feature is especially prominent on the front half of the body.

Nearly every scale on the head, body, and tail of this species is heavily keeled; the scales are sometimes almost pyramidal in shape, giving the snake a rugose appearance. A deep heat-sensitive pit is present on each side of the head between the eye and the nostril.

Most *Atropoides nummifer* have a series of large, rounded or rhomboidal spots on the middle of the back. In some individuals, these spots, which are dark brown to almost black in color, are fused to form a zigzag band. A row of similarly colored blotches is present on each side of the body. The dark markings of this species contrast sharply with the gray, tan, or light brown background color. A dark stripe is normally present behind the eyes. The chin, throat, and front of the body are white underneath; but further toward the tail, the belly gradually becomes clouded with pigment and is adorned with numerous squarish black spots. Small juveniles have a bright yellow tail tip that they wriggle like a worm to lure potential prey such as lizards and frogs.

This extremely thick, short snake has a maximum recorded total length of 810 mm (31⅞ inches). Most jumping pit vipers range between 450 and 650 mm (17¾ and 25⅝ inches) including the short tail.

Atropoides nummifer occurs in scattered locations at low and intermediate elevations, from Mexico to Panama. In Costa Rica, it occurs at elevations below 1,500 m (4,900 ft) in the northern half of the country, although some individuals have been discovered in the southern Pacific lowlands.

An encounter with an adult jumping pit viper is an unforgettable experience. These snakes have keen senses, and they constantly turn their head toward potential sources of threat. If disturbed, they employ an intimidating defensive display in which the mouth is gaped widely. If this does not deter the source of the threat, the snake may strike viciously. Jumping pit vipers owe their name to the erroneous belief that these snakes can strike great distances and that they actually launch themselves into the air, jumping toward an intruder. In reality, *Atropoides nummifer* is not capable of striking further than about half of its own body length.

The feeding strike of this species is different than that of many other terrestrial pit vipers, which release prey immediately after striking and follow the scent trail until they find the prey animal where it has succumbed to the snake's venom. In pit vipers with this feeding strategy, contact with the living prey may be reduced to about 0.3 seconds, thus minimizing the chance of the snake being injured by a struggling victim. On the other hand, the terrestrial *Atropoides nummifer*, and many arboreal pit vipers, hold the prey in the mouth and run a much higher risk of being bitten or scratched before the victim succumbs to the venom. In *Atropoides nummifer* and the eyelash pit viper (*Bothriechis schlegelii*) the heat-sensitive pits and part of the eyes are protected by folds of skin that cover these sensitive organs when the snake bites or has prey in its mouth.

The snakes of the genus *Atropoides* are live-bearers; *Atropoides nummifer* has been reported to give birth to broods of 5 to 27 babies measuring about 190 mm (7½ inches).

Jumping pit vipers are believed to have a relatively weak venom, and people bitten by these snakes mainly describe localized symptoms (pain, swelling) that usually disappear completely within days.

Bothriechis lateralis

Striped palm pit viper
Lora (plate 83)

This prehensile-tailed, green pit viper is similar in body shape and size to its close relative, the eyelash pit viper (*Bothriechis schlegelii*), although it lacks the pointed, eyelashlike scales over the eyes typical of that species. The presence of a thin white or yellowish line bordering the belly scales on each side of the body is typical for adults of this species, as is a series of alternating white bars along the midline of the back on an otherwise bright green background color. Juveniles typically are brownish with a contrastingly colored yellow or bluish-green tail tip that is presumably used as a lure to attract prey.

Striped palm pit vipers are found in the Tilarán, Central, and Talamanca mountain ranges of Costa Rica and adjacent Panama, at elevations between 850 and 2,000 m (2,800 and 6,550 ft). They are most frequently found coiled on vegetation above or near forest trails and streams.

Botriechis lateralis is common in Costa Rica, but because it is camouflaged and usually immobile, it is rarely seen.

Bothriechis schlegelii

Eyelash pit viper
Bocaracá (plate 83)

Three pit vipers of the genus *Bothriechis* occur in Costa Rica. The eyelash pit viper (*Bothriechis schlegelii*), the striped palm pit viper (*Bothriechis lateralis*), and the black-speckled palm pit viper (*Bothriechis nigroviridis*) were formerly placed in the genus *Bothrops*, but are now assigned to the genus *Bothriechis*; all have slender bodies and prehensile tails, are relatively small, and have arboreal habits. *Bothriechis lateralis* and *Bothriechis nigroviridis* are highland species that are found at higher elevations of Costa Rican mountain ranges, whereas *Bothriechis schlegelii* is found throughout the lowlands of Costa Rica.

The feature that most readily distinguishes an eyelash pit viper from all other Costa Rican snakes is the presence of (usually) two, eyelashlike pointed scales above each eye. The function of these scales is still a mystery. A plausible explanation is that they protect the snake's eyes from getting scratched when it is crawling through dense vegetation; the projecting scales would keep aerial roots and branches away from its eyes.

Bothriechis schlegelii is a medium-sized pit viper with a maximum total length of approximately 800 mm (31½ inches), although most adults measure between 500 and 600 mm (19⅝ and 23⅝ inches) in total length. It has a broad, triangular head that is distinctly wider than the slender, compressed body. The tail is strongly prehensile. Most scales on the head, body, and tail are heavily keeled. A deep loreal pit is present on each side of the head, between the nostrils and the eyes. The eyes are relatively small and have vertically elliptical pupils.

The coloration of this species is extremely variable; even within a single litter, different color forms may occur. The ground color is usually green, olive-green, brown, or grayish-brown with blotches, spots, or crossbands in various colors. One distinct color variety locally known as *oropel* exhibits a uniform bright yellow or golden color sprinkled with tiny black specks. Small juveniles have a brightly colored tail tip (cream, yellow, or greenish) that contrasts with the body coloration; these colors disappear with age.

The distribution range of *Bothriechis schlegelii* extends from the southern part of Mexico through Belize and northern Guatemala south to Ecuador and Venezuela, at elevations between sea level and 1,300 m (4,250 ft). This species is mainly found at low and moderate elevations on the Caribbean slope, but in sections of Costa Rica, Panama, and northwestern South America, it also inhabits the Pacific lowlands.

Bothriechis schlegelii is a common snake in the Caribbean lowlands of Costa Rica, although it is infrequently seen because of its excellent camouflage. Individuals coiled on a mossy branch are almost invisible to both predators and prey.

Like most pit vipers, eyelash pit vipers are sit-and-wait predators. They position themselves in a location where potential prey may pass and wait, sometimes for days on end, without changing position. These snakes are known to eat frogs, lizards (mostly anoles of the genus *Norops*), birds, and small mammals. Juveniles have been seen to use their brightly colored tail as a lure to attract lizards. The tail is wriggled in a wormlike fashion in front of the snake's head; when an unsuspecting prey animal comes within range, it is caught with a quick strike. Eyelash pit vipers tend to catch a prey and hold it in their mouth until the powerful venom starts to work. A fold of skin covers the heat-sensitive pit and part of the eye and protects those sensitive organs while the snake holds a struggling animal in its jaws. A similar skin fold is found in jumping pit vipers (*Atropoides nummifer* and *Atropoides picadoi*).

Eyelash pit vipers are arboreal snakes that can be seen coiled on branches, aerial roots, and large leaves, or in bromeliads, between 0.5 and 35 m (2 and 115 ft) above the ground. One individual found on the forest floor was trying to swallow a Central American whip-tailed lizard (*Ameiva festiva*) that was longer in total length than the snake itself. Eventually, after more than five hours, the pit viper succeeded in devouring the lizard.

Although *Bothriechis schlegelii* is a medium-sized snake, it has relatively potent venom. Snakebite incidents involving this species are not uncommon in Costa Rica, and every year three to six people are reported to have died after being bitten. A large percentage of the bites are sustained by people walking through dense vegetation; because this snake is arboreal, they are often bitten in the head, neck, shoulders, or chest. Occasionally, disturbed eyelash pit vipers will assume a defensive posture, with the mouth wide open, before striking.

Bothriechis schlegelii is live-bearing and produces litters of up to 20 young, each measuring between 210 and 240 mm (8¼ and 9½ inches), including the tail.

Bothrops asper

Fer-de-lance
Terciopelo, Barba amarilla (plate 84)

Bothrops asper is one of the most feared animals in Latin America. The fer-de-lance is a very large pit viper with a maximum known length of 246 cm (97 inches), including the nonprehensile tail. The large, slender head is triangular when seen from above, and

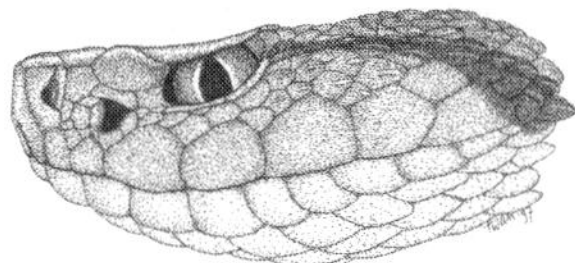

Fer-de-lance (*Bothrops asper*).

distinctly wider than the neck. There is a deep heat-sensitive pit between the eye and the nostril on each side of the head. The relatively large eyes have a vertically elliptical pupil. Most of the scales on top of the head, back, and tail are distinctly keeled.

The body is patterned with yellow or white stripes, forming a pattern of chevrons or X shapes that outline a series of dark-edged triangular blotches. The dark triangles are sometimes fused to form hourglass markings. The body, tail, and head are dark brown, with a velvety sheen (*terciopelo* means velvet in Spanish). The lip scales and the underside of the head and throat are cream or yellowish, gradually changing into the cream coloration of the belly. A dark stripe is present on each side of the head that starts behind the eye and extends to the corner of the mouth or slightly beyond.

The fer-de-lance ranges from northern Mexico to the Pacific lowlands of Colombia and Ecuador. In Costa Rica, this species is particularly abundant in the tropical rainforests of both Atlantic and Pacific regions, from sea level to at least 1,300 m (4,250 ft). It is scarcely observed in the dry forest of Guanacaste Province, and although it has been reported to inhabit the Nicoya Peninsula, there is no substantiating evidence.

The Tilarán, Central, and Talamanca mountain ranges constitute a geographic barrier that separates the Caribbean and Pacific populations of *Bothrops asper*, and striking differences exist between individuals from opposite sides of the country. Besides variation in the chemical composition of the venom and in scalation characteristics, there is also a distinct difference in the total length of the females. Females from Caribbean-slope populations measure on average 167 cm (66 inches); their smaller Pacific counterparts measure on average 142 cm (56 inches). There is also a distinct size difference between male and female individuals of all populations. On average, females are 20% to 25% longer than males. Since the litter size of these live-bearing snakes is positively correlated with the female's body size, fer-de lances on the Caribbean slope give birth to more young than on the Pacific side of the country. The mating season in Pacific populations, which takes place between September and November, seems to be unrelated to seasonal changes, whereas in Atlantic populations the mating appears to coincide with a relatively dry and warm period between February and April.

The gestation period for all Costa Rican fer-de-lances is between 6 to 8 months. This species is extremely prolific; litter size ranges from 5 to 86 babies. Newborn females are typically longer than newborn males. Young males have a conspicuous yellow tail tip.

Juvenile *Bothrops asper* predominantly eat frogs and lizards, although there are indications that they occasionally eat invertebrate prey as well. Adults feed on birds and mammals; they may take prey up to the size of opossums (*Didelphis marsupialis*) or rabbits (*Sylvilagus brasiliensis*).

Fer-de-lances are terrestrial snakes, although juveniles, and occasionally adults, will crawl into low vegetation. These pit vipers spend most of the day coiled and concealed in vegetation. They become active at dusk, when they move to their hunting sites, often at the side of a road or the edge of a trail, where they attempt to ambush prey. *Bothrops asper's* excellent camouflage makes them extremely hard to see when they are coiled in vegetation. Although they sometimes remain coiled in the beam of a flashlight when they are discovered at night, they tend to retreat within a few minutes of disturbance. Fer-de-lances flee with surprising speed and agility, usually toward the cover of dense vegetation. On entering the plant cover, they sometimes stop and turn around to face the perceived threat.

This species is originally a rainforest inhabitant, but it appears to adapt well to habitat changes. It is most frequently found in dense vegetation of all sorts, ranging from tall grass or scrub to virgin rainforest. Fer-de-lances are very common around human settlements throughout their distribution range and thus cause many snakebite incidents.

When threatened, individuals rapidly vibrate the tail, producing a clearly audible buzz. When further provoked, the snake strikes at its attacker with lightning speed. Its excitable disposition and strong venom make this an extremely dangerous snake. Fer-de-lances are responsible for numerous deaths in Costa Rica, although treatment of their bites has become increasingly successful. With proper medical treatment, most victims survive their unpleasant encounter, although long-term effects of the venom sometimes persist.

Cerrophidion godmani

Godman's montane pit viper
Toboba de Altura (plate 84)

Costa Rica is home to one member of the genus *Cerrophidion*. *Cerrophidion godmani* was previously included in the genus *Bothriechis*, and before that in the genus *Bothrops*. It is now assigned to the genus *Cerrophidion* because of its small size and moderately stout body, and because it lacks a prehensile tail and has enlarged irregular plates on top of the head.

Pit vipers of the genus *Cerrophidion* occur in mountainous habitats from southern Mexico to western Panama, at elevations from 1,300 to more than 3,000 m (4,250 to more than 9,850 ft). In Costa Rica, this snake is found at elevations above 1,500 m (4,900 ft) in the Central and Talamanca mountain ranges.

Cerrophidion godmani is a small- to medium-sized pit viper with a maximum known total length of about 789 mm (31 inches). Most individuals measure between 400 and 600 mm (15¾ and 23½ inches). The head is moderately broad, and wider than the neck. Most scales on the upper surfaces are keeled. Two distinct heat-sensitive pits are present, one on each side of the head between the nostril and the eye.

Godman's montane pit viper is a variable species, but most individuals have a series of pale greenish-brown blotches (outlined with very dark brown) that form a wavy band on a pale gray background. A row of similarly colored blotches is present on each side of the body. A distinct dark brown stripe starts behind the eyes and continues onto the neck, beyond the angle of the jaw. The underside of the head, throat, and belly are cream, but toward the tail this light coloration is increasingly suffused with dark pigment. In adults, the underside of the tail tip in adults is pale orange; in juveniles almost the entire tail is pale orange.

The natural history of *Cerrophidion godmani* is poorly understood. In Costa Rica, it is the only ground-dwelling pit viper that occurs at high elevations. The other montane pit vipers in the country, *Bothriechis lateralis* and *Bothriechis nigroviridis*, are both predominantly green, arboreal species. Godman's montane pit viper has been reported to be abundant locally, and is mostly seen active during the day. There are indications that these small pit vipers spend at least part of their life in underground burrows.

One individual *Cerrophidion godmani* was reported to bite and kill a green spiny lizard (*Sceloporus malachiticus*). Nothing further is known about the food preference of this species.

No bite accidents involving this species are known in Costa Rica, but reports from other countries indicate that *Cerrophidion godmani* most likely has a very mild venom that causes high fever and local swelling.

Crotalus durissus

Tropical rattlesnake
Cascabel (plate 85)

This is the only species of snake in Costa Rica with a rattle; very young individuals have a small button on the tip of the tail that later grows into a rattle. Even the youngest tropical rattlesnakes can be recognized by a color pattern that consists of dark, diamond-shaped spots on the back, combined with a pair of dark stripes on the head and neck.

Crotalus durissus is a large rattlesnake with a maximum size of about 180 cm (71 inches) including the short tail. The scales on the back of the head, body, and tail are very strongly keeled, giving this snake a rugose appearance. A distinct keel runs down the middle of the back. The head is almost triangular and significantly wider than the neck; a deep heat-sensitive pit is visible between the eye and the nostril on each side of the head. An ever-growing rattle is located at the tip of the tail; every time the snake sheds its skin, a segment is added to the rattle.

Crotalus durissus in defense posture.

Tropical rattlesnakes are tan, yellowish-brown, or grayish snakes with a pattern of two dark longitudinal stripes that originate on the head and extend onto the neck. These stripes are replaced on the body by a series of 18 to 35 diamond-shaped blotches.

This large pit viper can be found from Mexico to northwestern Costa Rica; it also ranges widely in South America, occurring as far south as Argentina. In Costa Rica, this species is only found in the dry savannas and deciduous forests of lowland Guanacaste Province, where it can be very common.

Crotalus durissus give birth to live young at the beginning of the rainy season, when prey is abundant. These impressive predators seem to feed mainly on mammals, such as rats and mice.

Crotalus durissus is an extremely dangerous snake: it is large, has an unpredictable character, and its venom is extremely toxic. There are indications that the composition of the tropical rattlesnake's venom changes throughout its vast distribution range; generally, however, it appears to consist of both hemotoxins and neurotoxins. One could say that the bite of a *Crotalus durissus* has the effect of being bitten by a fer-de-lance (*Bothrops asper*) and a coral snake (genus *Micrurus*) at the same time. Many fatalities in Central and South America can be attributed to the tropical rattlesnake, and this formidable animal should always be treated with the greatest care.

Lachesis stenophrys

Central American bushmaster
Cascabel Muda, Matabuey (plate 85)

Identifying characteristics of the bushmasters include an extremely large size, pyramid-like scales that cover the body and tail, and a long hornlike spike on the tip of the tail. Two species of the genus *Lachesis* live in Costa Rica, the Central American bushmaster (*Lachesis stenophrys*), which occurs on the Caribbean slope of the country, and the geographically isolated black-headed bushmaster (*Lachesis melanocephala*), which is restricted to the southwestern lowlands.

The Central American bushmaster is the largest member of the viper family, and the second largest venomous snake in the world. Only the king cobra (*Ophiophagus hannah*) surpasses this snake in size. A total length of more than 200 cm (79 inches) is not uncommon, and total lengths of up to 350 cm (138 inches) have been reported. The largest size ever measured for a bushmaster is 426 cm (168 inches), although the evidence supporting this claim has been lost.

In addition to their large size, bushmasters are characterized by a vertebral ridge down the middle of the back and the heavily keeled, almost pyramidlike scales. *Lachesis stenophrys* has a broadly rounded head and a relatively slender body. The tail is tipped with a distinctive long spine. On each side of the head, a deep heat-sensitive pit is present between the eye and the nostril.

Central American bushmasters may be grayish-brown, tan, or reddish-brown, patterned with a series of black diamond-shaped markings that have light triangular blotches in them. The resulting pattern, when seen from the side, looks like a series of black-outlined triangle-shaped markings. The head, which has a hue similar to the rest of the body, is marked on each side with a dark stripe that extends from behind the eye to the corner of the mouth, and sometimes beyond.

Lachesis stenophrys inhabits Panama, Costa Rica, and Nicaragua. Within Costa Rica, this majestic snake lives in the lowlands of the Caribbean slope, between sea level and about 1,000 m (3,300 ft).

Bushmasters are unique in being the only pit vipers that lay eggs. This may be one of the factors that limits the distribution of bushmaster species to hot and humid tropical forests, since the incubation of their eggs requires a high overall temperature and humidity.

Lachesis stenophrys is a shy, secretive species that inhabits dense virgin rainforest. These snakes are often found near large buttress-root trees, or large logs. Central American bushmasters are also found near the abundant understory palm *Welfia*. One of the most important seed-dispersal agents for this plant is the spiny rat (*Proechimys semispinosus*); since this rodent is among the favored prey of *Lachesis stenophrys*, these snakes are sometimes found near such palms.

As is indicated by its Spanish name, *cascabel muda* (silent rattlesnake), the bushmaster is closely related to rattlesnakes. Although *Lachesis stenophrys* does not have a rattle, the hard tip of the tail can produce a clearly audible humming sound when vibrated against leaves. This tail-vibrating behavior is part of the impressive defensive display of the bushmaster, which includes inflating the neck and lifting the head off the ground with the front part of the body coiled in an S-shaped curve. Bushmasters usually have a rather mild character, especially during the daytime. When they are disturbed during the night, these pit vipers are more prone to defend themselves and immediately assume the defensive posture. When harassed, they will not hesitate to strike at the source of the threat. Some unsubstantiated reports suggest that females may be more irascible during the breeding season and in the area where the nest is located. Females may be defending their eggs against trespassers.

Because these snakes are not common, people seldom are bitten by a bushmaster. However, the few reports on bite incidents indicate that the bite is invariably severe. Of the five cases reported in a Costa Rican study, four were fatal, even though all victims received hospital treatment and were administered antivenom. The venom of newly hatched juveniles of this species has a strong *coagulating* effect on human plasma; the venom of adults has an anti-coagulating effect.

A second species of bushmaster, the black-headed bushmaster (*Lachesis melanocephala*) was until recently thought to be a bushmaster subspecies, but is now considered a distinct species. Its distribution is limited to southwestern Costa Rica, predominantly on the Osa Peninsula and the adjacent lowlands. Black-headed bushmasters differ most conspicuously from their Caribbean slope counterpart, *Lachesis stenophrys*, in having the upper surface of the head, above the dark eye stripes, completely black. *Lachesis melanocephala* also appears to have a different disposition than Central American bushmasters, and is reported to be unusually aggressive when disturbed.

Porthidium nasutum

Hog-nosed pit viper
Tamagá (plate 86)

Three species of the genus *Porthidium* occur in Costa Rica, the hog-nosed pit viper (*Porthidium nasutum*), the slender hog-nosed pit viper or *toboba chinga* (*Porthidium ophryomegas*), and the recently discovered volcano hog-nosed pit viper (*Porthidium volcanicum*). All three species are small, stocky snakes with a distinctly upturned snout, terrestrial habits, and usually a pale line on the middle of the back that divides a series of staggered blotches.

The hog-nosed pit viper is the only snake in Costa Rica with a distinctly upturned snout that is at least twice as high as it is wide.

Females of this small, stout-bodied pit viper may reach a maximum size of 635 mm (25 inches); males remain considerably smaller, with a maximum total length of not more than 463 mm (18¼ inches). Females have a thick body and a slender, short tail; males have a thinner body, with a gently tapering, longer tail. In both sexes, the head is triangular when seen from above, and distinctly wider than the neck. Keels are present on virtually all scales on the head and body. A deep heat-sensitive pit is present on each side of the head, located between the eye and the nostril.

Hog-nosed pit vipers are brown, reddish-brown or grayish above, with a series of large, dark brown obscure blotches on the back that are

SNAKES

sometimes outlined in white. Usually a narrow, cream, orange, or red vertebral line divides these blotches, and occasionally the left and right halves of the blotches are offset on the middle of the back, producing a zigzag band. The upper surface of the head is frequently marked with a spear point of brown, outlined on the sides of the snout by pale orange stripes. The dark sides of the head are sometimes interrupted by rows of white spots forming irregular lines that radiate from the eye to various spots on the upper lip. The nonprehensile tail in this species is greenish in juveniles, but with age it becomes white with bold dark spots. Large females may have very obscure markings and often lack the vertebral stripe. Juveniles are noticeably brighter in coloration than adults.

Porthidium nasutum is found on the Caribbean slope, from Mexico to Colombia, and on the Pacific slope, from northern Costa Rica to Ecuador, from sea level to at least 800 m (2,600 ft).

Porthidium nasutum is a terrestrial snake that seems to prefer humid rainforest habitats. They are most often seen rolled up into a tight coil on the leaf litter that covers jungle trails. The color pattern of these snakes makes them blend in so well with a background of fallen leaves that they are difficult to spot.

An adult female of this species was noticed sitting in the middle of a trail in a reserve on the Caribbean slope. For 19 consecutive days, this individual was seen at exactly the same spot. On three occasions, she moved away during extremely heavy rains that flooded the forest floor, only to return to the location after the water had dissipated. During this time, the snake did not appear to have eaten anything.

Excellent camouflage helps *Porthidium nasutum* remain unnoticed by both predators and prey. Juveniles of this species have been observed to use their yellowish-green tail tip to lure potential prey to within striking distance. The sighting of three adult individuals that were missing the tail may indicate that these snakes sometimes attract predators as well as prey with their tail motions.

Juveniles eat mainly frogs and lizards, but have also been reported to eat earthworms. As they mature, food preferences change. Adults predominantly feed on mammals, though birds and other hog-nosed pit vipers may also be eaten occasionally. Like all pit vipers, individual *Porthidium nasutum* are capable of eating animals larger than themselves. A juvenile snake was reported to have eaten a spiny pocket mouse (*Heteromys desmarestianus*) weighing 129% of the snake's own body weight.

Porthidium nasutum is live-bearing, and Costa Rican females give birth to litters of up to 14 young.

In general, hog-nosed pit vipers are calm and sometimes almost lethargic. However, some individuals are very temperamental and strike at everything that comes within reach. Bites of this species have caused human fatalities, although this risk is likely not very high in healthy people.

A second species of this genus, the slender hog-nosed pit viper (*Porthidium ophryomegas*), lives in the dry deciduous forests of Guanacaste Province. A distinct preference for dry habitats and a shorter snout distinguish this species from *Porthidium nasutum*. A third Costa Rican *Porthidium*, the volcano hog-nosed pit viper (*Porthidium volcanicum*), has a very limited distribution. It was first described in 1994 from the Buenos Aires Volcano in the Valle del General (Puntarenas Province), where it lives between 400 and 450 m (1,300 and 1,475 ft). However, because of massive habitat destruction throughout its small range, this species is seriously reduced in numbers. Recent attempts to find individuals of this species have not been successful.

Literature

Bolaños & Montero 1970; Campbell & Lamar 1989, 1992; Chavez et al. 1993; Chiszar & Raddcliffe 1989; Greene 1997; Greene & Hardy 1989; Gutiérrez et al. 1990;

Hardy 1994; Lee 1996; Leenders 1995b; Nickerson et al. 1978; Porras et al. 1981; Sasa & Solórzano 1995; Solórzano 1990, 1993, 1994; Solórzano & Cerdas 1989; Taylor 1951, 1954b; Vial & Jimenez-Porras 1967; Wilson & Meyer 1985; Zamudio & Greene 1997; Zug 1993.

APPENDIX 1

Snakebite Prevention and Treatment

Although snakebite incidents are relatively common, fatalities are rare. In the United States, for example, there are roughly 8,000 incidents every year, resulting in just 10 to 15 deaths. The reason for this low fatality rate is mainly due to effective medical treatment. In Costa Rica, snakebite treatment has become increasingly effective, and the number of people who die after being bitten by venomous snakes has decreased dramatically in the last 50 years. At present, the mortality rate due to snakebite in the country is estimated to be approximately 0.2 per 100,000 inhabitants, almost 25 times lower than in the early 1950s. While the chances of surviving a bite by a Costa Rican venomous snake are good, there remains the grave danger of incurring serious permanent damage from the effects of the venom (see page 257 for information on venomous snakes and snake venoms). A bite from a pit viper or a coral snake should always be regarded as life-threatening.

In Costa Rica, the highest snakebite mortality rates occur in the Caribbean and southern Pacific lowlands. The most dangerous snake in the country, *Bothrops asper*, is not very common in the northern Pacific lowlands. The riskiest places tend to be areas that were formerly covered with rainforest and have been transformed into agricultural fields, and the vast majority of snakebite victims in Costa Rica are people who work those fields on a daily basis. The risk of being bitten by a dangerously venomous snake while visiting Costa Rica is very slim. However, there are a few simple, basic rules that may help decrease this already minimal risk.

How to minimize the risk of snake bites

When encountering a venomous snake, remain at a safe distance. No Costa Rican snake is capable of striking much beyond a length equal to half its body length. As a general rule, a safe distance is at least one full snake body length away from the animal.

Never handle a venomous snake, even when it appears dead! Many snakebite accidents happen during handling, or attempting to pick up, a venomous snake. In fact, most coral snake (*Micrurus*) bites occur when these snakes are picked up in the mistaken belief that they are harmless. Some snakes that play dead when threatened may suddenly bite when touched. Even truly dead snakes can be dangerous because of muscle reflexes that may occur up to several hours after the snake's death. A famous example of such reflex action is known from the United States, where a man died as a result of being bitten and envenomated by the severed head of a rattlesnake.

In Costa Rica, most bites occur on the feet and lower legs when snakes are inadvertently stepped on. Pit vipers are especially well-camouflaged, and even very large snakes are sometimes hard to see under the low light conditions that prevail in a forest interior. Note that, throughout the country, venomous snakes can also be expected on vegetation and rocks, not just on the ground. A common-sense rule to guard against bites from unseen snakes is "look before you grab and look before you step."

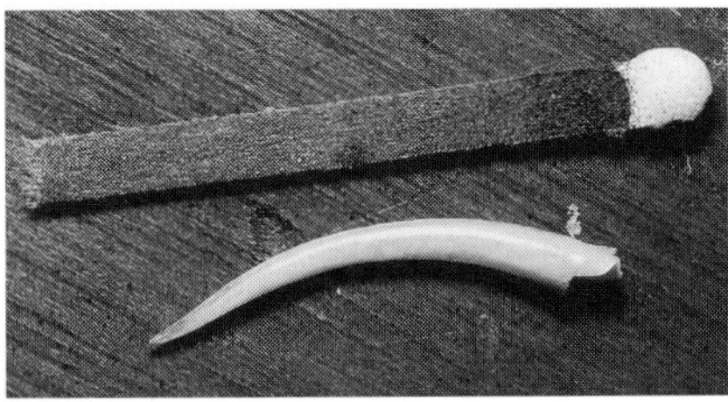
Fer-de-lance fang.

Coral snakes have relatively short fangs, and the chance of receiving a bite when not handling one is minute. Large individuals of species such as the fer-de-lance (*Bothrops asper*) have very long fangs, reaching up to 24 mm (1 inch), and such large snakes are capable of injecting venom through pants above the top of the boots. However, wearing sturdy shoes or boots and long, preferably baggy, trousers will help protect against bites from most other venomous snakes.

When walking at night, always use a flashlight to illuminate your path. Snakes reflect light well at night, and they are easily seen in the beam of a strong flashlight.

What to do in the case of a venomous snake bite

Few subjects in medicine are as controversial as the first-aid measures that should be taken between the time of a venomous bite and the time the victim arrives in a hospital. At present, the general consensus is that most of the previously advised and applied treatments—such as incision and suction, or applying tourniquets, electric shocks, or ice on or near the bite site—are often ineffective and may even have injurious effects on the victim.

Rapid evacuation of the patient to a medical facility should always have priority over first-aid measures, but the following suggestions for assisting the snakebite victim should be considered.

- Remain calm and reassure the victim. Many people believe that, after being bitten by a venomous snake, death will come fast and inevitably. However, medical treatment is available in most hospitals in Costa Rica and is effective in most cases.
- Remove rings, bracelets, watches, and tight-fitting clothes as soon as possible, before swelling commences.
- Immobilize the bitten body part, with a splint if necessary, and place any extremity that has been bitten below the level of the heart. In the case of a coral snake bite, it is advisable to lay the patient on his or her side, with the head bent back to avoid obstruction of the airway that may be caused by paralysis of the tongue.
- Do not give the victim alcohol, coffee, or aspirin. All these substances may cause increased bleeding and higher heart rate, both of which cause the venom to spread faster.
- Do not apply tourniquets or constriction bands. Such devices may rapidly cause unbearable pain, and their use has resulted in the loss of limbs in many cases.
- Although extractor kits have been known to remove some venom in laboratory tests, they remain to be proven effective under field conditions and in humans. However, they are not likely to do any harm and may be of some use. Extractor kits that utilize cutting and/or constriction bands should be avoided.

• If the patient develops shock before reaching a hospital, give him or her oxygen, if available. In the case of envenomation by a coral snake, respiratory arrest may occur. If necessary, apply standard cardiopulmonary resuscitation (CPR).

• Antivenom should be administered in the field only under very extreme circumstances. Only when the bite is inflicted by a large (over 1.2 m/4 ft long) *Bothrops*, *Lachesis*, or *Crotalus* species; when signs of envenomation such as pain, swelling, and vomiting are present; when the patient has no history of allergy to horse serum; and when the evacuation time to a medical facility will be more than 4 hours is it ever advisable to inject antivenom. In all other cases, such field treatment should never be undertaken.

• Bring the biting snake to the medical facility only if that can be done without risk. Since a polyvalent anti-Crotalinae serum, which is active against the venom of all Costa Rican pit vipers, and a serum against the venom of different coral snakes, are produced by Instituto Clodomiro Picado, it is not necessary to know exactly which species of venomous snake caused the bite incident to receive proper treatment.

Literature

Brown 1987; Campbell & Lamar 1989; Ernst 1992; Hardy 1994; Kitchens et al. 1987; Rojas et al. 1997.

APPENDIX 2

Rules and Responsibilities

The International Union for Conservation of Nature and Natural Resources (IUCN), which is an independent global organization, has a special division, the Species Survival Commission (IUCN-SSC), whose members are specialists on a variety of species and species groups. The commission's charter is to assess and monitor the status of all animal and plant species worldwide. After a species is surveyed, it is either assigned a conservation status or grouped in the category "deficient data." Since the number of animal and plant species is very large, the commission is unable to survey most species; the vast majority of the world's animal and plant species either have not been evaluated or have received a deficient data status. Therefore, the fact that a species does not appear on the IUCN Red Data List, which lists endangered species, does not necessarily mean that that species is not endangered.

The commission focuses research mainly on species that are obviously endangered or whose disappearance has been noted. The IUCN-SSC compiles a list of threatened animal species that lists all endangered animals. If sufficient data is available for a particular species, it is assigned to a conservation category or conservation status. These categories are extinct, extinct in the wild (individuals still survive in zoos, parks, etc.), threatened, or lower risk. Within the threatened category, animals are further categorized as critically endangered, endangered, or vulnerable.

The world's herpetofauna has received uneven attention from the specialists at IUCN-SSC. To date only the reptilian orders Crocodylia, Testudines, and Rhynchocephalia have received considerable attention. These three groups constitute less than 3% of the Earth's amphibians and reptiles. Although it is safe to say that there are many more species that are threatened, the current list of threatened animals includes only the Costa Rican reptiles and amphibians shown in table 9. Vulnerable species are those whose populations have declined by 20% over the last three generations. Endangered and critically endangered species are those whose populations have declined 50% and 80% respectively over the last three generations. Three other Costa Rican species placed at lower risk are shown in table 10.

Table 9: Costa Rican Amphibians and Reptiles Listed in the IUCN Red Data List as Threatened Species.

Name	*Common name*	*Status*
Crocodylus acutus	American crocodile	vulnerable
Caretta caretta	Loggerhead turtle	endangered
Chelonia mydas	Green turtle	endangered
Eretmochelys imbricata	Hawksbill turtle	critically endangered
Lepidochelys olivacea	Olive ridley	endangered
Dermochelys coriacea	Leatherback turtle	endangered
Kinosternon angustipons	Narrow-bridged mud turtle	vulnerable
Bufo periglenes	Golden toad	critically endangered

Table 10: Costa Rican Amphibians and Reptiles Listed in the IUCN Red Data List as at Lower Risk.

Name	*Common name*
Rhinoclemmys annulata	Brown wood turtle
Rhinoclemmys funerea	Black wood turtle
Trachemys scripta	Common slider

In spite of our poor knowledge of the status of most reptile and amphibian populations, IUCN preliminary data indicates that, worldwide, 25% of amphibian species and 20% of reptile species are threatened with extinction.

Among the many threats to wildlife is illegal trading and hunting. All species of sea turtles and crocodilians have suffered disastrous population declines at the hands of humans. The meat of most species, and the eggs of all species of sea turtle, are valued as a source of food. Hawksbills have been hunted to near extinction because of their gorgeous shells. In addition, the skin of many crocodilians and sea turtles is used in the leather industry or to produce generally tasteless souvenirs. The effects of the capture of many species of reptiles and amphibians for the pet trade are poorly known, but those effects, without question, are substantial in the case of some species. The Convention on International Trade in Endangered Species of Wild Flora and Fauna (CITES) was instituted as a tool to regulate the trade in endangered animals and plants.

A CITES display in an international airport warning tourists about products made from endangered animals.

CITES is an agreement between participating countries only. Government officials from those countries meet every five years to revise the CITES lists. While some nonparticipating countries are havens for illegal trade in plants and animals, most countries today endorse the CITES agreements. Participating countries issue permits for the export and import of listed species, but only for certain purposes, such as scientific research or conservation projects. Otherwise it is illegal to take any of these species across the borders of participating countries.

There are several levels of protectioin that apply to the species included in the CITES convention. The highest degree of protection is granted to the species listed in Appendix I of the CITES report; since these species are threatened with extinction, the trade of animals on this list is subject to extremely strict rules. Appendix II includes species that are not necessarily threatened with extinction now, but that may become so unless their trade is strictly regulated. This appendix also includes

Table 11: Costa Rican Amphibians and Reptiles Protected Under the CITES Convention

Appendix 1

Name	***Common name***
Bufo periglenes	Golden toad
Caretta caretta	Loggerhead turtle
Chelonia mydas	Green turtle
Eretmochelys imbricata	Hawksbill turtle
Lepidochelys olivacea	Olive ridley
Dermochelys coriacea	Leatherback turtle
Crocodylus acutus	American crocodile

Appendix II

Name	***Common name***
Dendrobates auratus	Green and black poison-dart frog
Dendrobates granuliferus	Granular poison-dart frog
Dendrobates pumilio	Strawberry poison-dart frog
Phyllobates lugubris	Striped poison-dart frog
Phyllobates vittatus	Golfodulcean poison-dart frog
Caiman crocodilus	Spectacled caiman
Iguana iguana	Green iguana
Boa constrictor	Boa constrictor
Corallus annulatus	Annulated tree boa
Corallus ruschenbergerii	Common tree boa
Epicrates cenchria	Rainbow boa
Ungaliophis continentalis	Central American dwarf boa
Clelia clelia	Mussurana

unthreatened species that resemble species that are otherwise protected, in order to ensure that protected species are not passed off as unthreatened species. Amphibians and reptiles in Costa Rica that fall under CITES-convention protection are listed in table 11.

The CITES regulations apply not only to both living and dead animals, but also to recognizable parts of protected animals. Thus the trade in crocodile-skin boots or sea-turtle eggs is just as illegal as the trade in those animals.

In addition to international regulations, most countries have also enacted national laws on collecting and transporting plants and animals. In Costa Rica, it is illegal to take any amphibian or reptile out of the country without a permit. It is also illegal to collect wild plants and animals, and the penalties are severe. Nevertheless, illegal trade in wild animals is unfortunately still a common practice in Costa Rica, as it is in other countries. IUCN and CITES lists alone will not stop the disappearance of these animals; the golden toad was added to Appendix I of the CITES convention in 1995, about six years after the last individual was seen in the wild. What is also needed is a radical change in our relationship to the natural world.

Literature
Baillie & Groombridge 1996; Schouten 1992.

APPENDIX 3

Amphibians & Reptiles of Costa Rica (Checklist)

An asterisk indicates species introduced to Costa Rica.

Amphibia (174)

Gymnophiona

Caeciliaidae (4)
Dermophis gracilior
Dermophis parviceps
Gymnopis multiplicata
Oscaecilia osae

Caudata

Plethodontidae (37)
Bolitoglossa alvaradoi
Bolitoglossa cerroensis
Bolitoglossa colonnea
Bolitoglossa compacta
Bolitoglossa diminuta
Bolitoglossa epimela
Bolitoglossa gracilis
Bolitoglossa lignicolor
Bolitoglossa marmorea
Bolitoglossa minutula
Bolitoglossa nigricens
Bolitoglossa pesrubra
Bolitoglossa robusta
Bolitoglossa schizodactyla
Bolitoglossa striatula
Bolitoglossa subpalmata
Nototriton abscondens
Nototriton gamezi
Nototriton guanacaste
Nototriton major
Nototriton picadoi
Nototriton richardi
Nototriton tapanti
Oedipina alfaroi
Oedipina alleni
Oedipina altura
Oedipina carablanca
Oedipina collaris
Oedipina cyclocauda
Oedipina gracilis
Oedipina grandis
Oedipina pacificensis
Oedipina paucidentata
Oedipina poelzi
Oedipina pseudouniformis
Oedipina savagei
Oedipina uniformis

Anura

Rhinophrynidae (1)
Rhinophrynus dorsalis

Bufonidae (14)
Atelopus chiriquiensis
Atelopus senex
Atelopus varius
Bufo coccifer
Bufo coniferus
Bufo fastidiosus
Bufo haematiticus
Bufo holdridgei
Bufo luetkenii
Bufo marinus
Bufo melanochloris
Bufo periglenes
Bufo valliceps
Crepidophryne epiotica

Centrolenidae (13)
Centrolenella ilex
Centrolenella prosoblepon
Cochranella albomaculata
Cochranella euknemos
Cochranella granulosa
Cochranella spinosa
Hyalinobatrachium chirripoi
Hyalinobatrachium colymbiphyllum
Hyalinobatrachium fleischmanni
Hyalinobatrachium pulveratum
Hyalinobatrachium talamancae
Hyalinobatrachium valerioi
Hyalinobatrachium vireovittatum

Dendrobatidae (8)
Colostethus flotator
Colostethus nubicola
Colostethus talamancae
Dendrobates auratus
Dendrobates granuliferus
Dendrobates pumilio
Phyllobates lugubris
Phyllobates vittatus

Hylidae (43)
Agalychnis annae
Agalychnis calcarifer
Agalychnis callidryas
Agalychnis saltator
Agalychnis spurrelli
Anotheca spinosa
Duellmanohyla lythrodes
Duellmanohyla rufioculis
Duellmanohyla uranochroa
Gastrotheca cornuta
genus *Hyla*
'albomarginata group'
Hyla rufitela
'boans group'
Hyla rosenbergi
'bogotensis group'
Hyla colymba
Hyla palmeri
'godmani group'
Hyla loquax
'lancasteri group'
Hyla calypsa
Hyla lancasteri
'leucophyllata group'
Hyla ebraccata
'microcephala group'
Hyla microcephala
Hyla phlebodes
'miliaria group'
Hyla fimbrimembra
Hyla miliaria
'pictipes group'
Hyla pictipes
'pseudopuma group'
Hyla angustilineata
Hyla pseudopuma
'rivularis group'
Hyla debilis
Hyla rivularis
Hyla tica
Hyla xanthosticta
'salvadorensis group'
Hyla legleri
'zeteki group'
Hyla picadoi
Hyla zeteki
Osteopilus septentrionalis *
Phrynohyas venulosa
Phyllomedusa lemur
Scinax boulengeri
Scinax elaeochroa
Scinax staufferi
Smilisca baudinii
Smilisca phaeota
Smilisca puma
Smilisca sila
Smilisca sordida

Leptodactylidae (46)
genus *Eleutherodactylus*
'biporcatus group'
Eleutherodactylus bufoniformis
Eleutherodactylus gulosus
Eleutherodactylus megacephalus
Eleutherodactylus rugosus
'cruentus group'
Eleutherodactylus altae
Eleutherodactylus caryophyllaceus
Eleutherodactylus cruentus
Eleutherodactylus moro
Eleutherodactylus pardalis
Eleutherodactylus ridens
'cerasinus group'
Eleutherodactylus cerasinus
'diastema group'
Eleutherodactylus diastema
Eleutherodactylus hylaeformis
Eleutherodactylus tigrillo
Eleutherodactylus vocator
'fitzingeri group'
Eleutherodactylus andi
Eleutherodactylus crassidigitus
Eleutherodactylus cuaquero
Eleutherodactylus fitzingeri
Eleutherodactylus phasma
Eleutherodactylus rayo
Eleutherodactylus talamancae
'gaigeae group'
Eleutherodactylus gaigeae
'gollmeri group'
Eleutherodactylus gollmeri
Eleutherodactylus mimus
Eleutherodactylus noblei
'melanostictus group'
Eleutherodactylus melanostictus
'rhodopis group'
Eleutherodactylus bransfordii
Eleutherodactylus persimilis
Eleutherodactylus podiciferus
Eleutherodactylus polyptychus
Eleutherodactylus stejnegerianus
Eleutherodactylus underwoodi
'rugulosus group'
Eleutherodactylus angelicus
Eleutherodactylus escoces
Eleutherodactylus fleischmanni
Eleutherodactylus punctariolus
Eleutherodactylus ranoides
Eleutherodactylus taurus
species of unknown affinity:
Eleutherodactylus johnstonei *
Leptodactylus bolivianus
Leptodactylus labialis
Leptodactylus melanonotus
Leptodactylus pentadactylus
Leptodactylus poecilochilus
Physalaemus pustulosus

Microhylidae (3)
Gastrophryne pictiventris
Hypopachus variolosus
Nelsonophryne aterrima

Ranidae (5)
Rana forreri
Rana taylori
Rana vaillanti
Rana vibicaria
Rana warszewitschii

Reptilia (221)

Crocodylia

Alligatoridae (1)
Caiman crocodilus

Crocodylidae (1)
Crocodylus acutus

Testudinata

Cheloniidae (4)
Caretta caretta
Chelonia mydas
Eretmochelys imbricata
Lepidochelys olivacea

Dermochelyidae (1)
Dermochelys coriacea

Emydidae (4)
Rhinoclemmys annulata
Rhinoclemmys funerea
Rhinoclemmys pulcherrima
Trachemys scripta

Kinosternidae (3)
Kinosternon angustipons
Kinsternon leucostomum
Kinosternon scorpioides

Chelydridae (1)
Chelydra serpentina

Squamata - Sauria

Eublepharidae (1)
Coleonyx mitratus

Gekkonidae (11)
Gonatodes albigularis
Hemidactylus frenatus *
Hemidactylus garnotii *
Lepidoblepharis xanthostigma
Lepidodactylus lugubris *
Phyllodactylus tuberculosus
Sphaerodactylus graptolaemus
Sphaerodactylus homolepis
Sphaerodactylus millepunctatus
Sphaerodactylus pacificus
Thecadactylus rapicauda

Corytophanidae (4)
Basiliscus basiliscus
Basiliscus plumifrons
Basiliscus vittatus
Corytophanes cristatus

Iguanidae (3)
Ctenosaura quinquecarinata
Ctenosaura similis
Iguana iguana

Polychrotidae (27)
Ctenonotus cristatellus *
Dactyloa chocorum
Dactyloa frenata
Dactyloa insignis
Dactyloa microtus
genus *Norops*
'auratus group'
- *Norops altae*
- *Norops aquaticus*
- *Norops cupreus*
- *Norops humilis*
- *Norops intermedius*
- *Norops lemurinus*
- *Norops oxylophus*
- *Norops pachypus*
- *Norops sericeus*
- *Norops townsendi*
- *Norops tropidolepis*

'biporcatus group'
- *Norops biporcatus*
- *Norops capito*
- *Norops fungosus*
- *Norops pentaprion*
- *Norops vociferans*
- *Norops woodi*

'fuscoauratus group'
- *Norops carpenteri*
- *Norops limifrons*
- *Norops pandoensis*
- *Norops polylepis*

Polychrus gutturosus

Phrynosomatidae (3)
Sceloporus malachiticus
Sceloporus squamosus
Sceloporus variabilis

Scincidae (3)
Eumeces managuae
Mabuya unimarginata
Sphenomorphus cherriei

Gymnophthalmidae (6)
Anadia ocellata
Bachia blairi
Gymnophthalmus speciosus
Leposoma southi
Neusticurus apodemus
Ptychoglossus plicatus

Teiidae (6)
Ameiva ameiva
Ameiva festiva
Ameiva leptophrys
Ameiva quadrilineata
Ameiva undulata
Cnemidophorus deppii

Xantusidae (2)
Lepidophyma flavimaculatum
Lepidophyma reticulatum

Anguidae (7)
Celestus cyanochloris
Celestus hylaius
Celestus orobius
Coloptychon rhombifer
Diploglossus bilobatus
Diploglossus monotropis
Mesaspis monticola

Squamata - Serpentes

Anomalepididae (3)
Anomalepis mexicanus
Helminthophis frontalis
Liotyphlops albirostris

Leptotyphlopidae (1)
Leptotyphlops goudotii

Typhlopidae (1)
Typhlops costaricensis

Loxocemidae (1)
Loxocemus bicolor

Boidae (5)
Boa constrictor
Corallus annulatus
Corallus ruschenbergerii
Epicrates cenchria
Ungaliophis panamensis

Colubridae (103)
Amastridium veliferum
Chironius carinatus
Chironius exoletus
Chironius grandisquamis
Clelia clelia
Clelia scytalina
Coluber mentovarius
Coniophanes bipunctatus
Coniophanes fissidens
Coniophanes piceivittis
Conophis lineatus
Crisantophis nevermanni
Dendrophidion nuchale
Dendrophidion paucicarinatum
Dendrophidion percarinatum
Dendrophidion vinitor
Dipsas articulata
Dipsas bicolor
Dipsas tenuissima
Drymarchon corais
Drymobius margaritiferus
Drymobius melanotropis
Drymobius rhombifer
Enuliophis sclateri
Enulius flavitorques
Erythrolamprus bizonus
Erythrolamprus mimus
Geophis brachycephalus
Geophis downsi
Geophis godmani
Geophis hoffmanni
Geophis ruthveni
Geophis talamancae
Geophis zeledoni
Hydromorphus concolor
Imantodes cenchoa
Imantodes gemnistratus
Imantodes inornatus
Lampropeltis triangulum
Leptodeira annulata
Leptodeira nigrofasciata
Leptodeira rubricata
Leptodeira septentrionalis
Leptodrymus pulcherrimus
Leptophis ahaetulla
Leptophis depressirostris
Leptophis mexicanus
Leptophis nebulosus
Leptophis riveti
Liophis epinephelus
Mastigodryas melanolomus
Ninia celata
Ninia maculata
Ninia psephota
Ninia sebae
Nothopsis rugosus
Oxybelis aeneus
Oxybelis brevirostris
Oxybelis fulgidus
Oxyrhopus petolarius
Pseustes poecilonotus
Rhadinaea calligaster
Rhadinaea decorata
Rhadinaea godmani
Rhadinaea pulveriventris

Rhadinaea serperaster
Rhinobothryum bovallii
Scaphiodontophis annulatus
Scolecophis atrocinctus
Senticolis triaspis
Sibon annulatus
Sibon anthracops
Sibon argus
Sibon dimidiatus
Sibon longifrenis
Sibon nebulatus
Spilotes pullatus
Stenorrhina degenhardtii
Stenorrhina freminvillii
Tantilla alticola
Tantilla armillata
Tantilla reticulata
Tantilla ruficeps
Tantilla schistosa
Tantilla supracincta
Tantilla vermiformis
Thamnophis marcianus
Thamnophis proximus
Tretanorhinus nigroluteus
Trimetopon gracile
Trimetopon pliolepis
Trimetopon simile
Trimetopon slevini
Trimetopon viquezi
Trimorphodon biscutatus
Tripanurgos compressus
Urotheca decipiens
Urotheca euryzona
Urotheca fulviceps
Urotheca guentheri
Urotheca myersi
Urotheca pachyura
Xenodon rabdocephalus

Elapidae (5)
Micrurus alleni
Micrurus clarki
Micrurus multifasciatus
Micrurus nigrocinctus
Pelamis platurus

Viperidae (14)
Agkistrodon bilineatus
Atropoides nummifer
Atropoides picadoi
Bothrops asper
Bothriechis lateralis
Bothriechis nigroviridis
Bothriechis schlegelii
Cerrophidion godmani
Crotalus durissus
Lachesis melanocephala
Lachesis stenophrys
Porthidium nasutum
Porthidium ophryomegas
Porthidium volcanicum

BIBLIOGRAPHY

Acuña-Mesén, R.A. (1990) The impact of fire and drought on the population structure of *Kinosternon scorpioides* (Testudines, Kinosternidae) in Palo Verde, Guanacaste, Costa Rica. Brenesia 20:85-98.

Acuña-Mesén, R.A. (1998) Las tortugas continentales de Costa Rica. Editorial de la Universidad de Costa Rica.

Aguilar, M.X. (1994) Efecto de la temperatura de incubación sobre la determinación del sexo en *Crocodylus acutus* y *C. moreletii*. Tesis de Maestría en Ciencias. Facultad de Ciencias, Universidad Nacional Autónoma de México, Mexico City.

Allsteadt, J. (1994) Nesting ecology of *Caiman crocodilus* in Caño Negro, Costa Rica. J. Herpetol. 28(1):12-19.

Alvarez del Toro, M. (1983) Los reptiles de Chiapas. 2nd ed. Gobierno del Estado, Tuxtla Gutiérrez, Chiapas, Mexico.

Andrews, R.M. (1971) Structural habitat and time budget of a tropical *Anolis* lizard. Ecology 52:262-270.

Andrews, R.M. (1979) The lizard *Corytophanes cristatus*: an extreme sit-and-wait predator. Biotropica 11:136-139.

Andrews, R.M. (1983) *Norops polylepis*. In: Janzen, D.H. (ed.) Costa Rican Natural History. Pp. 409-410. Univ. Chicago Press, Chicago.

Auth, D.L. (1994) Checklist and bibliography of the amphibians and reptiles of Panama. Smithsonian Herpetological Information Service # 98.

Avila-Pires, T.C.S. (1995) Lizards of Brazilian Amazonia (Reptilia: Squamata). Zool. Verh. 299:1-706.

Baillie, J. & B. Groombridge (eds.) (1996) 1996 IUCN Red List of Threatened Animals. IUCN, Gland, Switzwerland.

Ballinger, R.E., K.E. Marion, & O.J. Sexton (1970) Thermal ecology of the lizard *Anolis limifrons*, with comparative notes on three additional Panamanian anoles. Ecology 51:246-254.

Beckers, G. & T. Leenders (1994) Color patterns of Costa Rican Coral snakes. Studies on function and characteristics. Unpublished report # 320. Department of Ecology, Research Group Animal Ecology, University of Nijmegen, The Netherlands.

Beckers, G.J.L., T.A.A.M. Leenders, & H. Strijbosch (1996) Coral snake mimicry: live snakes not avoided by a mammalian predator. Oecologia 106:461-463.

Behler, J.L. & F.W. King (1979) The audubon society field guide to North American reptiles and amphibians. Alfred A. Knopf, New York.

Bezy, R.L. (1984) Systematics of Xantusid Lizards of the genus *Lepidophyma* in northeastern Mexico. Contrib. Sci. Nat. Hist. Mus. Los Angeles Co. 349:1-16.

Blaustein, A.R., P.D. Hoffman, D.G. Hokit, J.M. Kiesecker, S.C. Walls & J.B. Hays (1994) UV repair and resistance to solar UV-B in amphibian eggs: A link to population declines? Proc. Nat. Acad. Sci. USA. 91:1791-1795.

Bock, B.C. (1987) *Corytophanes cristatus*: nesting. Herp. Rev. 18(2):35.

Bock, B.C. & M. Quintero (1987) *Anolis limifrons* - Predation. Herp. Rev. 18(2):34.

Bolaños, R. & J.R. Montero (1970) *Agkistrodon bilineatus* Günther from Costa Rica. Rev. Biol. Trop. 16(2):277-279.

Boonman, J. (1993) De groene leguaan (*Iguana iguana*). Lacerta 51(3):65.

Boonman, J. (1998) Andere bladen: Een goddelijke hagedis. Lacerta 56(3): 74.

Brame, A.H. (1968) systematics and evolution of the Mesoamerican salamader genus *Oedipina*. J. Herpetol. 2:1-64.

Brodie, E.D. (1993) Differential avoidance of coral snake banded patterns by free-ranging avian predators in Costa Rica. Evolution 47:227-235.

Brodie, E.D., Jr. & P.K. Ducey (1991) Antipredator skin secretions of some tropical salamanders (*Bolitoglossa*) are toxic to snake predators. Biotropica 23(1):58-62.

Brodkin, M.A., M.P. Simon, A.M. DeSantis, & K.J. Boyer (1992) Response of *Rana pipiens* to graded doses of the bacterium *Pseudomonas aeruginosa*. J. Herpetol. 26:490-495.

Brown, C.W. (1968) Additional observations on the function of the nasolabial grooves of plethodontid salamanders. Copeia 1968(4): 728-731.

Brown, W.S. (1987) Hidden life of the timber rattler. Natl. Geogr. Mag. 172:128-138.

Bruemmer, F. (1995) La arribada. Nat. Hist. 104(8):36-43.

Brust, D.G. (1993) Maternal brood care by *Dendrobates pumilio*: A frog that feeds its young. J. Herpetol. 27(1):96-98.

Bunnell, P. (1973) Vocalizations in the territorial behavior of the frog *Dendrobates pumilio*. Copeia 1973:277-284.

Bustard, H.R. (1968) The egg-shell of Gekkonid lizards: a taxonomic adjunct. Copeia 1968(1):162-164.

Caldwell, J.P. (1996) The evolution of myrmecophagy and its correlates in poison frogs (Family Dendrobatidae). J. Zool. 240:75-101.

Campbell, J.A. (1973) A captive hatching of *Micrurus fulvius tenere* (Serpentes, Elapidae). J. Herp. 7:312-315.

Campbell, J.A. & W.W. Lamar (1989) The venomous reptiles of Latin America. Cornell University Press.

Campbell, J.A. & W.W. Lamar (1992) Taxonomic status of miscellaneous Neotropical viperids, with the description of a new genus. Occ. Pap. Mus. Texas Tech Univ. 153:1-31.

Carneiro, R.L. (1970) Hunting and hunting magic among the Amahuaca of the Peruvian montaña. Ethnology 9:331-341.

Chavez, F., J. Alvarado, R. Aymerich, & A. Solórzano (1993) Aspectos basicos sobre las serpientes de Costa Rica. Universidad de Costa Rica, Facultad de Microbiologia, Instituto Clodomiro Picado. San José, Costa Rica.

Chiszar, D. & C.W. Raddcliffe (1989) The predatory strike of the jumping viper (*Porthidium nummifer*). Copeia 1989(4):1037-1039.

Cloudsley-Thompson, J. (1995) Insects that mimic reptiles. British Herp. Soc. Bull. 53:31-33.

Cocroft, R.B., R.W. McDiarmid, A.P. Jaslow, & P.M. Ruiz-Carranza (1990) Vocalizations of eight species of *Atelopus* (Anura: Bufonidae) with comments on communications in the genus. Copeia 1990(3):631-643.

Coen, E. (1983) Climate. In: Janzen, D.H. (ed.) Costa Rican Natural History. Pp. 35-46. Univ. Chicago Press, Chicago.

Connors, J.S. (1989) *Oxybelis fulgidus* (Green Vine Snake): Reproduction. Herp. Rev. 20:73.

Crimmins, M.L. (1937) A case of *Oxybelis* poisoning in man. Copeia 1937:283.

Crump, M.L. (1986) Homing and site fidelity in a Neotropical frog, *Atelopus varius* (Bufonidae). Copeia 1986(2):438-444.

Crump, M.L. & R.H. Kaplan (1979) Clutch energy partitioning of tropical treefrogs. Copeia 1979:626-635.

Crump, M.L. & J.A. Pounds (1989) Temporal variation in the dispersal of a tropical anuran. Copeia 1989(1):209-211.

Das, B.B. (1998) Present status of Gahirmatha Beach in Bhitara Kanika sanctuary, Orissa. Marine Turtle Newsletter 79:1-2.

Davis, D.D. (1953) Behavior of the lizard *Corytophanes cristatus*. Fieldiana Zool. 35(1):3-8.

Dixon, J.R. (1970) *Coleonyx* Gray Banded geckos. Cat. Amer. Amph. Rep. 95:1-2.

Donnelly, M.A. (1994) Amphibian diversity and natural history. In: McDade, L.A., K.S. Bawa, H.A. Hespenheide, & G.S. Hartshorn (eds.) La Selva. Ecology and natural history of a Neotropical rain forest. Pp. 199-209. Univ. Chicago Press, Chicago.

Dowling, H.G. & I. Fries (1987) A taxonomic study of the ratsnakes. VIII. A proposed new genus for *Elaphe triaspis* (Cope). Herpetologica 43(2): 200-207.

Downs, F. (1967) Intrageneric relationships among colubrid snakes of the genus *Geophis* Wagler. Museum of Zoology, Univ. of Michigan.

Duellman, W.E. (1967a), Courtship isolating mechanisms in Costa Rican hylid frogs. Herpetologica, 23: 169-183

Duellman, W.E. (1967b), Social organization in the mating calls of some Neotropical anurans. Am. Midl. Nat. 77:156-163.

Duellman, W.E. (1968a) *Smilisca baudinii*. Cat. Amer. Amph. Rept. 59.1-2.

Duellman, W.E. (1968b) *Smilisca phaeota*. Cat. Amer. Amph. Rept. 61.1-2.

Duellman, W.E. (1970) The Hylid Frogs of Middle America. Monogr. Mus. Nat. Hist., Univ. Kansas, No. 1, 753 pp., 2 vols.

Duellman, W.E. & L. Trueb (1986) Biology of Amphibians. McGraw Hill.

Dugan, B. (1982) A field study on the headbob displays of male green iguanas (*Iguana iguana*): variation in form and content. Anim. Behav. 30:327-338.

Dunn, E.R. (1937) New or unnamed snakes from Costa Rica. Copeia 1937(4):213-215.

Dunn, E.R. (1941) Notes on *Dendrobates auratus*. Copeia 1941(2):88-93.

Durant, P. & J.W. Dole (1974) Food of *Atelopes oxyrhynchus* (Anura: Atelopodidae) in a Venezuelan cloudforest. Herpetologica 30(2):183-187.

Easteal, S. (1986) *Bufo marinus*. Cat. Amer. Amph. Rep. 395:1-4.

Eaton, T.H., Jr. (1941) Notes on the life history of *Dendrobates auratus*. Copeia 1941(2):93-95.

Echternacht, A.C. (1983) *Ameiva* and *Cnemidophorus*. In: Janzen, D.H. (ed.) Costa Rican Natural History. Pp. 375-379. Univ. Chicago Press, Chicago.

Eerden, H., van der, (1986) Opvallend gedrag van *Corallus enydris enydris* in het terrarium. Litt. Serp. 6(4):130.

Ernst, C.H. (1980a) *Rhinoclemmys annulata*. Cat. Am. Rep. Amph. 250:1-2.

Ernst, C.H. (1980b) *Rhinoclemmys funerea*. Cat. Amer. Amph. Rep. 263:1-2.

Ernst, C.H. (1983a) *Rhinoclemmys annulata*. In: Janzen, D.H. (ed.) Costa Rican Natural History. Pp. 416-417. Univ. Chicago Press, Chicago.

Ernst, C.H. (1983b) *Rhinoclemmys funerea*. In: Janzen, D.H. (ed.) Costa Rican Natural History. Pp. 417-418. Univ. Chicago Press, Chicago.

Ernst, C.H. (1988) *Chelydra* Schweiger, Snapping Turtles. Cat. Amer. Amph. Rept. 419:1-4.

Ernst, C.H. (1992) Venomous reptiles of North America. Smithsonian Institute Press, Washington, USA.

Ernst, C.H. & R.W. Barbour (1989) Turtles of the world. Smithsonian Institution Press, Washington D.C., USA.

Fabing, H.D. & J.R. Hawkins (1956) Intravenous injection of bufotenine in the human being. Science 123:886-887.

Ferwerda, W.H. (1993) De groene basilisk (*Basiliscus plumifrons*) en de helmbasilisk (*B. basiliscus*) in Costa Rica. Lacerta 51(6):179-182.

Fitch, H.S. (1973) A field study of Costa Rican lizards. Univ. Kansas. Sci. Bull. 50:39-126

Fitch, H.S. (1975), Sympatry and interrelationships in Costa Rican Anoles. Occ. Pap. Mus. Nat. Hist. Univ. Kansas, 40:1-60.

Fitch, H.S. (1983) *Sphenomorphus cherriei*. In: Janzen, D.H. (ed.) Costa Rican Natural History. Pp. 422-445. Univ. Chicago Press, Chicago, USA.

Fitch, H.S., A.A. Echelle, & A.F. Echelle (1976) Field observations on rare or little known mainland anoles. Univ. Kansas Sci. Bull. 51:91-128.

Fitch, H.S. & J. Hackforth-Jones (1983) *Ctenosaura similis*. In: Janzen, D.H. (ed.) Costa Rican Natural History. Pp. 394-396. Univ. Chicago Press, Chicago.

Fitch, H.S. & R.A. Seigel (1984) Ecological and Taxonomic Notes on Nicaraguan Anoles. Milwaukee Publ. Mus. Contr. Biol. Geol. 57:1-13.

Fleischman, L.J., E.R. Loew, & M. Leal (1993) Ultraviolet radiation in lizards. Nature 365:397.

Fleishman, L.J. (1985) Cryptic movements in the vine snake *Oxybelis aeneus*. Copeia 1985(1):242-245.

Foster, M.S. & R.W. McDiarmid (1983) *Rhinophrynus dorsalis*. In: Janzen, D.H. (ed.) Costa Rican Natural History. Univ. Pp. 419-421. Chicago Press, Chicago.

Fouquette, M.J., Jr. (1960) Isolating mechanisms in three sympatric treefrogs in the Canal Zone. Evolution 14:484-497.

Fouquette, M.J., Jr. (1969) Rhinophrynidae, *Rhinophrynus dorsalis*. Cat. Amer. Amph. Rept. 78:1-2.

Fouquette, M.J., Jr. & D.A. Rossman (1963) Noteworthy records of Mexican amphibians and reptiles in the Florida State Museum and the Texas Natural History Collection. Herpetologica 19:185-201.

Franzen, M. (1987) Froschlurche aus dem Monteverde-Nebelwaldreservat, Costa Rica. Herpetofauna 9(48):18-23.

Franzen, M. (1988) Beobachtungen an einigen Froschlurchen aus dem Santa Rosa-Nationalpark, Costa Rica. Herpetofauna 10(52):25-28.

Frost, D.R. & R. Etheridge (1989) A phylogenetic analysis and taxonomy of iguanian lizards (Reptilia: Squamata). Univ. Kansas Mus. Nat. Hist. Misc. Publ. 81:1-65.

Furst, P.T. (1972) Symbolism and psychopharmacology: The toad as earth mother in Indian America. In: King, J.L. & N.C. Tejero (eds.) Religion in Mesoamerica, pp. 37-45. XII Mesa Redonda, Sociedad Mexicana de Antropología, Mexico.

Furst, P.T. (1974) Comments. Curr. Anthropol. 15:154.

Glasheen, J.W. & T.A. McMahon (1996) A hydrodynamic model of locomotion in the basilisk lizard. Nature 380:340-342.

Glasheen, J.W. & T.A. McMahon (1997) Running on water. Sci. Amer. 27(3):68-69.

Goff, G.P., J. Lien, G.B. Stenson & L. Fretey (1994) The migration of a tagged leatherback turtle (*Dermochelys coriacea*) from French Guiana, South America, to Newfoundland, Canada, in 128 days. Can. Field-Nat. 108:72-73.

Goodman, D. (1971) Differential selection among immobile prey among terrestrial and riparian lizards. Am. Midl. Nat. 86:217-219.

Gradstein, S.R. & C. Equihua (1995) An epizoic bryophyte and algae growing on the lizard *Corytophanes cristatus* in Mexican rain forest. Biotropica 27(2):265-268.

Greene, H.W. (1997) Snakes: the evolution of mystery in nature. University of California Press, Berkeley, California.

Greene, H.W. & D.L. Hardy (1989) Natural death associated with skeletal injury in the terciopelo, *Bothrops asper* (Viperidae). Copeia 1989(4):1036.

Greene, H.W. & R.W. McDiarmid (1981) Coral snake mimicry: does it occur? Science 213:1207-1212.

Gregory, P.T. (1983) Habitat structure affects diel activity pattern in the neotropical frog *Leptodactylus melanonotus*. J. Herp. 17(2):179-181.

Gutiérrez, J.M. & R. Bolaños (1981) Polimorfismo cromosómico intraespecífico en la serpiente de coral *Micrurus nigrocinctus* (Ophidia: Elapidae). Rev. Biol. Trop. 29:115-122.

Gutiérrez, J.M., C. Avila, Z. Camacho, & B. Lomote (1990) Ontogenetic changes in the venom of the snake *Lachesis muta stenophrys* (bushmaster) from Costa Rica. Toxicon 28:419-426.

Guyer, C. (1986) Seasonal patterns of reproduction of *Norops humilis* (Sauria: Iguanidae) in Costa Rica. Rev. Biol. Trop. 34(2):247-251.

Guyer, C. (1994) The reptile fauna: diversity and ecology. In: McDade, L.A., K.S. Bawa, H.A. Hespenheide, & G.S. Hartshorn (eds.) La Selva. Ecology and natural history of a Neotropical rain forest. Pp. 210-216. Univ. Chicago Press, Chicago.

Hardy, D.L., Sr. (1994) *Bothrops asper* (Viperidae) snakebite and field researchers in Middle America. Biotropica 26(2): 198-207.

Hayes, M.P. (1991) A study of clutch attendance in the Neotropical frog *Centrolenella fleischmanni* (Anura: Centrolenidae). Ph.D. dissertation, Univ. of Miami, Miami, Florida.

Hayes, M.P., J.A. Pounds & W.W. Timmerman (1989) An annotated list and guide to the amphibians and reptiles of Monteverde, Costa Rica. Herpetological Circular # 17. Society for the Study of Amphibians and Reptiles. University of Texas, Tyler.

Henderson, R.W. (1972) Notes on the reproduction of a giant anole, *Norops biporcatus* (Sauria, Iguanidae). J. Herpetol. 6(3-4):239-240.

Henderson, R.W. (1984) *Scaphiodontophis* (Serpentes: Colubridae): Natural history and test of a mimicry-related hypothesis. Pp. 185-194 in: Seigel, R.R. et al. eds., Vertebrate Ecology and Systematics. Mus. Nat. Hist., Univ. Kansas Spec. Publ. 10:1-278.

Henderson, R.W. (1993a) *Corallus annulatus* (Cope). Cat. Amer. Amph. Rept. 573:1-2.

Henderson, R.W. (1993b) *Corallus enydris* (Linnaeus). Cat. Amer. Amph. Rept. 576:1-6.

Henderson, R.W. (1997) A taxonomic review of the *Corallus hortulans* complex of Neotropical tree boas. Carib. J. Sci. 33(3-4):198-221.

Henderson, R.W. & M.A. Nickerson (1976) Observations on the behavioral ecology of three species of *Imantodes* (Reptilia, Serpentes, Colubridae). J. Herpetol. 10(3):205-210.

Henderson, R.W., M.A. Nickerson, & L.G. Hoevers (1977) Observations and comments on the feeding behavior of *Leptophis* (Reptilia, Serpentes, Colubridae). J. Herpetol. 11(2):231-232.

Heselhaus, R. (1984) Pfeilgiftfrösche. Reimar Hubbing Verlag, Edition Kernen, Essen, Germany.

Heyer, W.R. (1967) A herpetofaunal study of an ecological transect through the Cordillera de Tilarán, Costa Rica. Copeia 1967(2):259-271.

Heyer, W.R. (1970) Studies on the genus *Leptodactylus* (Amphibia: Leptodactylidae). II. Diagnosis and distribution of the *Leptodactylus* of Costa Rica. Rev. Biol. Trop. 16(2):171-205.

Hillis, D.M. & R. de Sa (1988) Phylogeny and taxonomy of the *Rana palmipes* group (Salientia: Ranidae). Herpetol. Monogr. 2:1-26.

Hillman, P.E. (1969) Habitat specificity in three sympatric species of *Ameiva* (Reptilia: Teiidae). Ecology 50:476-481.

Himmelstein, J. (1980) Observations and distributions of amphibian and reptiles in the state of Quintana Roo, Mexico. Bull. N.Y. Herpetol. Soc. 16(2):18-34.

Ibañez, D.R. & E.R. Smith (1995) Systematic status of *Colostethus flotator* and *C. nubicola* (Anura: Dendrobatidae) in Panama. Copeia 1995(2):446-456.

Jackson, J.F., W. Ingram III, & H.W. Campbell (1976) The dorsal pigmentation pattern of snakes as an antipredator strategy: a multivariate approach. Am. Nat. 110:1029-1053.

Jacobson, S.K. & J.J. Vandenberg (1991). Reproductive ecology of the endangered Golden Toad (*Bufo periglenes*). J. Herpetol. 25(3):321-327.

Janzen, D.H. (1962) Injury caused by toxic secretions of *Phrynohyas spilomma*. Copeia 1962:651.

Janzen, D.H. (1980) Two potential coral snake mimics in a tropical deciduous forest. Biotropica 12(1):77-78.

Janzen, D.H. & C.L. Hogue (1983) *Fulgora laternia*. In: Janzen, D.H. (ed.) Costa Rican Natural History. Pp. 726-727. Univ. Chicago Press, Chicago.

Jaramillo, F.E., C.A. Jaramillo, & D.R. Ibanez (1997) The tadpole of *Hyalinobatrachium colymbiphyllum* (Anura: Centrolenidae). Rev. Biol. Trop. 45(2): 867-870.

Jaslow, A.P. & E.E. Lombard (1996) Hearing in the neotropical frog, *Atelopus chiriquiensis*. Copeia 1996:428-432.

Jiménez, C.E. (1994) Utilization of *Puya dasylirioides* (Bromeliaceae: Pitcairnoidea) as foraging site by *Bolitoglossa subpalmata* (Plethodontidae: Bolitoglossinii). Rev. Biol. Trop. 42(3):703-710.

Jörgens, D. (1994) Zur kenntnis der gelb-oliven Farbvarietät von *Dendrobates granuliferus* Taylor, 1958. Sauria 16(4):15-17.

Jungfer, K.-H. (1987a) Beobachtungen an *Ololygon boulengeri* (Cope, 1887) und anderen "Knickzehenlaubfröschen". Herpetofauna 9(46):6-12.

Jungfer, K.-H.(1987b) Herpetofocus: Wasseranolis. Herpetofauna 9(48):13.

Jungfer, K.-H. (1988) Froschlurche von Fortuna, Panama. 1. Microhylidae, Ranidae, Bufonidae, Hylidae (1). Herpetofauna 10(54):25-34.

Jungfer, K.-H. (1996) Reproduction and parental care of the coronated treefrog, *Anotheca spinosa* (Steindachner, 1864) (Anura: Hylidae). Herpetologica 52(1):25-32.

Kim, Y.H., G.B. Brown, H.S. Mosher, & F.A. Fuhrman (1975) Tetrodotoxin: occurrence in atelopid frogs of Costa Rica. Science 189:151-152.

Kitchens, C.S., S. Hunter, & L.H.S. van Mierop (1987) Severe myonecrosis in a fatal case of envenomation in the canebrake rattlesnake (*Crotalus horridus atricaudatus*). Toxicon 25:455-458.

Klemens, M.W. & J.B. Thorbjarnarson (1995) Reptiles as a food resource. Biodiv. Conserv. 4:281-298.

Kluge, A.G. (1981) The life history, social organization and parental behavior of *Hyla rosenbergi* Boulenger, a nest-building gladiator frog. Misc. Publ. Mus. Zool. Univ. Michigan, 160:1-170.

Kluge, A.G. (1991) Boine snakes phylogeny and research cycles. Misc. Publ. Mus. Zool. Michigan 178:1-58.

Knip, A. (1992) De Gouden pad (*Bufo periglenes*) in Monteverde. Lacerta 50(6):219-224.

Kofron, C.P. (1988) The Central and South American blindsnakes of the genus *Anomalepis*. Amphibia-Reptilia 9:7-14.

Köhler, G. (1995a) De soorten Zwarte Leguanen (*Ctenosaura*). Lacerta 54(1):13-28.

Köhler, G. (1995b) Freilanduntersuchungen zur Morphologie und Lebensweise des Fünfkiel-Schwarzleguans *Ctenosaura quinquecarinata* am Isthmus von Tehuantepec, Mexiko. Herpetofauna 17(97):21-26.

Koller, R.M. (1996) Herpetologische waarnemingen in Costa Rica (slot). Lacerta 54(4):111-118.

Kropach, C. (1975) The yellow-bellied sea snake, *Pelamis platurus*, in the eastern Pacific. In: Dunson, W., ed., The Biology of Sea Snakes. . Pp. 185-213 Univ. Park Press, Baltimore, Maryland.

LaBarre, W. (1970) The ghost dance: Origins of religion. Doubleday, Garden City, N.Y.

Lahanas, P.J. & J.M. Savage (1992) A new species of Caecilian from the Península de Osa of Costa Rica. Copeia 1992(3):703-708.

Lang, J.W. & H.V. Andrews (1994) Temperature-dependent sex determination in crocodylians. J. Exp. Zool. 270:28-44.

Lee, J.C. (1996) The amphibians and reptiles of the Yucatán Peninsula. Cornell University Press.

Leenders, T. (1994) The snakes of Rara Avis. I. Coral snakes (Elapidae, genus *Micrurus*). Litt. Serp. 14(4):107-116.

Leenders, T. (1995a) The herpetofauna of two localities in northeastern Costa Rica, with notes on the arboreal reptiles and amphibians. Unpublished Report for the Foundation for the Advancement of Herpetology, The Netherlands.

Leenders, T. (1995b) The snakes of Rara Avis. II. Pitvipers (Crotalinae). Litt. Serp. 15(1):4-12.

Leenders, T. (1996) The Central American arboreal herpetofauna. Unpublished Report for the Foundation for the Advancement of Herpetology, The Netherlands.

Leenders, T., G. Beckers, & H. Strijbosch (1996) *Micrurus mipartitus* (NCN). Polymorphism. Herp. Rev. 27(1):25.

Licht, L.E. (1968) Death following possible ingestion of toad eggs. Toxicon 5:141-142.

Licht, L.E. & B. Low (1968) Cardiac response of snakes after ingestion of toad paratoid venom. Copeia 1968(3):547-551.

Lips, K.R. (1993a) Geographical distribution: *Bolitoglossa compacta*. Herp. Rev. 24(3):107.

Lips, K.R. (1993b) Geographical distribution: *Bolitoglossa minutula*. Herp. Rev. 24(3):107.

Lips, K.R. (1993c) Geographical distribution: *Bolitoglossa nigriscens*. Herp. Rev. 24(3):107.

Lips, K.R. (1993d) Geographical distribution: *Oedipina grandis*. Herp. Rev. 24(3):107.

Lips, K.R. (1996) New treefrog from the Cordillera de Talamanca of Central America with a discussion of systematic relationships in the *Hyla lancasteri* group. Copeia 1996(3):615-626.

Lips, K.R. & J.M. Savage (1994) A new fossorial snake of the genus *Geophis* (Reptilia: Serpentes: Colubridae) from the Cordillera de Talamanca of Costa Rica. Proc. Biol. Soc. Washington 107(2): 410-416.

Lips, K.R. & J.M. Savage (1996a) A new species of rainfrog, *Eleutherodactylus phasma* (Anura: Leptodactylidae), from montane Costa Rica. Proc. Biol. Soc. Washington 109(4):744-748.

Lips, K.R. & J.M. Savage (1996b) Key to the known tadpoles (Amphibia: Anura) of Costa Rica. Stud. Neotrop. Fauna & Environm. 31:17-26.

Livezey, R.L. (1986) The eggs and tadpoles of *Bufo coniferus* Cope in Costa Rica. Rev. Biol. Trop. 34(2):221-224.

Lohmann, K.J. (1991) Magnetic orientation by hatchling loggerhead sea turtles (*Caretta caretta*). J. Exp. Biol. 155: 37-50.

Lourenco, W.R. (1995) Neotropical frog *Leptodactylus pentadactylus* eats scorpions. Alytes 12:191-192.

Lynch, J.D. (1975) A review of the broad-headed Eleutherodactyline frogs of South America (Leptodactylidae). Occ. Pap. Mus. Nat. Hist. Univ. Kansas, 38:1-46.

Lynch, J.D. & C.W. Myers (1983) Frogs of the *fitzingeri* group of *Eleutherodactylus* in eastern Panamá and Chocoan South America. Bull. Am. Mus. Nat. Hist. 175:481-572.

McCranie, J.R. & L.D. Wilson (1995) Two new species of colubrid snakes of the genus *Ninia* from Central America. J. Herpetol. 29(2): 224-232.

McDiarmid, R.W. (1983) *Centrolenella fleischmanni*. In: Janzen, D.H. (ed.) Costa Rican Natural History. Pp. 415-416. Univ. Chicago Press, Chicago.

McDiarmid, R.W. & K. Adler (1974) Notes on territorial and vocal behavior of Neotropical frogs of the genus *Centrolenella*. Herpetologica 30:75-78.

McDiarmid, R.W. & M.S. Foster (1975) Unusual sites for two Neotropical tadpoles. J. Herpetol. 9:264-265.

McDiarmid, R.W., T. Toure, & J.M. Savage (1996) The proper name of the Neotropical tree boa often referred to as *Corallus enydris* (Serpentes: Boidae). J. Herpetol. 30(3):320-326.

McVey, M.E., R.G. Zahary, D. Perry, & J. MacDougal (1981) Territoriality and Homing Behavior in the Poison Dart Frog (*Dendrobates pumilio*). Copeia 1981(1):1-8.

Miyamoto, M.M. (1982) Vertical habitat use by *Eleutherodactylus* frogs (Leptodactylidae) at two Costa Rican localities. Biotropica 14(2):141-144.

Miyamoto, M.M. (1983) Biochemical variation in the frog *Eleutherodactylus bransfordii*: geographical patterns and cryptic species. Syst. Zool. 32:43-51.

Morris, M.R. (1991) Female choice of large males in the treefrog *Hyla ebraccata*. J. Zool. 223:371-378.

Mrosovsky, N. (1988) Pivotal temperatures for loggerhead turtles (*Caretta caretta*) from northern and southern nesting beaches. Can. J. Zool. 66:661-669.

Mrosovsky, N. & J. Provancha (1989) Sex ratios of loggerhead sea turtles hatching on a Florida beach. Can. J. Zool. 67:2533-2539.

Mrosovsky, N. & C.L. Yntema (1981) Temperature dependence of sexual differentiation in sea turtles: Implications for conservation. Cons Biol. 18:271-280.

Mudde, P. (1989) *Anolis aquaticus*. Lacerta 48(1):1.

Mudde, P. (1992a) Bij de voorplaat: De stekelpad (*Bufo coniferus*). Lacerta 50(4):129.

Mudde, P. (1992b) Bij de voorplaat: De Vierstreepameiva (*Ameiva quadrilineata*). Lacerta 50(3):97.

Mudde, P. (1993) Bij de voorplaat: De Chiriqui-harlekijnkikker (*Atelopus chiriquiensis*). Lacerta 51(5):137.

Mudde, P. & M. van Dijk (1983) Herpetologische waarnemingen in Costa Rica (3). Pijlgifkikkers (Dendrobatidae) en klompvoetkikkers (Atelopodidae). Lacerta 42:42-46.

Mudde, P. & M. van Dijk (1984a) Herpetologische waarnemingen in Costa Rica (7). Schildpadden en krokodillen. Lacerta 42:221-223.

Mudde, P. & M. van Dijk (1984b) Herpetologische waarnemingen in Costa Rica (8). Gekko's (Gekkonidae) Lacerta 43:36-37.

Mudde, P. & M. van Dijk (1984c) Herpetologische waarnemingen in Costa Rica (9). Leguanen (Iguanidae). Lacerta 43:50-55.

Mudde, P. & M. van Dijk (1984d) Herpetologische waarnemingen in Costa Rica (10). Tejuhagedissen (Teiidae), skinken, (Scincidae) en hazelwormen (Anguidae). Lacerta 43:68-71.

Mudde, P. & M. van Dijk (1984e) Herpetologische waarnemingen in Costa Rica (11). Longloze salamanders (Plethodontidae). Lacerta 43:97-98.

Mudde, P. & M. van Dijk (1984f) Herpetologische waarnemingen in Costa Rica (12). Anolissen (Anolinae) Lacerta 43(7):121-136.

Myers, C.W. (1971) A new species of green anole (Reptilia, Sauria) from the north coast of Veraguas, Panama. Amer. Mus. Novitates 2470:1-14.

Myers, C.W. (1973) Anguid lizards of the genus *Diploglossus* in Panama, with the description of a new species. Am. Mus. Novit. 2523:1-20.

Myers, C.W. (1974) The systematics of *Rhadinaea* (Colubridae), a genus of New World snakes. Bull. Amer. Mus. Nat. Hist. 153:1-262.

Myers, C.W. (1982) Blunt-headed Vine Snakes (*Imantodes*) in Panama including a new species and other revisionary notes. Am. Mus. Nov. 2738:1-50.

Myers, C.W., J.W. Daly, & B. Malkin (1978) A dangerously toxic new frog (*Phyllobates*) used by Emberá Indians of western Colombia, with discussion of discussion of blowgun fabrication and dart poisoning. Bull. Amer. Mus. Nat. Hist. 161:307-366.

Myers, C.W. & W.E. Duellman (1982) A new species of *Hyla* from Cerro Colorado, and other tree frog records and geographical notes from western Panama. Am. Mus. Nov. 2752:1-32.

Nelson, C.E. (1962) Size and secondary sexual characters in the frog *Glossostoma aterrimum* Gunther. Transactions of the Kansas Academy of Science 65(1):87-88.

Nickerson, M.A., R.A. Sajdak, & R.W. Henderson (1978) Notes on the movements of some Neotropical snakes (Reptilia, Serpentes). J.Herpetol. 12(3):419-422.

Novak R.M. & D.C. Robinson (1975) Observations on the reproduction and ecology of the tropical montane toad, *Bufo holdridgei* in Costa Rica. Rev. Biol. Trop. 23:213-237.

Oftedal, O.T. (1974) A revision of the genus *Anadia* (Sauria: Teiidae). Arquivos de Zoologia 25 (4):203-265.

Opay, P. (1998) Legal action taken to stop the hunting of green turtles in Costa Rica. Marine Turtle Newsletter 79:12-16.

Pérez-Santos, C. & Moreno, A. (1988) Ofidios de Colombia. Monografie VI. Museo Regionale di Scienze Naturali, Torino, Italy.

Peterson, K.H. (1990) Conspecific and self-envenomation in snakes. Bull. Chi. Herp. Soc. 25(2):26-28.

Plotkin, P.T., D.C. Rostal, R.A. Byles, & D.W. Owens (1997) Reproductive and developmental synchrony in female *Lepidochelys olivacea*. J. Herpetol. 31(1):17-22.

Porras, L., J.R. McCranie, & L.D.Wilson (1981) The systematics and distribution of the hognose viper *Bothrops nasuta* Bocourt (Serpentes: Viperidae). Tulane Stud. Zool. Bot. 22:85-107.

Porter, K.R. (1970) *Bufo valliceps*. Cat. Am. Rep. Amph. 94.1-4.

Pough, F.H. (1976) Multiple cryptic effects of cross-banded and ringed patterns of snakes. Copeia 1976(3):834-836.

Pough, F.H., G. Kwiecinski, & W. Bemis (1978) Melanin deposits associated with the venom glands of snakes. J.Morphol. 155:63-72.

Pounds, J.A. (2000) Amphibians and reptiles. In: Nadkarni, N.M. & N.T. Wheelwright (eds.) Monteverde—ecology and conservation of a tropical cloud forest. Pp. 149-171. Oxford University Press, New York.

Pounds, J.A. & M.L. Crump (1987) Harlequin frogs along a tropical montane stream. Biotropica 19:306-309.

Pounds, J.A. & M.L. Crump (1994) Amphibian declines and climate disturbance: the case of the Golden Toad and the Harlequin Frog. Cons. Biol. 8(1):72-85.

Pounds, J.A., M.P.L. Fogden, J.M. Savage, & G.C. Gorman (1997) Tests of null models for amphibian declines on a tropical mountain. Cons. Biol. 11(6):1307-1322.

Pounds, J.A., M.P.L. Fogden, & J.H. Campbell (1999) Biological response to climate change on a tropical mountain. Nature 398:611-615.

Pröhl, H. (1997) Los anfibios de Hitoy Cerere, Costa Rica. Proyecto Namasöl, Cooperación Técnica Bilateral Holanda-Costa Rica.

Pyburn, W.F. (1970) Breeding behavior of the leaf-frogs *Phyllomedusa callidryas* and *Phyllomedusa dacnicolor* in Mexico. Copeia 1970(2):209-218.

Rand, A.S. (1983) *Physalaemus pustulosus*. In: Janzen, D.H. (ed.) Costa Rican Natural History. Pp. 412-415. Univ. Chicago Press, Chicago.

Rand, A.S. & H. Marx (1967) Running speed of the lizard *Basiliscus basiliscus* on water. Copeia 1967(1):230-233.

Rand, A.S. & C.W. Myers (1990) The herpetofauna of Barro Colorado Island, Panamá: an ecological summary. In: Four Neotropical Rainforests (A.H. Gentry, ed.), pp. 386-409. Yale University Press, New Haven.

Roberts, W.E. (1994) Explosive breeding aggregations and parachuting in a Neotropical frog, *Agalychnis saltator* (Hylidae). J. Herpetol. 28(2):193-199.

Robinson, D.C. (1983a) *Rana palmipes*. In: Janzen, D.H. (ed.) Costa Rican Natural History. Pp. 415-416. Univ. Chicago Press, Chicago.

Robinson, D.C. (1983b) *Sceloporus malachiticus*. In: Janzen, D.H. (ed.) Costa Rican Natural History. Pp. 421-422. Univ. Chicago Press, Chicago.

Rodríguez, L.O. & W.E. Duellman (1994) Guide to the frogs of the Iquitos Region, Amazonian Peru. Univ. Kansas Nat. Hist. Mus. Spec. Publ. No. 22. Pp. 1-80.

Rojas, G., G. Bogarin & J.M. Gutierrez (1997) Snakebite mortality in Costa Rica. Toxicon 35(11):1639-1643.

Ruiz-Carranza, P.M. & J. D. Lynch (1991) Ranas Centrolenidae de Colombia. I. Propuesta de una nueva clasificación genérica. Lozania 57:1-30.

Sasa, M. (1993) Distribution and reproduction of the gray earth snake *Geophis brachycephalus* (Serpentes: Colubridae) in Costa Rica. Rev. Biol. Trop. 41(2):295-297.

Sasa, M. & A. Solórzano (1995) The reptiles and amphibians of Santa Rosa National Park, Costa Rica, with comments about the herpetofauna of xerophytic areas. Herp. Nat. Hist. 3(2):113-126.

Savage, J.M. (1966) An extraordinary new toad (*Bufo*) from Costa Rica. Rev. Biol.Trop. 14(2):153-167.

Savage, J.M. (1968) The Dendrobatid frogs of Central America. Copeia 1968(4):745-776.

Savage, J.M. (1972a) The harlequin frogs, genus *Atelopus*, of Costa Rica and Western Panama. Herpetologica 28(1):77-94.

Savage, J.M. (1972b) The systematic status of *Bufo simus* O. Schmidt with description of a new toad from western Panama. J. Herpetol. 6(1):25-33.

Savage, J.M. (1974) On the leptodactylid frog called *Eleutherodactylus palmatus* (Boulenger) and the status of *Hylodes fitzingeri* O. Schmidt. Herpetologica 30:289-299.

Savage, J.M. (1986) Systematics and distribution of the Mexican and Central American rainfrogs of the *Eleutherodactylus gollmeri* group (Amphibia: Leptodactylidae). Fieldiana Zool. 33(1375):1-57.

Savage, J.M. (1997) A new species of rainfrog of the *Eleutherodactylus diastema* group from the Alta Talamanca region of Costa Rica. Amphibia-Reptilia 18(3):241-247.

Savage, J.M. & S.B. Emerson (1970) Central American frogs allied to *Eleutherodactylus bransfordii* (Cope): A problem of polymorphism. Copeia 1970:623-644.

Savage, J.M. & W.R. Heyer (1969) The tree-frogs of Costa Rica: diagnosis and distribution. Rev. Biol. Trop. 16:1-127.

Savage J.M. & A. Kluge (1961) Rediscovery of the strange Costa Rican toad *Crepidius epioticus*. Rev. Biol. Trop. 9:39-51.

Savage, J.M. & P.N. Lahanas (1989) A new Colubrid snake (Genus *Urotheca*) from the Cordillera de Talamanca of Costa Rica. Copeia 1989(4):892-896.

Savage, J.M. & P.N. Lahanas (1991) On the species of the colubrid snake genus *Ninia* in Costa Rica and Western Panama. Herpetologica 47: 37-53.

Savage, J.M. & K.R. Lips (1993) A review of the status and biogeography of the lizard genera *Celestus* and *Diploglossus* (Squamata: Anguidae), with description of two new species from Costa Rica. Rev. Biol. Trop. 41(3):817-842.

Savage, J.M. & R.W. McDiarmid (1992) Rediscovery of the Central American colubrid snake, *Sibon argus*, with comments on related species from the region. Copeia 1992(2):421-432.

Savage, J.M. & N.J. Scott (1985) The *Imantodes* (Serpentes: Colubridae) of Costa Rica: two or three species? Rev. Biol. Trop. 33:107-132.

Savage, J.M. & J.B. Slowinski (1992) The colouration of the venomous coral snakes (family Elapidae) and their mimics (families Aniliidae and Colubridae). Biol. J. Linnean Soc. 45:235-254.

Savage, J.M. & J.B. Slowinski (1996) Evolution of coloration, urotomy and coral snake mimicry in the snake genus *Scaphiodontophis* (Serpentes: Colubridae). Biol. J. Linnean Soc. 57:192-194.

Savage, J.M. & P.H. Starrett (1967) A new fringe-limbed tree-frog (Family Centrolenidae) from lower Central America. Copeia 1967(3):604-609.

Savage, J.M. & J.J. Talbot (1978) The giant anoline lizards of Costa Rica and western Panama. Copeia 1978(3):480-492.

Savage, J.M. & J.L. Vial (1974) The venomous coral snakes (genus *Micrurus*) of Costa Rica. Rev. Biol. Trop. 21:295-349.

Savage, J.M. & J. Villa (1986) Introduction to the herpetofauna of Costa Rica. Contributions to herpetology 3. Society for the Study of Reptiles and Amphibians, Oxford, Ohio.

Savage, J.M. & M.H. Wake (1972) Geographic variation and systematics of the Middle American caecilians, genera *Dermophis* and *Gymnopis*. Copeia 1972:680-695.

Savitzky, A.H. (1981) Hinged teeth in snakes: an adaptation for swallowing hard-bodied prey. Science 212:346-349.

Schmidt, A. A. & G. Köhler (1996) Zur Biologie von *Bolitoglossa mexicana*: Freilandbeobachtungen, Pflege und Nachzucht. Salamandra 32(4):275-284.

Schouten, K. (1992) Checklist of CITES Fauna and Flora. A checklist of the animal and plant species covered by the Convention on International Trade in Endangered Species of Wild Fauna and Flora. Revised edition. CITES Secretariat, Lausanne, Switzerland.

Schultes, R.E. & A. Hoffman (1973) The botany and chemistry of hallucinogens. Charles C. Thomas, Springfield, Ill., USA.

Schulz, K.-D. (1992a) Variation, distribution and biology of *Elaphe triaspis* (Cope, 1866), part 1, with remarks on the husbandry and breeding of the southern subspecies *Elaphe triaspis mutabilis* (Cope, 1885). Litt. Serp. 12(2):32-41.

Schulz, K.-D. (1992b) Variation, distribution and biology of *Elaphe triaspis* (Cope, 1866), part 2, with remarks on the husbandry and breeding of the southern subspecies *Elaphe triaspis mutabilis* (Cope, 1885). Litt. Serp. 12(3):54-68.

Schwartz, A. (1973) *Sphaerodactylus* Wagler Dwarf Geckos. Cat. Amer. Amph. Rep. 142:1-2.

Schwenk, K. (1994) Why snakes have forked tongues. Science 263:1573-1577.

Scott, N.J. (1983a) *Agalychnis callidryas*. In: Janzen, D.H. (ed.) Costa Rican Natural History. Pp. 374-375. Univ. Chicago Press, Chicago.

Scott, N.J. (1983b) *Bolitoglossa subpalmata*. In: Janzen, D.H. (ed.) Costa Rican Natural History. Pp. 382-383. Univ. Chicago Press, Chicago.

Scott, N.J. (1983c) *Bufo haematiticus*. In: Janzen, D.H. (ed.) Costa Rican Natural History. Pp. 385. Univ. Chicago Press, Chicago.

Scott, N.J. (1983d) *Clelia clelia*. In: Janzen, D.H. (ed.) Costa Rican Natural History. Pp. 392. Univ. Chicago Press, Chicago.

Scott, N.J. (1983e) *Conophis lineatus*. In: Janzen, D.H. (ed.) Costa Rican Natural History. Pp. 392-393. Univ. Chicago Press, Chicago.

Scott, N.J. (1983f) *Eleutherodactylus bransfordii*. In: Janzen, D.H. (ed.) Costa Rican Natural History. Pp. 399. Univ. Chicago Press, Chicago.

Scott, N.J. (1983g) *Eleutherodactylus diastema*. In: Janzen, D.H. (ed.) Costa Rican Natural History. pp 399. Univ. Chicago Press, Chicago.

Scott, N.J. (1983h) *Leptotyphlops goudotii*. In: Janzen, D.H. (ed.) Costa Rican Natural History. Pp. 406. Univ. Chicago Press, Chicago.

Scott, N.J. & S. Limerick (1983) Reptiles and amphibians: introduction. In: Janzen, D.H. (ed.) Costa Rican Natural History. Pp. 351-367. Univ. Chicago Press, Chicago.

Scott, N.J., Jr. & A. Starrett (1972) An unusual breeding aggregation of frogs, with notes on the ecology of *Agalychnis spurrelli* (Anura: Hylidae). Proc. So. Calif. Acad. Sci. (73):86-94.

Sexton, O.J. (1975) Black vultures feeding on iguana eggs in Panama. Am. Midl. Nat. 93(2):463-468.

Sexton, O.J., J. Bauman & E. Ortleb, (1972), Seasonal food habits of *Anolis limifrons*. Ecology 53:182-286.

Smith, R.E. (1968a) Studies on reproduction in Costa Rican *Ameiva festiva* and *Ameiva quadrilineata* (Sauria: Teiidae). Copeia 1968(2): 236-239.

Smith, S.M. (1975) Innate recognition of coral snake pattern by a possible avian predator. Science 187:759-760.

Smith, S.M. (1977) Coral-snake pattern recognition and stimulus generalisation by naive great kiskadees (Aves: Tyrannidae). Nature 265:535-536.

Smith, W.G. (1968b) A neonate atlantic loggerhead turtle, *Caretta caretta caretta*, captured at sea. Copeia 1968(4):880-881.

Solórzano, A. (1990) Reproduction in the pit viper *Porthidium picadoi* Dunn (Serpentes: Viperidae) in Costa Rica. Copeia 1990(4): 1154-1157.

Solórzano, A. (1993) Creencias populares sobre los reptiles en Costa Rica. San José, Costa Rica.

Solórzano, A. (1994) Una Nueva especie de serpiente venenosa terrestre del género *Porthidium* (Serpentes: Viperidae), del Suroeste de Costa Rica. Rev. Biol. Trop. 42(3):695-701.

Solórzano, A. (1995) A case of a human bite by the pelagic sea snake, *Pelamis platurus* (Serpentes: Hydrohpiidae). Rev. Biol. Trop. 43(1-3):321-322.

Solórzano, A. & L. Cerdas (1989) Reproductive biology and distribution of the Terciopelo, *Bothrops asper* Garman (Serpentes: Viperidae), in Costa Rica. Herpetologica 45(4):444-450.

Starrett, P.H. & J.M. Savage (1973) The systematic status and distribution of Costa Rican glass-frogs, genus *Centrolenella* (family Centrolenidae), with description of a new species. Bull. So. Calif. Acad. Sci. 72:57-78.

Stebbins, R.C. (1980) A field guide to western reptiles and amphibians. Peterson Field Guide Series.

Talbot, J.J. (1979) Time budget, niche overlap, inter- and intraspecific aggression in *Anolis humilis* and *Anolis limifrons* from Costa Rica. Copeia 1979(3): 472-481.

Taylor, E.H. (1939) A new species of the lizard genus *Lepidophyma* from Mexico. Copeia 1939(3):131-133.

Taylor, E.H. (1949) Two new teiid lizards from Costa Rica. Univ. Kansas Sci. Bull. 33:271-278.

Taylor, E.H. (1951) A brief review of the snakes of Costa Rica. Univ. Kansas Sci. Bull. 34:1-188.

Taylor, E.H. (1952a) The salamanders and caecilians of Costa Rica.Univ. Kansas Sci. Bull. 34(12):695-791.

Taylor, E.H. (1952b) A review of the frogs and toads of Costa Rica. Univ. Kansas Sci. Bull. 35:577-942.

Taylor, E.H. (1954a) Additions to the known herpetological fauna of Costa Rica with comments on other species. No. I. Univ. Kansas Sci. Bull. 36:597-639.

Taylor, E.H. (1954b) Further studies on the serpents of Costa Rica. Univ. Kansas Sci. Bull. 36:673-800.

Taylor, E.H. (1955) Additions to the known herpetofauna of Costa Rica, with comments on other species. No. II. Univ. Kansas Sci. Bull. 37:499-575.

Taylor, E.H. (1956) A review of the lizards of Costa Rica. Univ. Kansas Sci. Bull. 38:3-322.

Taylor, R.T., A. Flores, G. Flores, & R. Bolaños (1974) Geographical distribution of Viperidae, Elapidae and Hydrophidae in Costa Rica. Rev. Biol. Trop. 21(2):383-397.

Telford, S.R., Jr. & H.W. Campbell (1970) Ecological observation on an all female population of the lizard *Lepidophyma flavimaculatum* (Xanthusidae) in Panama. Copeia 1970:379-381.

Tihen, J. (1949) The genera of Gerrhonotine lizards. Amer. Midl. Nat. 41:579-601.

Troeng, S. (1998) Poaching threatens the Green Turtle rookery at Tortuguero, Costa Rica. Marine Turtle Newsletter 79:11-12.

Troyer, K. (1987) Small differences in daytime body temperature affect digestion of natural food in a herbivorous lizard (*Iguana iguana*). Comp. Biochem. Physiol. 87A(3):623-626.

Trutnau, L. (1988) Schlangen im Terrarium, Band I. Ungiftige Schlangen. 3rd. ed. Verlag Eugen Ulmer, Stuttgart, Germany.

Tuttle, M.D. & M.J. Ryan (1981) Bat predation and the evolution of frog vocalizations in the tropics. Science 214:677-678.

Tyler, M.J. (1976) Frogs. Collins, Ltd., Sydney, Australia.

Uzzell, T.M., Jr. (1966) Teiid lizards of the genus *Neusticurus* (Reptilia, Sauria). Bull. Am. Mus. Nat. Hist. 132(5):277-328.

Valerio, D.C. (1971) Ability of some tropical tadpoles to survive without water. Copeia 1971:364-365.

Verhoeven, K. (1995) Slangen van Rara Avis, Costa Rica. Lacerta 54(2):45-53.

Vial, 1968, The ecology of the tropical salamander *Bolitoglossa subpalmata*, in Costa Rica. Rev. Biol. Trop. 15:13-115.

Vial, J.L. & J.M. Jimenez-Porras (1967) The ecogeography of the bushmaster, *Lachesis muta*, in Central America. Amer. Midl. Nat. 78:182-187.

Villa, J. (1972) Un coral blanco y negra de Costa Rica. Brenesia 1:10-13.

Villa, J.D. (1977) A symbiotic relationship between frog (Amphibia, Anura, Centrolenidae) and fly larvae (Drosophilidae). J. Herpetol. 11:317-322.

Villa, J.D. (1984) Biology of a Neotropical glass frog, *Centrolenella fleischmanni* (Boettger), with special reference to its frogfly associates. Milw. Public Mus. Contrib. Biol. Geol. 55:1-60.

Villa, J.D. (1988) *Typhlops costaricensis* Jiménez and Savage. Costa Rican Blind Snake. Cat. Amer. Amphib. Rept. 435:1-2.

Villa, J.D. (1990) *Rana warszewitschii* (Schmidt). Cat. Amer. Amph. Rept. 459:1-2.

Villa, J.D. & N.J. Scott (1967) The iguanid lizard *Enyaliosaurus* in Nicaragua. Copeia 1967 (2):474-475.

Villa, J., L.D. Wilson & J.D. Johnson (1988) Middle American herpetology, a bibliographic checklist. University of Missouri Press, Columbia, USA.. 130 pp.

Vinton, K.W. (1951) Observations on the life history of *Leptodactylus pentadactylus*. Herpetologica 7:73-75.

Vogt, R.C. & O.F. Flores-Villela (1992) Effects of incubation temperature on sex determination in a community of Neotropical freshwater turtles in southern Mexico. Herpetologica 48:265-270.

Wake, D.B. & I.G. Dresner (1967) Functional morphology and evolution of tail autotomy in salamanders. J. Morphol. 122:265-305.

Wake, M.H. (1983) *Gymnopis multiplicata*, *Dermophis mexicanus*, and *Dermophis parviceps*. In: Janzen, D.H. (ed.) Costa Rican Natural History. Pp. 400-401. Univ. Chicago Press, Chicago.

Wassersug, R. (1971) On the comparative palatability of some dry-season tadpoles from Costa Rica. Am. Midl. Nat. 86:101-109.

Weimer, R., W. Feichtinger, F. Bolanos, & M. Schmid (1993a) Die amphibien von Costa Rica. Herpetologische eindrücke einer forschungsreise. Teil I: Einleitung, Hylidae (1). Sauria 15(2):3-8.

Weimer, R., W. Feichtinger, F. Bolanos, & M. Schmid (1993b) Die amphibien von Costa Rica. Herpetologische eindrücke einer forschungsreise. Teil II: Hylidae (2), Bufonidae, Centrolenidae, Dendrobatidae, Ranidae. Sauria 15(3):17-23.

Weimer, R., W. Feichtinger, F. Bolanos, & M. Schmid (1993c) Die amphibien von Costa Rica. Herpetologische eindrücke einer forschungsreise. Teil III: Leptodactylidae (1). Sauria 15(4):19-24.

Weimer, R., W. Feichtinger, F. Bolanos, & M. Schmid (1994) Die amphibien von Costa Rica. Herpetologische eindrücke einer forschungsreise. Teil IV: Leptodactylidae (2), zur evolutionsbiologie der Gattung *Eleutherodactylus*. Sauria 16(2):15-20.

Wijngaarden, R., van & S. van Gool (1994) Site fidelity and territoriality in the dendrobatid frog *Dendrobates granuliferus*. Amphibia-Reptilia 15:171-181.

Wilson, L.D. (1974) *Drymobius margaritiferus*. Cat. Amer. Amph. Rept. 172:1-2.

Wilson, L.D. & J.R. Meyer (1985) The snakes of Honduras. 2nd ed. Milwaukee Mus. Publ., No. 6.

Wood, J.R., F.E. Wood & K. Critchley (1983) Hybridization of *Chelonia mydas* and *Eretmochelys imbricata*. Copeia 1983(3):839-842.

Young, B. (1979) Arboreal movement and tadpole-carrying behavior of *Dendrobates pumilio* in northeastern Costa Rica. Biotropica 11:238-239.

Zamudio, K.R. & H.W. Greene (1997) Phylogeography of the Bushmaster (*Lachesis muta*: Viperidae): implications for neotropical biogeography, systematics, and conservation. Biol. J. Linnean. Soc. 62:421-442.

Zug, G. (1983) *Bufo marinus*. In: Janzen, D.H. (ed.) Costa Rican Natural History. Pp. 415-416. Univ. Chicago Press, Chicago.

Zug, G.R. (1993) Herpetology. An introductory biology of amphibians and reptiles. Academic Press, Inc. Harcourt Brace Jovanovich, Publishers.

Zweifel, R.G. (1964a) Distribution and life history of the Central American frog, *Rana vibicaria*. Copeia, 1964:300-308.

Zweifel, R.G. (1964b) Life history of *Phrynohyas venulosa* in Panama. Copeia 1964:201-208.

GLOSSARY

alkaloid A type of active chemical compound found in many animal toxins.

amplexus A general term describing the sexual embrace of frogs and toads, in which the male holds on to the female's back with his arms. In **axillary amplexus**, the male grabs the female under the armpits. In **inguinal amplexus**, the male grabs the female around the groin.

anal spurs Vestigial limbs found in some boas, which appear as a nail-like spur on each side of the vent.

annular folds Skin folds that encircle the body of all caecilians.

anurans The class of animals consisting of all tailless amphibians, the frogs and toads.

archosaur A group of extinct reptiles that included crocodilians, dinosaurs, and pterosaurs.

arthropod Any invertebrate that has jointed limbs and a segmented body, including insects, spiders, scorpions, and centipedes.

autotomy The ability to voluntarily break off part or all of the tail, an antipredator strategy found in many lizards. In **pseudoautotomy**, the tail breaks off only when it is restrained by a predator. This ability is seen in salamanders and some snakes.

axillary amplexus See **amplexus**.

axolotl A species of salamander, *Ambystoma mexicana*, that lives in the southern United States and Mexico. This interesting amphibian sometimes spends its entire life as an aquatic larva, never metamorphosing into an adult salamander.

background color The prevailing color of an animal (also referred to as **ground color**).

bromeliad Any member of the plant family Bromeliaceae, usually growing on tree branches.

bryozoan A small, mosslike aquatic invertebrate.

bufogenin A type of **bufotoxin**.

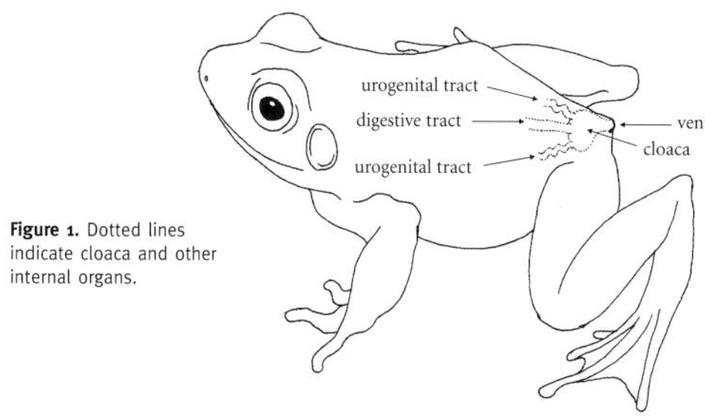

Figure 1. Dotted lines indicate cloaca and other internal organs.

bufotenin A **bufotoxin** with supposedly hallucinogenic properties.

bufotoxin Any toxic secretion produced by toads.

caecilian An order of wormlike, limbless amphibians. See description on page 36.

Figure 2. Shading indicates the eight costal scutes on *Chelonia mydas*. The costal scutes cover the ribs; the scutes on the center of the shell cover the vertebrae.

campesino *Spanish.* A farmer or peasant.

canopy The ecosystem formed by the overhanging branches of the trees in a forest.

carapace The shell that covers the sides and back of a turtle. See **plastron.**

chemoreception A faculty of sense perception widespread in amphibians and reptiles.

cloaca The body cavity where both the urogenital and digestive tracts terminate. The **vent** is the opening between the cloaca and the exterior of the body. See figure 1.

cloudforest A high-elevation forest characterized by cool temperatures and high annual rainfall.

coatimundi *Nasua narica.* A tropical relative of the raccoon.

costal fold Any skin fold between the ribs of salamanders.

costal scute Any plate on a turtle's shell that covers the ribs. See figure 2.

crossbands Bands that run perpendicular to the axis of the body.

cryptic *adj.* Serving to conceal.

dorsal *adj.* Pertaining to the back of an animal.

dorsal stripe A stripe running along the back of an animal. **Dorsolateral stripes** run between the back and the side of the animal. **Lateral stripes** run along the side of the animal. See figure 3.

dorsolateral stripe See dorsal stripe.

Duvernoy's gland A gland found in the upper jaw of some colubrid snakes that may secrete digestive enzymes and/or toxins.

ectoparasite Any parasite living on the outside of the body of its host.

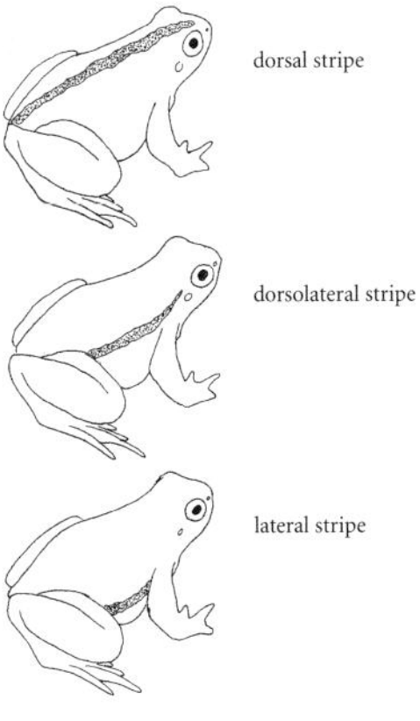

dorsal stripe

dorsolateral stripe

lateral stripe

Figure 3

ectothermous *adj.* Referring to animals that rely on external sources of heat to maintain their body temperature. All amphibians and reptiles are ectothermous. **Endothermous** animals generate body heat through an internal process called metabolism.

edge situation The boundary between two habitats.

endemic A species that only inhabits a restricted geographical area.

endothermous *adj.* See **ectothermous.**

epiphyte Any plant that obtains nutrients and water from the air, instead of the soil. Epiphytic plants usually grow on other plants.

eyespot A spot that indicates the location of the rudimentary eyes found in caecilians and blindsnakes, or any marking on the body of an animal that resembles an eye.

fossorial *adj.* Having burrowing, secretive habits.

gape The open mouth of a snake or lizard.

glandular skin Skin containing glands.

granular skin Skin covered with grainy bumps.

gravid *adj.* Pregnant.

ground color See **background color.**

hemipenis (*pl.* **hemipenes**) One of two reproductory organs in the tail base of male lizards and snakes. See figure 4.

herpetofauna The group of fauna that consists of amphibians and reptiles.

herpetology The study of amphibians and reptiles.

inguinal amplexus See **amplexus.**

Jacobson's organ The chemosensory organ found in the roof of the mouth of reptiles.

katydid An insect relative of grasshoppers and crickets.

keel A ridge on the scale of a turtle, lizard, or snake.

keratin A hard, hornlike material that is the main component of the top layer of turtle shells. Keratin is also found in human fingernails and hair.

lateral *adj.* Pertaining to either side of an animal.

lateral stripe See dorsal stripe.

larva (*pl.* **larvae**) The immature stage of an animal prior to metamorphosis. Frog and toad larvae are commonly referred to as tadpoles.

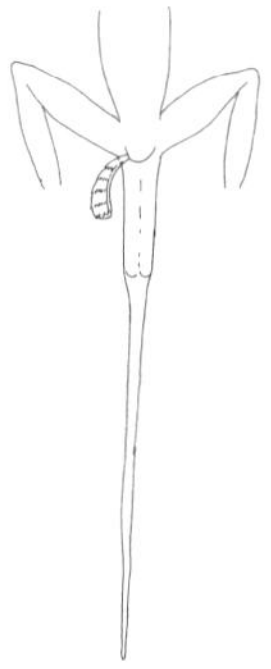

Figure 4. Tail base of male lizard with one hemipenis exposed. The second hemipenis is withdrawn in the tail base.

leaf axil The point on the main stem of a plant where the leaf or leaf stem joins it.

leaf litter The accumulated dead leaves that cover the forest floor.

liana Any species of woody vine growing in the canopy of tropical forests.

lichenous *adj.* Displaying a lichenlike pattern.

longitudinal *adj.* Running parallel to the axis of the body. Compare with **transverse**.

loreal scale A scale situated between the eye and the nostril of some snakes.

metamorphosis The transformation from larva to adult undergone by salamanders, frogs, and toads.

neotropics The New World tropics (found in Central and South America).

oviparous *adj.* Egg-laying. **viviparous** *adj.* Live-bearing. **ovoviviparous** *adj.* Producing eggs that are incubated inside the mother's body. The young hatch and leave the female's body as fully-formed juveniles.

oviposition The act of laying eggs.

ovoviviparous See **oviparous**.

paramó *Spanish.* A high-elevation habitat with shrublike, alpine vegetation.

parietal head scale The large plate or plates found on the top of the head of most snakes and lizards. See figure 5.

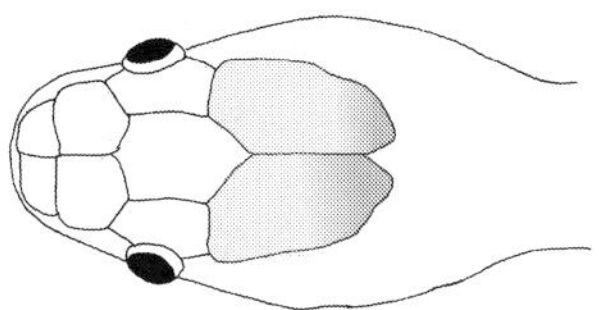

Figure 5. Shading indicates parietal head scales.

parthenogenesis The capacity possessed by the females of some species to produce offspring from an unfertilized egg. All offspring produced in this way are females.

pheromone trail The trail of volatile chemical compounds left by some animals.

plastron The part of a turtle's shell that covers the belly. See **carapace**.

prehensile tail A tail adapted for grabbing objects.

premontane *adj.* Pertaining to foothills.

primary forest Undisturbed, old-growth forest. Compare **secondary forest**.

pseudoautotomy See **autotomy**.

pustule A large wartlike structure.

rainforest Any forest that receives more than 2500 mm (100 inches) of annual rainfall.

reticulum A weblike pattern. A term used to describe the eye or skin pattern of some amphibians and reptiles.

scute A large scale.

secondary forest Partially logged or otherwise disturbed forest. Compare **primary forest**.

speciose *adj.* Containing a large number of species.

tarsus One of four segments of the hind limb of frogs and toads. The other segments are the thigh, lower leg, and foot. See figure 6.

taxon (*pl.* **taxa**) Generic name for taxonomic labels such as species or genus.

tetrapod Any animal with four limbs.

transverse *adj.* Running perpendicular to the axis of the body. Compare with **longitudinal**.

tubercle Any wartlike protuberance.

tunicate A group of nonmobile aquatic invertebrates with a saclike body.

understory The vegetation growing below the **canopy**.

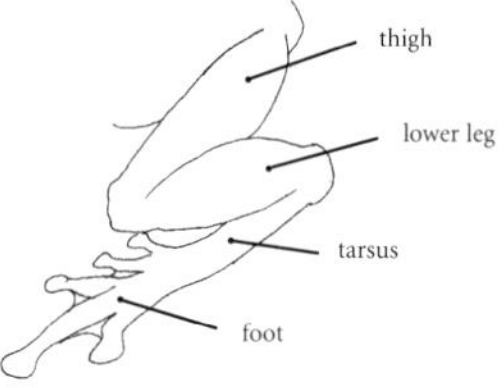

Figure 6. Four sections of anuran hind limb.

vent See **cloaca**.

ventral *adj.* (*n.* venter) Pertaining to the underside of an animal, the belly.

versant The slope or drainage system of a mountain range.

vertebral *adj.* Located on the spine.

viviparous See **oviparous**.

vocal sac A balloonlike, inflatable structure on the throat of some male frogs and toads that functions as a resonating chamber during calling.